D0918720

COMPETENCE CONSIDERED

COMPETENCE

CONSIDERED

EDITED BY

ROBERT J. STERNBERG

AND JOHN KOLLIGIAN, JR.

YALE UNIVERSITY PRESS

NEW HAVEN AND LONDON

Published with assistance from the Louis Stern Memorial Fund.

Designed by Nancy Ovedovitz. Set in Linotron 202 Baskerville type by Keystone Typesetting, Inc., Orwigsburg, Pennsylvania. Printed in the United States of America by Vail-Ballou Press, Binghamton, New York.

Library of Congress Cataloging-in-Publication Data

Competence considered / edited by Robert J. Sternberg and John Kolligian, Jr.

p. cm.

Includes bibliographical references.

ISBN 0–300–04567–0 (alk. paper)

1. Performance. 2. Self-perception. I. Sternberg, Robert J. II. Kolligian, John, 1960–

BF481.C63 1990

153.9—dc20 89–37261

CIP

The paper in this book meets the guidelines of permanence and durability of the Committee on Production Guidelines for Book Longevity of the Council on Library Resources.

10 9 8 7 6 5 4 3 2 1

CONTENTS

PREFACE

JOHN KOLLIGIAN, JR., AND
ROBERT J. STERNBERG

There's a lot of talk about competence these days. As a society, we worry about the competence of our students, our teachers, our leaders, and ourselves. Over the past few decades some researchers have gone so far as to characterize the search for competence as *the* basic motivation for behavior. Of course, there are different dimensions of competence, and it manifests itself in different ways. For instance, behaviorally, competence may take the form of maintaining control over external events; neurophysiologically, competence may be achieved through the brain's ability to establish order among the disparate stimuli received by the senses; sociologically, competence may consist of a healthy adaptation to an environment or social context; and psychologically, competence may be experienced through the ways in which one perceives, judges, and evaluates oneself. This volume focuses on the last important dimension of competence—that of self-perceptions and self-evaluations. It takes as a guiding premise that at all points in the life cycle it is one's construal of reality, rather than reality itself, that most accurately predicts self-concept, goals, academic performance, and overall mental health.

Many important, strikingly fundamental questions about competence have not previously been answered or even asked: What determines the nature of subjective perceptions of competence and incompetence? How does what we think about our competences depend on where we are in life? How do these perceptions develop, and what are their consequences? Why do some people perceive themselves as incompetent even though such negative perceptions are inaccurate or unfounded? In different ways, from diverse perspectives, the distinguished contributors to this book ask and grapple with these challenging questions.

In recent decades only a handful of isolated papers in the psychological literature has directly addressed issues related to the development and consequences of perceived competence and incompetence at different points in people's lives. But within the last few years, some distinguished scholars have begun to investigate the subject more thoroughly. We became convinced that although many new contributions have been made, they are not all as well known or as well integrated as they should be. Our conviction that the field is awakening and that there is a need to bring the various works on self-perception together motivated this book. Further, we believe the book is unique in assembling in one place alternative accounts of how questions of perceived competence can illuminate many dimensions of human experience.

In this collection of essays, the authors consider competence—its role, determinants, manifestations, and consequences—in the broader context of the developing, evolving person. The book's primary focus is on competence as it is viewed by the self as opposed to others. It also focuses on the processes and mechanisms that are at work (or that fail to work) when competence judgments are either accurately or inaccurately low—that is, when the self is viewed as incompetent. The intrapsychic and interpersonal dynamics that may be in operation in these self-perceptions are a central concern of the essays.

This volume documents the rapid strides that have been made in this field within the last decade. Considering that the topic has implications for most areas of psychology—particularly social-cognitive, developmental, educational, and clinical psychology—as well as psychiatry and sociology, the time is ripe for a collection of different scholarly perspectives that will lay a foundation for future work in this and related fields. The chapters are written both for psychologists and for others who, though they have a general background in psychology, do not necessarily have specialized knowledge about the subfields covered. Many of the chapters review existing studies, but the book is not intended to provide the kinds of literature reviews found in the *Psychological Bulletin* or the *Annual Review of Psychology*. The contributors—who are psychiatrists, psychoanalysts, and psychologists with many diverse specializations—have avoided such detailed literature reviews. Instead, their theorizing reflects our wish and encouragement for them to stretch their minds and those of their readers by freely expressing their emerging views on the topic. For this reason, we hope readers will find these chapters especially lively and provocative.

This book is intended as an intermediate-level text suitable for advanced undergraduate and graduate-level courses on child and adolescent development, self-concept, social cognition, and personality theory, and could serve as a supplementary text in courses on personality and on developmental, educational, and clinical psychology. It could also be a useful source book for psychologists, educators, and others who are interested in the nature of people's competencies, their positive and negative self-perceptions, and the consequences during different life phases.

The first section of the book is a single chapter by David Elkind. His introductory remarks on the question of competence present some of his current work on the attribution of competence in infants and young children in the contemporary United States. Elkind examines economic, social, and psychodynamic forces contributing to competence attributions, while pointing out the potential harm that competence-related stresses have on children in our society.

The second section, "Developmental Perspectives," comprises five chapters that examine the developmental course of perceived competence and incompetence. In the opening chapter, John G. Nicholls offers a developmental approach to the nature of ability and our mindfulness of it. He is concerned with developmental changes in children's and adults' conceptions of ability and intelligence, shows how these changes influence the growth of competence, and considers the emotional and behavioral consequences of these changes. By showing how differently children, adolescents, and adults construe issues of competence, he demonstrates the subject's complexity. Nicholls ultimately broadens the topic of perceived competence by stressing the importance of focusing on the value or meaningfulness of people's work, not just on their abilities as such.

Deborah A. Phillips and Marc Zimmerman next examine the developmental course and temporal stability of accurate and inaccurate self-perceptions and judgments of competence among competent children. They focus on the mediational role that subjective perceptions of competence play in determining a range of adaptive behaviors. Phillips and Zimmerman underscore how viewing oneself as competent to achieve valued goals and holding inflated notions of one's competence are essential to adjustment and ultimately to healthy development.

In the third developmental chapter, Susan Harter addresses the question of competence through an examination of the functional role of global self-worth from a life-span perspective. She examines the antecedents and determinants of one's level of self-worth, as well as the impact that self-worth has on one's affective and motivational orientation, and suggests a model of self-worth that addresses its antecedents and its functional role as they are applicable across the life span.

In the fourth chapter of this section, Paul M. Janos tackles the special competence dilemmas and perplexities experienced by a select group of individuals—exceptionally gifted young adolescents. Through an analysis of the self-statements of these uncommonly bright youngsters, he illuminates the cognitive and affective costs of intellectual precocity and the central role of social comparison theory and processes in these adolescents' experiences of themselves. Janos also translates his findings into general principles and practical suggestions for helping adolescents cope with giftedness.

Robert J. Sternberg, in the final chapter of this section, argues that the construct of competence is not a maximum level of performance nor incompetence a minimum level but, rather, that both are prototypes—profiles based on people's conceptions of the construct. Viewing competence and incompetence as a labeling phenomenon involving interactions among persons, tasks, and situations, Sternberg goes on to discuss the subcultural, cultural, and overall contextual determinants of children's competence in the schools.

The third section, "Social Perspectives," contains four chapters that investigate the socially related processes involved in self-perceptions of competence and incompetence. Ellen J. Langer and Kwangyang Park, in the opening chapter, grapple with conceptual foundations of the construct of incompetence, proposing that incompetence is predominantly a socially defined perception by the self and others of inadequate performance. The main point of their analysis is that there are at least four broad types of categories of personal incompetence, with each characterized by different causes and consequences. Langer and Park are careful to emphasize the plasticity of incompetence as a function of certain social settings and environments.

Karin S. Frey and Diane N. Ruble then examine variations in preferred standards of competence and the implications of particular standards for self-esteem maintenance. In the course of their analysis, they suggest that a high sense of competence and healthy functioning may depend on one's ability to exhibit flexibility in the choice of standards for comparison and evaluation. While discussing the utility of such a flexible approach, Frey and Ruble also underline the difficult nature of this competence-building process, suggesting that the readjustment of expectations can indeed be traumatic.

From a social-cognitive perspective, Julie K. Norem and Nancy Cantor discuss how a focus on the processes of motivation and ability can help illuminate the relationships among beliefs about competence, beliefs about tasks, motivation for performance, and actual performance. Specifically, they use the concept of "cognitive strategies" to describe the coherent patterns of appraisal, planning, retrospection, and effort that translate one's goals and beliefs into actions. Norem and Cantor show how strategic thinking helps one gain a sense of competence and mastery over one's environment and life tasks.

In the final chapter of this section, social psychologists Hazel Markus, Susan Cross, and Elissa Wurf examine the structures and processes of the self-system that are essential for creating and maintaining competence over the life span. They argue that "felt" competence is an important aspect of "actual" competence and is linked to instrumental action and effective performance in one's social environment. The authors also explore the role of the self-system in the development, maintenance, and breakdown of perceptions of one's own competence, illuminating the reciprocal relationship between self-system and competence. Their essential point—and one that resonates throughout the volume—is that competence is rooted not simply in one's attributes and abilities but also in the structures of the self-system that represent these attributes and abilities.

The next section, "Clinical Perspectives," contains four chapters that investigate the clinical processes and implications of self-perceptions of competence and incompetence. Carrie E. Schaffer and Sidney J. Blatt open this section by exploring ways in which competence in early interpersonal relationships serves as the foundation for the development of a sense of self and perceived self-efficacy. They discuss the crucial impact of the mother-infant relationship, as well as the physiological and affective dimensions of interpersonal relatedness, on the experience of self-efficacy. Schaffer and Blatt also examine the processes by which important relationships are internalized and contribute to the individual's sense of personal efficacy.

Viewing competence from a psychodynamic perspective, David W. Krueger examines some clinical factors that facilitate or impede people's ambition, effectiveness, and sense of competence over time. He traces the phase-specific expressions of ambition and effectiveness from mastery through childhood play to competence through adult work. Krueger focuses on the pathological manifestations of success inhibition and work compulsion at each life phase.

John Kolligian, Jr., then discusses the concept of perceived fraudulence and views it as a special case—as one possible manifestation—of the broader phenomenon of perceived incompetence. The conceptual relations among perceived fraudulence, perceived incompetence, and other negative self-perceptions are examined. A central point of this chapter is that authenticity concerns and fraudulent ideation in a variety of domains represent important aspects of people's general perceptions and judgments of competence. These concerns are associated with such clinical symptoms as depression and anxiety.

In the last chapter of this section, Marlene M. Moretti and E. Tory Higgins address the clinical side of competence by presenting a model of the development of emotional vulnerabilities within the framework of self-system development. This model charts the interaction between a child's developing cognitive capacity for mental representation and parental socialization practices. Moretti and Higgins consider how changes in one's self-regulatory and self-evaluative processes affect, and are influenced by, both cognitive and social factors in cases of developmental psychopathology. Especially given the relevance to the question of competence, the complexity of people's self-system networks could not have been considered in a more sophisticated manner.

Albert Bandura, in the final chapter of the book, offers a concluding and integrative commentary. He organizes and discusses the main themes of the contributors' views of perceived competence and incompetence and suggests some commonalities among their various perspectives. In bringing together the different ways in which the authors have begun to investigate the origins of perceived competence and the processes by which it affects human motivation, accomplishments, and dysfunctions, Bandura's synthesis of the nonability determinants of competence is unique—it paves the way for the advancement of this burgeoning field. Among other things, his perspective documents the progress that has been made in understanding and enhancing human competence and functioning, whereby many people have been invested with coping skills and resilient self-beliefs of capability, enabling them to exercise some control over their lives.

To conclude, we believe this book is the first text on perceived competence and incompetence that provides a broad and balanced exposure to the field. We hope the accounts here will stimulate further thinking along these and related lines—that they will encourage other scholars to consider the many fundamental, yet often neglected, questions surrounding the ways we reflect on our own and others' competences, real and imagined. This book is a beginning.

The editing for this volume represents a collaborative effort in which the editors shared equally in performing all editorial responsibilities. It was the publisher's decision to list the editors by seniority.

In editing a volume, one comes to appreciate that the muses inspiring writing are not always on schedule. We would like to thank Jeanne Ferris, our editor at Yale University Press, for her sound, sensible advice and her patience in seeing this project to fruition. Our special thanks to Cecile Watters for her thoughtful, meticulous editing of the manuscript. We also would like to thank Elizabeth Neuse and Sandi Wright for their impeccable administrative assistance; we could not have asked for two more highly competent and gracious technical assistants. We are, of course, grateful to the contributors to this book for taking time out from their busy schedules to write these chapters; we especially appreciated their willingness to take our editorial suggestions seriously. Most of all, we are indebted to Julie Sincoff, our colleague at Yale, for her tremendous support for the project; her involvement with us in all phases of this book has been indispensable.

COMPETENCE CONSIDERED

Introduction: Changing Conceptions of Competence

DAVID ELKIND

In my work on the origins and effects of stress upon children and youth in contemporary American society, I have found that an erroneous conception of childhood competence has arisen and that it likely has led to an increase in stress among young people. Accordingly, I will present here some evidence showing how pervasive the attribution of competence to infants and young children has become. I will then analyze some of the economic, social, and psychodynamic forces that have contributed to this conception of children and will conclude with a discussion of the harm it can do to young people.

THE ATTRIBUTION OF COMPETENCE TO INFANTS AND YOUNG CHILDREN

Philippe Aries, in *Centuries of Childhood* (1962), argues that in medieval society the idea of childhood did not exist—there was no awareness of the special nature of children and their difference from adults. This situation, Aries points out, was the result not of a misguided attribution of competence to infants and young children but rather, of the puerility of medieval society itself. In contemporary terms, the failure of medieval people to recognize the difference between children and adults was a failure of differentiation, not a higher-level attribution that presupposed such a differentiation. With the Renaissance, a new attitude emerged in which the child, "because of his sweetness, simplicity and drollery, became a source of amusement and relaxation for the adult" (128).

The difference between children and adults has been progressively elaborated since that time. What the difference consisted in, however, was a matter of dispute among both scientists and laymen. Some psychologists during the nineteenth century—notably G. Stanley Hall—believed that children recapitulated the history of the race. Others, like the Buhlers, saw children as simply the young of the species, whose development was very much affected by the child-rearing environment. Rousseau saw children as innocent and good, and adults as bad. Others, like Cotton Mather, thought children were born with original sin and warned parents, "Your child is not too young to go to Hell."

By the 1960s in this country, children were generally perceived in a humane, responsible way. Child labor laws were in place as were national programs of immunization, fresh-air camps, and subsidized school lunches. Federal Aid to Dependent Children legislation ensured a basic level of care for all children. There was discrimination and injustice to be sure, but it was not directed toward children per se. Moreover, children were regarded as innocent and in need of protection from the seamier side of life. Such television programs as "Leave It to Beaver," "Father Knows Best," and "Ozzie and Harriet" reflected this view of childhood.

Then a period of upheavals ensued in the sixties. For our purpose—the understanding of what brought about a transformation in our conception of children—two movements are of particular interest: the civil rights movement and the women's movement. Both grew out of long-standing resentments over discrimination, unequal educational and job opportunities, and negative, often puerile, portrayals in the media, which depicted both minorities and women as incompetent.

As women and minorities asserted their competence and demanded equal opportunity, what the learning psychologists used to call a "spread of effect" took place: many of their feelings of outrage "spread" to minority and female children. They, too, were now regarded as being discriminated against and denied equal opportunity, and advocates arose to speak on their behalf.

Perhaps the most well known of these spokespersons was Jerome Bruner. His statement in the best-seller *The Process of Education* (1962) that "you can teach any child any subject at any age in an intellectually honest way" gave expression and direction to the advocates of minority and female children. Adding to the force of this statement was Benjamin Bloom's argument in *Stability and Change in Human Behavior* (1964) that children attained half of their intellectual ability by age four. Further, because intellectual growth was more rapid at this age than at any later point in life, it was a critical time for instruction. Finally, J. McV. Hunt argued forcefully in *Intelligence and Experience* (1961) that intelligence was malleable and not fixed.

These writers, I am sure, had no awareness of the broader repercussions of their work but assumed only that they were aiding the cause of the disadvantaged. Certainly some positive results occurred: in 1964 Congress passed the first Head Start legislation and in 1965 a half million young children were enrolled in comprehensive programs of education and health care. These programs have had lasting beneficial effects, although it is clear, after decades of research, that they improve social skills and motivation rather than IQs or levels of academic achievement (McKay et al. 1985).

Nevertheless, the ideas that you can teach a child a subject at any age, that the early years are critical because intelligence is growing so rapidly, and that intelligence is potentially malleable were not lost on middle-income parents. If low-income children had a Head Start, should not middle-class children also be given a bit of a lead? One unfortunate consequence of this reasoning was that education has come to be seen as a race. Parents now believe that earlier is better, that an early start means an early and better finish—in sports and the arts as well as academics.

It is easy to document how widespread the notion of child competence has become. Programs such as Glen Doman's "Better Baby Institute" train parents how to teach their babies to read and do math. Swimming, exercise, ballet, music, and karate lessons for preschoolers are common around the country. "Educational materials" for young children are abundant and range from reading to computer programs.

One point about our changed conception of young children needs to be underscored. The changes in the conceptions and treatment of minorities and women came about in response to flagrant injustices. Although they have not all been eliminated, significant progress toward equality for both groups has been made. But the change in our conception of children did not come about because of any unbearable injustices being visited upon them. To the contrary: the middle decades of this century constituted a golden period for children in our society. By any measure—health, education, welfare—children are worse off today than they were in the fifties and early sixties.

An important factor in the acceptability of this new idea of childhood has been the transformation of the American family, which was at least partly a consequence of the women's movement. The traditional profile of the American family—two parents, only one of whom works outside the home, and an average of 2.5 children—characterized more than 50 percent of households in the 1950s but less than 10 percent today. The majority of contemporary American families have either one parent or two parents both of whom work outside the home.

The movement of large numbers of women into the work force was unprecedented and unplanned for. In particular, mothers with children under three years of age represent the fastest growing segment of the female labor force. Yet good, affordable child care is relatively scarce. Parents often have to make do with substandard day-care or latchkey arrangements. The government is moving sluggishly to provide the funds required to meet this basic need. In the meantime, working parents worry about finding child care and then about its adequacy—a situation conducive to parental anxiety and guilt. Moreover, though many contemporary parents have embraced feminist ideology, not all have fully abandoned the values that prevailed when they were growing up. The conception of children as innocent and in need of parental protection and guidance during the early years persists, compounding the guilt many parents feel when they must secure out-of-home care for their children. The concept of child competence helps relieve this guilt. If children are ready and able to handle all that life has to offer—indeed, if they profit from early exposure to everything and anything—then one does not need to feel guilty about putting them in day care or even about their watching television for many hours a day.

Another factor in the acceptance of the new idea of childhood derives from the parents' image of schools. Because schools have safe, regularly inspected buildings; licensed, trained, and reasonably paid teachers; and a history of stability and continuity, parents trust them and look to them for help with child care. In response, many schools have expanded their half-day kindergartens to full-day programs, and more than twenty-three states are providing or thinking of providing programs for four-year-olds.

But this expansion has to be paid for by taxpayers. The idea that young children are competent to engage in academic learning, and indeed benefit from it, is a strong selling point. Full-day kindergarten and prekindergarten are suddenly seen as *necessary* for preventing later school failure. This strategy is working because citizens and officials do not really understand early childhood education; they feel comfortable voting for academic programs but not for fingerpaints and gerbils. The schools, for their part, have accepted and reinforced the concept of the young child's academic competence.

A PSYCHODYNAMIC PUZZLE

A problem remains, however, in this interpretation of why the conception of child competence has taken hold in contemporary America. In his discussion of narcissism, Freud (1953) postulated that adults repress their tendencies toward helplessness and dependence as unacceptable adult behavior and then project these repressed tendencies onto children. Adults accept children as dependent and helpless—indeed, find these qualities endearing—because in so doing they vicariously satisfy their own needs.

How can we square this interpretation with the current attribution of competence to infants and young children? It would be hard to argue that contemporary adults repress their competence and project it onto children, for in our society, competence is highly valued. We must look for an explanation in a psychological dynamic that is developmentally earlier than repression and projection. When parents see the young as more competent than they really are, they fail to distinguish between their adult competencies and those of their offspring. This failure of differentiation between self and others appears earlier than projection and is a *form* of narcissism; it is the failure to go beyond one's own perspective and see another as a separate individual with different needs and points of view.

If this interpretation is correct, it would suggest that today's parents are more narcissistic than were parents in the past. One can make a strong argument that this is so. First, there has been a recent upsurge of clinical work on narcissism (e.g., Morrison 1986), which suggests greater prevalence. In addition, authors of works like *The Culture of Narcissism* (Lasch 1979) and "The Me Decade" (Wolfe 1982) have remarked on this trend. The eighties have been a period of more or less unrestrained materialism and conspicuous consumption—consider Ivan Boesky or Donald Trump, for example. Families in which both parents work have become common in part, at least, because they wish to keep up with the Joneses.

Moreover, infants and young children are used as evidence of the family's financial status. Parents purchase a particular brand of stroller or bassinet or buy perfume for their infants not so much for the baby's benefit as for the purpose of conspicuous consumption. Nor are these excesses limited to the wealthy; even low-income parents rushed to buy expensive Cabbage Patch dolls for their youngsters.

Parents who purchase these expensive "necessities" for their offspring often suggest that it is for the child rather than for themselves. Sometimes the reason given is peer group pressure: "If my child doesn't have Benetton clothes, she'll be ostracized by the others and have no one to play with." The parents confuse *their* anxiety about acceptance by *their* peer group with what the child is concerned about. Very young children are not really that concerned about their peer group's reaction to them, in part because they cannot fully appreciate the peer group reaction when it is different from their own.

Another component of parental narcissism has been called a "grandiose sense of self." Among parents this can entail a belief that the mother or father is almost totally responsible for the child's success or failure in life. The anxiety and guilt engendered by a grandiose sense of self make parents extraordinarily vulnerable to entrepreneurs eager to exploit their emotions (not to mention their children).

THE DAMAGE OF THE COMPETENCE CONCEPTION

Why should the attribution of competence to infants and young children be harmful? Given today's society with its problems of drugs, violence, degradation of the environment, foreign competition, and declining educational standards, maybe earlier *is* better. What is wrong with teaching four-year-olds about AIDS or nuclear war, for instance? How can we protect children if we don't educate them at an early age?

When I was trained as a clinician, I learned a valuable rule: "Never take anything away from a patient without giving him or her something in return." If a patient is deprived of a defense, he must be given another way of dealing with his anxiety or he has not been helped at all. And that is what we do to young children when we attempt to teach them about AIDS or nuclear war. We take away part of the child's sense of security without giving anything in return.

Young children cannot really understand the germ theory of disease. Talk of AIDS only says to them that there is something scary out there for them to be afraid of. There is nothing they can do about it; they are, after all, not sexually active. Nor can young children understand war, and certainly not nuclear war. When we tell young children about such things, we are only trying to relieve our own anxieties.

There is another way in which the ascription of competence to young children can do harm. Our public schools are pushing academic curricula, testing, grading, and homework into the kindergarten. Much of this downward extension is based on distorted notions of young children's intellectual competence, and that is what leads to harm.

Piaget and others have demonstrated that children believe adults are all-knowing and all-powerful. When adults tell a child she should be able to succeed in an academic task such as reading, and the child cannot do so for developmental reasons, what is the child's response? She does not think, "Hey, you dumb adult, wait a few months and I will breeze through this stuff." Rather she is more likely to think, "This all-knowing adult says I should be able to learn this and I can't. Something must be wrong with me—I guess I'm just dumb."

There is much evidence, some of it provided by authors in this book, that such self-appraisals can become self-fulfilling prophecies. It is this dynamic that helps explain the consistent finding that the youngest children in a kindergarten class do worse academically, in both the short and the long term, than the oldest children (Uphoff 1985). It happens because the curriculum is always geared to the oldest children. The youngest, regardless of intellectual potential, are at risk for the kind of negative self-evaluation described above.

CONCLUSION

I have given a social-clinical interpretation of the attribution of competence to infants and young children in contemporary America. Although I have talked about social forces and children in general, there are parallels with the discussions in later chapters of competence on the individual level. Perhaps the most striking is the discrepancy between ascriptions of competence and true competence. Many of the studies reported in this book attest to the fact that people who are competent often do not acknowledge their competence. Perceived fraudulence is a good example of the discrepancy between socially attributed and self-perceived competence. In the case of young children, unfortunately, the social ascription of competence is indeed unwarranted. Society, in effect, puts young children in the position of being impostors by attributing "impostors'" abilities to them that they do not possess.

Other parallels between attributions of competence at the social and individual level might easily be drawn. The only one I will add here has again to do with discrepancy—in this case, between what we know on a scientific basis and what we believe on an intuitive basis. The conception of child competence is totally at variance with what we know about child growth and development. At the social as at the individual level, intuitive psychologies exist side by side with scientific psychologies. With many of the authors in this book, I share an abiding curiosity about how and why such discrepancies between perceived and actual competence exist and are maintained in contemporary society.

PART ONE

DEVELOPMENTAL PERSPECTIVES

CHAPTER 1

What Is Ability and Why Are We Mindful of It? A Developmental Perspective

JOHN G. NICHOLLS

In this chapter, I examine developmental change in conceptions of ability and intelligence and describe the growth of competence in the understanding of ability and intelligence. I also consider the consequences for emotion and behavior of these changes in competence. Our competence at any given topic will not always predict how we will think about the topic. Individuals who know how to calculate the unit prices of goods, for example, do not always use their knowledge at the supermarket. Nor is there a simple relationship between the way ability is construed and the importance placed on ability as a cause of success and failure. That adolescents differ in the degree to which they see social status among their peers as dependent on their possessing an attractive car does not mean that they differ in their understanding of the nature of cars. In the same way, variation in beliefs about the importance of ability does not imply variation in the way ability is construed.

At the end of this chapter I will therefore take up the questions of when individuals use their most advanced conceptions of ability and when they see ability as an important cause of success. I will also consider the motivational and emotional consequences of emphasizing and using more versus less developmentally advanced conceptions of ability to evaluate one's performance. Although the more advanced conceptions provide better answers to questions such as how one can best distinguish individuals in terms of their ability, it does not follow that more advanced conceptions are better for every purpose. Indeed, in many circumstances there is much to be said for forgetting about one's ability and using childlike or even infantlike conceptions of competence. But before these latter matters can be discussed coherently, developmental change in conceptions of ability and intelligence must be described.

It is well known that infants who encounter an extremely unresponsive environment eventually stop trying to have any impact on it (Casler 1961). Young children, too, say "it's too hard" or "I can't" when facing tasks that are beyond them (Bird 1984; Bretherton & Beeghly, 1982). Such evidence could lead one to conclude that, like adults, they understand that their capacity limits what they can accomplish. There is evidence that young children get upset if they fail to meet another's challenge to win a race to build a block-tower (Heckhausen 1984). This might be taken to indicate that, like adults, they use social comparison information to judge ability. Young children also use the terms *know* and *guess* to distinguish occasions when they know something from occasions where they could only have guessed (Johnson & Wellman 1980). We might, therefore, leap to the conclusion that they have an adultlike comprehension of the difference between tasks that involve luck and those demanding skill.

We should acknowledge the competence that young children do have. They clearly have a working understanding of ability that has some affinity to that of adults. Yet, in each of the above cases we would be wrong to leap from evidence of similarity to the conclusion that the differences between adults and children are slight. Many years ago, Piaget claimed that young children's conceptions of number, space, and so on, differed dramatically from those of adults. When these claims first became public, they were greeted with skepticism by teachers, parents, and researchers. Recently, this skeptical view has attained the status of a revisionist position in developmental psychology. There is some basis for the view that Piaget focused more on what young children couldn't do than on their competencies. After all, the tendency had been to overestimate these competencies. Researchers can, however, still be fooled by young children's adultlike skills (Halford & Boyle 1985). I hope to show how different adults and young children are in their competence at construing matters of competence as well as how it is that they can often appear very similar.

THE QUESTION OF THE QUESTION

Before launching into an examination of developmental change in ability-related concepts, we need to be clear about what we are looking for change in. A researcher can ask many questions about this topic, and different questions demand different methods and lead to different answers—a fact that is often overlooked. Researchers who ask different questions often think they have simple disagreements about answers; then they have confusion as well as disagreement.

One type of question about perceptions of competence concerns the cues people use to judge ability (McArthur & Baron 1983). One could ask, for example, when and to what extent is visible evidence of smooth, apparently effortless performance taken as a sign of competence in basketball or other sports? Or, to what extent do eyeglasses or a studious air suggest intelligence? There might well be age-related changes in the attention paid to and use made of such information. Study of such questions would require (at least) visual presentation of behavior rather than the verbal descriptions that are the staple of much attributional research. Interesting though such questions might be, they have received little attention. More researchers have attended to the question of the rules or schemata children use to judge someone's level of ability given description's of, for example, their effort and performance (e.g., Surber 1984). The further question of developmental change in individuals' perceptions of how able they are and how confident they are of success has an appreciably longer history (Stipek 1984).

The question my associates and I have asked bears some relation to all the above but is not equivalent to any of them. It concerns the intensive content or meaning of ability and related concepts. Rather than asking: How do children judge ability? we asked: What do they think ability is? In Piaget's words, this work involved an attempt at "capturing the natural growth of logical thinking" by pursuing "a kind of logic of meanings. . . . a meaning is never isolated but always inserted into a system of meanings with reciprocal implications" (Piaget 1980, cited by Furth 1981, xv).

In advocating a developmental psychology of meanings, Piaget was turning his back on his own work on the logic of operations, which he described as "too closely linked to the traditional model of extensional logic and truth tables" (Furth 1981, xv). That work had been an attempt to generate abstract descriptions of child and adolescent logic that would be of universal applicability. An attempt to write a developmental psychology of the logic of meanings takes one in the opposite direction—toward an intimate concern with the unique features of specific concepts. One problem with abstract and general descriptions of cognition like Piaget's descriptions of the logic of operations is their limited value for predicting how children will construe any given topic. They are, for example, of little

for assessing competence. This assumption is so obvious that it scarcely seems worth mentioning. Yet the distinction between luck and skill is not fully established until early adolescence. The second aspect of the definition of ability involves the distinction between difficulty and ability and the third involves the concepts of effort and ability. After examining these three aspects, I will take up the question of intelligence.

LUCK AND SKILL

Weisz (1984) and Weisz and his associates (1982) have conducted studies of children's interpretations of outcomes on luck and skill tasks. Students from kindergarten through college age expected ability, effort, and practice to affect performance on a memory task. On a task where answers could only be guessed, kindergarteners and fourth-graders also expected ability, effort, and practice to affect outcomes. This tendency was barely present in eighth-graders and college students who distinguished sharply between the guessing and the memory tasks.

Nicholls and Miller (1985) employed a similar method and obtained similar results. A skill task wherein students had to match one of a number of slightly different drawings with a standard was compared with a luck version of the task where the drawings were turned face down so that one could only guess which matched the standard. Students from kindergarten through eighth grade attributed outcomes on the skill version to effort and ability. On the luck task, on the other hand, there was a decline, continuing up to eighth grade, in the tendency to attribute success or failure to ability or effort. There was a corresponding decline over the same age range in expectations of future success on the luck task but not on the skill task.

The above data do not, however, bear directly on the question of whether the meaning of luck and skill changes with age. One adult could be more inclined than another to attribute outcomes on academic tasks to luck without having a different understanding of the nature of luck. To address this question of meaning a little more directly, we conducted interviews that required children to explain their interpretations of outcomes on luck and skill tasks and to explain their predictions of what would happen if someone tried really hard on each type of task. The results obtained with this method converged with Nicholls and Miller's (1985) results and those of Weisz and his associates where only quantitative judgments were elicited. It was only at about twelve years that most

TABLE 1.1 Levels of Differentiation of Luck and Skill

1. Luck and skill per se are undifferentiated and are not the basis for distinguishing luck and skill tasks. Tasks are distinguised in terms of apparent difficulty. Effort is expected to improve outcomes on both tasks, but the skill task is seen as requiring more effort or as more difficult because of the complexity of its visible stimuli. The luck task, having no stimuli to compare, is seen as easier or as requiring less effort.
2. Skill and luck outcomes are partially differentiated, but the basis for the distinction is not articulated. Effort is expected to improve performance on both tasks, but the skill task is seen as offering more chance to do well through effort. This distinction, however, is not justified with reference to the fact that the luck task offers no chance to compare stimuli, whereas the skill task does.
3. Skill and luck outcomes are partially differentiated, and the basis for the distinction is made explicit. The skill task is seen as offering more chance to do well through effort because it is possible to compare stimuli on it but not on the luck task. Effort is, nevertheless, expected to improve performance on the luck task.
4. Skill and luck outcomes are clearly distinguished. It is seen that there is no way for effort to affect outcomes on the luck task, whereas effort is presumed to affect outcomes on the skill task.

students clearly distinguished skill from luck and argued that outcomes on a guessing task cannot be influenced by effort or ability. In all, four levels of understanding of skill and luck were identified (see table 1.1). Even at the lowest level, characteristic of five-year-olds, children clearly see luck and skill tasks as different. For one thing, they spend longer working on skill tasks, but this does not mean that the concepts are differentiated. In interpreting the tasks, children at the lowest level do not invoke the fact that there is no way to discern the answers to the guessing task. Instead, they note, for example, that the skill version of the task has complex stimuli that would be hard to analyze, whereas the luck version does not demand the same mental effort. Although five-year-olds see the tasks as different, their concepts of luck and skill are imperfectly differentiated.

The convergent age-trends for the qualitative judgment data and levels of meaning inferred from our interviews support the validity of each type of index. A lack of convergence might not mean that either method lacked validity. If different measures assess different things, they could well produce results that appear contradictory. This question, however, did not arise in this case.

The validity of the assessments of the conceptions of luck and skill was also indicated by the fact that they predicted persistence on luck and skill tasks. Children at level 4 persisted longer than those at the lower levels on a series of skill puzzles that appeared soluble but were impossible. On the other hand, they spent less time on a series of impossible guessing tasks than did the students with less differentiated conceptions of luck and skill. Stated another way, those children whose conceptions of luck and skill were most distinct from each other also employed effort most selectively: more than children with less differentiated conceptions, they reduced effort where adults would see effort as unfruitful and tried harder where adults would assume that effort would be fruitful.

The differentiation of the concepts of luck and skill seems of considerable adaptive significance. It means that effort is less likely to be "wasted" on luck tasks where it can have no impact. On the other hand, this development might make the emotional highs of success and the lows of failure on skill tasks more extreme. When young children expect that a failure on a skill task is about to reveal them as incompetent, this expectation may have some of the properties of an adult's expectation of receiving an unlucky hand of cards. Adolescents' expectations of appearing incompetent could be more starkly an expectation of incompetence and, thereby, have more negative effects on their emotional well-being.

DIFFICULTY AND ABILITY

Adults use the words *hard* and *easy* in different ways. At times, *hard* means "hard for me" and at other times, it refers to "tasks that most others cannot do." One even finds achievement motivation theorists using these two meanings inconsistently (Nicholls 1989). This difference in meanings captures much of the problem of maintaining feelings of competence. If what is hard for me is also hard for most others, I do not lack ability. But if what is hard for me is easy for most others, I lack ability. Thus, we need to distinguish the "self-referenced" meaning of *hard* from *hard* in the sense of "difficult for most members of a reference group." This is the second aspect of the definition of ability.

When, as adults, we set out to evaluate our own or another's ability, we employ the framework wherein high ability means ability to do tasks that others cannot do. The test of this conception (Nicholls 1978; Nicholls & Miller 1983; derived from Veroff 1969) required children to recognize that a puzzle which a small proportion of one's peers can do requires more

TABLE 1.2 Levels of Differentiation of Difficulty and Ability

1. *Egocentric.* Tasks are distinguished in terms of one's own subjective probability of success. Hard is equivalent to "hard for me" which is equivalent to "I'm not smart at it."
2. *Objective.* A continuum of levels of difficulty is recognized as demanding corresponding levels of ability. Difficulty is recognized independently of one's own expectations of success. Nevertheless, one cannot distinguish whether failure at a given task is due to low ability or high difficulty: the statement "it's hard" is not distinguishable from "it's too hard for me" which is not distinguishable from "I'm not smart at it."
3. *Normative.* Ability and difficulty are completely differentiated in terms of the success rates of others. Tasks that fewer peers can succeed on are judged harder and as needing higher ability. This means that "hard for me" can be distinguished from "hard."

ability than ones that larger proportions of one's peers can do. Although preschoolers will make social comparisons, show forms of rivalry, and become upset if others complete a task before they do (Heckhausen 1984), they cannot pass this test: they do not have normative conceptions of difficulty and ability. There is no contradiction here. The fact that a child compares her performance with that of another does not tell us how she construes ability. A desire to do better than another person does not depend on normative conceptions of ability and difficulty. All it requires is a belief that another's accomplishments indicate what one should be able to do—a form of normative conformity rather than an explicit recognition that ability and task difficulty are most precisely judgeable with reference to social comparison performance norms.

Two less differentiated conceptions of difficulty and ability were also distinguished (Nicholls & Miller 1983). The first, egocentric level (see table 1.2) is purely self-referenced in that *hard* means "hard for me." At the second objective level, children explicitly recognize hierarchies of difficulty of tasks on the basis of concrete properties such as the number of pieces in a jigsaw puzzle. At this point they identify the most complex of a series of puzzles as the hardest, whereas at the first level they do not. Both of these conceptions, however, are a perfectly adequate basis for the selection of tasks that are personally challenging and are sufficient to enable children to exercise and develop their skills (Schneider 1984).[2]

2. Researchers have tended to leap from evidence of young children's unrealistically optimistic statements about their competence or their chances of com-

These conceptions are also sufficient to allow young children to keep their places in dominance hierarchies (Strayer & Strayer 1976). All that is required is an ability to recognize whether one can or cannot beat others as one meets them.

The validity of the measure of the normative, or level 3 conceptions of difficulty and ability is suggested by evidence that children who "pass" this test are also more likely (than those who do not) to assert that a teacher would be impressed by people who solved a puzzle few others could do (Nicholls 1978, 1980). Furthermore, those with normative conceptions are more likely than those without to attempt unseen puzzles they are told that few or about half their peers can do. Children without the normative conceptions are more likely to choose tasks that most of their peers are said to be able to do (Nicholls & Miller 1983). Not seeing success on the more difficult tasks as more impressive, they have no reason for choosing them. Indeed, they might conclude that a puzzle on which most children succeed is the "right" one to choose.

It also seems likely that the increased responsiveness to social comparison cues that can occur around the age of seven (Boggiano & Ruble 1979; Frey & Ruble 1985) might in part be a consequence of the attainment of the normative conceptions of ability and difficulty. The proposition that the normative conception of ability would mean an increase in the systematic use of social rank to judge one's competence is also suggested by a study by Miller (in press). He found that students with the normative conception were less likely than those at lower levels to rank themselves top of their class in reading. This effect occurred despite the fact that those with the normative conception were rated as higher in reading attainment by their teachers. Furthermore, only those with the normative conception showed significant stability in rankings of their reading attainment over one year.

From the perspective of a society wherein the status of individuals depends on the relative competence of their performance, it is important that people should be able to recognize their rank in abstract hierarchies

pleting tasks to the generalization that they do not have a realistic sense of what they can and cannot do. Young children's optimism should be acknowledged. It is difficult, however, to see how they could ever move around in their worlds and select tasks that enable them to develop their competencies if they lacked a measure of "realism" about familiar tasks. It is, therefore, reassuring to have Schneider's evidence that, given appropriate tasks and measures of expectations of success, young children are sensitive to variations in objective difficulty.

of competence without engaging in direct contests with every other individual. People should, for example, be able to understand that if they have performed worse than others of their age, even if they have never seen them, they are less able than the others. By enabling such inferences, the normative conception of ability might help maintain the meritocratic tendencies of our society. But, from the point of view of the individual, the implications of this conception can often be negative. First, a heightened concern about one's standing relative to others and a decrease in self-referenced self-evaluation could lead to lower ratings of one's ability. Second, when the goal of one's efforts and accomplishments is to establish one's superiority over others, one's actions tend to be experienced as a means to this end (Butler 1987; Nicholls 1984a; Ryan 1982). Thus, the normative conception of ability might, by making children more susceptible to concerns about their standing, contribute to the decline in enthusiasm for learning that occurs over the school years (Eccles, Midgley, & Adler 1984; Harter 1981b).

ABILITY AND EFFORT

The third and final aspect of the definition of *ability* concerns the conception of ability as capacity—the notion that an increase in effort can increase how well we perform relative to others but only up to a limit that we take as an index of our current capacity. This conception is expressed in the belief that if someone can perform as well as others with less effort, he is more able than the others and could perform better than they if everyone applied the same amount of effort. Although commonsensical to adults, these understandings are not achieved until early adolescence.

There are always things we cannot do. But the mere fact that we cannot do something does not, in common usage, imply that we lack capacity. I have never come close to running a mile in three minutes, but that alone tells you nothing about my running ability. Even if I tell you that I have tried my best to do this and reduced my time dramatically, you still have no basis (on this information alone) for telling whether I lack capacity as a miler. It is only when you know that no one else has ever run a mile in three minutes that you know that my failure to reach this standard does not indicate a lack of capacity on my part. So, it is critical not to overlook the fact that, as it is commonly used, the concept of capacity refers to capacity relative to that of others. Note also that nothing is implied about genetic potential, ultimate capacity, or the levels one might ultimately reach given time, determination, and a favorable environment. As used here, the conception of ability as capacity is relevant to situations such as intelligence-testing sessions rather than to the processes involved in the acquisition of knowledge or skill. Accordingly, to determine whether children have this conception, they were given depictions of short-term performance situations in which one student who worked harder than another scored the same or more poorly than the other.

The questions asked about these stimuli were not simply intended to determine whether children judged the harder worker was more or less able. If that were the concern, it would have been sufficient simply to ask children how able they thought the two children were. But the answer to this question would have been of no value for determining how children construe ability and effort. A child could reason that, because more able students tend to work harder in school, the harder worker was probably more able. Interesting though such reasoning might be, it would be of no more use than the child's height for helping us judge whether she or he had the conception of ability as capacity. For this purpose we needed to confront children with a dilemma that could not be solved without the conception of ability as capacity. This was done by asking how it is that one person does as well as another (or better) despite less effort. It was also necessary to standardize interpretation of this problem. Students are, for example, prone to see cheating as an explanation of a lazier child's score. It was necessary (for our purpose) to make it clear that the situation depicted did not involve cheating, lucky guessing, or any other factor that would make effort and ability irrelevant as determinants of performance. And, to check on the initial answers, children were asked what score the students would get if, next time, they both tried hard. Then as a final check, we asked whether one student was smarter than the other at the task they were doing. (For more details of the idiosyncrasies of children's interpretations of these stimuli, see Nicholls 1989).

On the basis of these interviews, four levels of differentiation of the concepts of effort and ability were isolated with the conception of ability as capacity emerging at about ten to thirteen years (see table 1.3). The transition to level 2 occurs more or less simultaneously with the attainment of the normative conception of ability—at about six years (Nicholls 1978). Comparable age trends were obtained when, instead of reasoning about two others, children were interviewed about themselves and another who worked either harder or not as hard as they (Nicholls & Miller 1984b). So, these levels seem to describe the ways children construe their own ability as well as the ability of others.

TABLE 1.3 Levels of Differentiation of Ability and Effort

1. *Effort or outcome is ability.* Effort, ability, and performance outcomes are imperfectly differentiated as cause and effect. Explanations of outcomes are tautological. Children center on effort (people who try harder than another are seen as smarter even if they get a lower score) or on outcome (people who get a higher score are said to work harder—even if they do not—and are seen as smarter).
2. *Effort is the cause of outcomes.* Effort and outcomes are differentiated as cause and effect. Effort is the prime cause of outcomes: equal effort is expected to lead to equal outcomes. When attainment is equal but effort differs, this is seen as resulting from compensatory effort by students who try less (e.g., she worked really hard for a while) or misapplied effort by those who try harder (e.g., he went quickly and made mistakes).
3. *Effort and ability partially differentiated.* Effort is not the only cause of outcomes. Explanations of equal outcomes following different efforts involve suggestions that imply the conception of ability as capacity (e.g., the person trying less is faster or brighter). These implications, however, are not systematically followed through (e.g., children may still assert that individuals would achieve equally if they applied equal effort).
4. *Ability is capacity.* Ability and effort are clearly differentiated. Ability is conceived as capacity which, if low, may limit or, if high, may increase the effect of effort on performance. Conversely, the effect of effort is constrained by ability. When achievement is equal, lower effort implies higher ability.

In the case of the concepts of luck and skill, quantitative judgment methodologies and our method of assessing the meanings of skill and luck produced convergent findings. But this was not the case for the concepts of effort and ability. Surber (1984), for example, discusses evidence of little relationship between age and the inference that for a given performance, higher effort indicates lower ability between approximately six and twelve years (159). But it is hard to compare our research with the studies Surber reviews. Our interviews were not concerned primarily with inferences of ability from information about effort and performance.

Our interviews indicated that inferences of ability from effort and performance information could reflect diverse interpretations of the problem. A child might reasonably suspect that someone who did well with little effort was lucky on this occasion. She or he might not consider the performance information very relevant or very reliable and simply apply the generalization that harder workers are generally the more able students. These interpretations could both be legitimate and justify a judgment that higher effort indicated higher ability. But this would reveal nothing about a child's conceptions of ability and effort. The various studies of judgments of effort and ability do not explicitly present students with the problem of how someone can perform as well as or better than another with less effort and rule out interpretations such as cheating that make the situation explicable in terms of factors other than effort and ability.

Furthermore, in a number of studies of ability judgments, high effort was represented to children by saying that an actor had to try very hard (Kun 1977; Surber 1980). For children at a low level of understanding of difficulty, *hard* means "hard for me to do," which is close to "I'm not smart at this." Thus young children might see someone who "had to try very hard" as low in ability. But this would not mean that they understood ability as capacity. In this case, evidence of a lack of convergence between methods cannot be taken simply as evidence of lack of validity of one of the methods. Although, in this particular domain, users of quantitative judgment methodologies appear not to have been cognizant of the diverse interpretations that might underlie their findings, these findings remain important. They tell us about when students judge ability as high or low. They do not, as far as I can tell, have a clear bearing on the question addressed here—that of how children construe ability and effort.

An index of the validity of the present method of assessing conceptions of ability and effort can be gained by examining age-related changes in related evaluations or judgments. Research by others shows roughly parallel age-related change in evaluations of hypothetical students of different levels of effort and ability (Salili, Maehr, & Gillmore 1976; Weiner & Peter 1973). Judgments of ability based on evidence of teachers' feedback (Meyer et al. 1979) and emotion (Weiner et al. 1982) also show age changes that parallel and can be explained in terms of the differentiation of the concepts of effort and ability (see Nicholls & Miller, 1984a, for a review). More convincing, however, are studies where both conceptions of ability and evaluations or action were assessed.

In one approach to assessing achievement evaluations, students were asked (by a researcher with no knowledge of their conceptions of ability and effort) to predict how a teacher would evaluate students described as having succeeded with high effort and low ability or high ability and low effort. Students who did not differentiate effort and ability expected teachers to approve strongly of both students. But as ability and effort became partially (level 3) and fully differentiated (level 4), subjects expected teacher-approval of the student who was highly able but less industrious to decline. Presumably, for children who confound ability and effort, the description of someone as performing highly because of high ability (but despite low effort) does not imply a lack of industry as clearly as it does for level 3 and 4 children (Nicholls 1978).

Complementary results were obtained when, at the end of interviews, students were asked whether they would rather be like the student who worked harder or the student who was less industrious (Nicholls, Patashnick, & Mettetal 1986). Students at all levels were aware that teachers value effort and they do so themselves. The advantages of being able to do well with less effort than others were, however, largely lost on children at levels 1 and 2. Those at levels 3 and 4, on the other hand, were attracted to the possibility of needing less effort than others to do class assignments. Only 29 percent of level 4 and 57 percent of level 3 students preferred to be like the harder worker, whereas 97 percent of level 1 and 2 students did.[3] These results indicate the validity of the assessment of conceptions of ability and effort. Evidence on performance is also relevant to the question of validity.

When ability is construed as capacity, perception of oneself as lacking a given ability would, presumably, be more aversive and make it seem more unlikely that one could perform well on tasks demanding this form of ability. The attainment of the conception of ability as capacity could, therefore, lead to more decisively impaired performance in situations where students believe that their actions are highly likely to establish that they lack an ability that is important to them.

Miller (1985) tested this hypothesis using a paradigm developed by Frankel and Snyder (1978). Only one of the three conditions he created was calculated to make students think they were about to fail on a measure of intellectual ability *and* that (because the task was one that many children their age could do) their failure would indicate a lack of intelligence on their part. According to the above logic, this condition should lead to impaired performance in students with the conception of ability as capacity more than in those without this conception. A second condition was

3. Although accuracy of perception of competence is not the focus of this chapter, it is interesting that associations between children's rankings of their own reading attainment and teacher's rankings of reading achievement increase with level of differentiation of effort and ability: level 2, $r = .19$, n.s.; level 3, $r = .59, p < .001$; level 4, $r = .81$ (Nicholls 1978). Perhaps as the concepts of effort and ability become more differentiated, children judge their competence more on how they compare to others on concrete performance indexes than on the subjective experience of effortful accomplishment.

calculated to induce expectations of failure, but the sting of failure was reduced by saying that the task was one that hardly anyone the students' age could do well on. A third condition did not induce expectations of failure. The results were nicely in accord with expectations. For sixth-graders but not second-graders performance was poorest in the first condition, where failure would indicate lack of ability (comparable age trends in impairment of performance were reported by Rholes et al. 1980). The role of the conception of ability as capacity in the sixth-graders' results was indicated more directly when sixth-grade students were dichotomized into those who had completely (level 4) or partially (level 3) attained the conception of ability as capacity versus those who had not. There was no significant variation in performance across the three conditions for level 1 and 2 students. But those with the conception of ability as capacity (levels 3 and 4) performed worst in the condition where failure was both likely *and* where it would indicate low ability.

The concept of current capacity means that even tasks we are able to master as well as others can—if we expect others to need less time or effort—offer us no prospect of a sense of accomplishment. Furthermore, the harder we try to avoid low performance, the more convincingly will failure establish incompetence. Thus, when we expect to fail or take longer on tasks at which others succeed, hard work will be a less attractive option than it was at earlier ages. Even if we do not face failure, effort as such could be less inherently valuable when ability is construed as capacity. Effortful accomplishment still means virtue, but it does not connote competence as clearly as it does at less differentiated levels. And if we doubt our ability, we will—when we construe ability as capacity—have less faith in the power of effort to raise our performance relative to that of others. All of this adds up to the conclusion that, if we feel we lack ability, even though we might be able to learn we will see our best as not good enough. Furthermore, this deficiency of ability will be experienced as more fundamental than it was before we construed ability as capacity. This could make for an increased devaluing of activities where we might reveal our incompetence and lead to attempts to avoid such activities.

Sports organizations are voluntary and players apparently leave these in droves starting at about the age when the conception of ability as capacity develops (Roberts 1984). This trend is all the more dramatic when we note that adolescent males value competence in sports above competence in other domains (Coleman 1961; Roberts 1984). Thus, the dropping out in early adolescence is not likely to be the result of a lack of desire for competence in sport in general. The role of low perceived ability in disaffection and dropping out is suggested by evidence that youths who dropped out of U.S. Wrestling Foundation teams reported lower perceived ability and valued wrestling less than did those who continued (Burton & Martens 1986). Significantly, the two groups did not differ in the importance they placed on other sports. It was only wrestling, at which they felt less competent, that was valued less by dropouts. The development of the concept of capacity could be one of the factors contributing to the withdrawal of adolescents from sports.

In schoolwork, withdrawal must take more subtle forms. These could include the seeking of a sense of accomplishment in nonacademic domains such as sport and in membership in groups that actively resist the pressure for academic attainment. For those who have trouble finding any activity of some social esteem at which they can feel competent, adolescence might be bleaker than childhood.

INTELLIGENCE

The conceptions of ability I have discussed are general in that they apply to diverse skills. For example, whether one is interested in assessing intellectual or physical skills, one tries to ensure that test performance reflects skill rather than luck. One also endeavors to induce optimum effort so that performance reflects individual differences in current capacity rather than motivation during testing. Furthermore, a score or performance is normally interpreted as high or low with reference to the scores of others. These principles hold regardless of the type of ability involved. Second, these principles pertain to the process of assessing abilities rather than the problems of explaining the nature and development of the abilities that are thereby assessed. Psychometric researchers do not usually have doubts or diverse opinions about the principle that intelligence tests should be administered so as to elicit optimum motivation in those being tested. These are not matters that have concerned them. Such researchers do, however, argue about and seek to evaluate diverse views on the nature and determinants of different intellectual skills. They seek to learn if it is possible to distinguish aspects of intelligence involving reasoning and problem solving from those that reflect the amount of information a person can recall about specific topics. And, if this distinction can be made, how might these different aspects of intelligence be increased?

The conception of ability as capacity concerns the dynamics of effort and present competence in determining performance. Accordingly, the stimuli and questions we used to assess this conception were designed to focus students' attention on the immediate effects of effort on performance—on how unequal effort can lead to equal performance—not on the long-term development of abilities. Furthermore, the specific characteristics of the skill involved were not of concern in the interviews about conceptions of ability and effort. Thus, the methods and concepts I have discussed so far are as applicable to the domain of sport (Duda 1987) as they are to the domain of schoolwork. By way of contrast, the interview developed to assess conceptions of intelligence (Nicholls, Patashnick, & Mettetal 1986) focused on the specific properties of different types of intellectual skill and on the question of how these might be improved.

In different cultures, the word *intelligence* is applied to different forms of competence (Berry 1984; Goodnow 1980). This variation could reflect variation in the types of abilities that are valued and regarded as components of intelligence. In our society, there is variation in the types of competence that are taken as signs of intelligence. Adults are readier to take social competence as an indication of intelligence in young children than in adolescents (Siegler & Richards 1982). Adolescents also employ the term *intelligence* with more discrimination than do eight-year-olds (Murray & Bisanz 1987). From eight years on, children apply the term *intelligence* to examples of competence at academic and mental activities, but adolescents are less likely than eight-year-olds to apply the term to examples of social and physical ability. Our work was restricted to the development of the understanding of competencies that, in this society, would clearly be considered intellectual skills by both children and adults.

Sternberg and his colleagues' evidence (1981) that the first two factors in the conceptions of intelligence of both expert and lay North American adults corresponded rather well to the concepts of fluid and crystallized intelligence provided a starting point for the research I will discuss. Fluid intelligence consists mainly of abstract, nonverbal reasoning and problem-solving skills, whereas crystallized intelligence involves mainly verbal skills such as vocabulary and verbal comprehension. And, according to Horn (1968), "a relatively large population of the reliable variance in fluid intelligence reflects a pattern of physiological influences and a relatively small proportion of this variance reflects acculturation, whereas the opposite emphasis occurs for crystallized intelligence" (247–48).

In view of the salience of concepts analogous to fluid and crystallized intelligence among adults in the United States, Nicholls and his colleagues (1986) evolved a method that was intended to reveal such concepts in students who had them but that could also detect any different ways of construing these aspects of intelligence that might exist. The stimuli used were items from a verbal and nonverbal intelligence test that illustrate crystallized and fluid intelligence, respectively. Students, from first grade through college, were interviewed about two other students, one of whom was represented as more able than his classmates on the verbal test and less able on the nonverbal test. The second student's standing on these tests was reversed.

Three conceptions of intelligence were distinguished (see table 1.4). These form a series of increasingly differentiated levels. At level 1 there is almost no reference to the inherent properties of different types of intellectual ability: the subjective sense of difficulty predominates. Level 2 represents a conceptual advance in that it involves a specification of what makes intelligence difficult to acquire—namely, the amount of information that must be acquired through effort. (Level 2 also appears congruent with the second of three levels described by Leahy & Hunt, 1983, wherein level of motivation is seen as a major difference between people who are "smart" and those who are not.) Level 3b, which resembles fluid and crystallized intelligence, represents an advance over level 2 in that memory is clearly distinguished from problem-solving or reasoning ability. Level 3a appears as a less complete or transitional construction of this distinction: although abstract reasoning is seen as a significant type of skill and as more difficult to improve, it is not explicitly described as a problem-solving ability.

The conceptions of intelligence show some conceptual parallels with the conceptions of ability and effort. For example, the level 2 conception, wherein intelligence depends on effortful acquisition of information, parallels the level 2 conception of ability, wherein effort is seen as the prime cause of task outcomes. Furthermore, a belief in the limited value of effort for improving abstract intelligence is most evident in the most differentiated conception of intelligence (3b). In this respect, the latter conception parallels the differentiated conception of ability, wherein ability is construed as capacity that limits the effect of effort on performance. These conceptual parallels, however, are not manifest as empirical parallels. The most differentiated conception of ability is an achievement of early adolescence, whereas the corresponding conception of intelligence predominates only at about the age of sixteen—well after the concept of current capacity is established.

This finding is, perhaps, not surprising because understanding of

least three types of long-term change can be distinguished. Change can be judged in terms of things a person can do or understand. The concept of mental age exemplifies this concept—if one keeps improving on the types of skills that intelligence tests measure, one's mental age will keep going up. The general rule is that mental age increases during childhood. So, in this sense, change in intelligence is widespread. A second conception of change is change in social rank. One can learn new things and increase in mental age, but get lower and lower in social rank. One's IQ will decline, remain fixed, or increase depending on the rate at which one's mental age increases. But this is a zero-sum game. Children cannot all increase their IQs because they can't all be above average. Thus, a person could hold that change in the first sense is ubiquitous but that change in the second sense is less frequent. In our study of the conceptions of intelligence of 143 children and adolescents (Nicholls et al. 1986), all said yes when asked if people could improve their rank on verbal and nonverbal skills. In the first two senses, therefore, it seems that there are virtually no entity theorists.[4] The question of changeability could also refer to changeability of genetic potential. One might reject the possibility of this sort of change while allowing the first two forms. With respect to the third sense of change, presumably most of us are entity theorists.

It would be interesting to know what developmental changes occur in the understanding of these different forms of change. Simple questions about the changeability of intelligence will not enable us to distinguish the different types. At different ages, children will probably interpret questionnaire items about changeability differently. Age trends in responses to such scales would not be readily interpretable, and the absence of age trends (Bempechat 1985) could conceal differences in understanding of one or more of the different forms of intellectual change. Nevertheless, as Dweck and Elliott (1983) seem to suggest, reliable individual differences in beliefs about the alterability of intelligence might be identifiable and have important behavioral and emotional consequences (see also Rholes, Jones, & Wade, in press).[5]

4. The question about the possibility of change in rank on verbal and nonverbal skills was one of the questions that served merely to set the stage for the main questions. For this reason, and because of our subjects' unanimity, we did not report responses to this question. This also serves to highlight the differences between our work and that of Dweck. We assume that people see change in rank as possible. Our question then is which skills appear more changeable and why.

5. As Dweck and Bempechat have opted for a conventional psychometric instrument to assess theories of intelligence, evidence that it possesses conven-

Other studies of concepts of personal characteristics show age-related trends that have some convergence with some of those I have described. Barenboim (1981) presents evidence of a progression from behavioral comparisons—where children compare others in terms of actions—followed by the use of psychological constructs—such as "stubborn"—and finally, at ten and twelve years, social comparisons of psychological constructs. Although his method was different from those I have presented, Barenboim's analysis shows some correspondence with my description of conceptions of ability. The category of behavioral comparisons seems to correspond to the normative conception of ability, wherein "smart" means doing better than others. And, like the normative conception of ability and difficulty, it is found at about seven years. The conception of ability as capacity is a psychological construct that depends on social comparison. It and Barenboim's comparisons of psychological constructs both predominate at about twelve years. To emphasize this convergence could, however, conceal the fact that the conceptions of ability differ both in meaning and in pattern of development from conceptions of intelligence. The course of development of ability-related personal constructs cannot be encompassed by a single developmental sequence.

General descriptions of developmental change in personal constructs can probably never capture the richness and diversity of meanings of specific constructs. Perhaps if researchers examine the development of other specific constructs such as extroversion, industriousness, or honesty, greater richness and incommensurability will be found. In the achievement domain, for example, it would be of interest to know what subdomains of athletic ability are distinguished and how conceptions of athletic ability change. Informal interviews conducted by Patashnick indicate that adolescents see specific skills like running speed and lifting strength as very different from skill at games like basketball. But we seem to lack even a rough outline of how such skills might be construed. In view of the importance placed on athletic prowess by youths in our society, conceptions of athletic ability could have a significant bearing on psychological well-being (Duda, in press; Roberts 1984). Conceptions of social abilities might also prove a rewarding field for exploration.

Like different conceptions of ability, different conceptions of intel-

---

tional psychometric virtues, such as internal consistency and convergent and discriminant validity, is needed. To date, no such evidence has been presented. Do we know, for example, that endorsement of the entity view is not merely a statement of low performance expectations or low perceived ability?

ligence are accompanied by different evaluative judgments. At the end of the interview about intelligence, students were asked whether they would rather be good at the verbal or the abstract intelligence test. Overall, 67 percent of the students with conceptions akin to fluid and crystallized intelligence (level 3b) preferred abstract intelligence, whereas only 16 percent of those with level 1 and level 2 conceptions did (Nicholls et al. 1986). Findings similar to those of level 3 students were obtained for Taiwanese and Australian sixteen-year-olds and college students, most of whom would presumably be at level 3. Students of both nationalities saw abstract (spatial) responding as more important than verbal-educational ability and rote memory (Chen, Braithwaite, & Jong 1982).

The greater preference for abstract reasoning ability on the part of students with the conception resembling fluid and crystallized intelligence raises the possibility that, in Western culture if not others, the prestige accorded disciplines that appear to demand abstract intelligence might depend on this conception. The greater valuing of abstract reasoning might also make academic subjects such as mathematics especially threatening to those who doubt their fluid intelligence, and they might therefore avoid such subjects and occupations. Those who see themselves as high in abstract reasoning might seek to enhance their self-esteem by choosing subjects and occupations accordingly.

Conceptions of intelligence might also affect attitudes toward different teaching methods. For example, provided they do not doubt their competence, students with conceptions akin to fluid and crystallized intelligence appear more likely than others to favor teaching that fosters problem finding and solving rather than memorization. Younger children's conceptions of intelligence appear to dispose them to see virtue in memorization. Indeed level 2, "trivial pursuit" conceptions of intelligence might contribute to the resistance encountered by teachers who encourage self-directed problem finding and solving among younger students. On the other hand, level 2 conceptions might be sustained by the emphasis on memorization and on the following of teachers' rules that prevails in many schools.

WHEN AND WHY ARE WE MINDFUL OF OUR ABILITY?

It is one thing to describe the development of ability-related concepts. It is a different matter to explain either why development of ability-related concepts takes the forms it does or what influences rates of development of these forms. Because there are no relevant data, I can say nothing about these questions here, except that they should not—as has often occurred—be confounded. There is, however, a further important question to which we do have some answers: the question of when we employ our most differentiated conceptions of ability.

The assessment of the concept of capacity was designed to see if students had that concept, not to establish when that concept is used. Part of the argument above is that the differentiation of the concept of ability from effort, luck, and difficulty might lead, especially for those who doubt their competence, to reduced emotional well-being and less effective learning and performance. But these effects would occur only to the extent that, as the concept of ability becomes more differentiated, individuals consistently use it to evaluate their performance. And they do not always do so.

If we assume that the concepts we employ are a function of our purposes, it follows that we will not use complex conceptions where simple ones will serve (Nicholls 1984a). The concept of capacity is necessary if we want to tell how able we are. Without using this concept we cannot tell whether scores on tests reflect effort, task difficulty, or ability. This is why the logic of this concept is embodied in intelligence test administration and interpretation practices. Thus, if we are actively concerned about how able we are, we should employ this concept. We are likely to become actively concerned about how able we are if we think our ability (in a domain of personal relevance) is being tested, if an audience or evaluative comments focus our attention on our competence at a valued task, or if there is a climate of interpersonal competition.

In the absence of these conditions and when working on tasks that we find interesting, we should have no use for the concept of capacity. In such cases, we can function like little children and gain a sense of competence and accomplishment from the full exercise of our skills, from a gain in understanding, or from an increase in the efficiency of our performance.

A diverse body of research with undergraduates and adolescents (presented here in truncated form) supports these arguments (Nicholls 1984a, 1989). There is also some evidence of similar phenomena in young children. As Heckhausen (1984) has shown, rivalry can be stimulated so that young children adopt another person's performance as a standard of adequacy. These children would not have the normative conception of ability (let alone the conception of ability as capacity). Yet, when someone raises the question of their competence by implying that they should do as well as another, rivalrous behavior occurs and tasks they would happily work at alone can become a source of frustration and feelings of incompetence. It is interesting to contrast this tendency toward rivalry with the behavior described by Morrison and Kuhn (1983). They observed groups of four- to six-year-olds (each child working with a set of construction material) who had not been stimulated to rivalry. They worked on their individual projects, but they did observe others, especially those who were making more complex constructions than theirs. Most of these children appeared more concerned with learning from their peers than with evaluating their competence relative to their peers because observation of others was accompanied by gains in competence of constructions.

The contrast between these two concerns corresponds to the distinction between task involvement and ego involvement (Asch 1952; Maehr & Braskamp 1986; Nicholls 1984a). Ego involvement implies a concern with how one's ability compares with that of others—a desire to be superior as implied by lay terms like "ego trip" or "egotist." In task involvement, understanding a problem or performing one's best is the central concern. Spence and Helmreich (1983) make a similar distinction: competitiveness versus work and mastery orientations.

Although the implications of ego involvement should become more negative as the concept of ability becomes more developed, they appear likely to be negative across much of the life span. Young children's understanding of bribery and coercion undoubtedly undergoes considerable change from preschool to adolescence. There is, nevertheless, good evidence that preschoolers and adolescents alike have their interest in tasks undermined by rewards that smack of bribery (Kassin & Lepper 1984). We do not have the same amount of evidence on the undermining effect of competition—an emphasis on social comparison or public evaluations of competence—in young children. Yet it seems likely that it occurs.

In any event, there is considerable evidence that social conditions that produce ego involvement undermine interest in and enjoyment of task performance in adolescents and adults (e.g., Harackiewicz, Manderlink, & Sansone 1984). Similarly, there is evidence that the performance of individuals with low perceived ability is more impaired and their levels of aspirations more unrealistic in ego-involving conditions than in task-involving conditions (Nicholls 1984a, 1989). So the negative consequences of the differentiation of the concept of ability are more likely to be manifest in ego-involving than in task-involving environments. A task-involving climate increases the likelihood that even adults will evaluate their work in the self-referenced fashion of young children.

As Spence and Helmreich (1983) have shown, one can also distinguish individuals in terms of their dispositions to be concerned with their standing relative to others versus concerned about understanding as much as possible, performing one's best, or exercising one's skills as fully as possible. In this vein, we have devised scales of *ego orientation* and *task orientation* in schoolwork. These scales are either not associated or only slightly associated in college students (Nicholls et al., in press), high school seniors and freshmen (Nicholls, Patashnick, & Nolen 1985), highly academically able early adolescents (Thorkildsen 1988), fifth-graders (Nicholls & Thorkildsen 1987), and second-graders (Nicholls et al., in press). One additional finding of all these studies is of special interest here, namely, that perceived academic ability is either not associated or only slightly associated with task and ego orientations—that is, students who believe they are low in ability relative to their peers can nevertheless be highly oriented to understanding and working hard in order to learn.

Although conceptions of the nature of ability and intelligence undergo dramatic change over the school years, it seems that the distinction between task orientation and ego orientation can be made in a similar fashion at all grade levels. Furthermore, the correlates of these orientations are remarkably similar across the grades. Both high school and elementary students' beliefs about what leads to success in school are consistently related to motivational orientations. The beliefs that success in school depends on being smarter than other students and trying to beat them are associated with ego orientation. In other words, those whose goal is to be superior to others emphasize superior ability as a prerequisite of academic success. Task orientation, on the other hand, is associated with beliefs that academic success depends on interest, effort, collaborating with one's fellows, and trying to understand rather than just memorizing.

These results accord nicely with the ecological approach to social perception (McArthur & Baron 1983), which holds that perception is always a function of the perceiver's goals. This perspective does not imply that task- and ego-oriented individuals have different conceptions of effort, ability, or intelligence. Ability and effort attributions should (again) not be confused with conceptions of ability and effort. My proposal is that, for ego-oriented individuals, the limits imposed by current capacity are very important. These limits affect their chances of attaining their goal of superiority—their form of success—thus their emphasis on ability as a cause of success. For task-oriented individuals, however, effort and attempts to understand are necessary if they are to achieve their goals of gaining understanding or stretching their skills—thus their emphasis on effort and attempts to make sense of things.

These findings seem important for education because the only way for all students to have high perceived ability is for a lot of them to be deluded—they can't all be above average. High perceived ability (in the differentiated sense) seems, at best, a foolish criterion of educational success or personal well-being. Many self-esteem scales are dominated by questions about feelings of competence. To indicate self-acceptance on these scales, people must believe they are above average. This is the sort of criterion of adjustment that one might expect to be generated and used by researchers in a competitive, meritocratic society. If children reflect the preoccupation with ability that these scales symbolize, they will be ego-involved and unfortunate consequences will follow.

Rather than focusing on people's perceptions of competence, researchers could focus on their feelings about the value of what they are doing—the meaningfulness of their work. In the context of school, this would mean assessing students' feelings of satisfaction with their work rather than their evaluations of how competent they feel. We found satisfaction with learning in school to be positively associated with task orientation but not with ego orientation. Furthermore, the association between task orientation and satisfaction with learning in school was not altered when perceived academic ability was partialed out (Nicholls, Patashnick, & Nolen 1985; Thorkildsen 1988).

All the above statements about associations involving individual differences in task and ego orientation also apply when fifth-grade classes (instead of individuals) are the unit of analysis (Nicholls & Thorkildsen 1987). Task orientation and ego orientation are uncorrelated at the class level as well as at the individual level. Also, the more task-oriented a class is, the more the students in that class believe that success depends on effort, interest, attempts to understand, and collaboration with peers, and the more satisfied they are with learning in school. Ego-oriented classes are more inclined to believe that academic success depends on being smarter than others and trying to beat others. Furthermore, they have no advantage in terms of satisfaction with school learning. Thus, the same conclusions apply whether one speaks of the motivational climate of classrooms or individual differences in motivational orientation. There is much to be said for task-oriented classrooms—where students are concerned about making sense of things rather than being superior to their peers.

The above evidence might be considered along with evidence that task orientation more than ego orientation appears to foster free-choice participation in activities (Duda, in press), significant adult accomplishment (Spence & Helmreich 1983), and creativity (Amabile 1983). In light of this, one might wonder if the solution to the various problems attendant on low perceived ability is to divert attention away from the question of ability. Rather than thinking of ways to induce everyone to think they are highly able and to feel good about their ability, we might think of ways to help them find value in their work or to construct meaningful knowledge.

For example, Butler (1987) has shown that grades and praise foster ego involvement, whereas task involvement is fostered by comments that focus attention on the virtues of work already done and suggest directions for further development. There is scope for further exploration of this topic. Nicholls, Patashnick, and Nolen (1985) found that the belief (on the part of high school students) that school should make one a responsible, constructive member of society was associated with task orientation, whereas the belief that school should help one gain wealth and social status was associated with academic alienation. This raises questions about the possible role of parents' and teachers' views about the purposes of education in students' task or ego orientation. The finding that students who believe that school should help make them useful and knowledgeable citizens also tend to be task-oriented suggests that such students might be task-oriented to the extent that the subjects they study involve what they see as useful knowledge. One might, therefore, profitably explore students' understandings of the nature and purposes of different forms of knowledge. Such research might help in the development of curriculum materials that would foster task involvement.

These are but a few of the many questions researchers might ask if they wish to support teachers and parents who would foster involvement in learning for its own sake and minimize students' preoccupation with their standing in a hierarchy of ability (see also Deci & Ryan 1985; Nicholls, 1989). I have spent less time than I might on such questions. Instead of asking how preoccupation with one's ability can be reduced, I have focused on the question of how ability is construed, and my doubts about the worthwhileness of this work are growing. It is not that the work is worthless or lacking in interest, nor is it a question about the competence with which the work has been done. It is simply that more students might be gaining a sense of accomplishment and experiencing their work as meaningful if more researchers had been asking about the meaning of students' work rather than about their ability.

CHAPTER 2

The Developmental Course of Perceived Competence and Incompetence among Competent Children

DEBORAH A. PHILLIPS
AND MARC ZIMMERMAN

Viewing oneself as competent to achieve valued goals has been implicated repeatedly as essential to healthy development. It may even be that inflated notions of one's competence are associated with better adjustment throughout the life span. These assertions derive from two lines of research, one examining the effect of subjective perceptions of competence and another, the role of accurate versus inaccurate judgments of competence. Both areas of inquiry have documented that personal perceptions of competence mediate a wide range of adaptive behaviors throughout life.

In this chapter we explore the link between these two bodies of research with four goals in mind: (1) to trace the developmental course of accurate and inaccurate perceptions of academic competence among high-achieving elementary and secondary students, (2) to examine sex differences in the accuracy of self-perceptions during these school years, (3) to examine the temporal stability of these perceptions, and (4) to make

The research reported in this chapter was supported by grants from the Foundation for Child Development, the W. T. Grant Foundation, the National Institute of Health (Biomedical Research Support Grant to the University of Illinois School of Life Sciences), and the Arnold O. Beckman Research Award program at the University of Illinois. The authors wish to thank Robert Sternberg, John Kolligian, and Deborah Stipek for their helpful comments on this chapter.

some preliminary observations about the academic and motivational factors that accompany various patterns of change in perceived competence. We close by outlining a conceptual framework that adds the dimension of accuracy to models of the development of perceived competence.

This chapter examines self-perceptions in terms of both their level or valence (positive to negative) and their accuracy relative to objective, external indicators of competence. Whereas valence is a characteristic of perceptions independent of actual competence, the dimension of accuracy captures the *relationship* between actual and perceived competence. Low perceived competence, for example, may constitute an accurate perception of incompetence or it may be an underestimate of an individual who is, in fact, competent. Accordingly, underestimators have been portrayed as having an "illusion of incompetence" (Langer 1979; Phillips 1984, 1987). Thus, accurate perceptions may have either a positive or negative valence and inaccurate perceptions may constitute either overestimates or underestimates.

PERCEIVED COMPETENCE AND THE MOTIVATION LITERATURE

The vast literature on achievement motivation recognizes that academic success entails much more than sheer ability. Over the last decade interest has focused on efforts to decipher how children process and interpret information relevant to their abilities. Indeed, a central theme of cognitive-developmental models of achievement motivation is that a child's perception of reality, rather than reality per se, is the more potent predictor of how he will approach and react to achievement demands (Bandura 1977, 1981; Phillips 1984). In the case of perceived competence, this perspective implies that children's perceptions of their abilities may be more important than their actual abilities in determining their motivation and achievement in school. Perceived competence has been implicated broadly as integral to the pursuit and mastery of achievement goals.

It follows that negative perceptions of competence, or perceived *in*-competence, will be associated with impaired achievement striving. Available evidence supports this contention. Much of it has been generated by research in which primary attention is directed to the determinants and correlates of subjective perceptions of competence, with minimal emphasis on the *accuracy* of these perceptions. The central empirical issues have been whether and how social-cognitive variables, such as perceived competence, affect the achievement process, with the influence of actual ability generally being controlled.

This research has, however, contributed importantly to the growing evidence that motivational orientations are often independent of actual ability. The results of this research suggest that among children who are extremely academically capable, some will display motivational deficits, and among highly motivated children, some will not be especially bright. The relative independence of actual ability and motivational determinants of achievement provides a particularly compelling demonstration of the perception-reality distinction that is central to cognitive-developmental theories of achievement motivation. As such, children for whom a disparity exists between the quality of their academic functioning and their self-perceptions of academic competence afford the opportunity to examine the motivational significance of the *accuracy* of children's ability appraisals.

ACCURACY AS A COMPONENT OF PERCEIVED COMPETENCE

Assessments of accuracy presuppose an objective indicator against which over- and underestimates of competence can be determined. Accuracy, in this context, can be judged in terms of agreement with another individual who is in a position to judge actual ability (a teacher or parent), with standardized test scores, or with grades. As will be seen, we have relied on both teacher ratings of ability and test scores as markers of actual academic competence.

The literature addressing the *accuracy* of perceived competence has developed along two largely separate paths. The developmental path searches for universal age-related changes in the accuracy of children's self- and task-perceptions, with emphasis on the perceptions themselves, their nature, and the sequence of their development. The second path emphasizes factors that promote and sustain accurate versus inaccurate self-perceptions of competence. Pertinent research has relied largely on adult samples with the notable exception of the research on sex differences in achievement motivation. The emphasis in this adult literature has been on identifying the correlates of these perceptions rather than on their content and structure.

The overriding conclusion of the developmental research is that children's perceptions of their abilities grow more modest and more accurate from early to late childhood (Frey & Ruble 1987; Stipek 1984; Weisz 1983). This research was prompted by repeated observations of overoptimism in young children's expectancies and ability estimates.

Recently, speculation has turned to more "social" influences on the development of social cognitions. Higgins and Parsons (1983) have argued that the ways in which children interpret information are affected not only by their maturing cognitive abilities but also by parallel changes in socialization agents, social comparison opportunities, and social roles. They emphasize the significant influence of changing educational environments, in which emphasis is increasingly placed on normative evaluations and social comparisons, on the developing ability conceptions of children.

Research (Dweck & Licht 1980; Higgins & Parsons 1983; Ruble 1983) has shown that cognitive and social influences work in concert to foster the development of stable conceptions of ability that allow for less optimism for improvement in the face of negative feedback. This, in turn, appears to make children increasingly sensitive to the negative ramifications of low ability.

Low perceived ability has been found to lead to more severe motivational problems in older children (Rholes et al. 1980; Miller 1982). It is important here, however, to distinguish outcome expectancies from perceived competence, as noted by Weisz (1983). Both Rholes et al. (1980) and Miller (1982) assessed outcome expectancies—not perceived competence—and related age trends in these expectancies to developmental differences in conceptions of ability.

The second literature concerning the accuracy of competence beliefs focuses on individual differences in the accuracy of adults' perceptions of competence. Most theorists (Langer 1979; Schulz 1980) have adopted the stance that the elderly tend to underestimate their competence as a function of social stereotypes and more dependent living circumstances. Langer (1979) coined the phrase "illusion of incompetence" to capture the unrealistically negative self-perceptions that arise when control is relinquished or opportunities to behave competently are foreclosed.

Pertinent research that carefully distinguishes among perceptions of control, contingency, and competence is sparse (see Weisz 1983) and is distinctly nondevelopmental in its orientation. Nevertheless, available evidence suggests that exaggerated, and thus inaccurate, perceptions of competence in adulthood (Lewinsohn et al. 1980) and old age (Langer 1979) are associated with nondepressed affect.

Taken as a whole, this literature reveals that children's self-perceptions of ability grow more accurate and less uniformly positive with age, that accuracy derives from stable conceptions of ability that evoke heightened sensitivity to failure, and that adults who overestimate their personal competence and control are less likely to display signs of depression. Accuracy does not necessarily appear to be a virtue.

The development of these two strands of research on the accuracy of perceived competence has nevertheless produced a sizable gap in knowledge. Little is known about the origins and ramifications of individual differences in the accuracy of children's self-perceptions of competence, nor is there much in the way of developmental literature beyond the late elementary school years despite ample theorizing about life-span trends in the accuracy of subjective appraisals (Bandura 1981).

INDIVIDUAL DIFFERENCES IN CHILDHOOD

Three notable exceptions to the dearth of research on individual differences in the accuracy of children's perceived competence are provided by Stipek (1981), by Bierer (1982, reported in Harter 1983), and by our initial studies with high-achieving children who varied widely in perceived academic competence (Phillips 1984, 1987).

Stipek (1981) examined the developmental increase in the accuracy of children's competence appraisals using teacher ratings as the objective standard for comparison. She reports a significant relation between the self-teacher correspondence of second- and third-graders' competence ratings and the consistency of the teacher feedback to which the children had been exposed. Measurement of the consistency of feedback was operationalized by comparing the self-teacher correlations of children whom teachers placed in the top or bottom third of their classroom in ability with those placed in the middle third who presumably received a mix of positive and negative feedback. Consistency was thus confounded with placement in an extreme ability group and was not otherwise observed. These findings, however, highlight the value of examining factors, such as differing competence feedback, that may produce individual differences within the context of broad developmental changes.

In one of the few studies that examined directly the behavioral consequences of the accuracy of children's perceived competence (defined, as in Stipek, 1981, as the degree of congruence between child and teacher ratings), Bierer (1982, reported in Harter 1983) compared the challenge-seeking behavior of high-ability children who differed in perceived academic competence. She found that capable children who underestimated their abilities sought less challenging tasks than did children with accurate ability appraisals. Bierer concluded that these children's beliefs about

TABLE 2.1 Perceived Academic Competence and Achievement Test Scores of Children by Age and Perceived Competence Group

Group	Third Grade			Fifth Grade			Ninth Grade		
	N	Perceived	Actual	*N*	Perceived	Actual	*N*	Perceived	Actual
Total Sample	81	3.21 (.59)	90 (5.9)	117	3.15 (.48)	92 (5.4)	62	3.20 (.43)	94 (6.4)
Low Perceived Competence	18	2.34 (.35)	90 (5.7)	23	2.43 (.24)	90 (4.6)	10	2.51 (.24)	90 (12.3)
Average Perceived Competence	39	3.24 (.29)	91 (6.3)	64	3.13 (.18)	92 (6.2)	37	3.18 (.22)	94 (6.1)
High Perceived Competence	24	3.80 (.13)	93 (5.5)	30	3.75 (.19)	95 (4.2)	15	3.71 (.18)	97 (3.5)

Note: For each group, *N*s and mean scores are presented on the top line and *SD*s are presented in parentheses on the second line. "Perceived" refers to the children's perceived academic competence scores, and "actual" refers to their composite achievement test scores expressed as national percentile ranks. The achievement test scores of the three perceived competence groups differed significantly only for the fifth-grade sample.

second sample comprised children who were initially studied in fifth grade and seen again as they completed ninth grade. The determination of high (actual) academic competence in both samples was based on dual criteria: composite achievement test scores at or above the 75th national percentile, and ranking by their current teacher in the top third of their class in overall ability.

The children's perceived competence was assessed using the cognitive subscale from Harter's Perceived Competence Scale. Based on the subscale scores, which can range from 1.00 (low perceived competence) to 4.00 (high perceived competence), the children were divided into three groups: low (inaccurate), average, and high perceived competence. Cutoff scores for the three groups, based on the samples' distribution of scores, were selected to ensure that the low and high groups reflected unusually low and high perceptions of competence relative to Harter's standardization data for each age group.

For the third-graders, the cutoffs were established at 2.71 for the low group and 3.71 for the high group; for the fifth- and ninth-graders the cutoffs were set at 2.71 for the low group and 3.57 for the high group. To place these criteria in context, we found that, compared to Harter's third-, fifth-, and ninth-grade standardization samples, each of the high achievers who was assigned to the low perceived competence group scored below the mean cognitive subscale score obtained with normal samples of agemates.

The average perceived academic competence and actual achievement test scores at each age for the three perceived competence groups and the total sample are presented in table 2.1. The total sample scores indicate high consistency across grades in both perceived and actual competence among these highly capable students. Slightly less consistency characterizes the distribution of children across the three perceived competence groups. At each grade level, a sizable but declining proportion of the children were assigned to the low perceived competence group: 22 percent in third grade, 20 percent in fifth grade, and 16 percent in ninth grade. The correlation between perceived academic competence and the children's test scores also varied minimally across age groups: $r = .30$ at third grade, r's = .27 for the complete fifth-grade sample and .28 for the fifth-graders in the longitudinal sample, and $r = .36$ at ninth grade.

INDIVIDUAL DIFFERENCES IN THE ACCURACY OF PERCEIVED ACADEMIC COMPETENCE

Given our emphasis here on the accuracy of perceived academic competence, an initial question concerns the relative disparity between the perceived and actual abilities of the children assigned to the three perceived competence groups. The sample selection and assignment to groups were guided by the assumption that the children in the low perceived competence group exemplified inaccurate perceptions—that is, underestimates—of their abilities, whereas those in the average and high perceived competence groups exemplified more accurate self-perceptions.

To test this assumption, disparity scores were calculated using the children's perceived competence scores and their achievement test scores. As recommended by Kenny (1975), all scores were standardized prior to computing the disparity score. As revealed in table 2.2, the assumptions regarding accuracy were only partially confirmed. Children assigned to the low perceived competence group did, in fact, underestimate their abilities relative to their actual achievement test performance. And children assigned to the average group had accurate views of their abilities as

TABLE 2.2 Average Disparity Scores Based on Perceived Academic Competence and Achievement Test Scores of Children by Age and Perceived Competence Group

	Third Grade		Fifth Grade		Ninth Grade	
Group	*N*	Mean Disparity	*N*	Mean Disparity	*N*	Mean Disparity
Low Perceived Competence	18	−1.10	23	−1.04	8	−0.83
Average Perceived Competence	39	0.21	64	−0.02	34	0.05
High Perceived Competence	24	0.81	30	0.84	15	0.66

Note: The means represent the difference between two *Z*-scores. Positive scores indicate that perceptions overestimate test scores; negative scores, that perceptions underestimate test scores. Five ninth-grade children lacked test data.

indicated by their very small mean disparity scores. Contrary to our assumptions, however, the children assigned to the high group also revealed inaccurate perceptions; they overestimated their actual abilities somewhat.

This pattern was consistent for the three age groups studied. One-way ANOVAS run on the children's disparity scores confirmed these differences, with F's ranging from 23.02 ($p < .0001$) for the fifth-graders to 5.71 ($p < .01$) for the ninth-graders. It appears that, even among a sample of children in which the range of actual competence was deliberately restricted, both the illusion of incompetence and the illusory glow revealed in Lewinsohn's adult sample (Lewinsohn et al., 1980) were evident.

SEX DIFFERENCES IN ILLUSORY INCOMPETENCE

In contrast to the consistencies across age groups revealed in tables 2.1 and 2.2, a striking developmental trend is evident in table 2.3, which presents the sex composition of the perceived competence groups by grade level. At third and fifth grade, nonsignificant chi-squares revealed that equal proportions of boys and girls were assigned to each group. Moreover, no within- or between-group sex differences in perceived academic competence were found for these two elementary-age samples.

TABLE 2.3 Distribution of Boys and Girls across Perceived Competence Groups by Grade Level

	Third Grade			Fifth Grade			Ninth Grade		
Group	Total	Boys	Girls	Total	Boys	Girls	Total	Boys	Girls
Low Perceived Competence	18	8	10	23	10	13	10	0	10
Average Perceived Competence	39	19	20	64	22	42	37	12	25
High Perceived Competence	24	7	17	30	13	17	15	9	6

Note: The ninth-grade sample ($N = 62$) is a subset of the fifth-grade sample ($N = 117$) which participated in a longitudinal followup.

At ninth grade, in contrast, significant sex differences characterized the competence group assignments (chi-square = 9.73, $df = 2$, $p < .01$), such that girls composed 100 percent of the low perceived competence group and 40 percent of the high perceived competence group relative to their 66 percent share of the ninth-grade sample. The mean perceived competence scores of the boys and girls in the ninth-grade sample (M for boys = 3.38 and for girls = 3.11) provides further evidence of the emergence of sex differences.

This dramatic departure in the assignment of boys and girls to the extreme perceived competence groups at ninth grade is particularly compelling given the lack of sex differences in both the original sample of children seen at fifth grade ($n = 117$) and also in the fifth-grade perceived competence scores of the subgroup ($n = 62$) of these children who were seen longitudinally. This finding fits squarely within the heritage of results yielded by sex differences research. Girls have consistently been found to underestimate their abilities, while boys err in the direction of overestimation (Crandall 1969; Deaux 1976; Eccles 1983; Parsons et al. 1976).

The sex differences literature is inconsistent, however, regarding the age at which sex differences reliably emerge. Entwisle and Baker (1983) found sex differences in achievement expectations as early as first grade in a middle-class sample: girls showed unwarranted pessimism in their expectations for math performance relative to their actual grades, whereas boys were overly optimistic. Frey and Ruble (1987) found sex differences in kindergarteners' self-appraisals of competence using both observations of spontaneous remarks while working on classroom assignments and standardized questionnaire measures. Ladd and Price (1986) found sex differences in generalized perceptions of academic and social competence in third- and fifth-graders. In contrast, however, the multiage studies of Eccles (1983), Fennema (1974; Fennema & Sherman 1977), and Stevenson and Newman (1986) did not reveal stable sex differences in self-perceived math ability prior to junior high school.

In order to claim that the emergence of sex differences in perceived competence is unwarranted on objective grounds, the absence of actual ability differences must be documented. We therefore examined the question of whether the sex difference in the ninth-graders' self-perceptions—a sample that was not selected *at ninth grade* to be uniformly high in actual ability—could be traced to actual differences in the achievement of boys and girls. Group differences and interaction effects were examined for boys and girls across the three perceived competence groups for their ninth-grade composite achievement test scores, quantitative achievement test scores, and final-year grades (average of grades in math, English, social studies, science, and language). No significant main or interaction effects for sex were found on these measures of composite and math achievement.

Attention was then turned to nonintellectual mediators of the observed sex difference in perceived competence found at ninth grade. Among the most prominent factors examined in the empirical literature are parent socialization (Block 1979; Parsons, Adler, & Kaczala 1982), differential patterns of teacher feedback (Dweck & Licht 1980), internalization of sex-role standards (Parsons, Frieze, & Ruble 1976), attributional predilections in which girls are more likely than boys to ascribe poor performance to lack of ability (Dweck, Goetz, & Strauss 1980; Eccles 1983), and the salience of social comparison cues in one's environment (Lenny 1977). In the present sample, two of these mechanisms were explored: the socializing influence of parents and the sex-role identity of the children.

Family Socialization

Parents have been found to exert a substantial influence on children's developing self-perceptions of ability (Fox 1976; Parsons, Adler, & Kaczala 1982; Phillips 1987). In particular, both mothers and fathers have been found to hold differing attitudes toward sons' and daughters' ability to achieve in math, which in turn have been causally associated with children's self-concepts, expectancies, and future course plans in math. Parents' perceptions of their children appear to be more powerful predictors of children's self-perceptions than are objective indicators of ability such as grades and test scores (Parsons et al. 1982; Phillips 1987). Moreover, Astin (1974) found that in a sample of youth selected specifically on the basis of high mathematical and scientific aptitude test scores, boys were encouraged to pursue college coursework and careers more than girls. Others (Raymond & Benbow 1986; Sherman 1980), however, have not found evidence of differential parent treatment of sons and daughters with respect to mathematics.

Is there evidence in the current study of high achievers to suggest that parents socialize daughters, but not sons, to disparage their abilities? At ninth grade, both mothers and fathers were asked a series of questions about their perceptions of their own and their children's abilities. Following Eccles (1983), both modeling and socializing influences were examined. The modeling hypothesis is premised on the existence of actual differences in mothers' and fathers' self-assessments of ability. In the present sample, no evidence suggested that mothers, as compared to fathers, present a model of disparaging self-perception to daughters. Mothers and fathers did not differ significantly in their generalized assessments of their own abilities across the total sample, nor did subsamples of parents of daughters and of sons.

On the other hand, our evidence suggests that parents contribute to sex differences in perceived competence by conveying sex-linked beliefs about their children's abilities and likely achievements. Analyses of covariance (Sex X Perceived Competence Group with ninth-grade composite achievement test scores covaried) run on both the parents' perceptions of their children and the children's perceptions of these parental beliefs revealed a cluster of significant main effects for sex of child. Specifically, both mothers and fathers of girls rated school as more difficult for their child than did parents of boys. The parents of girls and boys did not differ, however, in their ability judgments or expectations for their children.

Significant sex differences were found also in the children's beliefs about their parents' expectations. Girls perceived that their mothers, but not their fathers, expected significantly less of them compared to the boys' perceptions. Girls, as compared to boys, also perceived that their mothers held them to less stringent achievement standards. Recall that boys and girls did not differ significantly in actual achievement assessed with national test scores and year-end grades.

This pattern of results resembles the sex-differentiated parent and child perceptions, unrelated to actual ability differences, that Eccles (1983) and her colleagues (Parsons, Adler, & Kaczala 1982) found to be predictive of girls' disparaging ability and task perceptions in the area of math. Assertion of a predictive relation between these parent and child perceptions must await causal analyses. In particular, the children's perceptions of their parents' appraisals may derive from their self-perceptions rather than from their parents' sex-linked difficulty judgments. Nevertheless, these initial results, when placed in the context of prior research (Eccles 1983; Phillips 1987), suggest that parents may unwittingly socialize their daughters to adopt unwarranted perceptions of incompetence. Why this influence did not manifest itself at fifth or third grade remains an open question.

Sex-Role Identity

The influence of sex typing on achievement attitudes and behaviors has received considerable attention, particularly with respect to math achievement (Eccles 1983; Fennema & Sherman 1977, 1978). The premise of this work is that academic achievement, and math achievement in particular, involves sex-stereotyped behaviors, values, and goals which are more consistent with traditional male than female characteristics. To the extent that children view achievement-related activities in accord with these stereotypes and acquire sex-role identities that correspond to their gender, the achievement patterns of boys and girls should diverge in a manner that favors the continued achievement of boys. This is, however, a controversial area of inquiry, with some investigators reporting that mathematics is not significantly sex-typed (Raymond & Benbow 1986; Stein 1971) and that sex typing is related to subsequent pursuit of math coursework for boys but not for girls (Pedro et al. 1981).

Our variation on this theme involved examining whether children's sex-role identities were associated with their perceived competence status. Each ninth-grader completed the Personal Attributes Questionnaire and was assigned to one of four groups: masculine, feminine, androgynous, and undifferentiated (see Spence & Helmreich 1978). Table 2.4 presents the percentage of each perceived competence group composed of children in the four sex-identity groups. A chi-square revealed significant differences in the sex-role identity of the children in the three perceived

TABLE 2.4 Composition of Each Perceived Competence Group and Total Sample by Ninth-Grade Sex-Role Identity

Perceived Competence Group	N	Sex-Role Identity Feminine (%)	Masculine (%)	Androgynous (%)	Undifferentiated (%)
Low	10	60	20	20	0
Average	37	19	30	32	19
High	15	7	33	53	7
Total Sample	62	23	29	35	13

competence groups (chi-square = 16.23, $df = 6, p < .05$). Children with feminine sex-role identities were overrepresented in the low perceived competence group and underrepresented in the high group. Specifically, "feminine" children composed 60 percent of the low perceived competence group and 7 percent of the high group compared to their 23 percent share of the total sample. Conversely, children with androgynous identities were overrepresented in the high group and underrepresented in the low group.

Not surprisingly, all the children with feminine sex-role identities were girls (34 percent of the girls in the sample), whereas girls and boys were represented among the androgynous group in numbers proportionate to their 2-to-1 representation in the sample as a whole. The chi-square was rerun on the subsample of girls, given this confounding of real gender and gender identity, to examine whether the association between low perceived competence and femininity held for this group. The chi-square was nonsignificant (chi-square = 5.47, $df = 6, p > .10$), although several cells had fewer than five subjects. Absolute cell sizes did, however, show an interesting pattern. Of the girls with low perceived competence, 60 percent had feminine sex-role identities compared to 17 percent of the girls with high perceived competence. Conversely, 20 percent of the girls with low perceived competence had androgynous identities compared to 50 percent of those with high perceived competence.

Taken together, these results provide considerable evidence that the sex differences that emerged at ninth grade in this sample of high achievers can be ascribed to social rather than strictly cognitive sources. No evidence of sex differences in the children's actual achievement, including their achievement in math, was found. Nevertheless, parents of daughters viewed school as more difficult for their children compared to parents of sons, girls tended to believe that their parents expected less of them in school than did boys, and the feminine sex-role identities that were adopted by many girls (but no boys) were associated with negative perceptions of ability. These results, therefore, directly contradict the conclusions reached by Benbow and her colleagues (Benbow & Minor 1986; Benbow & Stanley 1980; Raymond & Benbow 1986) that actual sex differences in mathematics ability, rather than environmental or socialization influences, account for boys' higher levels of mathematics achievement. It is important to note, however, that the present sample of high-achieving children is not comparable to the truly gifted children studied by these investigators.

STABILITY OF ILLUSORY INCOMPETENCE

The emergence of sex differences at ninth grade suggests a certain degree of instability in children's perceived competence. The fifth-to-ninth-grade longitudinal assessments provide the opportunity to assess developmental trends in the stability of accurate and inaccurate perceptions of competence as children make the transition from elementary to high school. Table 2.5 presents the sample sizes and perceived competence scores for the nine groups of children defined jointly by the children's fifth- and ninth-grade perceived competence group assignments.

It is apparent that children's perceptions of their abilities can change dramatically between late elementary and early high school. Only 28 percent of the children assigned to the low perceived competence group as fifth-graders remained in the low group as ninth-graders. Among the children assigned to the high group in fifth grade, 39 percent retained this classification in ninth grade. The average group showed the greatest stability: 63 percent of those with average perceived competence in fifth grade remained in this group in ninth grade. The low correlation between the fifth- and ninth-grade perceived competence scores (r = .28) also indicates poor stability.

The issue of stability in children's self-conceptions has received extensive empirical attention (Damon & Hart 1986; Harter 1983; Rosenberg 1979). Indeed, self-perception research generally assumes some reasonable degree of consistency over time in how individuals view themselves. The data reported here appear to document quite the opposite—namely, that the illusion of incompetence, or more generally the accuracy with which children perceive their abilities, is not necessarily an enduring

TABLE 2.5 Fifth-to-Ninth-Grade Trends in the Composition, Perceived Competence Scores, and Achievement Test Scores of Perceived Competence Groups

Perceived Competence Group		N		Perceived Academic Competence		Achievement Test Change Score
Fifth Grade	Ninth Grade	Boys	Girls	Fifth Grade	Ninth Grade	
Low	Low	0	4	2.36	2.57	−3.00
	Average	3	4	2.41	3.02	3.14
	High	2	1	2.24	3.86	9.67
Average	Low	0	6	3.07	2.48	−1.75
	Average	6	16	3.15	3.16	5.16
	High	4	3	3.16	3.63	4.57
High	Low	0	0	—	—	—
	Average	3	5	3.73	3.23	0.38
	High	3	2	3.91	3.74	1.40

Note: This table includes only the 62 children who were studied as fifth- and ninth-graders. Comparisons of the sex composition, competence group distribution, achievement test scores, and perceived competence scores for the total fifth-grade sample and the fifth-graders who participated in the longitudinal sample showed no evidence of selective recidivism. *T*-tests comparing the fifth-grade perceived competence and achievement scores of the children included and not included in the followup study were not significant.

characteristic or cognitive style. Yet this presupposes a relatively restricted view of stability that fails to acknowledge any flux—lawful or otherwise—over time.

A more promising approach, for developmental purposes, involves the search for lawful patterns in the organization and functions of self-perceptions over time (Damon & Hart 1986; Harter 1983). Predictable change and logical associations rather than absolute constancy thus become the targets of inquiry. Applying this developmental perspective to the issue of inaccuracy, one might ask whether individual differences in the persistence or impermanence of illusory incompetence among capable children relate consistently to distinct patterns of behavior and attitudes.

An initial attempt to assess these issues was made by examining relations between changes in children's perceived competence status and changes in their achievement test scores. Table 2.5 also presents the fifth- to ninth-grade change scores in the children's standardized achievement test scores for the nine groups. Perceived competence and objective competence appear to follow parallel patterns of change. Declines in perceived competence and persistence of low perceived competence are accompanied by declines in achievement. Improvements in perceived competence, particularly from low to high and average to high, are accompanied by improved achievement. An exploratory two-way analysis of variance was run using the children's fifth-grade and ninth-grade perceived competence group assignments as independent measures and the children's achievement test change scores as the dependent measure. None of the main or interaction terms attained significance, although the very small cell sizes substantially reduce the power of this analysis.

The issue of the causal primacy of actual or perceived competence in this pattern of change is of central importance. The preponderant evidence on this issue suggests that actual achievement predicts perceived ability (Caslyn & Kenney 1977; Eccles 1983; Harter & Connell 1984), although, as Harter and Connell (1984) have suggested, different relations among these two constructs may emerge for accurate versus inaccurate raters, and also for children at different ability levels. The current sample is too small to assess direction of effects with any accuracy, but the apparent association between actual and perceived competence highlights the value of designing future studies to permit testing of competing causal models.

CORRELATES OF DEVELOPMENTAL CHANGE IN PERCEIVED COMPETENCE

To further explore these patterns of change in perceived competence, we divided the longitudinal sample into three groups based on the children's perceived competence group assignments (low, average, or high) in fifth and ninth grade. Specifically, three groups were created by combining (1) children who either had low perceived competence in both the fifth and the ninth grade or dropped from one group to another (e.g., high to low, high to average, or average to low) between fifth and ninth grades, (2) children who were assigned to the average perceived competence group in the fifth and the ninth grade, and (3) children who either had high perceived competence in both the fifth and the ninth grade or rose from one group to another (e.g., low to high, low to average, or average to high) between fifth and ninth grade. (Of course, other groupings suggest themselves as well, such as children whose self-perceptions decline versus those whose self-perceptions improve.) For ease of presentation, these groups are labeled "low-drop," "average-stable," and "high-improve," respectively.

The distribution of children across these three groups again revealed a sex difference which is evident in table 2.5. Of the eighteen children in the low-drop group, fifteen were girls and three were boys. Of the twenty-two children in the average-stable group, sixteen were girls and six were boys. And of the twenty-two children in the high-improve group, ten were girls and twelve were boys. A significant chi-square (chi-square = 7.00, df. = 2, $p < .05$) confirmed that girls were overrepresented in the low-drop group relative to their share of the total sample, and boys were overrepresented in the high-improve group.

To examine achievement orientations at ninth grade that are associated with these trends in perceived competence status, all ninth-grade outcome measures were analyzed for significant group (low-drop, average-stable, and high-increase) and sex differences using a series of multivariate analyses, with the children's fifth- and ninth-grade achievement test scores covaried. The outcome measures encompassed a wide range of motivational, scholastic, and psychosocial measures and were designed to provide convergent assessments of self- and other perceptions among children and their parents. For example, measures of classroom behavior and adjustment, psychosomatic symptoms, involvement in extracurricular activities, achievement attitudes, and coping styles were included in the broader study from which this discussion is drawn.

Of the total of nineteen multivariate analyses, four showed significant effects for fifth-to-ninth-grade perceived competence group (see table 2.6) and three showed significant effects for sex. Univariate effects were then examined only for the variables included in these significant multivariate analyses. The interaction term did not attain significance for any of the analyses and was thus dropped.

Table 2.6 presents the fifth-to-ninth-grade perceived competence group means for the significant univariate effects found for this independent variable. The pattern of results suggests that the children who sustained self-perceptions that seriously underestimated their actual abilities and children whose self-perceptions declined between the fifth and the ninth grade were viewed by their mothers as less capable and viewed by both parents as failing to perform up to their capacity relative to their more confident peers, including those whose self-perceptions improved over this four-year time span. Children in the low-drop group accurately perceived that their parents judged their abilities relatively less favorably, expected lower levels of success, had lower generalized perceptions of

TABLE 2.6 Fifth-to-Ninth-Grade Perceived Competence Group Means and Standard Deviations for Ninth-Grade Outcomes

Measure	Perceived Competence Group		
	Low-Drop	Average-Stable	High-Improve
Ability perceptions:			
Mother's rating of child's academic competence			
M	3.19	3.71	3.73
SD	.11	.09	.07
Mother's rating of child's ability relative to classmates			
M	17.29	20.98	21.31
SD	1.01	.85	.64
Mother's rating of whether child is performing up to capacity			
M	3.47	5.65	5.06
SD	.58	.48	.36
Father's rating of whether child is performing up to capacity			
M	4.05	5.85	4.93
SD	.58	.48	.36
Child's perception of mother's judgment of child's ability			
M	3.18	3.53	3.67
SD	.15	.13	.09
Child's perception of father's judgment of child's ability			
M	3.19	3.69	3.59
SD	.16	.13	.10
Achievement expectancies and standards:			
Expectancy of success			
M	83.76	89.25	88.77
SD	1.47	1.33	1.19
Nonacademic perceived competence:			
Generalized perceived competence			
M	2.63	2.87	3.10
SD	.12	.11	.10
Importance ratings:			
Importance of social skills			
M	8.53	7.13	8.06
SD	.39	.35	.30

Note: $N = 56$ for the ability, expectancy, and perceived competence measures, and $N = 42$ for the importance measure. All means are adjusted for standardized fifth- and ninth-grade achievement test scores.

competence (compared only to the high-improve group), and placed greater importance on social skills relative to the average-stable group (but not the high-improve group). Unless otherwise noted, the low-drop group mean differed significantly from the means of the other two groups, but the average-stable and high-improve groups did not differ significantly from each other.

Although these analyses cannot support causal conclusions, they reveal the negative correlates of the enduring tendency to disparage one's abilities and of shifts in self-perception from over- to underestimates of ability. The associations extended beyond the children's own competence and task perceptions to encompass their parents' views of the children and also the children's perceptions of their parents' ability judgments. Prior research (Parsons, Adler, & Kaczala 1982; Phillips 1987) has demonstrated that this constellation of interlocking self- and other views among parents and children may provide the type of self-perpetuating feedback that can sustain inaccurate perceptions of academic competence among bright children. It is also important to note, however, that the majority of the achievement and social measures assessed with the ninth-grade sample failed to show significant effects for the perceived competence trend scores as presently analyzed.

With respect to sex differences, three clusters of measures showed significant multivariate effects: (1) the children's perceptions of their parents' and teachers' expectancies and standards, (2) measures of anxiety and psychosomatic symptoms, and (3) the children's nonacademic perceived competence ratings. The univariate analyses revealed that girls, compared to boys, believed that their math and physical education teachers expected lower levels of achievement from them, believed that their mothers expected poorer school performance and set lower performance standards for them, reported fewer psychosomatic symptoms, and had more positive perceptions of social competence, but more negative perceptions of physical competence. That girls view significant adults as holding low expectations for their achievement is a robust finding in the sex differences and achievement literature (Deaux 1976; Eccles 1983; Crandall 1969).

The perceived competence results raise an interesting question about whether self-perceptions in nonacademic domains compensate for negative ability perceptions. It is possible that some girls make greater personal investments in social activities and thus gain self-confidence despite disparaging perceptions of their academic competence. Along these lines,

Accuracy again enters the model as how accurately parental judgments of academic competence and of the difficulty of school, for example, are perceived and ultimately internalized by children. Competent children who are viewed by their parents as being relatively incompetent may *not* accurately perceive these disparaging parental appraisals, in which case the illusion of incompetence would not be manifested. On the other hand, accurate perceptions of disparaging parental appraisals provide another avenue by which capable children may come to underestimate their abilities.

We maintain, as we have suggested elsewhere (Phillips 1987), that children's self-perceived competence is affected by their perceptions of their parents' ability appraisals. To date, however, research that effectively distinguishes directionality between these two child perceptions (self-perceptions and perceptions of parental judgments) has not been reported. Children undoubtedly project their perceived academic competence onto their views of their parents' appraisals. Children are also likely, however, to show individual differences in the tendency to equate their self-perceptions with their parents' appraisals. Elsewhere (Alessandri & Wozniak 1987), this link has been examined in the context of developmental trends in the ability to distinguish self-views from others' views of the self. For the present purposes, it is important to add this link to our model given that the influence of parents' positive ability judgments may be derailed if children perceive *in*accurately that their parents judge their abilities unfavorably and then incorporate these inaccurate perceptions into their self-appraisals. The final section of the model illustrates the four patterns of perceived academic competence—accurate with low actual and perceived competence, accurate with high actual and perceived competence, overestimators, and underestimators.

Finally, a developmental model of perceived competence must address age-related changes in factors that influence the course of perceived competence and incompetence. These factors include children's maturing cognitive capacities, their exposure to numerous new sources of competence feedback at school entry, changing achievement demands across the school years, and their increasingly salient sex-role orientations.

FUTURE DIRECTIONS FOR RESEARCH

The evidence we have presented in this chapter has underscored the need to assess both the level or valence of children's perceived competence and its accuracy. Not only are children's actual and perceived abilities often at odds with each other, but the tendency to underestimate or overestimate one's competence is in and of itself a predictive, though not necessarily stable, cognitive style. We presented a preliminary developmental model that incorporates accuracy as a central dimension of competence-related perceptions in order to foster more systematic attention to these issues in future empirical work.

Within this approach, numerous issues warrant empirical attention. One concerns the generalizability of tendencies to over-, under-, or accurately estimate one's competence across different domains of behavior. Do the patterns found in our study, as well as in prior work (Bierer 1982; Ladd & Price 1986), constitute a pervasive perceptual style, or are they confined to particular domains? Does the generality of these tendencies vary with the developmental level of the children studied, given that older children appear more capable of maintaining contradictory perceptions (see Harter 1985a)? Perhaps some styles (e.g., the tendency to overestimate) are more domain-specific than others.

In our research, intercorrelations among the cognitive, social, physical, and global self-worth subscales of the Perceived Competence Scale revealed some intriguing differences across various groups of children. At fifth grade, for example, the underestimators' perceived competence scores correlated highly with their global self-worth (r = .76) and physical perceived competence (r = .56) scores, whereas the overestimators' perceived academic competence scores correlated only modestly with their global and physical perceived competence (r's = .27 and .07, respectively). A more specific test of the generalizability of perceptual styles regarding *accuracy* would require obtaining perceived and actual competence data in several domains and examining the overlap among children in the four patterns of perceived academic competence. These correlations, however, suggest that underestimation may be a more pervasive style (among bright children) than is overestimation.

A related question, raised in the discussion of sex differences, concerns the dynamics of self-perceptions across domains. For example, among children who underestimate their academic abilities, is there any evidence of a compensatory role for more positive self-perceptions in nonacademic domains? This speculation evokes the stereotypic image of the poor high school student who becomes the quarterback of a winning football team, thereby gaining popularity and self-esteem. The personal importance assigned to different areas of competence undoubtedly figures in to the dynamics of cross-domain perceptions of competence as well.

A second avenue warranting empirical study focuses on differing patterns of change over time in perceived academic competence. Some of the children in our research who remained low in perceived competence across the fifth- to ninth-grade time span of the longitudinal study maintained high levels of achievement, nevertheless. This speaks directly to the issue of resiliency: what factors compete with these children's negative and inaccurate self-perceptions to enable them to sustain their high achievement?

Along these lines, some of the new work on the impostor phenomenon (Clance 1985; Kolligian & Sternberg 1989) suggests that the disparity between children's actual and perceived competence may serve to motivate highly effortful achievement for some children who feel undeserving of their strong academic performance. In effect, these children work extremely hard to avoid confirming their worst fears about their "true" abilities. Given their strong abilities, high effort ensures that they will do extremely well. It would be ironic to discover that what, on the face of it, is a maladaptive and inaccurate self-perception serves as a positive motivator of achievement for some children.

Finally, the cross-sectional research that predominates in the achievement motivation literature, including that which focuses on perceived competence, requires replication and extension using longitudinal designs. The small sample of children that we followed from fifth to ninth grade, while inadequate to permit causal analyses, illustrates the importance of attending to changes in the stability of perceived competence across the life span. Only then can we answer compelling questions about the causes and consequences of differing developmental patterns in perceived competence, about the remediation of illusory incompetence, and about the role of these perceptions in mediating adjustment to the changing array of achievement settings that individuals face as they age.

CHAPTER 3

Causes, Correlates, and the Functional Role of Global Self-Worth: A Life-Span Perspective

SUSAN HARTER

During the past decade, there has been a resurgence of interest in the self that has focused on the study of individual differences as well as developmental change. Much of this work can be subsumed under the rubric of the "self-concept," where there has been a proliferation of theoretical and methodological activity, leading to a growing body of empirical evidence on the self. These efforts have either provided a descriptive account of how the dimensions on which the self is based change with age (the developmental focus) or have documented the correlates of self-concept among a particular age group (the individual-difference focus). This chapter attempts to integrate these orientations to the self-concept, adopting a life-span perspective, which attends to developmental similarities and differences and addresses the role of individual differences at given developmental levels.

The particular focus will be self-esteem, or what I have termed global self-worth in my own work (Harter 1986b, 1987). By global self-worth, I mean the overall value that one places on the self as a person, in contrast to domain-specific evaluations of one's competence or adequacy. How the two sorts of self-evaluations are related will be a major topic here. But I will move beyond competence to reveal other dimensions that are equally critical to one's feelings of self-worth.

Another goal of this chapter will be to suggest a model of self-worth that addresses its antecedents as well as its functional role. Much of the literature on self-concept has been less than gratifying (see Wylie 1979), given its preoccupation with predictors or correlates. There have been few efforts to reveal the antecedents or determinants of one's level of self-esteem or to establish its functional role. Are such constructs merely epiphenomenal, contributing little to other affective, motivational, or behavioral systems of interest to psychologists? Does self-esteem really make a difference? Does it affect the day-to-day happiness or functioning of the individual at various stages across the life span? If one's cognitive construction of the self has little functional value, then the flurry of activity devoted to its assessment in recent years may be misguided—a pessimistic perspective not adopted here. Rather, I raise the issue to highlight the fact that the zeal with which the self has been conceptually embraced in the past decade has not been matched by a consideration of the precise role the self may play. Why should we care about the self and devote our energies to its study?

Thus, I will examine not only the antecedents or determinants of one's level of self-worth but also the impact that self-worth has on one's affective and motivational orientation. I will begin with the theoretical emergence of a model that has found considerable empirical support among older children and adolescents. More recently, my colleagues and I have extended our inquiry to younger children, college students, and adults, making it possible to test the applicability of the model across the life span and to chart developmental similarities and differences in the determinants and functional role of self-worth.

DIMENSIONS OF SELF-EVALUATION ACROSS THE LIFE SPAN

Within the literature on the self there has been a contrast between the spontaneous self, best represented by relatively open-ended self-descriptions, and the more reactive, evaluative self in which individuals are asked to make judgments about their competence or adequacy across a variety of content areas. I will focus here on the evaluative self, which can be more generally referred to as the self-concept. (For developmental differences in self-description, see Damon & Hart 1982; Harter 1983, 1988; Rosenberg 1985.)

Some theorists proposing models of the self-concept (e.g., Coopersmith 1967) have concluded that it is a unidimensional construct, best assessed by combining an individual's self-evaluations across items tapping a range of content. Items are given equal weight, and it is assumed that the total score adequately reflects an individual's sense of self across the various areas of his or her life.

This unidimensional view has been challenged by those who argue that such an approach masks important evaluative distinctions that individuals make about their competence in different domains of their life. Proponents of this multidimensional perspective have proposed models, and adopted measurement strategies, that identify the particular domains of self-evaluation, assessing each separately (see Harter 1985b; Mulliner & Laird 1971; Shavelson, Hubner, & Stanton 1976). Such an approach provides a *profile* of self-evaluations across those domains identified by a given investigator.

An alternative model can be found in the work of Rosenberg (1979), who has emphasized global self-esteem—the general regard one holds for the self as a person. Rosenberg has acknowledged that such a global judgment is likely the product of a complex combination of discrete judgments about the self. He has opted, however, not to examine these underlying judgments, assuming that the individual is probably unaware of the processes through which these elements are weighted and combined. Rather, he has concluded that a global self-evaluation of one's esteem is a phenomenological reality for adults and can be assessed directly.

Our model of the self-concept represents an integration of two approaches: we emphasize the need to consider the multidimensional nature of self-evaluative judgments as well as the individual's overall sense of self-worth. It is critical to appreciate the fact that global self-worth is a construct, in and of itself, namely an overall judgment about one's worth as a person (consistent with Rosenberg's conceptualization). It is assessed, therefore, *not* by combining domain-specific judgments but by asking an independent set of questions that tap the construct of self-worth directly. These items inquire about the extent to which one likes oneself as a person, likes the way one is leading one's life, is happy with the way one is, etc. By conceptually and empirically separating domain-specific judgments of competence or adequacy from the more global judgment of one's worth as a person, we are in a position to determine the relationship that specific competencies bear to global self-worth. Toward this end, our work has proceeded on two fronts—empirical and theoretical. The model we have developed will be presented in the next section. But before describing it, we must identify what specific domains are to be included at each developmental period across the life span, as well as the age at which judgments of global self-worth can be reliably obtained.

The Proliferation of Domains across the Life Span

A central theme in the developmental literature involves the extent to which psychological systems undergo ontogenetic change with regard to both differentiation and integration. The self-system can be considered within such a framework. Theory and research have indicated that, with development, an increasing number of self-concept domains can be *articulated* as well as *differentiated.* (I will return to the issue of how they are integrated into an overall judgment of self-worth).

In our work, for example (Harter & Pike 1984), we have demonstrated that four- to seven-year-olds can make reliable judgments about the following four domains: cognitive competence, physical competence, social acceptance, and behavioral conduct. Thus, these four dimensions are meaningful to young children in that they can articulate their judgments about the self. Interestingly, however, judgments across the domains are not yet clearly *differentiated.* Factor analyses reveal that cognitive and physical items combine into one competence factor—i.e., young children do not seem to make a clear distinction between their cognitive and their physical skills. Moreover, social acceptance and behavioral conduct items also combine into a second factor, suggesting that they too are not yet differentiated.

Children in this age range are also incapable of making judgments about their self-worth. (Here it needs to be clear that I am referring to the conscious, verbalizable concept of one's worth as a person.) This cognitive construction, as tapped by items that require judgments about self-worth, is not available to the young child. It is not until middle childhood that one can make meaningful and reliable judgments about this global construct, a finding that is consistent with the evidence on children's emerging cognitive abilities to form concepts.

This does not mean, however, that young children do not *possess* a sense of self-worth. We have been misunderstood on this issue, in part because in previous writings we have not been sufficiently clear. It is our conviction, bolstered by recent empirical work (Haltiwanger & Harter 1988), that young children "exude" a sense of overall self-worth as manifested in certain behaviors. This "presented self-worth" will be examined later, but the point here is that young children do not have a verbalizable concept of their self-worth, as tapped by self-report measures. This is not merely a measurement issue but rather a cognitive limitation of young children just as is their inability to differentiate discrete domains of the self-concept.

During middle childhood, the structure of the self-concept changes. More domains are differentiated, and the ability to make judgments about self-worth emerges. Factoring procedures applied to our Self-Perception Profile for Children (Harter 1985b) reveal that children between the ages of eight and twelve clearly differentiate the five domains included on this instrument: scholastic competence, athletic competence, peer social acceptance, behavioral conduct, and physical appearance. (It is likely that they can discriminate additional domains as well, e.g., different forms of scholastic competence, as suggested by the Shavelson et al., 1976, model, a claim that requires further research.) In addition to these emerging discriminations, children's responses to items asking about their global self-worth indicate that this concept takes on meaning in middle childhood.

During adolescence, there is further articulation and discrimination. Our instrument, the Self-Perception Profile for Adolescents, includes three new domains, close friendship, romantic appeal, and job competence, in addition to the five named above. All eight subscales define separate factors for adolescents. Of particular interest is the finding that although close friendship items are comprehended by older children, they are not differentiated from more general peer acceptance items, suggesting that the distinction between popularity and close friendship does not emerge until early adolescence.

Among college students, there is a further proliferation of domains that are articulated and differentiated, so that our Self-Perception Profile for College Students requires twelve domains in addition to global self-worth (Neemann & Harter 1986): scholastic competence, intellectual ability, creativity, job competence, athletic competence, physical appearance, romantic relationships, peer social acceptance, close friendship, parent relationships, sense of humor, and morality. Factoring procedures reveal that each of these domains defines its own factor, with high loadings of items on the designated factor and negligible cross-loadings. Of particular interest is that college students make clear differentiations among scholastic competence (how well they are actually doing in coursework), intellectual ability (how smart they are), and creativity (how inventive or original they are).

Such distinctions force one to consider both the role of cognitive-developmental advances as well as environmental influences in producing differentiation within the self-system. While the cognitive apparatus becomes increasingly capable of discriminations, one's environmental circumstances may also support such distinctions. The college experience, for example, may well reinforce the distinction between academic performance, in the form of grades, and intellectual ability, which may or may not be applied to scholastic goals. Creativity presumably becomes distinguishable in college because feedback makes salient the distinctions among originality, intellectual potential, and the mastery of academic content. It would be interesting to pursue the identification of discrete domains in a comparison group of young adults who are not attending college.

When we devised an instrument that would be sensitive to the concerns of older adults (ages twenty-five to fifty-five), we found it necessary to make fewer distinctions along some dimensions (e.g., the cognitive domain) and more distinctions that involved the domains of work, home management, and family. Thus, our Adult Self-Perception Profile (Messer & Harter 1985) includes the following eleven domains, in addition to self-worth: intelligence, sense of humor, job competence, morality, athletic ability, physical appearance, sociability, intimate relationships, nurturance, adequacy as a provider, and household management. Each subscale defined its own discrete factor, with the exception of humor and sociability, which combine to form a single factor.

The need for a structure on the adult scale that was different from the college version reflects developmental differences across the life span, although we have conceptualized these differences as changing concerns and life circumstances rather than as differences that involve cognitive-developmental processes. Thus, the need to distinguish among facets of the intellect that involve academic performance, intellectual potential, and creativity would appear to diminish, normatively, among middle-aged adults, whereas such dimensions as nurturance, adequacy as a provider, and household management increase in salience and must be included in order to yield a comprehensive self-concept profile.

A summary of the changing structure of our instruments to match the most salient dimensions of the self-concept at each of five developmental periods is presented in table 3.1. Next we will deal with precisely how the domain-specific evaluations are related to one's global self-worth, an important link in our understanding of how self-judgments are integrated into a more comprehensive view of the self.

TABLE 3.1 Domains of the Self-Concept at Each Period of the Life Span

Early Childhood	Middle/Late Childhood	Adolescence	College	Adult
Cognitive competence	Scholastic competence	Scholastic competence	Scholastic competence	
			Intellectual ability	Intelligence
			Creativity	
		Job competence	Job competence	Job competence
Physical competence	Athletic competence	Athletic competence	Athletic competence	Athletic competence
	Physical appearance	Physical appearance	Physical appearance	Physical appearance
Peer acceptance	Peer acceptance	Peer acceptance	Peer acceptance	Sociability
		Close friendship	Close friendship	Close friendship
		Romantic relationships	Romantic relationships	Intimate relationships
			Relationships with parents	
Behavioral conduct	Behavioral conduct	Conduct/morality	Morality	Morality
			Sense of humor	Sense of humor
				Nurturance
				Household management
				Adequacy as a provider
	Global self-worth	Global self-worth	Global self-worth	Global self-worth

A MODEL OF THE DETERMINANTS OF SELF-WORTH

Having conceptualized self-concept as a collection of domain-specific judgments about one's competence as well as a global judgment of one's worth, we were curious about the relationship between the two types of self-evaluative statements. For example, does global self-worth merely represent an additive combination of domain-specific judgments, or is the whole greater than, or different from, the sum of its parts?

Rather than reinvent the theoretical wheel, we turned to two historical scholars of the self, James (1892) and Cooley (1964 [1902]). Each of these theorists was explicit on the point that one possesses a global concept of self, over and above more specific self-judgments. Their theoretical formulations, however, suggested very different determinants of one's global sense of self. For James, the origins of one's overall sense of esteem lay in how one weighted one's *competencies,* whereas Cooley focused primarily on the *social* origins of the self, highlighting the incorporation of the attitudes of significant others.

According to James, one's overall sense of esteem did not involve the mere averaging of one's competencies. Rather, he suggested that one places a different *value* on success within the various domains of one's life, a factor that leads to a different personal equation for each individual. Global self-esteem, therefore, was conceptualized by James as the ratio of one's competencies or successes to one's "pretensions"—namely, the value that one places on success within each competence domain. This metaphorical ratio led James to postulate that if one's demonstrated level of success across domains was equal to, or commensurate with, one's aspirations for success, then one would experience high self-esteem. Conversely, if one's pretensions vastly exceeded one's actual level of success, one would suffer from low self-esteem. Implicit in this model, therefore, was the notion that individuals compare their level of competence to the importance of success across numerous domains, and the degree of congruence or discrepancy that results will determine their level of self-esteem.

It should be noted that James's theorizing was intended to shed light on the processes underlying the formation of *adult* self-esteem. Thus, it is reasonable to assume that adults have constructed a hierarchy of perceived competencies across several domains, as well as a hierarchy of values with regard to the importance of success in each of them. Moreover, adults should possess the cognitive capacity to compare these two hierarchies in order to assess congruences and discrepancies and arrive at a summary statement that will affect their global sense of worth. At what point in development, does one possess the capacity to make such comparisons? Are there cognitive-developmental limitations that preclude the applicability of such a model in young children? We will return to this issue when we examine the appropriateness of James's model for each period of the life span.

In contrast to James who focused exclusively on individuals' own evaluations, Cooley postulated that the origins of the self were primarily social in nature, that they resided in the attitudes of significant others. One is motivated to appraise others' attitudes toward the self, opinions that one then imitates or incorporates and that become one's own sense of self. For Cooley, therefore, these reflected appraisals represent what he termed the "looking-glass self," since significant others are the social mirror into which one gazes for information that defines the self. This resembles Mead's (1934) concept of the "generalized other," which represents the pooled or collective judgments of significant others toward the self.

Cooley's formulation, like James's, was intended to provide an explanation for the level of *adult* self-esteem. From a developmental perspective, therefore, one needs to address the issue of what particular processes are necessary for one to adopt the attitude of others? Is the mechanism one of simple imitation? Does it involve higher-level processes such as perspective-taking, as Mead suggested in his formulation of the generalized other? What type of internalization process is required for individuals to incorporate others' attitudes, and might these processes differ as a function of developmental level? Is the individual *aware* that the bases of one's sense of self may partially lie in those opinions of others toward the self that one has incorporated? Or are such processes more automatic, more unconscious in nature, and might the answer to this question depend on our consideration of developmental level? These are all issues to which I shall return, after reviewing the evidence to date on the applicability of the model at different stages of the life span.

EMPIRICAL EVIDENCE DURING MIDDLE CHILDHOOD AND EARLY ADOLESCENCE

Our empirical efforts to examine the applicability of James's and Cooley's models began with elementary school children, grades three through six, and young adolescents in middle school, grades six through eight. We began with the assumption that the competence–importance of success discrepancy formulation put forth by James and the looking-glass self formulation postulated by Cooley are not necessarily competing explanations for how one's sense of global self-esteem is formed. Thus, to give each a fair hearing, we set out to operationalize the constructs in both models.

To test James's model with children, we needed to operationalize both perceived competence or success and the importance attached to success across the various domains of the child's life. Perceived competence was defined on the basis of the scores obtained on our Self-Perception Profile for Children (Harter 1985b), tapping scholastic competence, athletic competence, peer social acceptance, physical appearance, and behavioral conduct.

The construct of pretensions, in James's parlance, was operationalized as the *importance of success* in each of these same five domains. Children were given a separate rating scale in which they were asked to make judgments about how important it was to do well in each domain in order to feel good about themselves. Thus, we obtained five competence/adequacy judgments and five importance ratings that could be compared for each domain to determine whether the relationship between competence and importance of success predicted global self-worth. Self-worth was assessed by another set of items tapping how much one liked oneself as a person, was happy with the way one was, liked the way one was leading one's life, etc. (See Harter, 1985b, for details including the psychometric properties of these instruments.)

In order to capture James's ratio between successes and pretensions, we calculated a total discrepancy score (competence minus importance) averaged across just those domains that the child considered *important.* (In James's formulation, competence, high or low, in domains deemed unimportant should not affect one's global self-esteem.) The bigger the discrepancy score in a negative direction—i.e., the more one's importance scores exceed one's competence/adequacy judgments—the lower one's level of self-worth should be. High self-worth should be associated with scores close to zero, indicating that one's hierarchy of perceived competencies is congruent with one's hierarchy of judgments concerning the importance of success.

In operationalizing Cooley's formulation, we defined the construct of others' opinions toward the self as the degree to which children felt that others acknowledged their worth as a person. Thus, we were interested in tapping the perceived positive regard as well as the emotional support that others displayed toward them in order to determine if this predicted their self-esteem. Four sources of such regard or support were identified: parents, teachers, classmates, and close friends. Items tapped the extent to which the subjects felt that others treated them like a person who matters, felt that they were important, listened to what they had to say, liked them the way they were, cared about their feelings, etc. (See the Social Support Scale for Children, Harter, 1985c.)

It should be noted that social support can be, and has been, defined in many ways. Our intent here was to operationalize that form of regard from others most analogous to the regard one holds for the self—i.e., to make these two constructs as conceptually parallel as possible. If one wishes to test the hypothesis that self-worth involves the incorporation of the attitudes of others toward the self, the content of both measures should ideally be similar.

It should be noted, therefore, that, by design, our measure did not tap support in the form of network strength or support conditional on particular levels of performance, number of persons available, or other potential dimensions of social support. This point is critical since often, in the zeal for measures, one uses an instrument whose title seems to bear some resemblance to the constructs in which one is interested without carefully examining its actual content.

Specific Findings

We examined the relationship between the competence/importance discrepancy score (derived from James's model) and self-worth, as well as the relationship between positive regard or socioemotional support (derived from Cooley's formulation) by utilizing several converging statistical procedures. These included correlational procedures, path-analytic techniques, and analyses of variance. Each approach yielded the same pattern of results—they provided clear support for the formulations of both James and Cooley.

In support of James, we obtained correlations between the competence/importance discrepancy score and self-worth in the range of $-.72$ to $-.55$ across several samples of children between eight and fifteen. Thus, the larger the negative discrepancy score—the more an importance rating exceeded perceived competence—the lower the level of self-worth. The smaller the discrepancy score—the closer it moved to zero—the higher the child's sense of worth. More direct evidence on the psychological processes underlying the magnitude of these discrepancy scores revealed that low self-worth children were unable to *discount* the *importance* of those areas in which they were not competent (see Harter 1986b). In contrast, high self-worth children appeared able to discount the importance of domains in which they were less competent, while touting the value of those areas in which they were successful. Causal modeling techniques applied to these data suggested that the competence/discrepancy score is indeed a determinant of self-worth—that global judgments of worth are based upon one's prior evaluation of how competently one is performing in domains deemed important.

In support of Cooley's conceptualization, we found that correlations between overall positive regard and self-worth ranged from .50 to .56 across several samples. Thus, the more persons felt that *significant others* had regard for them, the higher their self-worth—i.e., the more the *individuals* had regard for themselves. Path-analytic procedures suggested that the regard from others was casually prior to regard from the self, supporting the interpretation that children and young adolescents incorporate the attitudes of significant others toward them.

Interestingly, the pattern of findings reveals that the impact of the competence/importance construct on self-worth is quite similar to the influence of the positive-regard construct in magnitude. Moreover, the contributions of these two constructs appear to be relatively independent, as revealed by the low correlations between the competence/importance discrepancy score and the socioemotional support/positive regard score. Thus, an additive model seems best to capture the effects in that these two constructs combine to produce one's level of self-worth.

In order to explore specifically how particular levels of discrepancy and regard or support combine to produce different levels of self-worth, we turned to an analysis of variance model. We created a three-by-three matrix, dividing children into groups defined by high, medium, and low discrepancy scores crossed with high, medium, and low social support scores (see Harter, 1987, for details). Figure 3.1 presents the mean self-worth scores for all nine subgroups, separately for elementary and middle school children, where the patterns were virtually identical. The effects of the competence/discrepancy construct and the regard/support construct are additive and highly systematic, revealing no evidence of an interaction.

These findings imply that both constructs are critical in determining

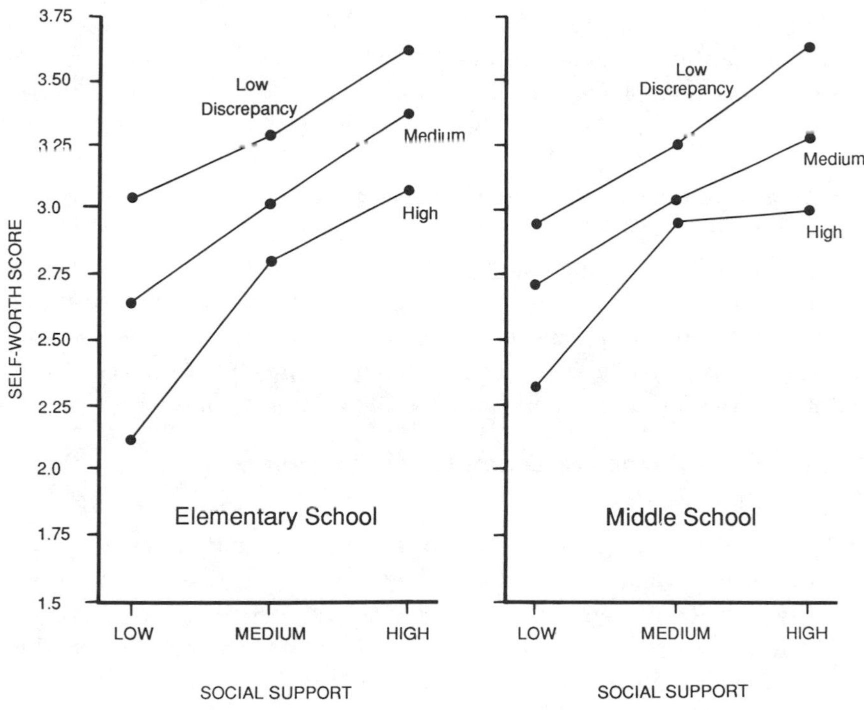

Figure 3.1. Self-worth as a function of levels of social support and competence/incompetence discrepancy among elementary and middle-school children.

self-worth and that one does not offset, or compensate for, the other. Thus, the self-worth of a child with very little discrepancy between competence judgments and importance ratings, a child who is doing well in domains deemed important, will suffer some loss of self-worth if socio-emotional support is also not forthcoming. The congruence between the child's competence and importance hierarchies, therefore, does not totally insulate her against the impact of low support or regard from significant others.

Similarly, high levels of support or regard in and of themselves do not guarantee that a child will have positive self-worth in the sense that such support does not totally protect him against the impact of a high discrepancy score. A large discrepancy between competence and the importance of success will take its toll, lowering self-worth, despite the fact that a child may be receiving social support from significant others.

As Figure 3.1 indicates, therefore, the child with the highest level of self-worth (approximately 3.5) was one who possessed a combination of high support/regard *and* a low discrepancy score. The opposite pattern, low support/regard combined with a high discrepancy score, characterized those children with the lowest levels of self-worth (approximately 2.2). The difference in self-worth between these two extreme groups was marked, revealing the impact of both determinants, combined, on the child's global sense of worth as a person. Thus, these findings imply that in our attempts to directly influence a child's self-worth, we need to attend to the competence/importance discrepancy construct as well as the emotional support provided by significant others in the child's social environment, if we wish to maximally enhance a child's sense of worth.

The Impact of Particular Competence/Adequacy Domains on Self-Worth

In first exploring the Jamesian notion that the discrepancy between one's competence or adequacy and the importance of success is a determinant of self-worth, we operationalized the discrepancy construct as the average of the discrepancies across five domains. Of further interest is whether certain domains contribute more than others as predictors of self-worth. We addressed this issue by examining the correlations of discrepancy scores, calculated separately for each domain, and self-worth for both the elementary and the middle school samples.

The findings revealed that certain domains systematically contributed more to self-worth than others and that the ordering of domains was similar for both groups of students. Physical appearance was the most important contributor for both elementary ($r = -.66$) and middle school ($r = -.57$) students. Thus, the discrepancy between the importance of being good-looking and one's evaluation of one's perceived appearance or attractiveness would seem to be a major concern for children in the age range of eight to fifteen, as judged by its impact on self-worth.

Social acceptance was the second most critical domain, as judged by the relationship between the discrepancy score and self-worth, although its impact was slightly higher among the young adolescents in middle school ($r = -.45$) than among elementary school pupils ($r = -.36$). Scholastic competence, athletic competence, and behavioral conduct contributed least to self-worth, as judged by the correlation of their discrepancy scores and self-worth (ranging from $-.24$ to $-.35$ across the two samples).

This pattern is interesting since it suggests that competencies per se are less powerful determinants of self-worth at these ages than one's physical appearance and social acceptability. This is not to say, however, that these children considered cognitive competence or behavioral conduct as unimportant. To the contrary, they judged both domains to be extremely important. Nevertheless, the discrepancy construct—the level of competence/adequacy in relation to the importance judgment—did not affect self-worth nearly as significantly as physical appearance in particular.

These findings raise intriguing questions with regard to how the value of attractiveness, and to a somewhat lesser degree, social acceptance, come to dominate as determinants of a child's sense of global worth as a person. The emphasis the media place on appearance and its relationship to acceptance may well be a culprit. Movies, television, rock videos, and magazines tout the importance of attractiveness in the form of physical features and dress, glamorizing the popular role models one should emulate. The biggest consumers of these media messages appear to be teens and preteens. As Elkind (1979) has pointed out, the importance of physical appearance among young people has escalated in recent years and has become evident at increasingly younger ages. Our findings, indicating that children's and adolescents' judgments of their attractiveness are highly predictive of their global self-worth, would certainly support this contention.

To anticipate our findings for both college students and adults, the relationship between physical appearance and global self-worth was extremely robust. In fact, across the entire age range we have examined to date, ages eight to fifty, the correlations between appearance discrepancy score and self-worth have been dramatically similar, all about $-.65$. We were particularly surprised to find in a study of third- and fourth-grade intellectually gifted children who had been placed in segregated classes to meet their scholastic needs that physical appearance (rather than scholastic competence) continued to be the best predictor of self-worth ($r = -.67$).

This overall pattern of unexpected findings reveals a very interesting developmental *similarity* across the life span that warrants further consideration. It raises the possibility that the relationship between physical appearance and self-worth may represent an issue more profound than mere media effects in the socialization of both children and adults. As a tentative framework, we are moving toward the view that physical appearance represents the manifestation of the *outer self,* whereas self-worth represents the *inner- self,* both globally defined. As such, appearance seems to be qualitatively different from our other competence/adequacy domains in that it is not merely one discrete, relatively situation-specific area of performance in which one manifests the appropriate behavior, but an omnipresent feature of the self that is always on display.

From a developmental perspective, the primacy of the physical self is revealed in studies of the emerging infant self (see Lewis & Brooks-Gunn 1979). This body of work (also reviewed in Harter 1983) documents a sequence of stages in which the infant first comes to appreciate the capabilities of its bodily self and then later, at about eighteen months to two years, develops facial recognition skills to identify the self in mirrors and later in photographs. Moreover, studies (see Langlois 1981; Maccoby & Martin 1983) reveal that others react to infants and toddlers on the basis of their physical appearance or attractiveness. Those who are attractive, by societal standards, are responded to with more positive attention than those who are judged to be less physically attractive. Thus, from a very early age, the physical or outer self appears to be a highly salient dimension that not only is linked to one's capabilities but provokes psychological reactions from others that may well be incorporated into the emerging sense of one's inner self.

This speculative analysis implies that the outer self develops prior to, and therefore has an impact on, the inner, psychological self. During the early years, this may well be the case, but the directionality of effects may not be so predictable in later childhood, adolescence, and adulthood. That is, although one's perceptions of one's appearance or attractiveness may well influence one's judgments of one's worth as a person, it is also plausible to speculate that one's perceived psychological worth—judgments about the inner self—may well affect one's views of one's appearance, or outer self.

These would be intriguing questions to pursue, particularly from a developmental and an individual-difference perspective. It may well be that the directionality of the relationship between outer and inner self changes with development. At certain developmental levels it is also possible that the impact of one on the other differs across individuals. For some, perceptions of their appearance may be more causally predictive of their worth as a person, whereas others may view the inner self as causally prior to their judgments of the outer self. We are pursuing these questions in our current research in an attempt to unravel the nature of the very robust relationship between physical appearance and self-worth across a very large portion of the life span.

THE IMPACT OF PARTICULAR SOURCES OF SUPPORT ON SELF-WORTH

In our initial examination of Cooley's formulation it was established that a composite of social scores was predictive of self-worth. An analysis of the relative contribution of each source of support was also illuminating, however, among both older children and young adolescents, the pattern was relatively similar. Parent and classmate support was the biggest contributor to self-worth (correlations ranging from .42 to .46). These were followed by close friend support and then teacher support (*r*'s = .27 to .37), revealing that these latter sources had less impact on self-worth.

As discussed in Harter (1987), it is of interest to note that the influence of parent support is at least as strong as peer classmate support in early adolescence, ages thirteen to fifteen. Although peers definitely have a major role in early adolescence, thoughtful attention to the particular function played by different sources of support would suggest that parents are still critical in their impact on their child's sense of worth. We have yet to pursue this relationship at the high school level, a topic that will be of interest developmentally.

In distinguishing between the two peer sources, classmates versus close friends, it is noteworthy that classmates seem to have more of an influence on self-worth than do close friends. The acknowledgment from peers in the more public domain seems more critical than the personal regard of a close friend with whom one can share more intimate details of one's life. Given that, by definition, one's close friends provide such support, it may well be that their regard is not perceived as necessarily self-enhancing. Rather, one must turn to somewhat more objective sources as feedback to validate the self. The processes underlying the impact of both classmates and close friends warrants further scrutiny, however, since this pattern is not limited to the period of childhood and adolescence.

THE DETERMINANTS OF SELF-WORTH AMONG COLLEGE STUDENTS

We turn now to our models of global self-worth in relation to college students. As described earlier, among this group, twelve competence or adequacy domains are necessary to capture the complexity of the self-concept (see table 3.1).

Our socioemotional support or positive-regard construct among college students was operationalized by identifying five sources of support similar to those included in our studies of older children and adolescents: parental support (separate scales for mother and father), instructor support, close friend support, and support from peers in campus organizations.

As a first step in exploring the applicability of our model to college students, we examined the correlation between our competence/importance discrepancy score, combined over domains, and global self-worth, as well as the correlation between the total social-support score, combined across sources of support, and self-worth. Interestingly, we found that the competence/importance discrepancy score was a better predictor of self-worth ($r = -.62$) than was the social-support composite ($r = .33$), a finding obtained for two college campuses (University of Denver and Colorado State University at Fort Collins). In contrast to older children and young adolescents, therefore, the self-worth of college students seems to be more heavily determined by how adequately one is performing in domains of importance than it is by the positive regard of significant others.

Of particular interest is the relative contribution of each particular competence/adequacy domain, and each source of support, to self-worth, since there was considerable variation in their impacts. The two domains that were most highly related were *physical appearance* ($r = -.80$) and *peer social acceptance* ($r = -.60$). It is noteworthy that these are the same two domains that were most highly predictive of self-worth for older children and young adolescents. The next cluster of contributors (correlations between $-.44$ and $-.52$) comprised job competence, romance, and the three intellectual subscales—creativity, general intellectual ability, and scholastic competence. Close friendship ($r = -.40$) and morality ($r = -.38$) were somewhat less highly correlated with self-worth, followed by the remaining three subscales, parent relationships ($r = -.31$), humor ($r = -.24$), and athletic ability ($r = -.19$).

Of special interest is the fact that the two domains most predictive of self-worth did not reflect competencies per se in the sense of skills, despite the fact that this was a college population where competence was undoubtedly a salient dimension. As with our younger normative samples, one's outer self, as reflected by one's physical appearance and one's acceptance by peers, played the more critical role. Thus, these findings bolster our carlier analysis on the importance of further examining the processes underlying the contribution of these dimensions to self-worth.

Two further distinctions are of interest in this regard. Our findings revealed that the two separate aspects of the physical self, appearance and athletic ability, functioned very differently in relation to self-worth. Appearance was by far the single most important contributor ($r = -.80$), whereas athletic ability was the least critical domain ($r = -.19$). Thus, while some theorists have suggested physical self-concept as a meaningful dimension, our findings clearly indicate the need to consider the possible components of this dimension separately. Not only did appearance and athletic competence function very differently in regard to their contribution to self-worth, but they were not highly correlated with each other among our college sample ($r = -.24$).

A second distinction concerns the general category of peer relationships where our findings revealed that peer social acceptance, defined as the ability to demonstrate social skills that will cause one to be generally accepted by peers, was a more critical predictor of self-worth than was the ability to sustain an intimate relationship with a close friend.

A similar pattern was obtained when we examined the relative predictability of the five sources of social support. Support from peers in campus organizations was the strongest correlate of self-worth ($r = .49$), whereas support from a close friend was the weakest predictor ($r = .28$). The contribution of support from father ($r = .47$), mother ($r = .32$), and instructors ($r = .33$) fell in between these two sources of peer support.

It would appear, therefore, that the ability to garner the acceptance and support of peers, in general, provides a much greater path toward self-enhancement in the form of self-worth than does the ability to develop a relationship with, and receive support from, a close friend. These findings raise intriguing questions about the role of close friendships. To the extent that they represent comfortable opportunities to express one's problems, to let one's hair down, and show one's less exemplary side on occasion, such support may not directly translate into self-worth. These suggestions are merely speculative, however, and indicate the need for more thoughtful consideration of why one's public social self contributes more heavily to one's sense of self-worth than one's private or intimate social self.

THE DETERMINANTS OF SELF-WORTH AMONG ADULTS

Our strategy for examining the relative contribution of the competence/importance discrepancy construct and social support or positive regard to self-worth was similar among our samples of adults in the world of work and the family. As can be seen in table 3.1, our parsing of the adult self-concept yields eleven domains, in addition to global self-worth (Messer & Harter 1985). With regard to the sources of support, our studies revealed the need to distinguish among the following: spouse or significant other, parents/relatives, friends, coworkers, members of one's church or civic group, and children (Hamm 1986).

The findings reveal that the overall contribution of the competence/importance discrepancy (averaged over domains) is similar ($r = -.50$) to the contribution of the combined social-support index ($r = .46$). When one examines the relative contribution of the different competence/adequacy domains, physical appearance once again heads the list as the best predictor of self-worth ($r = -.61$). Interestingly, the second highest predictor was intimate relationships ($r = -.56$), although sociability was also relatively high ($r = -.50$). This pattern is similar to the one obtained for children, adolescents, and college students in that both appearance and social relationships appear to contribute most to global self-worth. The difference, however, is that intimate relationships play a more critical role in adulthood as a source of one's esteem or worth as a person.

Intelligence ($r = -.55$) and adequacy as a provider ($r = -.53$) were also strong predictors of self-worth among adults, whereas the domains of morality ($r = -.47$), job competence ($r = -.42$), humor ($r = -.40$), and nurturance ($r = -.39$) were somewhat less highly correlated. Interestingly, one's ability to provide for one's family was somewhat more important than one's job competence per se. The least powerful predictors of global self-worth for adults were household management ($r = -.28$) and athletic competence ($r = -.12$).

The relative contribution of each source of social support to self-worth formed an interesting pattern that was similar to the one obtained for college students. Support from individuals within one's church or civic group ($r = .52$) and support from one's coworkers ($r = .46$) were most highly predictive of self-worth. Next came support from adults within the family, one's parents ($r = .41$) and one's spouse or significant other ($r = .38$). Least critical to self-worth was support from one's friends ($r = .33$) and one's children ($r = .29$). Thus, the more public sources of support seem to represent the most critical avenues to feelings of self-worth, just as with college students, in that the support of those in campus organizations was the best predictor. Family support, while not trivial, predicted slightly less well, and friend support was the least predictive among adult sources of support, consistent with the college data. Interestingly, across all age groups, more *public peer group support*—classmates for children and adolescents, peers in organizations for college students, and peers in church/civic organizations as well as coworkers for adults—played a greater role in determining levels of self-worth than did the support of a close friend. These findings warrant further study since they may have important implications for the very formation and maintenance of one's perceptions of worth as a person, particularly with regard to incorporation of the attitudes of significant others.

SELF-WORTH AMONG YOUNG CHILDREN: TOWARD AN IDENTIFICATION OF DETERMINANTS

Most recently we have been interested in a downward extension of our model of self-worth to children between the ages of four and seven. To what extent do competence and social support contribute to self-worth formation in the young child? Any sensitive analysis of the relationships among these constructs must begin with an inquiry into whether such constructs are even meaningful for this age group. Here we need to distinguish between two uses of the term *meaningful*—availability in the cognitive/verbal repertoire of the child versus their overt manifestation in behavior. That is, can we assess children's concepts of themselves through self-report measures, or do we need to employ more observational techniques for those constructs the young child cannot verbalize? The answer to this question is "both," in that although young children have conscious access to certain self-perceptions, other facets of the self have not yet reached the level of verbal awareness and therefore require alternative methodologies.

The growing literature on the young child's self-concept can be summarized as follows:

1. Young children (ages four to seven) are able on self-report measures to make judgments about their competence or adequacy if these are couched in terms of concrete, observable behaviors (Montemayor & Eisen 1977; Damon & Hart 1982; Harter 1983, 1986b; Harter & Pike 1984). With regard to the domains we have identified, young children can make such judgments about their cognitive competence, physical competence, and behavioral conduct if pictorial stimuli depicting concrete manifestations of the relevant behaviors are presented (Harter & Pike 1984).

Our findings also indicate, however, that such judgments are likely to be inaccurately high—young children tend to inflate their sense of adequacy. We have thought that this tendency reflects age-appropriate distortion in that the young child naturally confuses the wish to be competent with reality. At this age, the child is unable to utilize accurately social comparison information for the purpose of self-evaluation (Ruble 1983; Suls & Sanders 1982). Moreover, benevolent socializing agents typically provide extremely positive feedback concerning the young child's displays of competence, often making favorable comparisons with the child's past level of accomplishment. Such praise serves to reinforce the young child's egocentric perceptions of competence. Whether such inaccuracy is cause for concern depends upon the investigator's perspective and the nature of the questions that are addressed. If one adopts the view that the child's self-perceptions are more critical than his or her actual competence level, then judgments obtained from self-report indexes may well be appropriate independent of their level of accuracy. At a more philosophical level, if one believes that positive self-perceptions serve to motivate the child toward greater levels of mastery, then inflated self-judgments are to be touted as growth-promoting heroes rather than psychometric villains that attenuate correlations.

2. Young children can also make judgments about the socioemotional support they receive from significant others—parents, peers, teachers—*if* the content involves judgments of very concrete, behavioral actions of others. In our own construction of measures of support from parents, peers, and teachers, we have initially asked young children to describe how they know that these other people like them (or love them, in the case of parents). The resultant items have been based on behavioral manifestations that are commonly mentioned in these open-ended descriptive protocols. Interestingly, these items involve such activities as playing with the child, listening to the child, reading bedtime stories, taking the child to favorite places, cooking the child's favorite foods, caring about the child's feelings—responses that involve socioemotional support rather than direct validation of the child's competence.

3. Although young children can make judgments about their competence, concretely depicted, they do not appear to have the ability to make discriminating judgments about the *importance* of different domains, in contrast to older children who attach different values to success across the domains we have tapped. Thus, the competence/importance discrepancy construct is not meaningful for young children.

4. Perhaps most critical (if not potentially distressing, given our own

goal of examining the applicability of our model to young children) is the fact that the young child does not have a concept of his or her worth as a person. The ability cognitively to construct a concept of one's self-worth represents a developmental acquisition that does not emerge until middle childhood, according to our findings. Here it is important to appreciate the fact that we are referring to the lack of a conscious, verbalizable concept of one's worth as a person in the young child. We are claiming not that self-worth is nonexistent at these early ages but that it is manifest in the child's *behavior*, a suggestion that has implications for our methodological approach to assessing self-worth in young children. Our efforts to examine the determinants of self-worth through entirely self-report procedures have been thwarted by the cognitive limitations of the young child. As a result, it was necessary to turn our attention to the development of a more behavioral index of self-worth prior to examining the relationships among the constructs of interest.

A BEHAVIORAL INDEX OF PRESENTED SELF-WORTH IN YOUNG CHILDREN

Our initial goal was to identify prototypic behaviors that characterize both the high and low self-worth child (Haltiwanger & Harter 1988). Toward this end we invoked the aid of nursery school and kindergarten teachers who have had considerable experience with young children. In talking with them, we found that early childhood educators frequently make reference to children's self-esteem and that this is a very meaningful concept that distinguishes children from one another.

Thus, as a first step, we conducted open-ended interviews with about twenty teachers in order to generate an item pool from which we would eventually select those that best discriminate between high and low self-worth children. With teachers, we employed the term *self-esteem* rather than *self-worth,* since the former was more familiar. Teachers were asked to describe those behaviors that characterize the high self-esteem child, those that characterize the low self-esteem child, and those they felt did not allow them to discriminate between the two groups. This phase was successful in that teachers had definite opinions about behaviors that were both relevant and irrelevant to this construct.

From these interviews we culled eighty-four behavioral descriptors, phrases that represented behaviors ranging from those that teachers felt did discriminate between high and low self-esteem children in varying degrees to those that they felt were not relevant. We next employed a Q-sort procedure in which we asked a separate set of teachers to sort these eighty-four items into those that were most descriptive of the high self-esteem child at one end of the distribution, those that were most like the low self-esteem child at the other end, and those that were neither like or unlike the high or low self-esteem child in the middle. Thus, teachers performed a single sort based on their view of the *prototype* of both the high and low self-esteem child.

An initial goal of this methodological approach was to determine whether there was any consistency in teachers' judgments. Could they agree on a subset of items that clearly discriminated the groups (as well as on items that did not)? Our results were encouraging in that reliability analyses indicated very substantial agreement among teachers.

Items that Discriminate between High and Low Self-Esteem Children

Our next goal was to examine the content of those items that did discriminate in order to determine whether it could be meaningfully interpreted. The findings revealed an intriguing pattern. There were two primary categories of items that defined the *high self-esteem child.* Following are examples of mentioned behaviors:

1. *Active displays of confidence, curiosity, initiative, and independence:* trusts his or her own ideas, approaches challenge with confidence, initiates activities confidently, takes initiative, sets goals independently, is curious, explores and questions, is eager to try doing new things. Two other items seemed to convey the more general manifestation of these attributes: describes self in positive terms and shows pride in his or her work.

2. *Adaptive reaction to change or stress:* able to adjust to changes, comfortable with transitions, tolerates frustration and perseveres, able to handle criticism and teasing.

Similar categories describing the *low self-esteem* child representing the converse of these two sets of items emerged, although not *every* contrasting item emerged:

1. *Failure to display confidence, curiosity, initiative, independence:* doesn't trust his or her own ideas, lacks confidence to initiate, lacks confidence to approach challenge, is not curious, does not explore, hangs back, watches only, withdraws and sits apart, describes self in negative terms, does not show pride in his or her work.

2. *Difficulty in reacting to change or stress:* gives up easily when frustrated, reacts to stress with immature behavior, reacts inappropriately to accidents.

Behaviors Judged Irrelevant to High versus Low Self-Esteem

Equally instructive, if not surprising, were the categories of behaviors that teachers felt did *not* discriminate between high and low self-esteem children. These included the following: (1) *competence:* performs tasks competently, shows difficulty performing tasks, uses materials in imaginative ways; (2) *attention:* listens, pays attention, wanders off mentally or physically; (3) *motivation to complete tasks:* stays on task until finished, tries to do very best, does not complete things; (4) *activity level:* acts or moves in a lively way, does not talk very much; (5) *friendships:* has good friends, needs support of other children; and (6) *need for teacher encouragement:* asks for help from teacher, needs encouragement to tell about experiences.

This content analysis is particularly illuminating given what it reveals about the nature of self-esteem as seen through the collective eyes of experienced teachers. They suggest two primary dimensions, one active and one more reactive. The active dimension represents a style of approach rather than the display of skills per se. That is, the high self-esteem child manifests confidence in the world, whereas the low self-esteem child avoids challenge, novelty, and exploration of the world. The reactive dimension involves the response of the child to change, frustration, or stress. The high self-esteem child reacts more adaptively, whereas the low self-esteem child reacts with immature, inappropriate, or avoidant behaviors.

Of particular interest are the categories of behaviors that do not seem to discriminate between high and low self-esteem children, according to teachers. The fact that competence per se is not a correlate of overall self-esteem in young children is striking. It would appear that *confidence,* as a behavioral style, is not synonymous with competence, at least at this age level. Nor do task completion and attentional dimensions appear to be relevant. This overall pattern is illuminating since it suggests that the origins of a sense of confidence during early childhood do not necessarily reside in the display of skills, more objectively defined. During later childhood, the link between confidence in the self and one's level of competence apparently becomes stronger. This developmental pattern, therefore, suggests that we search for the origins of the young child's sense of confidence within his or her socialization history, a search that has implications for our developmental analysis of the determinants of self-worth.

Implications for a Model of Self-Worth among Young Children

Having identified those behavioral manifestations that appear to discriminate high from low self-esteem children, we next translated the twenty-four items that best differentiated the two types of children into a four-point rating scale in order to assign a behavioral self-worth score to individual children (Haltiwanger 1989). We are currently embarking on a study of the relationship between competence (perceived as well as "objective," i.e., rated by teachers) and behavioral or presented self-worth, and the relationship between social support (perceived as well as objectively rated) and behavioral self-worth. At present, we can only speculate on the outcome and its implications for our understanding of the origins of the young child's self-worth.

Several lines of thinking lead to the expectation that social support will have a major impact on self-worth, as defined by our behavioral composite involving confidence, initiative, curiosity, independence or their absence, whereas competence level per se will *not* represent a very strong predictor for young children. The first suggestive evidence comes from our finding that competence or skills did not emerge as a relevant dimension in identifying those behaviors most characteristic of high and low self-esteem children at this age level. A second line of evidence comes from our previous findings revealing that perceived cognitive and physical competence did not correlate that highly with perceived social acceptance from mother and peers (as tapped by self-report measures among four-to-seven-year-olds). That is, competence and social acceptance defined separate factors.

Social acceptance *does,* however, correlate with perceived affect level (happiness/sadness) at this age level (Harter 1987), a third finding that is relevant since our larger model postulates that affect, so defined, is highly related to self-worth. Perceived competence, in contrast, did not correlate highly with affect at this age level. If self-worth serves as the mediator of affect, as we are predicting, then we anticipate that social acceptance will have an impact on behavioral self-worth, which will in turn influence affect level. In contrast, competence should bear little relationship to our behavioral index of self-worth just as it bears little relationship to affect, as documented in our previous findings.

Finally, although our efforts to identify behavioral dimensions of self-worth in young children were empirical, by design, rather than theoretical, there are some interesting theoretical convergences that have implications for a model of self-worth. The very behaviors that our Q-sort identified as discriminating features of high and low self-esteem children are highly reminiscent of the behaviors that discriminate securely and insecurely attached infants according to attachment theory (Ainsworth 1979; Sroufe 1979). Thus, although we had no a priori theoretical predilections about the categories that would emerge to define global self-esteem, the resulting behaviors—e.g., exploration, initiative, reactions to stress—are precisely those that one might expect from an attachment-theory perspective. Extrapolating from this literature, parent variables that would lead young children to display the type of confidence that characterizes self-worth, as we have now defined it behaviorally, are similar to the social-support dimensions that are included on our parent social acceptance subscales for young children. Thus, we anticipate that our indexes of parent support, in particular, should be highly predictive of our behavioral self-worth composite.

At present, we can only provide an argument drawing upon these several lines of evidence, one that strongly suggests that during the early years, parental social support in particular will be a much more powerful determinant of self-worth, as behaviorally manifested, than will competence per se. Thus, our model of self-worth during these early years differs from the network of constructs that emerge in middle childhood and beyond in that perceived competence and/or adequacy are not viewed as critical in the earliest formation of self-worth. They do, however, *come* to play a critical role in shaping and/or maintaining self-worth during subsequent periods of development.

SELF-WORTH AS A MEDIATOR OF AFFECT AND MOTIVATION

Although the documentation of the determinants of self-worth has been a major goal in our model-building, equally critical has been the demonstration that self-worth, in turn, has an impact on other systems of interest. We have sought to examine the functional role of self-worth, based on the assumption that it is not merely epiphenomenal in nature. Because much of this work has been reported elsewhere (see Harter, 1986b, 1987), I will merely summarize it here. But I will present our most recent efforts that extend the model to include suicidal ideation.

Our goal has been to examine the hypothesis that self-worth serves as a mediator of one's general affective and motivational states. Our inquiry is consistent with those recent sequential models demonstrating that a self-judgment can elicit an affective reaction that, in turn, mediates one's motivation of behavior (Bandura 1978; Kanfer 1980; Wicklund 1975). The particular *affective* state of interest to us has been represented by the continuum of cheerful to depressed. Our *motivational* construct has involved the energy to engage in age-appropriate activities. Each of these constructs has been operationally defined by its own subscale on our self-report measure, the Dimensions of Depression Profile for Children and Adolescents (Harter & Nowakowski 1987a). Thus, our interest in the larger theoretical model of self-worth was partially spawned by our studies of childhood depression and its correlates.

Utilizing correlational as well as causal modeling techniques, we have found that self-worth has a major impact on one's mood or affective state. In fact, the correlations across four samples of older children and young adolescents have all fallen between .75 and .82. Moreover, factor analysis of the five subscales of the depression profile reveals that self-worth and mood consistently form one factor. Thus, the individual who likes himself as a person will invariably be quite cheerful, whereas the individual with low self-worth will be affectively depressed. The findings also reveal that affect, in turn, has a critical impact on children's energy level, our motivational construct. Children and adolescents who report happy or cheerful affect also report much greater energy levels than those who appear to be depressed. Thus, this chain of effects reveals that self-worth does have a functional role, given its impact on affect and subsequent motivation.

Implications for Depression

The relationship between self-worth and affect is of particular interest given some controversy in the literature over whether negative self-attitudes or self-deprecatory ideation should represent a cardinal symptom of depression, particularly for children. The DMS-IIIR, for example, does not require that such negative self-attitudes be part of the primary symptom constellation necessary for the diagnosis of depression. Dysphoric mood and/or loss of interest and pleasure in usual activities represent the defining features. In contrast, Weinberg et al. (1973) have proposed a diagnostic system in which both dysphoric mood and self-deprecatory ideation are the cardinal features of childhood depression.

Given the extremely strong relationship between self-worth and affect that has been obtained in our own studies (see Harter & Nowakowski 1987a, 1987b), it would appear that the vast majority of those children and adolescents in normative samples who have low self-esteem also report depressed affect. Thus, the findings support the claim of Weinberg et al. (1973) regarding self-deprecatory ideation. It should be noted, however, that since the concept of global self-worth as a self-reported cognitive evaluation of the self does not emerge until the age of eight, the link between low self-worth and depressed affect may emerge only in middle childhood.

Interestingly, those children with depressed affect and low self-worth report other indications of self-deprecatory ideation, consistent with our model. They have a large discrepancy between their perceived competence and the importance of success, and they report dissatisfaction with their physical appearance in particular. In addition, their social-support scores are low.

Although the relationship between self-worth and depressed affect is quite strong (correlations between .75 and .83), there does exist a very small subgroup of children who report depressed affect but *without* accompanying low self-worth. This subgroup also does not report other forms of self-deprecatory ideation, although they do report relatively low social support.

These two groups of children with depressed affect, those with and those without low self-worth, are reminiscent of Freud's (1916) distinction between mourning and melancholia. In melancholia one suffers from depression accompanied by low self-esteem (as exemplified by our larger group). In mourning, depression may be due to the loss of significant others, but it is not accompanied by negative self-attitudes (as in our smaller subgroup with adequate self-worth, where lack of social support is the primary correlate). Thus, while the majority of depressed children in our samples report low self-worth and related negative self-attitudes, it is important from a diagnostic perspective to identify the second, small subgroup where depression may be a reaction to loss of or lack of support since the implications for treatment may be quite different. (We are currently in the process of clinical validation study to investigate these issues more thoroughly.)

Extension to Suicidal Ideation

Recently, we have extended our model to examine the larger network of constructs among young adolescents who manifest suicidal ideation (Harter & Marold 1986; Marold 1987). Our first study yielded an interesting pattern, with one unexpected finding. As anticipated, we did find that young adolescents who report high levels of suicidal ideation also report depressed affect and low self-worth. They also report a large discrepancy between perceived competence/adequacy and the importance of success. Unexpectedly, however, they did *not* report low levels of social support.

Drawing upon her clinical experience with families in which adolescent suicidal ideation has been an issue, Marold hypothesized that the *level* of social support, particularly from parents, may not be as predictive as the *conditionality* of support. Her observations suggested that suicidal ideation may be manifested by adolescents when parental support is conditional on performance that meets high parental expectations: support is periodically withdrawn when the adolescent does not perform in accordance with expectations. Adolescents who experience such a conditional pattern of support and who feel that they cannot meet high performance standards are likely to feel that they are letting their parents down, which, in turn, causes them to engage in suicidal ideation.

In her dissertation, Marold (1987) found some support for this pattern. Those children most heavily engaged in suicidal thinking reported the highest levels of conditional parental support. In addition, the discrepancy between competence/adequacy and the importance of their success *to their parents* was a better predictor of suicidal ideation than was the discrepancy between competence/adequacy and importance of success for the self.

We are currently pursuing a study of this pattern and are particularly intrigued by the role of conditional support within the context of high parental expectations. In addition, we have added the construct of hopelessness to our model, especially the hopelessness that adolescents may feel about being able to meet their parents' expectations. We are now testing the hypothesis that adolescents engaged in suicidal thinking will manifest the following pattern of perceptions: low competence/adequacy in areas deemed important by the parents, conditional support for meeting high parental expectations, hopelessness about meeting these expectations, low self-worth, and depressed affect. Although the correlation between suicidal ideation and depressed affect is relatively high (.60 to .65 in our samples), depressed affect is not necessarily accompanied by suicidal thinking. Thus, we are interested in determining whether these other dimensions add to the prediction, thereby pointing to a constellation of factors that may help us identify those children who are at risk for suicide and in need of some form of intervention.

In extending these efforts to the issue of suicidal ideation, we have recognized the fact that self-worth does indeed play a functional role, one that may have serious consequences in the lives of adolescents. Moreover, we have discovered the need to expand our more normative model to include constructs such as the conditionality of parent support, the importance of adolescent success to the parents, and the degree to which the adolescent feels hopeless or hopeful about meeting parental expectations, in order to better understand the constellation of risk factors leading to suicidal thinking and behavior. These refinements will lead to a more comprehensive picture of the relationships among these constructs as well as to diagnostic information that will allow us to better understand the role of self-worth, in general, as well as to intervene in the lives of individual children and adolescents who may be at risk.

CHAPTER 4

The Self-Perceptions of Uncommonly Bright Youngsters

PAUL M. JANOS

American teenagers must figure out standards for success as students and as social beings and use them to make complicated judgments about themselves. The lucky ones are provided with healthy, if not clear-cut rules for doing so. Most of the time, though, young people must imagine what is commonly expected of those their age and try to observe what their agemates are doing. The standards they derive from these reference points for "social comparison" (Festinger 1954) may be inconsistent, and they are, much worse, almost always seriously neglectful of individual differences. Certain youngsters find it difficult or impossible to conform to such norms. It is almost inevitable that their self-esteem will suffer. Even when their—statistically speaking—deviant behavior derives from a highly valued trait such as intelligence, punishment for nonconformity may be prompt and persistent.

This chapter analyzes perplexities like these as illustrated in the words of exceptionally intellectually talented individuals, who have been singled out in the historical literature on so-called gifted children (e.g., Hollingworth 1942; Janos & Robinson 1985; Terman & Oden 1947). Robinson's (1981) label for them, "*uncommonly* bright," captures the element of deviance and thus will be used here. Uncommonly bright youngsters have typically earned scores on individually administered IQ tests roughly four

Additional unnamed coauthors of this chapter are all the students in the Early Entrance Program at the University of Washington, especially those who submitted to the "nine-pencil" interviews specifically pertaining to this chapter.

or more standard deviations above the mean or have progressed through school three or more grade levels ahead of typical agemates.

Several cautions are in order. In the first place, the risks inherent in deviation from norms—even positive deviation—are emphasized, and what are, properly managed, creative and self-enhancing aspects are intentionally downplayed. Second, the chapter sidesteps discussion of other influences on self-perceptions, like familial beliefs and values, modeling, and the structuring of contingencies, which are indubitably more powerful than social comparison, particularly in families fostering uncommon intellectual talent (Albert & Runco 1986; Bloom 1985). These problems notwithstanding, it should emerge that factors that are, like social comparison, norm-referenced must operate curiously indeed among a population defined as outliers on an important psychological dimension.

THE PSYCHOLOGICAL IMPLICATIONS OF STANDARDS FOR PERFORMANCE

Normally, parents base guidelines for children's school performance pretty much on prevailing practices, emphasizing this or that aspect slightly more or less. It is uncommon for them to have, early on, so successfully cultivated intellectual development that what classmates are doing becomes virtually irrelevant. By school age, parents almost have to discourage such points of reference if certain youngsters are to progress at rates commensurate with their ability. As John Stuart Mill committed to his autobiography: "[My father] kept me, with extreme vigilance, out of the way of hearing myself praised, or of being let to make self-flattering comparisons between myself and others. . . . the standard of comparison he always held up to me was not what other people did, but what a man could and ought to do. . . . I was not at all aware that my attainments were anything unusual at my age. . . . If I thought anything about myself, it was that I was rather backward in my studies, since I always found myself so, in comparison with what my father expected from me." (1964, 44).

High expectations, then, can stimulate exceptional performance. Even so, youngsters may not know it. Without obvious confirmation of success, which would follow naturally from comparisons with other youngsters, they can readily learn to focus on defects in their performance vis-à-vis ideals and fail to reward themselves for veritable gains. This can be destructive in the long run. Mill claimed that never feeling he had done well enough contributed to his breakdown at age twenty. His recovery was based in part on adopting standards that permitted a better balance in his life. This personal growth may have been as essential to his subsequent brilliant generativity as his earlier rigorous education.

Mill's autobiography suggests that achievement expectations exceeding chronological age norms are not, like the noble gases in chemistry, benignly inert. Although they probably play a necessary role in the development of talent, they must be employed with supreme sensitivity, for they can easily precipitate a solitary, painful quest for compromises that fulfill emotional needs. This has been underscored by other cases. Norbert Wiener, for example, who matriculated at Tufts University when he was eleven years old, recounted in his autobiography, "I knew well that I was to be judged by standards according to which a moderate degree of success would take on the appearance of failure. Thus I did not escape the floundering that generally goes with adolescence; and although this floundering was at a far higher intellectual level than that of the majority of teenagers, it represented a more than usually severe and doubtful struggle with the forces of uncertainty and my own inadequacy" (1953, 215–16).

The personal experiences reported above are consistent with systematic investigations. Uncommonly bright children do, in fact, communicate predominantly with adults rather than with peers from an early age (Bloom 1985; Fowler 1981). Usually parents try to compensate for this, and they are more often than not successful in promoting adequate emotional and social adjustment (Burks, Jensen, & Terman 1930; Janos 1986; Terman & Oden 1947). Nevertheless, casualties of achievement-oriented socialization practices have been prominent (Montour 1977; Wallace 1986), and hurrying children can generate compromising quantities of stress (Elkind 1987, 1981). Moreover, a signal minority of uncommonly bright children—disproportionately large in comparison with normative samples—appears to suffer from serious psychological and social difficulties (Hollingworth 1931, 1936; Janos 1983; Janos & Robinson 1985; Selig 1959; Zorbaugh, Boardman, & Sheldon 1951).

Uncommonly bright youngsters manage to fulfill extraordinary expectations; in this positive way, they deviate from the norm. They are also different in other ways, which may not be so positive. Joan Freeman (1979), for example, reported that the question "Do you think your child feels different from other children?" was the most discriminating of 217 variables employed in her study of gifted children. Yet children so characterized manifested many signs of distress, including disturbed sleep patterns, hyperactivity, showing off, and peer maladaptiveness. Of the maladjusted children in her sample, in fact, 52 percent were judged by their parents to feel different from other children.

Impressed by Freeman's findings, in 1982 we asked 271 high IQ (mean Stanford-Binet IQ = 140) elementary- and middle-school-age children themselves whether they felt "different" (Janos, Fung, & Robinson 1985). A very sizable minority (37 percent) indicated that they did and described the differences in straightforwardly conventional terms that appeared, on the surface, to be unambivalently positive (e.g., "I'm smarter"). Yet, in comparison with children who did not indicate feeling different, they evidenced *diminished* levels of self-esteem across a variety of domains. They also more often reported having too few friends, that being smart made it harder to make friends, that their friends were usually younger or older, and that they rarely played with other children.

As suggested above, social alienation appears to provide the negative coloration for the inside experience of differentness among "able misfits" (Pringle 1970). For example, Norbert Wiener described himself as "in some sense a misfit" (1953, 75), elaborating, "I was naturally awkward, both physically and socially; and my training did nothing to alleviate this awkwardness and probably increased it. Moreover, I was intensely conscious of my shortcomings and of the great demands upon me. These gave me an unmitigated sense of difference, which did not make it easy for me to believe in my own success" (289).

Social comparison theory suggests that one source of uncommonly bright individuals' feelings of alienation may be a peculiar type of praise. When comparisons between individuals are explicit and difficult to terminate, distort, or ignore, they are highly capable of intruding unpleasantly upon the self-perceptions of everyone who hears them (Mettee & Smith 1977). Especially when the construct of superiority is invoked, an individual and the group to which he or she is "favorably" compared may suffer. Bloom (1985) provided an illustration:

> Well, I was always singled out by the rest of the people in the class. I was somehow always described as the brain and all that sort of thing. And everybody related to me in a slightly strange way. I guess as time went on, it became more specifically related to math. But I wasn't all that comfortable with it. It set me apart from everybody and made me feel awkward and in fact uncomfortable. I think I preferred to have the ability and do the stuff and not to be singled out. I think I had enough self-confidence that it didn't

> make me feel that I had to live up to anything, but I didn't cope too well with the social results. It definitely made me feel very different. (311–12)

It is always treacherous to generalize from select cases, but empirical studies provide a convergent line of evidence. The literature is, admittedly, disappointingly skimpy. One must turn to studies at "commonly bright" levels of talent (e.g., IQs of 120–140), where it has been repeatedly observed that self-perceptions of social qualities are often less positive than are perceptions of academic qualities (Brounstein & Holahan, 1987; Ross & Parker 1980; Winne, Woodlands, & Wong 1982). Self-perception is, obviously, a multifaceted construct. Each of its aspects finds more or less support from pivotal agents, like parents, and from more diffuse environmental influences, like the so-called peer group on the playground and in the neighborhood. Varying levels of security in the differing realms of competency are thus inevitable. Parents of uncommonly bright youngsters must be ever attentive to the balance.

THE CLINICAL INQUIRY CONDUCTED AMONG EARLY COLLEGE ENTRANTS

Overview of the Inquiry

Uncommonly bright youngsters might be insightful informants along several lines of inquiry suggested by the literature. First, they can talk about how high expectations affect the development of their self-perceptions. Second, they can reflect on having been subjected to alienating comparisons with other youngsters. They can, obviously, also provide many details regarding their social experiences in general.

About twenty students, uncommonly bright in that they had entered college markedly early, were asked about their experiences and perceptions. They were drawn from the Early Entrance Program (EEP) at the University of Washington, which may be one of the most unusual educational milieux in the world. It facilitates the higher education of groups of able and—usually, but not always—academically devoted youngsters, who range in age at university matriculation from roughly twelve to fifteen years. Applicants to the EEP must evidence outstanding college aptitude test (e.g., SAT) scores relative to their agemates, excellent achievement in junior high school, and, through a variety of necessarily imprecise assessments, above-average maturity and appreciation for the consequences of their choices. Empirical research has shown that for such youngsters, early entrance to college, in addition to matching curricula to talents (Robinson 1983; Robinson & Robinson 1982; Stanley 1976), also appears to provide unusually well for psychosocial development and career achievement (Daurio 1979; Janos 1987; Janos, Carter, et al. 1988; Pollins 1983; Stanley & Benbow 1983a, 1983b).

Because students entering college so young are rightly regarded as vulnerable on several counts, a fundamental tenet of the EEP has been the provision of intensive social and psychological support. As its primary providers, we have enjoyed multitudinous exchanges over the last ten years with every one of the approximately 150 formally designated early entrants admitted to the University of Washington to date. Most of that communication has consisted of routine meetings and informal conversations about course selection, career planning, and countless personal concerns. Additionally, we asked students to reflect on aspects of their own competence, and made verbatim transcripts of what they had to say.

These materials constituted the basis for the ideas formulated in this chapter. Unfortunately, there was inadequate time to conduct empirical research. The chapter, then, is replete with the strengths and limitations characterizing *la méthode clinique*. It was written with two objectives in mind: to captivate a broader audience with an extraordinary population and to stimulate further empirical investigations.

Conceptions and feelings about oneself seemed ordained to reflect the impact of an academic placement certifying, in many people's minds, unmitigated deviance as an intellectual achiever and as a social being. Joining the EEP had, in fact, for most students (whom we affectionately call "EEPers") merely provided a rare context to which they were, in many respects, well matched. In fact, they liked their newfound "normalcy" and were a little resistant to probing differences from agemates; most had become adept at minimizing or denying them. After some coaxing, however, and reassurance that it was not the purpose to parade them as special, they transcended this well-rehearsed defense and shared the awarenesses and sentiments each had acquired according to a uniquely personal timetable. Many gave examples of the subtle stresses deriving from high expectations, and drew attention to how they were still operating in their lives. Most, if not all, vividly recalled incidents in which intellectual competencies had been disbelieved or singled out in a fashion deemed compromising to relationships with classmates. They conveyed a sense of having found a welcome home among full-fledged peers.

Self-Perceptions and High Expectations

Although this section is oriented primarily to considerations of vulnerability, it seems appropriate enough to begin by illustrating, in the words of a precocious graduate in journalism, how constructive it can be for individuals *to whom youngsters are fondly attached* to model high standards by example: "My grandmother truly believed that 'God was in the details.' She never let a thing slip by that wasn't just right. Naturally, she wanted and needed my help in doing lots of things, like gardening, cleaning gutters and windows, and all that. I *never* got things perfect. She would just come along, and say 'let me help you finish,' as she put it. I adored her, so, of course, that was OK. But believe me, I learned how to do things the *right* way. It's affected everything I've ever done."

Among the EEPers, youngsters who perceived expectations as divorced from emotional support appeared particularly vulnerable to insecurity and distant or hostile peer relations. Having learned the maladaptive habit of imputing emotional and social significance to what ought to be purely intellectual performances, they had suffered regardless of whether their private assessments of relative position among agemates were high or low. Self-confidence and social participation were thereafter seriously compromised, regardless of whether the results of competitive comparisons were shared with peers or kept to oneself. For example, a boy of sixteen, already a highly paid consultant to a major biomedical company, recounted, "My dad had always been stressing to my sister, and to me later, education, education, education. He has always been pressuring me to do well. When I agreed to enter the gifted class, it was because I knew he wanted me to do it. I was taught that life's one big game, a competition, that there was a limited amount of jobs out there. Everybody wants 'em and few will get 'em. I was good in math. That was important to me. I hoped it would keep me above the pack. But I never felt as good as they seemed to."

This youngster was not saved from the ill effects of competitive comparison by objective superiority on certain academic tasks. Others, too, reported how threatening it was to encounter veritable intellectual peers. They had, apparently, lost the skill of comfortably integrating information about themselves when it was derived from comparison with peers. Although, of course, affiliative motivations were simultaneously awakened, and usually won out, as shall be documented below, the two were in strong competition. The following account, taken from the same boy quoted above, dramatizes the downside: "We passed our papers around during class. It was a super humbling experience for me. I remember being embarrassed. Just not wanting others to see how I had done. At the end of the first quarter, I burned everything I had. The day I got my grades, I was extremely shocked. I can feel it now. That year was more or less like that. I kinda felt that others were always laughing at me."

Dr. Halbert Robinson, who founded the EEP, believed that one of the most trying tasks facing child prodigies is formulating realistic and rewarding standards for adult performance. By and large, such youngsters become the victims of an insidious expectation inflation. Because they were dazzling at learning in school, people find fault with them for not acting like "geniuses" as adults. Yet no one can be expected to entertain his or her fellows with superhuman performance throughout a lifetime, and setting up youngsters to expect themselves to do so is extremely destructive. Much time and energy must be devoted to getting out of a trap that need not have been set. The quotes from Mill and Wiener were so exemplary in this respect that only one EEPer account is included to document its timeless operation. It was voiced by a young man of seventeen, then a junior at an Ivy League college, who confessed to being seriously drained by such reflections: "I always thought that what I most wanted to do was write something that would have an impact 200 years from now. But I have these friends. . . . They're just better than me at *everything*. As far as I can tell, in any area I pick there are people who are infinitely better than me."

This boy had been taught to identify with those who had already succeeded and with acts of achievement. That left him in a bind, because he could never control the myriad factors determining recognition, even though his self-esteem, at this point in his development, seemed to depend upon it. Perhaps youngsters are better served by being taught to appreciate themselves per se and the process of striving, independent of its outcome.

Self-Perceptions and Intrusive Social Comparison

Mettee and Riskind (1974) have argued that self-evaluation via social comparison often occurs as a result of the intrusion of unsolicited feedback and that it tends to arouse potentially negative competitive sentiments. The EEPers reported that they had been frequently subjected to such feedback at every grade level. In typical situations, their competence had been publicly heralded, but usually in ways having demeaning implications for others. The assessment that such well-meaning praise had made their social adaptation difficult was unanimous, and their feelings were accordingly unappreciative.

In this vein, a thirteen-year-old girl who recently qualified for admission to the EEP related:

> In the first grade, we used to be restricted to what books we could check out. The librarian eventually let me take out other books. But one day, she reminded our class, "Everyone but Allison must take out books beginning with the letter of their last name." It made me feel different from everyone else. When you're different from everyone else, they don't want to be around you. It wasn't fair to me or them that she told me in front of them. It felt like it was making me apart—putting up a blockade so I couldn't be friends. It made me embarrassed, like she was making me out to be a great person.

Another young woman, on her way at eighteen to a social sciences department at a top-notch graduate school in the Midwest, shared an experience that had occurred during her eighth-grade humanities class: "The teacher said, 'If I hadn't graded on a curve, only one person would have gotten an *A*.' The whole class chimed out, 'Rosemary!' They said it in a derogatory way, accusing me of being the only person who could have gotten it. I was uncomfortable about the class regarding me in that way. I wanted to fit in, but they wouldn't let me."

During the preschool and elementary years, uncommonly bright youngsters may themselves make comments that backfire. In most cases, the EEPers suggested, they quickly learn not to. Yet, because it is entirely appropriate to communicate about performance at school, such exigencies often saddle youngsters with unpleasant affect, which they apparently increasingly keep to themselves. Thus uncritically internalized, this can induce marked uncertainty about how one should perform, or has. In the three selections quoted below, observe the progression from the uncensored expressiveness at kindergarten age to the frustrated protestations at the third-grade level to the defeated silence during the fifth grade.

One eighteen-year-old female senior at the university, who in the spring of 1986 presented original social science research at an international conference of educators, recalled:

> In kindergarten, we were learning how to follow instructions. We were drawing a giraffe, the teacher telling us to move one unit up, two units over, etc., on graph paper. I tore it up. I thought this was a stupid game. I

was angry and frustrated. I had gotten the point, and I didn't want to draw a giraffe anyway. Everyone else said, "That was really fun," and asked me why I didn't like it. But the teacher, whom I always adored, came down hard on me. She said, "You pick that out of the garbage and do it." I felt very bad because I felt very unloved. That was about the only time a teacher ever got mad at me.

A seventeen-year-old female senior presently engaged in research on blood clotting reported, "In second and third grade, I was in the highest reading class—a group of about seven or eight. I finished *Caddie Woodlawn* a LONG time before anyone else. No one would believe me. I felt put down. I got angry, but I didn't express it. I was a very quiet child."

A barely seventeen-year-old male senior, undecided about his career plans, appears to have experienced a bit of discrimination based on the stereotype of the bookworm: "In fifth grade, we had for PE various stations, climbing rope with your legs straight out, situps, pushups, etc. I buzzed through pretty easily. They had a chart on the wall with your name on it where they put stars. The kid after me on the list of names was an athlete. I was a nerd. Even though I had way more stars than he did, the PE teacher assumed the stars on my chart had been put up from his name by mistake. He moved them down to his name. I was a little upset about it. But I didn't say anything. I thought, maybe I didn't do them right."

Virtually everyone agreed that, by the time they were thirteen or fourteen, they had learned not to advertise their accomplishments in public. After joining the EEP, they expressed a huge relief at no longer needing to be always so self-censoring.

Differentness in the Realm of Social Functioning

It doesn't take long for children to notice one among them who marches to the beat of a different drummer. Indexes like size, advanced language, and immaturity in social presence are readily discriminable, and group reactions, unregulated by compassion, may be interpreted personally and hurtfully. Hollingworth (1942), for example, tells the sorry tale of a boy who got his hair pulled for trying, probably a little too hard, to interest his first-grade colleagues in books beyond them. Usually, however, such non–meetings of the minds are marked by ripples, not waves.

When elementary school is typified by the type of social experiences depicted above, it appears that youngsters gradually temper their gregarious instincts. By middle-school age, for many EEPers, social support consisted of a few carefully chosen friends. Many had acquired a distaste for "cliques" and the "intragroup codes" imposed on "in-group" members. They often felt like "misfits" or "outcasts," as a seventeen-year-old female M.B.A. candidate suggested: "In 8th grade, I was not 'with it' socially. I didn't dress right, I didn't care for the things that they were interested in. I don't remember doing a single thing with anybody. I didn't get along with anyone—oh, wait. There was an African girl who was as outcast as I."

The intrinsically reinforcing qualities of intellectual exercise can make it an attractive compensation for unpleasantness in the social domain. The first of the quotes below, taken from a seventeen-year-old female psychology major, suggests that academic talent can prove a lifesaver when acute distress characterizes social experience. The second account, from a seventeen-year-old male anthropology major, seems more typical of the longing, but not tortured, stance exhibited by youngsters who can regard their situations with a modicum of detachment.

> Everyone in 7th grade hated me, with some exceptions. My friends were in the "out" crowd. The popular kids looked down on me. I felt dirty, unclassy, unfeminine. It was worse in 8th. The one thing my ego was based on was being smart.

> I remember feeling left out of all of the cliques in middle school. To some extent I had my own group. It was basically the misfits, those not accepted by primary groups for one reason or another. We largely rejected the norms that they judged things by. . . . Once teachers assigned us to compete by making devices to walk on water. Our group succeeded. But some of the people in our group were not misfits. They learned to appreciate me. It changed my status in the overall group. Suddenly I had done something that we were all evaluating in the same way. It was important to me and at the same time also important to them. It was sort of a milestone in that before we had been pursuing different sorts of goals, activities, ideas, and whereas in the past I could say, "This is what I've achieved," they could say, "That doesn't matter to us." Suddenly, I had achieved a goal that they had been trying to achieve also. Later, by the way, our group used the device to earn $300 for a charity campaign by walking across Greenlake.

Affiliation among Full-Fledged Peers

Most EEPers wanted to participate normally in the social lives of their precollege schools, but they seemed discouraged from manifesting it assertively. In about half the cases, it appeared that alienation entered determinatively into the decision to seek early college enrollment. Perhaps because of the contrast afforded by social difficulties endured earlier in development, virtually all early entrants attached among themselves. Although elements of threat often had to be overcome, usually the EEPers confidently opened up to each other. The importance of this opportunity can hardly be overestimated. Because it met such long pent-up needs, EEPers, even those experiencing difficulties in their studies, found the social prospects of the EEP and the university incalculably attractive.

A young woman who had at age twenty passed a state bar examination in the East pointed out that time, propinquity, and a receptivity to one another are prerequisites for the in-group feeling to develop. For many EEPers, college presented this constellation for the first time:

> I've thought about this a lot, the feeling of being secure in the universe, which for me began when I was 16, with the whole thing of hanging out at the HUB [the university student center] morning, noon, and night. HUB time was sacred. People would actually schedule their classes around it. It probably took two years, over which we built up this repertoire of friends that was all really a base. You just had a *place* where you were recognized, where people knew you well enough to talk to you for extended periods of time, and have fun. What is it when people gather around, drink coffee, jabber, read the *Daily,* sing Monty Python songs, do lots of laughing? It's not that self-conscious a thing; that's what these places are about. It must have helped that it was integrated with the rest of campus. We could bring in new friends, strange ones with forceful personalities, who were secure enough not to deal in groupthink.

We have studied the development of friendships among early entrants and their older college classmates (Janos, Carter, et al. 1988). Sixty-three EEPers supplied data on the number and ages of their friends, the amount of time spent together in various activities, the number of times various sensitive topics were discussed, and the degree of shared intimacy. Striking differences appeared during the first and second years between the proportions of the friendships invested with agemates and with older university classmates. By junior year, however, and thereafter, early entrants appeared to have established relations with other students of breadth and depth at least equivalent to those already existing with agemates. Graduates of the EEP were pronouncedly more invested in relationships with older individuals. These findings suggested that uncommonly bright youngsters preferentially associate among comparably able agemates, when available, for a couple of years, up until about age sixteen. Thereafter, that their friends be of comparable age is probably less important;

they then feel more competent to develop friendships with older students, with whom they appear to have substantially caught up in social maturity.

While they were utilizing newfound, full-fledged peers as a secure base for developing other friendships, early college entrants were often simultaneously revising long-standing perceptions of themselves as social misfits. The process was, apparently, subject to predictable glitches. Innocent questions related to age seemed to perturb them, perhaps by highlighting an element of deviance which they were striving to bury; EEPers reported avoiding, evading, and bungling such questions. In short, they exhibited marked deficits in their ability to handle them constructively or gracefully. The following example suggests that a deep-seated insecurity may underlie this ineptness:

> In law school, I was not thrilled with people's reactions to my age. The way they asked questions, what it seemed like to me was that they had a conception of why *they* were [in law school], a career plan or something, a lot of investment, and I had just walked in, eight years younger, not professing any particular dream about the law, and the average person—they still ask me these questions—halfway expected me to have these plans, and I just don't, and I don't know what they take that for—it doesn't feel good. You can't take it too seriously, or let it get under your skin. They're just sorta asking out of general curiosity, and I'm actually fairly insecure about it. I'm still having trouble with it.

Fortunately for them, with the advent of young adulthood, the physical cues that tip people off to certain anomalies become fewer and eventually disappear altogether. Thereafter, such questions rarely come up, as we were told with some relief by those who had reached the ripe old ages of twenty-two and twenty-three.

DISCUSSION

Uncommonly bright youngsters have been identified as a population at risk for psychological difficulties. One reason appears to be that subtle sources of vulnerability attend developmental tasks typically referencing chronological age norms. This chapter has attempted to examine such vulnerability within the framework of social comparison. A central assumption has been that uncommonly bright youngsters, like others, naturally compare themselves to prevailing standards and to peers, but are left largely to their own devices for evaluating and managing deviations reliably attributable to themselves. Without adequate preparation, then, they may be hampered in constructing relatively accurate and satisfying self-perceptions.

We have directed attention to two main sources of perplexity. The first derives from the potential inappropriateness of standards that may be invoked when agemates are relegated to the status of essential irrelevance in evaluating performance. Certainly, when vigorous direction away from natural objects of comparison is practiced, it must be accompanied by adequate solicitude for overall emotional needs. Without such support, youngsters may determine themselves to be utterly unsuccessful.

Even when the major perplexity is "only" that expectations take a while to fulfill, reinforcement, although substantial in the end, may be so delayed that dispiritedness characterizes the period of striving. An additional source of discouragement may be the ambiguity attending evaluation of interim states of performance. In contrast, when agemates constitute the basis of comparison, self-enhancing information may be continuously accessible during the extended periods over which performances take place.

Albert and Runco (1987) have suggested that a close and realistic fit between familial expectations and children's talents and ambitions provide the most favorable developmental start toward a significant and satisfactory career. Our own work with early college entrants further suggests that when expectations reflect adequate knowledge of a child's capacities and are introduced in a playful and stimulating context, accompanied by plentiful social and emotional support, they appear to play a constructive role in development. Properly communicated, then, they appear to be internalized early and without untoward conflict. By the early teens, however, it appears that uncommonly bright youngsters, like most adolescents, are less receptive to expectations that are perceived as imposed by external authorities. They may occasionally need someone to remind them of their capabilities when they are feeling undirected or demoralized, but they appreciate respect for their self-direction and self-motivation. What they eagerly seek, and probably profit greatly from receiving, are genuine expressions of interest and encouragement and the provision of multiple educational and extracurricular options.

The second source of perplexity focused on in this chapter was intrusive social comparison which, regardless of whether issuing from authority figures, peers, or uncommonly bright youngsters themselves, tends to compromise social relations. Such comparisons may unwittingly provoke competitive dynamics among groups of youngsters who might otherwise be guided toward common appreciation. They may also saddle individual youngsters with conceptions of individual differences that they, irrespective of intelligence, must be specifically equipped to conceptualize adequately and work out affectively. All of these detrimental consequences foster alienation during the particularly vulnerable years of childhood and youth, when approval of agemates appears to be a sine qua non of well-being.

In a chapter best regarded as exploratory, it has not proved possible to elucidate developmental aspects of the targeted sources of perplexities. Our observations suggest that high expectations and social isolation begin to operate relatively early, although their toll is gradually and increasingly exacted until appropriate support is sought and provided. Parents and other well-meaning adults undoubtedly attempt to help youngsters cope with the stresses peculiar to uncommon brightness, but their efforts may be impaired by adolescents' disinclination to disclose experiences judged to reflect negatively on their own competence. Meanwhile, compensatory investment in academics may as readily mask as signal the build-up of difficulties.

Uncommonly bright adolescents, like most adolescents, are granted little power to control the factors resulting in even predictable perplexities. Socializing agents define the tenets of expectations. Youngsters must conform to programs in school, whether they meet their academic needs or not. Similarly, they must adapt to social groups as they find them. Faced with these inevitable limitations, young people often good-naturedly resign themselves to waiting for better situations to develop, immersing themselves in reading, seeking out adult company, and otherwise providing for their own advancement and emotional support. These strategies are more or less palliative, depending on a plenitude of personal and situational factors. It seems that those lucky enough to maintain a sense of agency and work toward constructive changes probably fare better than those who provoke battles or externalize responsibility for devising solutions. The need for adult sponsorship of these goals, however, cannot be too heavily emphasized, as youngsters can generally make only token progress on their own.

Youngsters who unflaggingly struggle to develop their talent and fulfill their social needs can be expected to make it, but what an unenviable job that can be! Much can be done to better support their efforts. Rather than make piecemeal suggestions, we have attempted to generalize a practice that has worked moderately well at the Early Entrance Program: consciously assessing students' self-defined intellectual and social needs, providing developmentally appropriate levels of challenge or support, and attempting continuously to incorporate feedback as to outcomes. This strategy of intervention tends to be solicitous of and responsive to information arising from insightful adolescents themselves, which differentiates it from many of the more widespread prescriptive approaches.

In the academic arena, this principle has been called the "optimal match" (Robinson & Robinson 1982). It rests on the "axiomatic" (Robinson 1983) assumptions that learning proceeds best when instruction:

1. is organized as a succession of coherently designed tasks;
2. maintains motivation by being neither too easy nor too hard;
3. is responsive to individual differences in patterns of talent and interest.

Rapid progression through school frequently results when learning opportunities are tailored according to the principal of the optimal match. This method of meeting the needs of uncommonly bright youngsters has yielded impressive achievements, judged by the criteria of grades and honors in college and graduate school (e.g., Daurio 1979; Janos & Robinson 1985; Stanley & Benbow 1983a) and by the more stringent criteria of ultimate career success (Pressey 1967; Stanley & Benbow 1983b). Naturally, not all who qualify for early entrance find college an academic haven; a substantial minority of students who matriculate have pressing developmental and emotional concerns to work out, and grades and career progress may diverge from what certain people expect (Janos, Sanfilippo, & Robinson 1986). Furthermore, an overwhelming majority of uncommonly bright youngsters probably choose not to accelerate their education to the extent of early entrance to college. They provide a useful reminder that there are multiple routes to success, because they seem to catch up eventually with early college entrants in career achievement (Janos 1987; Janos, Shluter, et al., in press), at least when they enjoy comparable levels of environmental support.

Adherence to the principle of matching challenge to readiness may reduce problems associated with inordinately high expectations and the ambiguity attending comparisons with agemates. First, it tends to focus attention on learning tasks relatively closely linked in sequence, and it tends to be responsive to youngsters' indications of interest. As an example of how the matching principle might issue in utterances to children, consider the following inquiry: "Now that you've successfully finished X, you may well attempt tasks A or E. They lead to somewhat different, but by no means mutually exclusive options. If you choose to attempt task A, tasks B and C constitute the logical progression thereafter. If you choose to attempt task E, tasks F and G constitute the logical progression thereafter. In which direction would you like to proceed? Remember, you can complete either one of these short sequences and still economically attempt the other."

The approach suggested above has a number of useful properties. First, it requires that the inquirer clearly understand and communicate sequences by which progress obtains in given domain(s) of talent. Persons with such knowledge and skills rarely need to invoke unhelpfully vague and distant goals. Second, it permits accurate assessment and due regard of youngsters' manifest mastery and inclinations—on a timetable that precludes the development of enormous disparity between competence and expectations. Thus, it permits youngsters to make choices and identify themselves with immediate programs of action. The approach is, by its nature, interactive, specific, and inviting; it provides personally relevant and attainable criteria for performance without introducing distracting references to other youngsters.

We are presently developing guidelines for extending the optimal-match principle into the social and emotional domains. The task is obviously formidable, for convincing articulations of sequences in these domains have proved elusive. Additionally, normal developmental needs may be differently expressed and met when young adolescents are exceedingly deviant intellectually and spend most of their waking hours in the company of individuals significantly older. What has clearly worked at the university's EEP is the provision of a home base populated by optimally matched agemates, the other EEPers. Among these full-fledged peers, uncommonly bright youngsters have experienced, often for the first time, "non"-cognitive kinds of connection that may thereafter be generalized to agemates in general. For some, the connection is rapid; others need much exposure for it to take, and for some, of course, it never does. Overall, few of the youngsters have appeared consciously intent on taking advantage of the rare social opportunities set before them. What occurs is largely below the threshold of consciousness, at the level of easy exchange and interplay that characterizes normal social relations, and for which experiences there appear to exist pent-up needs. This natural connection probably provides a sound basis for acquiring or honing social skills that will serve them well elsewhere.

Assessment of developmental status in noncognitive domains poses the seduction of applying stereotypical notions about children in general. For example, one might inadvertently impose obstacles based on the assumption that attendance at the high school prom is critical, or that adolescent girls are at risk in encounters with young men of fraternities. Hence, the value of sensitivity in listening and restraint in intervening cannot be overemphasized. To develop rapport with adolescents, it is useful to accept what they say about themselves at face value and then try to elicit the invitation jointly to reflect on such statements. We have learned that discussions proceed most constructively when clear distinctions are maintained among manifest achievements, the imputed meanings, and the attached affect. Youngsters do not always, or even often, conceptualize accomplishments as adults do, and they rarely limit feelings to the predictable, positive ones. Stirring around inside them are usually admixtures of inappropriately negative feelings, like shame, guilt, resentment, differentness, obligation, etc. In this clinical interview study, for example, we found that, in determining how one thinks and particularly how one feels about oneself, incontrovertible evidence of intellectual superiority (such as bursting through the ceilings of standardized tests, earning straight As in school, securing glowing recommendations from teachers, participating in prestigious programs, and winning substantive competitions) may compete weakly with experiences of inconvenience and distress occasioned by poorly fulfilling, in others' minds and one's own, expectations for greater ordinariness in achievement and social intercourse.

As the above example suggests, it is worthwhile to find out how individual children view and evaluate their own accomplishments, rather than make assumptions or project one's own feelings onto them. By conveying an information-sharing attitude, one may be permitted to engage in deeper levels of processing. Meanwhile, one is less likely to engage in inappropriate control or to make insensitive remarks that promote alienation among groups of youngsters. One may instead promote attachment among a variety of adolescents by acknowledging differences brought to one's attention, and then orienting to the observer's needs. Insofar as achievement has prompted one youngster to remark about another, one might say something like, "Johnny and Mary probably feel very happy/productive that they accomplished so-and-so. Everyone has his own special means of feeling that way. Since we're on that topic, do you mind my asking what makes you feel competent and successful?"

Having touched upon what we regard as interesting psychological issues pertaining to uncommonly bright youngsters, it would be remiss not to note that the lives of children not so designated are characterized by what they too experience as unique perplexities, many of them similar to those sketched above. Likewise, caring methods of inquiry and effective responses to the information acquired can probably be applied to help them develop more optimally, particularly if they possess extraordinary, highly visible attributes. These procedures cannot succeed, however, without excellent understanding of the factors affecting adolescent development in general. Needless to say, only further empirical research can foster the goal of achieving such excellence.

CHAPTER 5

Prototypes of Competence and Incompetence

ROBERT J. STERNBERG

We tend to think of competence and incompetence as characteristics of a person. For example, we might say "Joe is such an incompetent schlep!" and thereby signify that we think that Joe is an exceptionally incompetent person. That competence and incompetence are not really characteristics is shown by the interpretive possibilities of the statement, "Joe scores at the fourth-grade level on the Iowa Silent Reading Test." Whether Joe is viewed as competent or as incompetent will depend on a number of variables, many of which go beyond the characteristics of a person. For example, the way Joe is perceived will depend on his grade (reading at the fourth-grade level would be impressive for a first-grader but unimpressive for a tenth-grader), his native language, and the situation in which the testing occurred (e.g., we would want to know whether there was any distraction, or whether the lights went out, or whether Joe took the test seriously, etc.). We would also want to know just how important it is for Joe to read at a certain level. Whereas our culture, for example, values reading, some cultures do not, and some may not even have a written language.

Clearly, competence and incompetence involve, at a minimum, an interaction among person, tasks, and situation. But more important, competence and incompetence are ascriptions to performance. They

Preparation of this article was supported by Contract MDA90385K0305 from the Army Research Institute. Requests for reprints should be sent to Robert J. Sternberg, Department of Psychology, Yale University, Box 11A Yale Station, New Haven, CT 06520.

represent a labeling phenomenon. Thus, it is not the same thing to understand *performance* in, say, mathematics as to understand *competence* in mathematics. Performance pertains to how well a person does, whereas competence (in one of its meanings) refers to how well that person is perceived to do by someone, whether the self or another. To understand competence or incompetence is to understand a labeling phenomenon.

It is also important to realize that incompetence is not necessarily a bad thing. The acquisition of competence usually starts out with a recognition of incompetence and a desire to do something about it. Learning requires the prior recognition of ignorance.

The general theme of this chapter, then, is that competence is not a maximum level of performance nor incompetence a minimum level, but rather, both are prototypes—i.e., profiles based on people's conceptions of a construct. In the first part of the chapter, I describe a method for discovering prototypes and describe our research on prototypes of one kind of competence that is of signal importance to our society, namely, intelligence. In the second part, I discuss the culture of competence in the schools, pointing out how children's cultural and subcultural backgrounds contribute to the extent to which teachers perceive these children as competent or incompetent. Next, I argue that children considered to be competent in our schools are not ones who are necessarily at or near the maximum in terms of the abilities that schools should look for. Last, I summarize my main points and draw conclusions.

PROTOTYPES OF INTELLECTUAL COMPETENCE

Adults' Prototypes

In a first series of studies on the nature of people's conceptions of intellectual competence, Sternberg et al. (1981) sought to determine the structure and use of people's implicit theories of intelligence. First, we asked laypersons entering a supermarket, commuters in a train station, and students in a college library to list behaviors they believed characterized an extremely intelligent, academically intelligent, or everyday intelligent individual. We then compiled a master list of behaviors and asked new samples of subjects to rate how characteristic each behavior was of an ideally "intelligent person," "academically intelligent person," and "everyday intelligent person." A separate set of samples was asked to rate how important each behavior was to defining intelligence, academic intelligence, and everyday intelligence. We were particularly interested in two samples: laypersons and experts (renowned university professors) in the field of intelligence, broadly defined. From these studies, we learned some interesting facts about people's implicit theories of intelligence.

First, laypersons have quite well-defined implicit theories of intelligence. Three factors emerged clearly from their rating data: practical problem-solving ability (e.g., reasons logically and well, identifies connections among ideas, sees all aspects of a problem, gets to the heart of problems), verbal ability (e.g., speaks clearly and articulately, is verbally fluent, converses well, reads with high comprehension), and social competence (e.g., accepts others for what they are, admits mistakes, displays interest in the world at large, is on time for appointments).

Second, there is a high correlation between lay and expert views of intelligence: The median correlation between the response patterns of professors specializing in the study of intelligence and those of laypersons was .82. There were two main differences between the two groups, however. The first was that the experts considered motivation to be an important ingredient in academic intelligence, whereas no motivation factor emerged for the laypersons. Behaviors central to the motivation factor for experts included, for example, displays dedication and motivation in chosen pursuits, gets involved in what he or she is doing, studies hard, and is persistent. The second difference was that experts placed somewhat less emphasis on the social-cultural aspects of intelligence than did the laypersons. The latter mentioned behaviors such as sensitivity to other people's needs and desires, and frankness and honesty with self and others, but the experts seldom did.

In order to get a better sense of how experts and laypersons differ in their views of intelligence, I went back to the original ratings of the importance of the various behaviors to people's conceptions of intelligence. I was particularly interested in those kinds of behaviors that received higher ratings from laypersons than from experts, and in those that received higher ratings from experts than from laypersons. The pattern was clear. Consider first some of the behaviors that laypersons emphasized more than did experts in defining intelligence: acts politely, displays patience with self and others, gets along well with others, is frank and honest, and emotions are appropriate to situations. These behaviors, typical of those rated higher by laypersons, clearly show an emphasis on *inter*personal competence in a social context. Consider next some of the behaviors that the professors typically emphasized more than did laypersons: reads with high comprehension, shows flexibility in thought and action, reasons logically and well, displays curiosity, learns rapidly, thinks deeply, and solves problems well. These behaviors clearly show an emphasis on *intra*personal competence in an individual context. To the extent that there is a difference, therefore, it is clearly in the greater emphasis among laypersons on intelligence as an interpersonal and social construct.

Third, the three kinds of intelligence are correlated, but differentially. For laypersons, the correlations between ratings of characteristicness were .75 between intelligence and academic intelligence, .86 between intelligence and everyday intelligence, and .45 between academic intelligence and everyday intelligence. For experts, the correlations were .83 between intelligence and academic intelligence, .84 between intelligence and everyday intelligence, and .46 between academic intelligence and everyday intelligence. Two conclusions emerge from these correlations. First, the professors view intelligence as closer to academic intelligence than do laypersons. Second, academic and everyday intelligence are viewed as related but clearly distinct constructs.

Fourth, a fine-grained analysis of our data reveals not only distinguishable differences between experts and laypersons, but also distinguishable subpopulations among laypersons. Students, we found, gave greater weight to academic ability as a component of general intelligence than did commuters. Commuters, on the other hand, considered everyday intelligence—the ability to function well in daily life—more important.

Although the experts in our initial studies were all college professors, their fields were almost exclusively psychology and education. They had clear notions of what they looked for when they looked for intelligence in their students. But would these notions be the same across fields? Would professors of philosophy, for example, look for the same kinds of attributes as would professors of, say, physics, in evaluating the intelligence of a student? In order to address this question, I conducted a separate set of studies in which professors of art, business, philosophy, and physics were asked to list behaviors that were characteristic of highly intelligent individuals in their fields. Once the behaviors were compiled, new samples of professors in the same fields were asked to rate the characteristicness of each behavior in the repertoire of an extremely intelligent person (Sternberg 1985b). I found differences in emphasis across fields.

Whereas the professors of art emphasized knowledge and the ability to use it in weighing alternative possibilities and in seeing analogies, the business professors emphasized the ability to think logically, to focus on essential aspects of a problem, and to follow others' arguments easily and to see where they lead. The emphasis on assessment of argumentation in the business professors' implicit theories is far weaker in the artists' implicit theories. The philosophy professors emphasized critical and logical abilities very heavily, and especially the abilities to follow complex arguments, to find subtle mistakes in them, and to generate counterexamples to invalid arguments. The philosophers' view clearly emphasizes those aspects of logic and rationality that are essential in analyzing and creating philosophical arguments. The physicists, in contrast, placed more emphasis on precise mathematical thinking, the ability to grasp quickly the laws of nature. In short, professors in different fields had a core view of the nature of intelligence, but there were also important and intuitively plausible differences among the fields in what kinds of behaviors were emphasized in the assessment of intelligence.

The studies described above queried teachers regarding their conceptions of intelligence, but, of course, all the teachers were at the undergraduate and graduate levels. One might well wonder how teachers of younger students conceive of intelligence, and whether there are differences as a function of the grade level of the students whom the teachers teach. Fry (1984) addressed this question in a series of studies in which she used the Sternberg et al. (1981) procedures with teachers at different levels of schooling ranging from the elementary to the college level. Her results generally replicated those of Sternberg et al., but she found clear differences in emphasis as a function of the grade level at which the teachers taught. At the elementary level, teachers emphasized the social competence aspects of intelligence in their evaluations, at the secondary level, verbal skills, and at the college level, problem-solving skills. These results have potentially important implications for understanding what is valued in the schools at different levels. In particular, they suggest that in the elementary school grades, noncognitive factors carry a large weight in teachers' conceptions of intelligence. (My own experiences with the teachers of my children are consistent with this finding and have often resulted in my great frustration as my discussions of cognitive progress with these teachers seemed always to turn to discussions of social skills, whether I wanted this turn in the conversation or not!)

In sum, both laypersons and teachers at all levels have rather well-defined notions of intelligence. These notions display a common core, but are shaded according to the individual's walk of life. In particular, teachers' conceptions of intelligence vary as a function of the level of teaching and as a function of the field of teaching at the upper levels. There is not one "school's-eye" view of intelligence, but several such views, and they color the ways in which teachers perceive the intelligence of their students. Views of intelligence also vary across cultures, as shown by the work by Berry (1984) and Serpell (1977).

Use of Implicit Theories

Clearly, people have well-defined implicit theories of intelligence. But do they actually use these implicit theories in evaluating themselves and others? My collaborators and I sought to address this question in our research (Sternberg et al. 1981).

To find out whether or not what people say intelligence is actually has any relation to their judgments of the intelligence of others, we sent lay subjects a series of personal sketches of fictitious people, employing behaviors taken from the master list. These sketches in some ways resembled brief telegraphic letters of recommendation one might get if one sought written evaluations of people's intelligence. Consider two typical sketches:

SUSAN:
She keeps an open mind.
She is knowledgeable about a particular field.
She converses well.
She shows a lack of independence.
She is on time for appointments.

ADAM:
He deals effectively with people.
He thinks he knows everything.
He shows a lack of independence.
He lacks interest in solving problems.
He speaks clearly and articulately.
He fails to ask questions.
He is on time for appointments.

The respondents' task was to rate the intelligence of each person on a scale from 1 (low) to 9 (high). Our task was to find out whether respondents' ratings were consistent with laypersons' conceptions of intelligence. If they were, then behaviors that received higher characteristicness ratings for intelligence should lead to higher ratings of the intelligence of the fictitious persons. "Keeps an open mind," for example, had been rated 7.7, whereas "shows a lack of independence" had been rated just 2.7. Averaging the characteristicness ratings for each of the fictitious persons, we came up with a score of 6.0 for Susan and of 4.3 for Adam. By comparison, our respondents rated Susan's intelligence at 5.8 and Adam's at 4.3. Overall, when we calculated the correlation between the two sets of ratings (expected values on the basis of the average characteristicness ratings for the described persons, on the one hand, and actual ratings of the described persons, on the other), we obtained a coefficient of .96. In other words, laypersons' ratings of other people's intelligence were indeed firmly grounded in their implicit theories about intelligence.

We also used multiple-regression techniques in order to determine the weights for each of the three factors in laypersons' implicit theories. As independent variables, we used approximation factor scores of each of the described individuals on each of the factors of the implicit theory (as well as on intelligence). The multiple correlation was .97. The standardized regression (beta) weights for three factors were .32 for problem-solving ability, .33 for verbal ability, and .19 for social competence. (There was also a weight for unintelligent behaviors of −.48.) These weights indicate the psychological importance assigned to each of these factors by the subjects in the study. All weights were statistically significant and all signs were in the predicted directions, with only unintelligent behaviors showing a negative weight. As expected, the unintelligent behaviors had the highest regression weight, because there was only one independent variable for such behaviors, as opposed to three for intelligent behaviors. Moreover, as anyone who has read letters of recommendation knows, even one negative comment can carry quite a bit of weight. Of the three kinds of intelligent behaviors, the two cognitive kinds (problem solving and verbal ability) carried about equal weight and the noncognitive kind (social competence) carried less weight.

Do people use their implicit theories of intelligence in evaluating their own intelligence? Sternberg et al. (1981) had one group of subjects rate themselves on each of the behaviors in the master list, and also had them rate themselves on intelligence, academic intelligence, and everyday intelligence. In order to get a score from the behavioral ratings, we correlated each individual response pattern with the prototypical response pattern for the ideally intelligent person (obtained from the subjects described earlier). One might view the correlation between the individuals' self-descriptions and the prototypical response pattern as measuring the degree to which a given subject resembles the prototype of an intelligent person. Higher scores represent closer resemblance between the individual and the prototype.

The mean correlation of subjects' response patterns for themselves compared to the prototypical response pattern was .40 for intelligence, .31 for academic intelligence, and .41 for everyday intelligence. On the average, then, people saw themselves as having a moderate degree of resemblance to each of the prototypes. The range in degree of resemblance was quite large, though. For intelligence, for example, the range of correlations for individual subjects was from −.05 to .65.

These prototype scores were then correlated with both self-ratings of intelligence, academic intelligence, and everyday intelligence, and with IQ. The respective former correlations were .36, .42, and .17 for intelligence, academic intelligence, and everyday intelligence, and the latter correlations were .52 for the intelligence prototype score, .56 for the academic intelligence prototype score, and .41 for the everyday intelligence prototype score. Thus, IQ tests come closest to measuring what people conceive of as academic intelligence, and least close to measuring what people conceive of as everyday intelligence.

In sum, people not only have, but use their implicit theories of intelligence in evaluating others. These implicit theories are important in the judgments of both laypersons and teachers. But how about the students? Do they have implicit theories, and if so, how do these theories match up with those of the schools?

Children's Prototypes

Of several studies done on children's conceptions of the nature of intelligence, three are particularly relevant.

Yussen and Kane (1983) conducted a series of studies on children's conceptions of intelligence. In the first, they conducted interviews with children in the first, third, and sixth grades. All were lower-middle to middle-middle class. They found that younger children's conceptions of intelligence were less differentiated than those of older children. Older children were also more likely to characterize intelligence as an internalized quality of the individual. In other words, the younger children were more likely to believe that a person's level of intelligence can be assessed by things the person does or says than were the older children. There was also a monotonically decreasing trend in levels of self-ratings with grade level.

In a second study, Yussen and Kane asked first- and sixth-graders to imagine either of two children, one of whom is smart and the other not smart. They were then to assess the performance of the children on various tasks. For example, suppose the hypothetical target child is Susan. She may be imagined to be either smart or not smart. Subjects would be asked questions such as "Suppose Susan is having a jumping contest with her friends. How often will she jump the farthest and win the contest?" or "Suppose Susan hears a new song. How much of it will she remember the next day?" The questions were divided into four categories: physical, social, academic, and cognitive. The two sample questions above are physical and cognitive, respectively. In this second study, three clear-cut findings emerged. First, in all descriptive categories, smart children were judged as better than children who are not smart. Second, the gap between smart and not smart children is relatively small for the physical behaviors.

In a last study, children in grades three and six, as well as college-age adults, were asked to characterize an intelligent individual as an infant, as a ten-year-old, as an adult, and as an older adult. The results of this study were complex and can only be presented here in barest outline.

Consider first the infant. Everyone agreed that gross and fine sensorimotor control, the tendency to do things without help, and precocious language acquisition are important to intelligence. Both groups of grade-school children, but not the adults, also emphasized the importance of the infants' knowing what they should and should not do under particular circumstances. But only the adults mentioned motivation and curiosity as signaling infant intelligence.

Consider next the ten-year-old. All age groups agreed that superior school performance is typical of the intelligent child. But whereas everyone mentioned general kinds of knowledge and performance indicators, only the children emphasized the importance of excellence in the specific pursuits of reading and mathematics. All the groups mentioned certain social skills, such as being helpful to others and being an adaptable member of a group. But only the children mentioned physical skills, as in sports, as typifying the intelligent individual, whereas only the adults mentioned motivation, learning, thinking abstractly, showing interest and affiliation with peers, exhibiting independence, and creativity.

The greatest divergence between the children's and adults' characterizations were for their conceptions of the intelligent adult. The children emphasized the importance of performance on specific tasks, such as managing the household, excelling at a job, earning money, and teaching

be a recipe for disaster, as shown in the brilliant work of Shirley Heath (1983) on language development in three U.S. subcultures.

Heath studied language development in three communities in the Piedmont Carolinas, Trackton (lower-class black), Roadville (lower-class white), and Gateway (middle-class white). I can present here only a few of the observations she made on the effects of match and mismatch between what constitutes intelligent behavior from the point of view of the school and from the point of view of the community in which a child is raised.

Trackton children do not expect adults to ask them questions, in general, because in Trackton, children are not seen as information-givers or as question-answerers. Thus, the very act of being asked a question is strange to them. When Heath asked Trackton children to do tasks she gave them, the children often protested, seeing no reason for doing them. They particularly have trouble dealing with indirect requests, such as, "It's time to put our paints away now," because such unfamiliar kinds of statements may not even be perceived as requests. These children also have difficulty with "Why?" questions, because adults in Trackton do not engage children in conversations in which such questions are asked, in stark contrast to typical middle-class upbringing.

In Roadville, as in Gateway, the situation young children confront is very different. Adults see themselves as teachers, and thus ask and answer questions, including "Why?" By the time they go to school, these children have had considerable experience with both direct and indirect requests. Unfortunately, parents in Roadville do not persist in this attitude. Once their children start school, they more or less abdicate their role as teachers, leaving it to the school to do the job.

Trackton children are also at a disadvantage when they start school from the standpoint of understanding similarities and differences between objects and skills that are important in school and critical on typical intelligence tests. They never spontaneously volunteer to list the attributes of two objects that are similar to or different from each other. Instead, they seem to view objects holistically, comparing them as wholes rather than attribute by attribute. Although they may be sensitive to shape, color, size, and so on, they do not use these attributes to make judgments as to how the two objects are similar or different. Their unfamiliarity with abstraction, and their viewing of things in holistic contexts, impedes progress in reading as well as in reasoning. The Trackton child experiences a holistic coherence with respect to printed words such that if the print style, type font, or even the context of a given word changes, the child notices the change and may become upset. At the same time, the child fails to realize the symbolic equivalence of the print under these transformations, which, although relevant to the child, are irrelevant to the meaning of the printed word. Each new appearance of a word in a new context results in a perception of a different word.

The holistic perceptual and conceptual style of Trackton children also interferes with their progress in mathematics, where one object plus one object may be perceived as yielding one object, in that the two objects are viewed as a new whole rather than as composed of two discrete parts resulting from the summation. Rather than carrying rules over from one problem to another, children may see each problem as a distinct whole, needing new rules rather than transfer of old ones.

The situation is different in Roadville. Adults encourage children to label things, and they talk to the children about the attributes of these things. A primary goal in adults' play with children is to encourage them to define the attributes of the play stimuli, and the toys the adults give the children encourage them to match attributes such as color, shape, size, etc. Gateway parents, too, give their children educational toys from an early age. Children are encouraged to note points of similarity and difference between objects, and to label these differences as they are encountered. Gateway parents talk to children about names of things in books as well as in the world, discussing matters of size, shape, and color as they arise.

Like the Trackton children, members of the Kpelle tribe in Africa also seem to view certain kinds of problems holistically, which inhibits the transfer of problem-solving skills to other contexts that appear to be dissimilar. Cole and his associates showed that the Kpelle were stymied by a problem in inferential combination that utilized an unfamiliar apparatus, but successfully solved an analogous problem that involved familiar objects (Cole et al., 1971). The American apparatus consisted of a box with three compartments. When a button was pushed on one of the compartment doors, a marble would be released. Pushing a button on a second door resulted in the release of a ball bearing. Insertion of a marble into a hole in the third door led to the release of a piece of candy. Though the Kpelle learned how to obtain the item from each compartment individually, they were almost always unable to figure out how to start with nothing and end up with a piece of candy (i.e., by pushing the button to get the marble and then inserting the marble into the hole in the other door). The second version of the problem was constructed so as to require identical steps for its solution. In this case, the candy was in a box locked with a red key. Each of two nearby matchboxes contained a key, one red and the other, black. To solve this problem, the red key had to be removed from its matchbox and used to unlock the box containing the candy. After learning what the individual containers held, nearly all the Kpelle subjects solved this problem spontaneously. The lack of transfer to the American version of the problem can be attributed to the subjects' failure to compare the problems on a point-by-point basis. Holistically viewed, the American version seemed to be a totally different problem.

Trackton children are disadvantaged in reading as much by attitudes toward reading as they are by their perception of the reading material. In Trackton, reading is a group affair. Those who choose to read on their own are viewed as antisocial. Solitary reading is for those who are unable to make it in the Trackton social milieu. Moreover, there are few magazines, books, or other reading materials, so that children have little opportunity to practice reading or to be read to. Whereas Roadville parents frequently read to their children, especially at night, such a practice would be most unusual in Trackton.

McDermott (1974) has noted that reading is an act that aligns the black child with the wrong forces in the universe of socialization. Whereas reading is a part of the teacher's agenda and a game the teacher wishes the students to play, it is not a part of the black students' agenda and the games they wish to play. Not reading is accepting the peer group's games over the teachers' games, and Trackton children are likely to make just this choice.

Attitudes toward reading differ in Roadville and Gateway, but the attitudes of the two communities also differ within themselves. Once children start school, parents in Roadville generally stop reading to their children, expecting the school to take on this task. Adults encourage children to watch "Sesame Street," one means for the children to pick up reading, but the adults themselves scarcely set examples to model. Heath notes that the two outstanding features of reading habits in Roadville are, first, that everyone talks about it but that few do it, and second, that few take any followup action on the reading they do. Unlike homes in Trackton, those in Roadville do have reading matter, such as magazines, but they usually pile up unread and are thrown out during housecleanings.

Attitudes toward reading are different yet again in Gateway. There, children are coached before they enter school in both reading and listening behaviors. They are encouraged to read, to learn the structures of stories, and to use what they learn in their lives.

A major difference between communities is in the preferred mode of communication. In Trackton, there is a heavy emphasis upon nonverbal, as opposed to verbal, forms of transmission of knowledge. Adults pay little attention to a baby's words. Even sounds that are clearly linked to objects are ignored. In contrast, adults pay careful attention to babies' nonverbal responses, praising responses such as coos and smiles that seem appropriate to a situation. People talk *about* babies but rarely *to* them. During the first six months to a year of life, babies are not even directly addressed verbally by adults. Signs of aggressive play in children are acknowledged and generally encouraged. Babies sit in the laps of adults frequently during the first year, and during that time, the child literally feels the nonverbal interaction of the conversationalist. Children are expected to pay close attention to nonverbal signals about the consequences of their actions and to act accordingly. When older children show younger children how to do things, they do not usually describe the required actions in words. Rather, they exhibit the behavior, and simply tell the younger children to follow suit. Watching and feeling how to do things are viewed as more important than talking about how to do them.

In Roadville, there is much more stress on verbal interaction and development. When babies respond to stimuli verbally, adults notice the responses, and ask questions and make statements directed at the baby. When the children start to combine words, usually between eighteen and twenty-two months, adults respond with expansions of these combinations. Children are encouraged to label things and, just as important, to communicate their needs and desires verbally.

Habits of verbal learning in Roadville, despite these desirable features, do not match up with what will later be expected in school. Home teaching and learning are modeled not upon the schools' modes of knowledge transmission but upon those of the church. Children are expected to answer questions with prescribed routines. The measure of a child's understanding of things is his or her ability to recite back knowledge verbatim. The style of learning is passive: one listens, repeats back, and thereby is expected to learn. The sign of learning is memorization, not understanding. Even in their play, Roadville children use language in the same way as in more serious endeavors: they tell stories in strict chronological order and do not embellish them either with evaluations or creative fictions.

In Gateway, modes of learning are different, yet again. As in Roadville, early language use is encouraged and reinforced. Mothers talk to babies and assume that the babies are listening to them and will want to respond.

Parents believe that a child's success in school will depend, in part, upon the amount of verbal communication directed to and received from the child. But whereas Roadville parents discourage fantasy, Gateway parents encourage it and praise children's imaginary tales. When they ask questions, adults answer at some length and probe the children's knowledge to assess just what is known and what needs to be known. The goal is to encourage understanding rather than verbatim recall.

Consider next studies that have been done outside the bounds of U.S. culture. Cross-cultural studies of classification, categorization, and problem-solving behavior illustrate the effects of three processes I have labeled selective encoding, combination, and comparison (see Davidson & Sternberg 1984; Sternberg 1985a). *Selective encoding* is at issue in studies of attribute preference in classification tasks. In these tasks, a subject may be shown a red triangle, a blue triangle, and a red square, and asked which two things belong together. Western literature shows a consistent developmental trend such that very young children choose color as the decisive (or relevant) stimulus attribute, whereas older children shift their preference to form by about age five (cf. Suchmann & Trabasso 1966). Cross-cultural studies, on the other hand, often fail to show this color-to-form shift (Cole et al. 1971). Cole and Scribner (1974) suggest that the preference for form versus color may be linked to the development of literacy (where alphabetic forms acquire tremendous importance), which differs widely across cultures.

Luria (1976) provides an illustration of *selective combination* in a categorization task. Shown a hammer, a saw, a log, and a hatchet, an illiterate Central Asian peasant was asked which three items were similar. He insisted that the four fit together, even when the interviewer suggested that the concept "tool" could be used for the hammer, saw, and hatchet, but not for the log. The subject in this instance combined the features of the four items that were relevant in terms of his culture, and arrived at a functional or situational concept (perhaps one of "things you need to build a hut"). In his failure to combine the "instrumental" features of the tools selectively into a concept that excluded the log, however, the subject was not performing intelligently—at least, from the perspective of the experimenter's culture.

In many of Luria's studies, the unschooled peasants have great difficulty in solving the problems given them. Often, they appear to be thrown off by an apparent discrepancy between the terms of the problem and what they know to be true. For example, take one of the math problems:

"From Shakimardan to Vuadil it is three hours on foot, while to Fergana it is six hours. How much time does it take to go on foot from Vuadil to Fergana?" The subject's response to this problem was, "No, it's six hours from Vuadil to Fergana. You're wrong . . . it's far and you wouldn't get there in three hours" (Luria 1976, 129). In terms of *selective comparison,* performance suffered precisely because the subject was comparing incoming data to what he knew about his world, which was irrelevant to the solution of the problem. As Luria put it, the computation could readily have been performed, but the condition of the problem was not accepted.

We have seen the diversity of prototypes that exists for intellectual competence of school-age children. The critical fact is that how competent a child is perceived to be will be, in large part, a function of the match between prototypes of intelligence in the home and in the school. The greater divergence in the prototypes, the more room there is for a child to be perceived as competent in the home and community but not in the school environment. Is it possible to formalize these observations and to delimit some of the various profiles of competence that are differentially rewarded in our culture and, especially, our school culture?

PATTERNS OF COMPETENCE AND INCOMPETENCE: SCHOOL AND CULTURAL PROTOTYPES

Consider three aspects of potential scholastic competence: intelligence, intellectual style, and motivation. Each of these aspects plays a role in how competent (or incompetent) children are judged to be. By intelligence, I mean the effectiveness with which an individual purposively adapts to, selects, and shapes environments. By intellectual style, I mean the way in which this intelligence is expressed. By motivation, I refer to the push an individual exerts on his or her intelligence or other skills.

Profiles of Intelligence

Consider three students—Alice, Barbara, and Celia—who are or have been real students in our psychology graduate program at Yale (with their names changed to protect the innocent!). In analyzing the profiles of these students, two questions will be addressed: which students, if any, are intelligent in the objective sense, and which are intelligent in the subjective sense?

Alice was an admissions officer's dream. She was an easy admission to our graduate program, for she came with stellar aptitude test scores, outstanding college grades, excellent letters of recommendation—close to a perfect record. Alice proved to be, more or less, what her record promised. She had excellent critical, analytical abilities, which helped her earn outstanding grades in her coursework during her first two years at Yale. In taking tests and writing term papers, she had no peer among her classmates. But later on, Alice no longer looked quite so outstanding. In our graduate program, as well as in others, the emphasis shifts after the first two years. Standard coursework requires critical, analytical ability, just the kind of thing that intelligence tests measure fairly well. The third year, however, calls for a more creative, synthetic sort of intelligence. It is not enough to be able to criticize other people's ideas or to understand concepts that others have proposed. One must start coming up with one's own ideas and figuring out ways of implementing them. Alice's synthetic abilities were inferior to her analytic ones, but there would have been no way of knowing this from the kinds of evidence available in the admissions folder. Conventional measures can give us a fairly good reading on analytic abilities, but virtually none on synthetic abilities. Thus, Alice was "IQ-test" smart, but she was not equally intelligent in all senses of the word and, in particular, in the synthetic side of intelligence.

Barbara, on the other hand, presented a dilemma to the admissions officer. When she applied to Yale, she had good grades, but abysmal aptitude test scores, at least by Yale standards. Despite these low scores, she had superlative letters of recommendation, in which she was described as an exceptionally creative young woman, someone who had designed and implemented creative research with only minimal guidance. Moreover, her résumé showed her to have been actively involved in important publishable research. Her referees assured us that this research was a sign of her own ability to generate and follow through on creative ideas, not merely a sign of the ability of her advisers. The first time Barbara applied to Yale, her case was discussed at length. The long discussions in the admissions committee meeting seemed almost an attempt by the members to salve their collective conscience, for they knew that ultimately they would reject her. The vote was five to one against her admission.

Unfortunately, most people like Barbara are rejected not only from our program but from other competitive programs as well. As a result, they enter a program that is much less competitive or a different field altogether. This pattern is not limited to graduate school. There are thousands of people like Barbara (although perhaps not quite so gifted on the synthetic side) who are similarly rejected from law schools, business schools, medical schools, and the like (including jobs requiring selection tests). Some of them never even get to the point of applying, having been rejected earlier from competitive colleges.

In Barbara's case, however, an unusual thing happened. The one person who voted for her admission (myself, of course) was so convinced of her talents that he hired her as a full-time research associate. She also enrolled in two courses, two-thirds of the standard first-year graduate schedule. Her accomplishments that year should have been an embarrassment to the admissions committee. She was one of the best students in both her classes, despite working full time. Although not as good in classes as Alice, she was significantly above average. Moreover, she showed the outstanding research abilities her referees had promised: she independently engaged in creative, enterprising research. The next year, Barbara reapplied to Yale and to other graduate programs. This time around, the vote for her admission was unanimous, and she was admitted to other equally competitive programs. We were most pleased when she decided on Yale. Although never as excellent as Alice in her early coursework, Barbara was equipped for the third-year change in the graduate program. Indeed, she was in her element, for she greatly surpassed Alice in synthetic abilities.

Celia, on paper, appeared to fall somewhere between Alice and Barbara in terms of her suitability for admission to the graduate program. She ranked very well on almost every measure of ability to succeed in graduate school, but not outstanding on any of them. We admitted her, expecting her to come out near the middle of the class. But, as it turned out, Celia also proved to be outstanding, although in a way different from Alice or Barbara. Her expertise lay in figuring out and adapting to the demands of a complex environment—demands that are not always what they would seem to be on paper. Placed in a new setting, Celia determines what is required of her and then acts accordingly. In conventional parlance, Celia is "street-smart"—she excels in practical intelligence. She made mistakes, but relatively few, and corrected them quickly. Moreover, she made sure that everyone was convinced that she had the abilities it would take to obtain a good academic job and then do well in it. Although possessing neither Alice's analytic abilities nor Barbara's synthetic ones, she applied the abilities she had to the everyday environment of academia better than practically anyone else who had come to our program within the recent past. For example, she made sure that she would have three excellent letters of recommendation, the number customarily required for job applications. In contrast, Alice and Barbara never quite ensured that three recommenders were so aware of their accomplishments they could be counted on for strong letters.

These informal vignettes tell us something about intelligence, as it is both objectively and subjectively defined. First, the perceived nature of intelligence can change with level of schooling. Through college, analytic abilities weigh heavily in teachers' evaluations of intelligence; they are important in standardized ability and achievement tests, in some teacher-made tests, in classroom discussions, and the like. Later on, whether in school or on the job, synthetic abilities become more important—one must come up with new ideas and ways of implementing them. There is a transition from the particular valuing of Alices to the particular valuing of Barbaras that, although not complete, is nevertheless noticeable.

Second, conventional standardized tests measure analytic abilities fairly well, but they scarcely measure synthetic abilities at all. Nor is it clear, at the present time, how synthetic abilities can be measured in a nontrivial way. But, because they lack adequate predictor measures, teachers and administrators fall back on measures of analytic ability to predict success, even when they are inappropriate. Alices almost always have the edge in prediction.

Third, conventional standardized tests also fail to measure very well the student's propensity to make the most of his or her latent abilities and to implement them in everyday settings, whether inside or outside the school. Making the most of one's abilities in practical and social settings is important to intelligence as it is manifested in behavior and is in itself a kind of practical intelligence. At least some of Celia's skills are necessary if one is to use one's intelligence and have an impact upon the world.

Fourth, schools may be rewarding ability patterns that pay off very well in the short run, especially in early schooling, but not those that pay off in the long run, especially in later schooling and adulthood. The great contributions in most fields are probably made by Barbara-like individuals, not by Alice-like individuals. Many of the latter do extremely well in school and then disappear into the woodwork, never to be heard from again.

Fifth, this pattern of rewards may ultimately have pernicious effects on society, given the contributions it needs. The reason for this derives from reinforcement theory. Through the early years of advanced graduate education (in whatever field), students like Alice tend to be continually reinforced for their analytic abilities because these are the ones the school values. As a result, such individuals develop a pattern of use and capitalization upon these abilities. When the reward system changes, as it eventually does, the Alices come to be intermittently, rather than continually, reinforced for their analytic abilities, for they continue to matter—just not so much. But reinforcement theory predicts that intermittent reinforcement will sustain a given pattern of functioning more, rather than less, than continual reinforcement. As a result, Alice-like individuals may well not seek other abilities in themselves that would lead to greater success in later life. Barbara- and Celia-like individuals, on the other hand, will be only modestly reinforced for their abstract analytic abilities early in their schooling because these abilities are not so well developed. As a result, they may realize that they need to find other abilities within themselves upon which to capitalize. When the reinforcement pattern changes later in life, therefore, they may be more prepared than Alice-like individuals to capitalize upon their synthetic or practical abilities. The sad part of this story is that Alice might potentially have at least some of the abilities of Barbara or Celia, but never find or develop them because of the pattern of reinforcement she receives in her schooling.

Finally, there is the danger that students like Barbara and Celia may come to perceive themselves as not particularly intelligent because of their lesser test scores and the lesser reinforcement they receive in school. When, later on, they do succeed, they are potentially at risk for perceiving themselves as "impostors,"—people who succeed despite the fact that they are not very capable. They may view themselves as putting one over on the world rather than as capable people in their own right.

The view of intelligence presented here is based upon my triarchic theory of human intelligence, according to which it comprises three main aspects—a componential one, relevant especially to memory and analytical reasoning abilities; an experiential one, relevant especially to synthetic and insightful-reasoning abilities; and a contextual one, relevant especially to practical, everyday reasoning abilities (Sternberg 1985a). People are not solely like Alice, Barbara, or Celia, but rather, some blend of the three. Thus, a given individual will vary in the extent to which he or she exhibits each of the three aspects of intelligence. Other views of intelligence make at least some of these distinctions. Memory and analytical-reasoning abilities, for example, are the hallmark of traditional psychometric conceptions of intelligence, such as those of Spearman (1927) and Thurstone (1938). The importance of insightful thinking and coping with novelty, in general, has been stressed by cognitive theorists such as Raaheim (1974), but also by Piaget (1972). The role of practical skills in intelligence is discussed at some length in the collection edited by Sternberg and Wagner (1986), which deals exclusively with practical intelligence. Hence, although my partitioning of abilities may be somewhat novel, the abilities I identify appear in other theories as well.

In sum, the vignettes show that the subjective side of intelligence does matter, having substantial effects upon the way in which rewards are distributed by the schools and, ultimately, by the students, both to themselves and to others.

Profiles of Intellectual Style

Consider next profiles of three intellectual styles and how they relate to perceptions of competence. Throughout the author's four years in college, three roommates more or less stuck it out with one another. The roommates—Alex, Bob, and Cyril (only one of these names is unchanged)—looked remarkably similar intellectually when they entered college. All had high Scholastic Aptitude Test scores and very high academic averages in high school; they seemed to have similar strengths and weaknesses intellectually. For example, all three were more verbal than quantitative, good reasoners, but rather weak spatially. Thus, in terms of standard theories of intelligence, the three roommates looked similar. Moreover, today, all three are successful in their jobs and have achieved some national recognition for their work. Thus, one could not attribute whatever differences might exist among them simply to motivational differences. Nevertheless, if one looks beyond their intellectual similarities, one cannot help but notice some salient differences that have profoundly affected their lives. Let's consider some of those differences.

Alex, a lawyer, could be characterized (and would characterize himself) as fairly conventional, rule-bound, and comfortable with details and structure. He does well what others tell him to do, as a lawyer must, and has commented that his idea of perfection is a technically flawless legal document or contract whereby those who sign on the dotted line are bound to the terms of the contract without loopholes. In a nutshell, Alex is a follower of systems and follows them extremely well, as shown by the facts that he is a former Rhodes scholar and a partner in a major national law firm. Alex can figure out a system and work almost flawlessly within it.

Bob, a university professor, is quite different stylistically from Alex. He is fairly unconventional and dislikes following or even dealing with other people's rules. Moreover, he has relatively few rules of his own. Although he has some basic principles that he views as invariants, he tends not to take rules very seriously, viewing them as conveniences to be changed or even broken as the situation requires. Bob dislikes details and is comfortable working within a structure only if it is his own. He does certain things well, but usually only if they are the things he wants to do rather than what someone else wants him to do. His idea of intellectual perfection is the generation of a great idea and a compelling demonstration that the idea is correct or at least useful. In brief, Bob is a creator of systems and has designed some fairly well-known psychological theories that reflect his interest in system creation.

Cyril, a psychotherapist, is like Bob but not Alex in being fairly unconventional. Like Bob, too, he dislikes others' rules, but unlike Bob, he has a number of his own. He tends to be indifferent to details. He likes working within certain structures, which need not be his own, but must be adjudged by him to be correct and suitable. Cyril does well what he wants to do. His idea of perfection is a difficult but correct psychological diagnosis, followed by an optimal psychotherapeutic intervention. In sum, Cyril is a judge of systems. His interest, perhaps passion, for judging was shown early in his career when, as a college student, he constructed a test (which he called the "Cyril Test") to give to others, and especially to dates, to judge the suitability of their values and standards. Cyril was also editor of the college course critique, a role in which he took responsibility for the judgment and evaluation of all undergraduate courses at the university.

Although Alex, Bob, and Cyril are all intellectually able and similarly competent, even these brief sketches serve to illustrate that they use their intelligence in different ways. Alex is a follower or executor, Bob, a creator or legislator, and Cyril, a judge of systems. They differ in terms of their intellectual style or ways in which they direct their intelligence. Although people do not exhibit one or another style exclusively, they do tend to prefer some styles to others, exhibiting them in a broader range of situations than the less preferred styles. A style, then, is not a level of intelligence, but a way of using it—a propensity. When one is talking about styles rather than levels, one cannot talk simply about better or worse. Rather, one must speak in terms of "better or worse for what?"

How might one use the concept of style, as well as the aspects of application of styles to problems, to generate a theory of how styles differ in terms of mental self-governance?

The Legislative Style. The legislative style characterizes individuals who enjoy creating, formulating, and planning for problem solutions. Such individuals tend to gravitate naturally toward legislative activities. In general, they tend to be people, like Bob, who (a) like to create their own rules, (b) enjoy doing things their own way, (c) prefer problems that are not prestructured or prefabricated, (d) like to build structure as well as content in deciding how to approach a problem, (e) prefer creative and constructive planning-based activities, such as writing papers, designing projects, or creating new business or educational systems, and (f) enter occupations that enable them to utilize their legislative style, such as creative writing, science, art, investment banking, policy-making, or architecture.

The Executive Style. Individuals with an executive style are implementers. Like Alex, they (a) like to follow rules, (b) like to figure out which of already existing ways they should use to get things done, (c) prefer problems that are prestructured or prefabricated, (d) like to fill in content within existing structures, (e) prefer activities that are already defined for them, such as solving algebra-word problems, applying rules to already structured engineering problems, giving talks or lessons based on others' ideas, or enforcing rules, and (f) prefer executive types of occupations, such as those of lawyer, police officer, builder (of others' designs), surgeon, soldier, proselytizer (of others' systems), and manager (lower echelon).

The Judicial Style. The judicial style, as shown by the psychotherapist, Cyril, involves judgmental activities. Judicial types (a) like to evaluate rules and procedures, (b) like to judge existing structures, (c) prefer problems in which one analyzes and evaluates existing things and ideas, (d) like to judge both structure and content, (e) prefer activities that exercise the judicial function, such as writing critiques, giving opinions, judging people and their work, and evaluating programs, and (f) tend to gravitate toward occupations involving large amounts of judicial activity, such as those of judge, critic, program evaluator, admissions officer, grant or contract monitor, systems analyst, and consultant.

The issues that apply to jobs apply as well to schools. I would argue that schools most reward executive types—children who work within existing rule systems and seek the rewards that the schools value. To some extent, the schools create executive types out of people who might have been otherwise. But whether the rewards will continue indefinitely for the executive types will depend in part upon their career path—one reason school grades are not very predictive of job success. One's ability to get high grades in science courses involving problem solving, for example, probably will not be highly predictive of one's success as a scientist, an occupation in which many of the rewards go to those who generate the ideas for the problems in the first place. Judicial types may be rewarded somewhat more in secondary and especially tertiary schooling, where at least some judgmental activity is required, as in paper writing. Legislative types, if they are rewarded at all, may not be rewarded until graduate school, where there is a need to come up with one's own ideas in a dissertation and other research. But some professors—those who want students who are clones, or at least disciples of themselves—may not reward legislative types even in graduate school, preferring executive types who will carry out their research for them in an effective, diligent, and nonthreatening way.

The fit between student and teacher, as between principal and teacher, can be critical to the success of the teacher-student system or of the principal-teacher system. A legislative student and an executive teacher, for example, may not get on well at all. The legislative student may not even get along with the legislative teacher if that teacher happens to be one who is intolerant of other people's legislations. During the course of my career, I have found that although I can work with a variety of students, I probably work best with students whom I now, in retrospect, would classify as legislative. I can work reasonably well with executive types as well. I am probably weakest with judicial students, who to me seem more eager to criticize than to do research. The general point is that educators need to take into account their own style in order to understand how it influences their perceptions of and interactions with others. Clearly, certain children benefit from certain styles. A gifted executive-type student might benefit more from acceleration, where the same material is presented at a more rapid pace. A gifted legislative-type student might benefit more from enrichment, where the opportunity to do creative projects would be consistent with the student's preferred style of working.

Schools should take into account not only fit between teacher and student (or principal and teacher) style but also the fit between the way a subject is taught and the way a student thinks. A given course often can be taught in a way that is advantageous (or disadvantageous) to any given style. Consider, for example, an introductory or low-level psychology course. This course might stress learning and using existing facts, principles, and procedures (an executive style of teaching), or designing a research project (a legislative style of teaching), or writing papers evaluating theories, experiments, and the like (a judicial style of teaching). The general principle of style of teaching reflecting the teacher's preference is not limited to psychology or even science. Writing, for example, might be taught in a way that emphasizes critical (judicial) papers, creative (legislative) papers, or expository (executive) papers.

Sometimes, there is a natural shift in the nature of subject matter over successive levels of advancement, just as there is in jobs. In mathematics and basic science, for example, lower levels are clearly more executive, requiring solution of prestructured problems. Higher levels are more clearly legislative, requiring formulation of new ideas for proofs, theories, or experiments. What is of concern is that some of the students screened out in the earlier phases of education might actually succeed quite well in the later ones, and vice versa.

Perhaps the most important point to be made is that we tend to confuse level with style of intelligence. For example, most current intelligence and achievement tests reward the executive style by far the most—they require solution of prestructured problems. One cannot create one's own problems or judge the quality of the problems on the test (at least not at the time of the test). Judicial types get some credit for analytical items, but legislative types hardly benefit at all from existing tests and may actually be harmed by them. Clearly, style will affect perceived competence, but as noted earlier, style is independent of intelligence, in general, although not within particular domains. Certain styles work better within a given domain than do others. Style ought to count as much as ability and motivation in recommending job placements, although probably not in making tracking decisions that deal with issues of ability rather than style. Most of all, we need to be sensitive to how our perceptions of competence can be affected not just by abilities but by the styles with which these abilities are manifested in the everyday world.

The conception of intellectual styles presented here is based upon my theory of mental self-government (Sternberg, 1988). There are, however, other theories that overlap with my own and that also underscore the importance of styles in judgments of competence (e.g., the Myers-Briggs *Introduction to Type,* 1986; see also Jung 1923). Style, then, has been and continues to be an important aspect of perceived competence.

Prototypes of Motivation

Consider two real students, David and Melissa. Both are similar in their level and profiles of intelligence, and similar as well in their profiles of intellectual style. Nevertheless, they exhibit a key difference.

David's primary motivation is intrinsic. He is motivated in school by a desire to learn and does what he thinks he needs to do in order to learn. Some of the time, what he believes results in learning does not correspond to what his teacher believes results in learning. But he finds it difficult and even unprincipled to do things that he believes amount to no more than busy work, and so he does as much as he needs to do in order to learn, but what he does may or may not correspond to what the teacher wants. Sometimes he does more than is required, but it is not necessarily the same in kind as what is required. Hence, the teacher does not give him full credit for what he does. As a student, he is considered good but not great. The teacher views him as something of an underachiever and as rather rambunctious in that he sometimes seems to enjoy thwarting her goals, at least from her perspective. To some extent she is correct: David is concerned with what he learns, whereas his teacher is concerned with how he learns it and, in particular, that how he learns it corresponds to what she wants. David is somewhat exceptional in that the use of rewards and punishments has not undermined his intrinsic motivation. He is content with lower grades so long as he believes he is learning.

Melissa has little of David's intrinsic motivation, but she is as motivated as he from an extrinsic point of view. Because she wants to look good in the teacher's eyes, she does what the teacher wants. She probably would do little of what she is doing were it not for the rewards the teacher has to offer her. She does not view herself as unmotivated or as selling out to the school. Rather, she believes that the teacher knows what is best and that by doing what the teacher requires, she will learn. It is not the learning but the pleasing of the teacher that motivates her to perform. Were the teacher to be taken away, her motivation might be undermined.

The teacher does not see David and Melissa as equally motivated. She sees Melissa as the much more motivated of the two students, but she is wrong. Ironically, it is David rather than Melissa who is more interested in learning, although the teacher would have great difficulty believing it. The culture of competence in the school rewards Melissa's extrinsic motivation rather than David's intrinsic motivation.

Work summarized by Amabile (1982), as well as others, suggests that to the extent we wish to encourage creative performance on the part of our children, we should emphasize the development of their intrinsic motivation. Nothing tends to undermine creativity quite like extrinsic motivators do. They also undermine intrinsic motivation: when you give extrinsic rewards for certain kinds of behavior, you tend to reduce children's interest in performing those behaviors for their own sake (Greene & Lepper 1974).

CONCLUSIONS

Competence and incompetence represent labeling phenomena. They cannot be understood as entities in themselves, apart from the people who ascribe them. Although certain kinds of performance can be measured objectively, competence cannot be, because competence is not itself an objective phenomenon. What is competent in one culture may be incompetent in another, and not only levels but even dimensions of performance may differ across cultures in terms of the extent to which they are viewed as relevant for judging competence.

I started this chapter by discussing how implicit theories of intelligence shape our conceptions of competence. Whether or not our implicit theories are "right" (and it is not always clear what *right* means in this context), they are our main bases for evaluating the competence of others. And these implicit theories differ from one group to another. I then discussed the work of Shirley Heath and other anthropologically oriented investigators. Although their goals in their research were variable, what their projects all show are the profound effects of socialization upon perceptions of competence, both directly and indirectly through their effects on implicit theories. I then discussed three constructs—intelligence, intellectual style, and motivation—and how differing patterns of these constructs affect our perceptions of competence. We tend to view certain kinds of intelligence and intellectual styles as more desirable than others, views that are, of course, largely subjective. To understand perceptions of competence, then, we need to understand the implicit theories that underlie them, where these theories come from, and how they interface with explicit theories of intelligence, intellectual styles, and motivation.

Competence is ascribed through the creation of prototypes, which apply to constructs as diverse as intelligence, intellectual style, and motivation. These prototypes differ from one culture to another, but our schools as they now exist have rather fixed and stereotypical prototypes for what is considered competent within the school setting. What's worse, the prototype of competence in the school is arbitrarily extended to apply outside the school. But research on practical intelligence (Rogoff & Lave 1984; Sternberg & Wagner 1986) suggests that the prototype of competence in the school is different from what it is outside. Indeed, the view of the school is limited in terms of what might be considered competent or incompetent. We will better understand and utilize our children's capabilities when we broaden the set of prototypes we view as competent, within school and without.

PART TWO

SOCIAL PERSPECTIVES

CHAPTER 6

Incompetence: A Conceptual Reconsideration

ELLEN J. LANGER
AND KWANGYANG PARK

John can't fix the wurblet, Tim can't fix it, and neither can Mary.

Because these people do not know each other, they cannot be comforted by the fact that they are not alone in their incompetence. They would not take comfort even if they did know each other since John is twenty-eight years old, Tim is six, and Mary is seventy-six. To John, Tim is a mere child and Mary is an old lady, reason enough for incompetence. To Mary, John and Tim are children. Tim does not yet know the comfort available through making social comparisons; his brother can fix a wurblet and he wants to as well. They are all unhappy because of their incompetence. It is certainly true that each is presently unable to fix it.

To understand more deeply what it means not to be able to do something that one wants to do and that one has some expectation of being able to do, we must draw finer distinctions. By incompetence we mean the self-perception or that of another of inadequate performance, which is considered a stable attribute of the performer; it may refer to either specific or global behavior. Further, we believe incompetence is socially defined, and thus the difference between actual and perceived incompetence is more apparent than real.

There are at least four broad categories of what is considered personal incompetence, each beginning with a different psychological past and each leading to potentially different psychological consequences. First is *precompetence,* which is incompetence on its way to competence. There is *mundane incompetence* (undercompetence), which can be competence under mindful circumstances. In contrast to this, there is *overcompetence,* which is competence "in fact" but looks like incompetence in certain contexts. And, finally, there is *disability,* or *objective incompetence:* someone may successfully arrive at the desired goal, but because of a disability, does not do so in the traditional way. We will consider each kind of incompetence, noting similarities and differences, and examine how each may become another. Part of our purpose in doing this is to consider how to increase the perception of being competent.

A discussion of incompetence usually begins with how to help or improve the performance of the incompetent, or the disabled person. Although some researchers do examine the etiology of incompetence (e.g., Abramson, Seligman, & Teasdale 1978; Dweck 1975; Seligman 1972), few question whether those who are considered incompetent are in fact incompetent. We believe, however, that before helping the incompetent person, we must understand the logical structure and empirical process of judging incompetence. The categories above will help us do so.

Perhaps not in all, but surely in some important cases, we cannot much help or improve the state of the "incompetent" person without questioning the label "incompetent." The point is not that all human incompetence, or disability, can be eradicated by some conceptual reorientation; instead, we note the plasticity of "incompetence" in certain social settings. Some people now labeled "incompetent" will be transformed into "not incompetent" people, to be distinguished from the "ex-incompetent" person after "treatment." An advantage of using this conceptual reorientation is avoiding the unexpected damaging effects of "helping." Research has shown that helping people to accomplish simple tasks has the negative effect of inducing the perception of incompetence in the person being helped (Langer & Avorn 1981; Langer & Benevento 1978; Langer & Chanowitz 1987). Such help not only prevents the helpee from getting involved in the task and learning how to accomplish it but underscores the helpee's relative lack of skill. Helping may erroneously lead to the self-label "incompetent" even when the person is able to perform the task without help.

Categorizing people requires some discriminating cue; it is also true, however, that any categorization is a crude dissection of a continuous reality. There can be many possible ways of categorizing people as competent or incompetent in addition to the one being used. The label "incompetence" encourages the illusion of a fixed reality. Assuming an objective reality completely independent of human presence also encourages the precise labeling of people and objects, when, in fact, the labeling process is an interaction between the perceiver and the perceived. Assumptions, perspectives, expectations, motivations, informational state, and the like in the perceiver interact with certain perceptible aspects of the object, resulting in the specific categorization created. A look at some of the categories of incompetence should make clear its context-dependent nature.

PRECOMPETENCE

Children who cannot perform an *adult* skill are typically seen by adults as people in the midst of the learning process; failures are typically forgiven and attributed to their age. Anyone whose student or apprentice status is salient and appropriate, in fact, also will be seen in this way. This category of incompetence is taken to be temporary, and the social environment becomes coordinated to support this dynamic view. Precompetent people are encouraged by themselves or others to try harder or to try again. When the precompetent person is a child, it seems clear to adult observers that she or he will at some point be able to accomplish the task. Precompetent people are often considered inexperienced, and, as such, they are often explicitly told not to take their failures seriously. For them, incompetence is merely a behavioral description of the present, not a prescription for the future. In fact, once people are perceived as precompetent, the judgment of their performance as competent or incompetent becomes irrelevant—i.e., the evaluation is not considered in the first place.

There is a counterpart to precompetence: *postcompetence,* or beyond-competence. Suppose someone is told he is wonderful at spelling three-letter words. Most educated adults will not be impressed by this response to their ability (cf. Feather 1969; McClelland 1961; Atkinson 1964); the compliment is not absorbed. Most people are confident they can accomplish this task successfully, so they do not have to think about it. In other words, they are beyond the point where competence-incompetence is a relevant distinction. Precompetence and postcompetence are not "qualified" for a judgment of competence-incompetence for different reasons. We will focus on precompetence because of the problems that result from its similarity to incompetence.

Interestingly, if one assumed that any incompetence is a behavioral description and not a psychological explanation, then one would be more inclined to search for a cause to explain the incompetence (cf. Heider

1958). Incompetence is currently treated like an internal stable attribution. As soon as self or other searched for a reason for the incompetence, however, and found (created) it, an attribution of precompetence would be more likely to follow. For example, if a man had trouble banging a nail into a board, one might call him incompetent. But if one simply asked *why,* one may find that he never learned (or forgot) how to hold the hammer properly. Such explanations suggest that learning could change the outcome and, if so, the more appropriate attribution by self or other is precompetence, not incompetence. Consider some reasons one might offer for another's incompetence: she was never taught it; his parents, for behavioral or deep-seated reasons, made it hard for him to focus on this sort of problem; he is afraid of it; she has learned not to like it. The more reasons there are, the more likely that at least one will be external. As a result, it may occur to the person that though he could not do it before, *now he is trying to learn it* (i.e., the person is precompetent, not incompetent). Simply asking about possible causes of incompetence can lead to a judgment of precompetence.

The cues of learning, then, may produce a judgment of precompetence. The relationship between the perceived and the perceiver is also important in drawing such a judgment. Those who generally are confident would seem to attribute their failures and those of their friends (in-group members) to inexperience, or precompetence. Research on defensive attributions (e.g., Harvey, Ickes, & Kidd 1976; Shaver 1970; Weary 1979), and ethnocentric attributions (Hewstone & Ward 1985; Pettigrew 1979), in fact, tells us that, in general, people take responsibility for their own and in-group members' successes and blame failures on external, unstable factors. A precompetence judgment is not exactly an external attribution for the incompetence performance. It simply says that the actor is not yet prepared to do it correctly, so it is unfair and premature to label it as "failure." A judgment of precompetence by self or other, however, may serve the same function as an external attribution in protecting the individual from the negative effects of being labeled "incompetent." An attribution to precompetence provides the actor with the opportunity to learn by trial and error without fearing failures. In this way, the same behavioral performance leads us to see the opportunity of learning, not the end of learning.

An attribution to precompetence is highly desirable in that failure in learning is not stigmatizing. Indeed, neither internal nor external attributions are likely because the person is involved in the task at hand. When failures are noticed, they are likely to be forgiven regardless of whether an internal or external attribution for them is made. Failures become clues along the way to a successful outcome. If people paid attention to why they did what they did when they did it, they could always make an attribution of precompetence for themselves. Yet many people—for example, children and students—suffer from perceived incompetence. If perceived precompetence is desirable and available, one may reasonably ask why this more valuable attribution is not readily seized upon.

Just as the status of the actor and the relationship between the actor and the observer is important in a judgment of precompetence, the state of mind of the actor is important in the self-perception of precompetence. In order to understand this, we need to explain mindfulness/mindlessness theory (for a more detailed discussion, see Langer 1979, 1989b).

Mindlessness/Mindfulness Theory

When one is trying to do some task without actively considering alternative ways of doing it, without differentiating the various aspects of the task, but rather taking the behavior single-mindedly as a whole, based on a past construal of the situation, one is behaving mindlessly (Langer 1989a, 1989b). This typifies the incompetence most of us experience. To try and fail basically the same way each time, without a conscious appreciation of alternative available responses, is mindless incompetence. Holding the task constant in this way leads to disengagement with that task. Engagement in a task would seem to be incompatible with feelings of incompetence (or competence, for that matter).

When behaving mindfully, in contrast, aspects of the environment are *not* available as rigid, structural cues that can trigger well-defined sequences of behavior. To operate mindfully is to recognize the underdefined and ready-to-be redefined character of objects in the environment. Routine action is not possible, because the person is involved in choosing what to do, how to do it, and the resources available to do it with. There is an awareness of alternative actions and of alternative ways for viewing the objects of the environment. The exercise of choice that follows from mindfulness inescapably involves the person in a certain kind of cognitive activity not available under routine circumstances. Mindless and mindful engagements with the environment can be distinguished, then, in terms of the radical absence versus the ever presence of possibility.

A distinction between mindless and mindful activity does not imply that during mindless activity the mind is somehow absent. Rather, the mind abstains from performing in certain ways that are, in principle, available. This abstinence has consequences for one's ongoing capacity to control the environment. When mindless, the person operates in a routine fashion. The environment is seen as presenting a series of well-structured cues that invite rigid, well-defined performance. It does not occur to the person that choice is available. The objects of the environment are seen as rigidly signifying only one thing as the person single-mindedly pursues the goal.

Much of the incompetence people experience must be of the mindless sort, because mindful failures tend to be seen as part of the process of accomplishing the goal (Chanowitz & Langer 1980) and thus, as part of the task. If they are noticed as failures at all by the actor, they should be attributed by her or him to precompetence because task learning is so salient to the individual. The erroneous assumption people typically make for themselves is that there exists some "not incompetent" object which is a standard for the judgment of competence and incompetence. When someone is eventually successful, people say that any prior failure provided a good lesson for the person—the failure was a necessary component of the success. What happened before success was achieved is another matter: mistakes were taken as evidence of incompetence. If someone is mindfully engaging in the task (learning something), however, then she can be in the precompetence stage until she succeeds.

Mindfulness can be used self-destructively. Imagine someone going through a task, mindfully considering alternatives that bear no fruit: "I've gone through all this work and I still can't figure this problem out—I must really be stupid." But there are always new, untried ways. Being mindful in trying to find a task's solution is *engaging* and at the least will result in *incidental learning*. These two outcomes should work to make a mindful task activity less vulnerable to self-incrimination than mindless activity, even if no solution is found (Langer 1989b). Moreover, although people often self-handicap (behave in ways to provide excuses for potentially poor performance, e.g., intentionally drinking alcohol or not studying before an exam) when faced with important but difficult tasks (Berglas & Jones 1978), there is no evidence that if they were encouraged not to self-handicap (or to be mindful) they would be worse off in any way if failure did occur. (We will discuss the importance of this mode of performing tasks later.)

MUNDANE INCOMPETENCE (UNDERCOMPETENCE)

In contrast to the precompetence case, the person here is implicitly perceived by self and/or others as qualified to be judged as competent or incompetent. Mundane incompetence on the *surface* is most familiar to us; it derives from (initially) unexpected personal failures for which an internal attribution is made. Mundane incompetence is mindless and may be real or illusory. We want to emphasize, however, that this incompetence can be competence under mindful circumstances. We will demonstrate this with three kinds of mundane incompetence: (1) learned helplessness, (2) outcome-oriented incompetence, and (3) observer-determined incompetence.

Learned Helplessness

Learned helplessness may be seen as mundane mindless incompetence. According to learned-helplessness theory, people perceive response/outcome independence in situations that are response-dependent because of their prior experience with (seemingly) uncontrollable aversive outcomes. The individual equates the present situation with one in the past and, because he was not able to control the outcome then, he concludes he cannot control it now, even though others can readily identify the opportunity for control (Alloy & Abramson 1979; Garber & Seligman 1980; Miller 1985; Seligman 1975; Wortman & Brehm 1975). If instead of mindlessly holding the past constant, the person considers each situation new (at least new enough to need mindful attention to detail), it is unlikely that an illusion of incompetence in the form of learned helplessness could result (see Langer, 1979, for a discussion of the illusion of incompetence).

Learned helplessness, however, may appear to differ from mindless incompetence because at the beginning of the helplessness training the individual cannot affect the environment no matter how hard she tries; thus, mindfulness would seem to be useless. No matter how much conscious appreciation one has for alternative available responses, it is a no-win situation. But this kind of reasoning in the uncontrollable situation (learned-helplessness environment) probably would not result in learned helplessness. More likely it would be "learned inaction," which would look the same but have different implications. It can be a mindful response to an unresponsive environment. As we will discuss below, one cannot be sure that an outcome is indeed uncontrollable no matter how unresponsive the environment may be; one can conclude only that such control is indeterminate.

Outcome-Oriented Incompetence

When individuals feel incompetent, they long to feel competent; however, perceived competence and perceived incompetence may be, like all opposites, in many ways very much the same thing. When one is feeling very *competent,* one is also vulnerable to the fear and negative experience of failures. The perception of incompetence is not possible without certain expectations of competence, and vice versa. This contrasting complementarity is especially true when the outcome is the sole criterion of whether the performance is competent or incompetent. Thinking about failing or thinking about succeeding are the same: the focus is on the outcome, not the process. If one actively perceived competence (attending to self, not task), one would remain vulnerable to future failure and to potentially unflattering social comparisons—to people who are more skilled than past comparison others (Festinger 1954).

If one concentrated on process, the question of incompetence probably would not arise. A process orientation is the strategy one uses when one is doing a task with no well-defined end. It is also the strategy one uses when playing a game. One may want to win the game, but if the game is not involving and if it is over quickly, it will not be enjoyable. ("Routine fun" is a contradiction in terms since routines are typically engaged in to free the individual from thought about the task.) To prevent the perception of incompetence, then, one might consider tasks to be related so that the idea of ending becomes unimportant and process becomes the goal. If one writes a paper to achieve some goal without attention to the writing process, one is more vulnerable to a good or bad evaluation of the product. If, however, one saw that as soon as one is finished with the first paper, thoughts are continued in the next paper, then there would probably follow a different, more involving orientation to the task. As such, subsequent evaluation necessarily should be less important, because behavior that is involving is itself rewarding.

Observer-Determined Incompetence

In addition to mindless incompetence, the mundane experience of incompetence can also be illusory. An illustration from Shakespeare will demonstrate how:

> Corin: And how like you this shepherd's life, Master Touchstone?
> Touchstone: Truly, shepherd, in respect of itself, it is a good life; but in respect that it is a shepherd's life, it is naught. In respect that it is solitary, I like it very well, but in respect that it is private, it is a very vile life. Now in respect it is in the fields, it pleaseth me well; but in respect it is not in the court, it is tedious. As it is a spare life, look you, it fits my humor well; but as there is no more plenty in it, it goes much against my stomach. Hast any philosophy in thee shepherd?
>
> *As You Like It,* act 3, scene 2

Here we see affection and dislike for what seem to be two sides of the same thing. Touchstone likes the forest because it is solitary, yet thinks it vile because it is private. The way this dual characterization contributes to the perception of incompetence will become clear. It may be that almost all characteristics can be cast in both a positive and a negative context, which, however, does not mean there are positive and negative elements to everything. Rather, the same element is simultaneously positive and negative, depending on perspective. To be consistent, one must be rigid. To be spontaneous, one must be impulsive. But to act like a fox, one cannot act like a hedgehog. One cannot engage in mutually exclusive behavior.

Perceived incompetence may often stem from the desire to change those behaviors or characteristics that are, in fact, valued when called by another name (Langer 1989b). One may strain to be more flexible, but as long as one values being consistent, these attempts should meet with failure. To test this hypothesis, Langer and Thompson (1987) presented subjects with a list of negative traits and asked them to indicate for each whether it was one they tried to change but could not, tried to change and did, or considered irrelevant. Subsequently, subjects were given a random list of traits that represented the positive casting of each of the traits on the former list. They were asked to indicate how much they valued each of these characteristics. Results revealed that those negative characteristics that people wanted to change but apparently could not were actually traits they valued in themselves when called by another name. This finding may explain why people who are truly motivated to change and who possess the skills required for change have so much difficulty. Change is often not called for. Or to put it differently, their incompetence is illusory.

People typically do not intentionally act in negative ways. If, however, people behave mindlessly without an active awareness of why they are doing what they are doing, they become vulnerable to other people's characterizations of their behavior. If one is aware of being "planful," one becomes less vulnerable to accusations of being plodding. What this suggests, then, is that incompetence by one name may be competence by another. Further, it suggests that if people were aware of how their behavior could be alternatively cast, the frequently experienced struggle of change could become instead a simple decision. One would decide whether to be inconsistent and flexible or to be consistent and rigid. People often mistakenly think they are deciding between something positive and something negative—being flexible or rigid. Given this alternative, we have all been taught to choose to be flexible.

Others have looked at this actor/observer difference on the group level. The study of sex differences (e.g., Gilligan 1982) and race differences (e.g., Katz & Taylor 1988) has shown that behavior initially considered incompetent by the culture at large in fact was motivated by a different set of concerns. The difference between an Asian culture and the American culture with respect to individualism is an example. Asians may appear more conforming than Americans. To Asians, however, they are being more harmonizing than Americans. Indeed, research conducted with the elderly made this same point (Langer, Rodin, et al. 1979). We found that memory improved when there was reason to remember; that is, a lack of relevance masqueraded as memory loss.

In an even more elaborate investigation, we brought elderly men to a retreat in New Hampshire (see Langer et al. 1989). Some people arrived looking as though they were at death's door. After five days in a new context and after being treated with positive expectations for ultimate success, the people were far more active and healthy looking.

Thus, much of the mundane incompetence we experience is illusory. If people mindfully engage themselves in their tasks, this illusion of incompetence would largely be dispelled. Of course, if the belief in incompetence leads to disengagement from the task and thus prevents new learning, competent performance eventually will be absent. This belief in incompetence is frequently seen with elderly adults. It would be hard for an elder to be rude to the kind nurse trying to help her by showing her competence. Moreover, nurses communicate their perceptions of the elders' incompetence by subtle or not so subtle cues. Caporael et al. (1983) found that care givers who think the receiver has a low level of ability use more baby talk. It would be hard to betray the expectation of the person especially when the person is trying to "help" the "incompetent." Moreover, "good" patients—those who are passive and compliant—get more lessly—i.e., without self-referent thought (Bandura 1981; Langer 1979). But presumed incompetence in this case is devastating because it concerns tasks the person felt expert on.

Research by Langer and Imber (1979) supports this view. They tested the hypothesis that there exists a curvilinear relationship between amount of task experience and vulnerability to competence-questioning aspects of the environment. Subjects were given either no practice on a task, a moderate amount of practice, or enough practice to overlearn the task. They were then assigned an inferior label to encourage them to question their competence. Those subjects who either had no experience on the task or who had overlearned it performed poorly once they questioned their competence.

These findings were explained in terms of mindlessness. As one practices a task, its individual components coalesce so that, over time, the individual steps are not available for conscious use. It is these steps, however, that are used as evidence of task competence. One way to know you can do a task is to run through the steps in your head. But once it becomes overlearned, evidence of competence in this form is no longer available. In a second study, subjects also were led to question their competence on an overlearned task. For half of them, we made the steps of the task salient and for half we did not. By making the components of the task salient, we eliminated the perception of incompetence.

In another investigation, subjects purportedly in an experiment looking at voice quality, were asked to speak about an overlearned or a novel issue under one of two circumstances. Either they were to pause first and think about what they were going to say or they were to speak immediately into a tape recorder. The results revealed that subjects were less fluent when thinking about what could be spoken mindlessly—the overlearned issue (Langer & Weinman 1981). Similar work on nonintellectual tasks has been conducted by Baumeister (1984).

These studies suggest that people may become incompetent on tasks for which they have already demonstrated competence (where they are "objectively" competent). Thus, competence and incompetence for them is a matter of context. This work also suggests that such incompetence can be prevented either by discouraging mindlessness in the first place (Langer, Hatem, et al. 1987; Langer & Imber 1979; Langer & Piper 1987) or by educating people to recognize its potentially debilitating consequences. People who demonstrate overcompetence can perform the tasks on which they are failing. They must simply let themselves perform reinforcements for their dependency than do angry, demanding] Therefore, patients become increasingly "incompetent" as they re a long-term-care setting (Baltes & Skinner 1983; Raps et al. 1982 of our research has shown that helping may hurt those helped (/ Langer 1982; Langer 1983; Langer & Avorn 1981; Langer & Be 1978). People may initially be able to perform tasks they are "help not being able to accomplish.

In contrast to precompetence and postcompetence, the perce incompetence is relevant for mundane incompetence. It can be ered incompetence in that the intended action fails. But compete incompetence are relative to each other; each can be perceive other, depending on the context. For example, being "consistent' petent until someone calls it "rigid." Or if you think you finally not to react in a learned-helplessness situation, then you are not (incompetent) any more. Changing from the outcome-oriented r performance to the process-oriented mode can change the perce failure to that of learning. The fixed-observer point of view is factor preventing us from seeing the relative nature of compete incompetence. Entertaining multiple perspectives helps us to see tence (e.g., observers may see "rigid" behavior; actors intend to l sistent"). By and large, consideration of mundane incompetence s the context-dependent nature of the perception of incompetence ideas about postcompetence complement those of precompet complete the picture we will explore a counterpart to mundane in tence (undercompetence) by considering overcompetence.

OVERCOMPETENCE

Overcompetence is a fragile state, that point in skill attainment a the behavior is overlearned and is unintentionally mindlessly e Like mundane incompetence, it is a relative state, so that it also incompetence in certain contexts. But it differs from mundane in tence primarily because it emphasizes that period in skill attainme one considers oneself expert at the task at hand. If circumstances overcompetent person to question his performance, the result failure. Renewed attention to that which is overlearned, even for i tual tasks, is debilitating (Langer & Imber 1979; Langer & W 1981). Failures resulting from overcompetence are illusory becau petent behavior would have ensued had the individual performe mindfully throughout (stay as learners and not become nonlearners) or inhibit self-referent thought. Unfreezing one's rigid conception about competence and incompetence can be the first step to becoming "competent."

We have now examined four logical cells relevant to a discussion on incompetence: two instances that are *not* in the incompetence-competence category (precompetence and postcompetence) where a judgment of incompetence does not arise in the first place, and two instances that are most relevant to the competence-incompetence category (undercompetence and overcompetence). We focused on precompetence rather than on postcompetence because an important purpose here is to consider how to lessen the negative effect of incompetence and how to increase competence. In discussing undercompetence and overcompetence we tried to make clear the relative nature of competence and incompetence. Mindfulness, considered here primarily as process-oriented multiple-perspective taking, is suggested as an effective way to deal with negative effects of a judgment of incompetence.

"OBJECTIVE" INCOMPETENCE: DISABILITY

Because people categorize and label the objects around them (Brown 1956; Bruner 1951) mainly by comparison, it is not surprising that some people are designated "incompetent" and some "competent." We have argued that such categorizing is relative. We must first decide whether the performance is in the category of competence-incompetence—a decision not so clear-cut. Even after the performance is subjected to a competence judgment, there are many perspectives from which to see the performance. Is there, however, real and objective incompetence independent of context? Although success may be achieved in some unusual way, it is true that a blind person would be "incompetent" at finding by looking for a hidden figure in a picture puzzle. Disability, in contrast to incompetence, carries a sense that there is an excusable, physiologically based cause for the failure. The attribution of incompetence seems to us also to imply something about the competence of the evaluator, whereas disability does not. As such, the attribution to incompetence may be interactive and more obviously social (or relative). Just as it is not easy to decide between precompetence and incompetence from the observer's perspective, it is not always easy to decide between aspects of labeled disability that represent objective competence and illusory incompetence.

Disability raises questions about physical and physiological limits. The popular idea of limited capacity in psychology also suggests the existence of objective incompetence. There are many examples, however, that show that the objective incompetence displayed, measured, and assumed because of a capacity limit can be changed by changing the context in which the behavior appears. Karsten (1928) showed that people can continue a task after being fatigued if there is a change in context. She had subjects become exhausted writing ababab . . . Once she changed the context and asked them simply to sign their name, subjects had no difficulty doing so. She also found that, with a change in context, subjects could complain in a clear voice after their voices had just become hoarse from reading poems. And it is a familiar story that the level of pain of the same wound is reported differently by soldier and civilian (Beecher 1956).

Premature Cognitive Commitment

Research suggests that the way we learn about the world of ideas, people, and things determines how we use that information (see Chanowitz & Langer 1981; Langer & Piper 1987; Strube, Berry, & Moergen 1985). If we originally take in information in an absolute way, we may be able to use that information only in the same way in the future. In contrast, if we initially accept information in a more conditional and uncertain way, we may be able to use it more flexibly in the future (Langer, Hatem, et al. 1987; Langer & Piper 1987). These rigid mind-sets are called premature cognitive commitments. Whether people become mindless over time with repetition or mindless on a single exposure when they form premature cognitive commitments, information previously available when mindful is now no longer available for conscious use.

When information is presented by a person who is perceived to be irrelevant or by a trusted authority, or when it is simply stated in an absolute way, people have no apparent reason actively to think about the information. Instead, people form premature cognitive commitments and thus unwittingly take in the information in a rigid form. In the first study conducted on premature cognitive commitments, Chanowitz and Langer (1981) presented subjects with information that was either apparently irrelevant to them or not. Later, the information became relevant and its mindful use was important to competent performance. Those people for whom the information was initially irrelevant performed poorly, whereas those discouraged from making premature cognitive commitments did not. Subsequent measures revealed that both groups had processed the same information, but whether they processed it mindfully or mindlessly determined how competent their performance was. Accepting information uncritically may render people incompetent. If this information is passed on, generations of people may be rendered incompetent.

Basic categories of social reality (good/bad and high/low) and their evaluation are usually acquired in early stages of socialization when children are not aware of their identity in those categories. They accept the given view of the world as natural, so that they live under the burden of a stigma, perceiving themselves in the "wrong," "bad," "low," "inferior" side of the world. Actors have been overridden by observers. One characteristic of mindlessness is not making novel distinctions, but just applying old distinctions again and again. Mindlessness produced by premature cognitive commitments, therefore, inhibits resisting a self-damaging worldview. This may explain why people remain on the "inferior" side of the world.

In contrast to forming premature cognitive commitments, and the incompetence almost endemic to it, one may remain mindful by remaining somewhat uncertain. In a recent study by Langer and Piper (1987), subjects were introduced to novel objects in either an absolute or a conditional way. When novel use of those objects was called for, only those subjects introduced to objects in a conditional way thought to use them creatively. The remaining subjects were trapped by their premature cognitive commitments to what the object "was." For example, in one experiment, subjects were introduced to an object and were told either "this is a dog's chew toy" or "this could be a dog's chew toy." Subsequently, an eraser was needed. The question being asked was, who would think to use the "dog's chew toy" as an eraser? The answer was, only those people in the conditional group. For the other subjects it *was* a dog's chew toy and therefore it was not anything else. Another need was introduced and the conditional group again thought to use the same object in a novel way. Other studies have introduced ideas, not objects, conditionally or unconditionally and made the same point (Langer, Hatem, el al. 1987).

Many of the ideas we have about our abilities were initially taken in as premature cognitive commitments and often lead to the more pernicious mundane incompetence already discussed rather than to the more benign precompetence. We shall discuss the relationship between premature cognitive commitments and mundane incompetence before showing how premature cognitive commitments can lead to the misperception of universal incompetence.

When people are first introduced to a work setting, for example, they are told how to do their jobs. They are rarely told, "You could do it this way or that way." They are given one way and therefore typically mindlessly form premature cognitive commitments to the information. Once they learn how to do it the given way, they are expected to finish practicing and begin doing it. They are no longer novices. Once that change takes place, routines can set in because development has halted. Although this may seem advantageous, it is more costly than not and paves the way for mundane incompetence and overcompetence. The institutional or cultural change from learner to nonlearner robs the individual of the obvious attribution of precompetence as a comforting explanation for failure. And the possibility of finding better ways of doing things is forestalled. Routines work to protect those in power, those who learned to use the routines to their advantage. To the extent that routines work to promote the perception of incompetence in subtle ways, incompetence will be very hard to change on the group level. For individuals, however, it is a different story.

As children, we are told many things by adults—information we took in uncritically, unaware of how we may have been entrapped by it if we later need to rethink it. Information taken in as a premature cognitive commitment feels like absolute truth. Most of us assume that psychokinesis, for example, is impossible not because it violates our deep appreciation of the principles of physics but because we were probably instructed that it cannot be done (whether it can or cannot is beside the point).

In questioning premature cognitive commitments about abilities, we have found that memory does not necessarily worsen with age (Langer 1982; Langer, Rodin, et al. 1979). More recently, we have questioned whether eyesight may be improved by psychological means (Langer, Dillon, et al. 1987). Interestingly, when we asked people whether they would believe a study that showed that one could improve vision by psychological means, those who know almost nothing about the eye and the experts, ophthalmologists, were more likely to say yes than were general-practice physicians. A little knowledge may be limiting.

That study not only questioned whether there was a limited premature cognitive commitment regarding vision but also used premature cognitive commitments to bring about the improvement. Subjects (members of ROTC) in the experimental group were instructed to be pilots. They donned fatigues and flew a flight simulator. Rigid beliefs regarding pilots include that they have excellent vision. Subjects were given eye tests as part of a general physical before the study and then again when in the pilot context. They were asked to read the markings on the plane ahead of them. (These markings were actually part of an eye chart presented in the shape of a wing.) Vision improved for about 40 percent of this group, but not for control subjects.

Many of the beliefs we hold are of this rigid sort (see Langer 1989b). They are beliefs we take for granted and do not even think to question. Yet many of them may be unnecessarily competence-reducing. Therefore, it is important to remember that the most we can say about incompetence with respect to its being real or illusory is that, if an action has not been competently executed, whether or not it ultimately can be is indeterminate. Indeed, all conclusions about limited capacity are indeterminate. Similarly, Navon (1984) recently has argued in the cognitive psychological literature against the idea of limited capacity. The concept of capacity is post hoc; when one exceeds a capacity, the earlier capacity is said to have been in error.

FINAL THOUGHT

Accepting the different forms of incompetence we have discussed, rather than seeing incompetence in a unitary way, is equivalent to accepting that one's failure is controllable (e.g., by changing the context) or at least not uncontrollable. It may be useful to note explicitly that this view implies that the etiology of all incompetence is social. One cannot judge what is poor performance without an appreciation of what the larger group values and thereby deems desirable to achieve. For instance, if children prefer poems that rhyme, writers of nonrhyming children's poems are unable to write poetry that pleases them. We use this example to make obvious that incompetence for one group, here children, may be considered competence by another. Incompetence based on in-group standards displayed by out-group members is met with disapproval that is likely to affect adversely the self-esteem of the out-group. When in-group members perform poorly, however, the task rather than the person may be denigrated. For example, if academics were not able to perform a coding task, we would probably be told that as academics we were overqualified for the task; if we could not play sports, we would be led to believe brains and brawn are mutually exclusive. These culturally given face-saving devices reveal the context-dependent nature of competence. Behavior originates with reference to a particular social milieu. When this is overlooked, the instances where incompetence is illusory are overlooked as well.

CHAPTER 7

Strategies for Comparative Evaluation: Maintaining a Sense of Competence across the Life Span

KARIN S. FREY AND
DIANE N. RUBLE

Until his knees gave out, the husband of the first author participated in daily track and road races with a running club at work. One runner figured prominently in the daily anecdotes. The author's husband, twelve years his junior, was one of the few who could keep up with him, and then only for a little while. At forty-eight, this runner was gradually slowing down and was having a hard time adjusting to that. Retaining his unchallenged status as the fastest runner did not seem to help much. This was intriguing to us as researchers in motivation.

Current theorizing about motivation suggests that the orientations or goals with which one approaches an activity influence the interest and enjoyment derived. One approach contrasts intrinsic to extrinsic orientations: whether one approaches a task with a sense of self-determination, as an end in itself, or as a means to another end, such as anticipated rewards, positive self-presentation, and various controlling events (Deci & Ryan 1985; Lepper & Greene 1978; Pittman, Ruble, & Boggiano 1983). A more recent, related approach distinguishes between two types of orientations: task involvement versus ego involvement (Nicholls 1979b) or learning versus performance goals (Dweck & Elliot 1983). The basic idea is that concern with evaluation (ego or performance goals) interferes with the intrinsic pleasure of mastering a task.

An interesting feature of these approaches is that the *criteria* that are used to assess competence are integral in distinguishing between goals.

With learning goals, for example, competence is judged in terms of mastery and effort, leading naturally to a focus on temporal or autonomous (self-focused) standards indicating whether or not progress is being made. In contrast, with performance goals, competence is evaluated through normative or social comparison. The assumption is that one will experience greater pleasure if one uses temporal rather than social comparison as the standard of evaluation. This is one reason the discontent of the runner described above, who clearly favored temporal over social comparison standards, was intriguing to us. The goal of this chapter is to examine variations in preferred evaluative standards. We suggest that healthy functioning may depend on the ability to exhibit flexibility in the choice of evaluative comparisons in order to maintain a sense of competence and high self-esteem.

A DEVELOPMENTAL ANALYSIS OF STANDARDS OF COMPETENCE

Several lines of reasoning suggest that standards of evaluation are directly related to level of development. Veroff (1969), for example, suggested that children begin with autonomous standards but shift to social comparison after considerable social reinforcement in school. Finally, the two standards are integrated in middle elementary school. Similarly, according to Nicholls (1984b) and Dweck and Elliott (1983), competence and satisfaction are defined in terms of progress and effort for the young child. Competence is later evaluated through social comparison norms.

Moreover, it is consistently documented that young children have high self-perceptions of competence and expectations for success and seem to be resilient to failure (Parsons & Ruble 1977; Rholes et al. 1980), as if they were buffered from failure by a reliance on temporal self-evaluation. Interestingly, downward shifts in children's perceived academic competence occur at about the same time as well-documented increases in social comparison (Frey & Ruble 1985). The possibility of a causal link is suggested by individual differences found in second- and fourth-grade children, showing that higher levels of comparative information seeking are associated with lower perceived competence (Frey & Ruble 1985). Finally, there is even some evidence that young children's orientations toward tasks are more likely to be intrinsic. Evidence from Harter (1981a) suggests that measures of intrinsic orientation show a decrease with age.

But is there any direct evidence that the performance standards of young children are based predominantly on autonomous standards—i.e., temporal comparison and effort? In fact, there is not much. Results of a study by Ruble, Feldman, and Higgins (in preparation, described in Ruble et al. in press) showed that young children can use both temporal and social comparison when judging performance, using social comparison as much as autonomous standards. Indeed the oldest group, fourth-graders, evidenced the greatest preference for reliance on temporal comparisons when evaluating themselves.[1] Similarly, in an ongoing longitudinal study, we have asked children about their affective reactions to temporal versus social comparison feedback. Kindergartners and first- and second-grade children showed a clear preference for social comparative feedback. Only the fifth-grade children reported that they would feel happier to be told they had done the best job they had ever done than to be told they had done the best job of anyone in the class. Finally, a study by Ruble and Flett (1988) looked at children's interest in different kinds of feedback, rather than the impact of that feedback. Children in second, fourth, and sixth grades were given an opportunity to examine evaluative information in a free-choice situation. Once again, the shift was toward greater personal temporal comparison with age, rather than the reverse as would be predicted.

Thus, there was no support for the idea of a linear shift from temporal to social bases of evaluation. There was also no support for the idea that the youngest children would be most interested in and most influenced by temporal bases. Of course, it may be that these were inadequate tests of the basic hypothesis because, for example, we did not include kindergarteners in the information-seeking study. Further, it may be that the setting was too obviously evaluative, thereby diminishing children's natural preferences for temporal standards (Nicholls 1984b). It may also be time, however, to reevaluate some of the hypotheses.

ANALYSIS BASED ON PHASES OF SKILL DEVELOPMENT

A possible interpretation of the above results is that the developmental predictions are correct, but that in order to predict standards of evaluation, one must consider the phase of skill development at a task. Regard-

1. These conclusions apply to judgments of the specific success/failure outcome of the task and affective reactions to that outcome. Judgments of competence, more generally, showed a much more complex pattern with use of social comparison increasing with age, consistent with previous studies. There was still no evidence of greater use of temporal standards by younger children, however.

less of individual developmental differences, it does not seem likely that an individual would be oriented toward the same type of standards, or even that standards would have the same relation to affect and pleasure, when one is just learning an activity, relative to when one is at a performance plateau or even past one's prime.

Albert's theory of temporal comparison (1977) proposes that temporal comparison is most likely to occur during times of rapid change, particularly if the change is indicative of progress or growth. The most important goal of someone undertaking a new activity is to improve. This should result, then, in a strong focus on temporal comparison, especially since social comparison is not likely to impart much useful information about ability when one's skill level is rapidly changing. Furthermore, social comparison is unlikely to provide much opportunity for obtaining gratifying feedback unless other novices are available for comparison. Social comparison will be more salient, for example, if initial learning occurs in a class, particularly if improvement is difficult to observe until some basic skill level is attained, such as remaining upright on a bicycle. The feedback provided by social comparison depends more on situational variables. Thus, social comparison is less likely to be a consistent source of satisfaction than temporal comparison and will be less important as a personal standard during the initial stages of skill acquisition.

This does not mean that comparative standards are necessarily irrelevant at the earliest stages. Social comparison is a way of obtaining information about the activity itself. Young children in particular are likely to rely on observation of others as a way of finding out *how* to do a task (Feldman & Ruble 1977; Frey & Ruble 1985). Comparative standards may come into play even before a person attempts an activity for the first time. For example, a kindergarten child, observing that some children already know how to read, may be interested in knowing when *most* children learn to read, thereby forming future expectations and determining whether lack of the skill is cause for embarrassment. A fifty-year-old woman who is considering running as a form of exercise may be interested in the experiences of other women her age as a means of assessing her own chances of running without injury.

Once the basic elements of a skill are acquired, the evaluative function of social comparison is likely to assume greater importance. Knowledge of comparative norms is essential to assess ability realistically, which is itself required for making adaptive choices about the future. Knowledge of comparative performance level, for example, may prevent an individual from making a major commitment to a field of endeavor in which success is highly unlikely (Trope 1986). It is probable that even the kindergartners in the Ruble et al. (in press) study had some familiarity with their skills at puzzle-type games. Thus, they may have already been past the stage where only personal standards are relevant to assessing performance and affect. The length of the comparative assessment phase may vary considerably, however. Uncertainty regarding ability should prolong the focus on comparative assessment. Once competence is assessed, the individual can focus on doing the task as well as possible, and temporal standards may once again become paramount. (See Ruble & Frey, in press, for a more extended analysis of skill-acquisition phases.)

Further analyses of Ruble and Flett's (1988) data support the usefulness of a phase-of-skill analysis. In this study, children were categorized into math ability levels, and interest in different standards was examined as a joint function of ability level and developmental level. The results showed that differences in orientation toward autonomous information as a function of age occurred primarily for high-ability children. Low- and medium-ability children maintained an interest in social comparison. In one sense, this result seems odd. As a strategy for maintaining a sense of competence, low- and medium-ability children seem to have everything to lose (and high-ability children everything to gain) by emphasizing social comparison. Our interpretation is that the high-ability children were past the need for normative assessment, whereas the low- and medium-ability children were not. When asked to indicate how certain they were of their abilities, high-ability children were more certain than the others.

Virtually all our data suggest that older children return to more autonomous forms of assessment. This appears to be the strategy the high-ability children used in the information-seeking study. As a strategy for maintaining motivation, temporal comparison has its advantages. It provides opportunities for improvement and success, thereby promoting mastery and competence. This should serve to increase motivational differences across ability levels.

This analysis is admittedly speculative. It represents a reexamination of data that did not support original predictions. An alternative explanation of these data is that avoidance of social comparison by older children constitutes their increased concern with self-esteem rather than mastery.

In other words, avoidance of social comparison may be a strategic, ego-saving response available to older children.

In the studies dealing with children, skill level development increases with age. Although age in adults should roughly covary with phase of skill development, exceptions will be more common than in children. Raynor (1982) suggests that older people who are in the initial stages of a career path are "psychologically young"—i.e., their level of motivation and temporal perspective will be similar to that usually found in a chronologically young person. The father of one of the authors, having been a mediocre skier for forty-five years, took his first ski lessons at age seventy-seven. One of the oldest members of his ski club, he nevertheless captured the trophy for the "most improved skier" at the end of an intensive week. His laughing disclaimer that he was the worst to begin with did not hide his obvious pride. By taking up the sport anew, he unlinked the expected relationship between age and skill development, experiencing consistent progress. As long as improvement is readily discerned, temporal comparison should be a major source of satisfaction.

A comparison of the skier to the runner leads us to consider another phase in skill development. Stagnation occurs when performance reaches a plateau and episodes of improvement decrease in frequency. Lack of rapid change lessens the need for temporal comparison (Albert 1977), and interest in temporal comparison may eventually diminish. Although interest may remain high for a while if the person believes there is still opportunity for occasional improvement, when performance is seen as consistently declining, temporal comparison may become a source of discouragement. Increased difficulty getting to the net or placing a serve does not just mean you have to work harder, as it might for a novice; it may mean you have "lost it," that efforts to improve or maintain performance are in vain.

Does this mean it is impossible to sustain feelings of competence and accompanying motivation when performance is declining? Apparently not. One of the authors played golf last year with an elderly man (perhaps eighty-five) who, although a lifelong player, not surprisingly, could not hit the ball very far. Nevertheless, he loved it; he was a genuine golfing enthusiast. Interestingly, he seemed obsessed with social comparison. He kept asking, "How old do you think I am?" and then referred to Bob Hope and other well-known older golfers as youngsters. Regardless of his actual performance, or the declines he had likely suffered, he seemed to be enjoying himself thoroughly, presumably because he was doing extremely well for an eighty-five-year-old.

According to temporal comparison theory (Albert 1977), the golfer is likely to deemphasize comparisons over time, since those comparisons give evidence of a major decline in his game. Meanwhile, attention to social comparison should increase. Because age has a negative effect on performance, as people become quite old they are likely to rely increasingly on comparison with agemates for motivation. The social comparison literature has demonstrated the importance of comparisons with others who are similar on attributes related to performance (Goethals & Darley 1977). Furthermore, age becomes an increasingly distinctive attribute among athletes, suggesting that the oldest athletes will be most likely to serve as a reference group for each other (Miller, Turnbull & McFarland 1987). In fact, some evidence suggests that old adults are more responsive to age norms than young or middle-aged adults (Davis 1967).

Particularly in physical activities, age may be more predictive of comparative goals and satisfactions when performance is declining. A forty-year-old runner who is slowing down, for example, may encounter forty-year-old beginners who are still improving. Thus, peer comparison may not offer as much solace as it might to a sixty-five-year-old runner, whose peers are experiencing similar declines. Furthermore, as agemates retire from participation because of lack of interest or physical inability, the chances for obtaining individual recognition increase.

In the three examples we have described (the runner, the skier, and the golfer) different modes of comparison led to different conclusions about competence. The runner and the skier focused primarily on temporal information, to the dissatisfaction of the runner and the satisfaction of the skier. Information that has different implications for competence (e.g., comparison with most other participants in the sport) appears to have little impact on them. For the golfer, the implications of temporal comparison or comparison with most other golfers are both negative, but those criteria appear to be less salient and have less impact on self-satisfaction than the positive implications of comparison with agemates. We might tentatively suggest, therefore, that responsiveness to different goals is partly strategic, enabling persons to maintain motivation, satisfaction, and a sense of competence. Moreover, a developmental perspective emphasizes that the implications of any set of goals and criteria will differ markedly with age and developmental level. Temporal comparisons were formerly a source of satisfaction for the now disheartened runner, whereas comparisons with agemates may have been less pleasurable for the golfer at thirty-five than they are at eighty-five.

A STUDY OF RUNNERS

In order to explore skill level and age-related variation in the self-assessments of adults, we undertook a study of 237 long-distance runners between twenty and seventy-seven years of age.[2] Since race times provide a highly accurate means of making temporal comparisons, comparisons with selected others, and comparisons with all other racers, we expected to see several strategies of self-evaluation. Regardless of age or performance level, runners who are improving should emphasize temporal goals and comparison, and experience greater satisfaction with their performance, than those whose performance is stable or declining. We expected declining runners to deemphasize temporal comparison in favor of comparison with peers. A shift toward socially comparative goals and standards should be particularly evident among older runners.

Performance Phase and Level of Satisfaction

Not surprisingly, age was a strong predictor of performance phase. Runners whose performance was declining were older than those whose performance was improving or stable. There was a fair amount of overlap, however. One third of the runners over fifty-five were improving. Runners whose performance was improving were more satisfied with their performance over the last year and in the last race than runners whose performance was stable or declining. Stable runners were also more satisfied with their previous year's performance than declining runners. With performance phase statistically controlled, satisfaction with performance did not differ by age, nor was there an association with the interaction of age and performance phase. Thus, being able to improve in an activity is a powerful predictor of satisfaction, one shared by adults of all ages.

Temporal versus Social Comparison

Not surprisingly, runners who were no longer improving were the most likely to be considering a new sport that would offer renewed oppor-

2. Numbers in the analysis are slightly lower, owing to omitted questions.

TABLE 7.1 Proportion of Runners Making Spontaneous Temporal and Social Comparisons as a Function of Performance Phase

	Performance Phase		
	Improving	Stable	Declining
Pre-race goals			
Targeting a finish time	.84	.76	.64
Targeting a specific competitor	.20	.21	.42
Post-race satisfactions			
Improvement/lack of decline in time	.28[a]	.08	.00
Age-related competition	.06	.06	.22
Most satisfying possible achievement			
Shorten times	.52	.40	.29
Be more competitive in age division	.03	.03	.12

a. Runners could cite more than one goal, satisfaction, or achievement.

tunities for mastery. Runners could also maintain their interest by adopting new performance goals commensurate with their capabilities. Strong support for a shift in performance standards comes from spontaneous comparisons made by runners. Our questionnaire asked them to describe the satisfying aspects of their last race, the goals they set for that race, and their most satisfying possible achievement. For each measure (see table 7.1), runners with declining performance were more likely than improving or stable runners to mention competition and less likely to mention changes in finish times as a goal or satisfaction. With age, runners were also more likely to cite the satisfaction of beating competitors and less likely to form temporal goals. Age and performance did not interact. Rankings of racing and training goals showed a very similar pattern. Declining and older runners emphasized comparison with agemates and deemphasized comparison with their own past performance.

Thus, the running study demonstrated that the evaluation standards adopted for an activity and the satisfactions derived from it are closely tied to the direction of performance change. The results provided strong support for the hypothesis that adults will shift their focus from temporal comparison to social comparison as the phase of performance shifts from improvement to decline.

These results conflict with Suls's (1986) findings that adults over sixty-five years are more oriented to temporal comparison than are younger persons. One possible explanation for the discrepancy concerns differences in activities. Suls included reading, figuring numbers, and making conversation, activities people do not typically subject to comparative scrutiny, unlike running race results. Furthermore, it is unclear how important the skills were to the individuals involved. Wood (in press) argues that the use of standards that emphasize the uniqueness of one's accomplishments is favored only when the activity is one that is personally important and desirable. Otherwise, comparison with similar others is favored. Suls's subjects preferred social comparison at all ages, whereas runners in our study preferred temporal comparison, again suggesting that different processes were operating. Finally, it is possible that Suls's results are an accurate reflection of *most* older adults, whereas ours speak to a sample of unusually active, involved citizens. In line with Raynor's theory of personality change (1982), older people display more variability in achievement-related behavior than is found in younger age groups (Davis 1967).

Thus, it may be that our results were due to self-selection of older individuals who are highly competitive, rather than to a shift in standards over time. Perhaps those who are initially more competitive will be most likely to persist in an activity when performance is declining and temporal comparison no longer provides incentives to continue. We find this explanation less compelling, however, in part because the competitiveness of older runners seemed qualitatively different from that of younger runners, owing to the emphasis on age.

Age Norms as Standards of Comparison

Conversations with older runners, as well as the notes and letters they appended to our questionnaire, suggested that the importance of age for evaluative standards goes well beyond successful competition in one's age division. McGuire and McGuire (1981, 1987) have shown that distinctive or nonnormative attributes like extreme age tend to be the ones that people spontaneously use to describe themselves, suggesting that such attributes are more central to self-identity than are nondistinctive ones. At races, older runners were unique in their tendency to volunteer their age enthusiastically when handed a questionnaire. Told simply that this was a study of motivation and runners, one man immediately responded, "I'm sixty-two. I've been running for two years and I haven't peaked yet!"

Responses to the questionnaire also indicated that age was a particularly salient aspect of comparison for older people. Older runners were increasingly likely to see age as an important factor when they were satisfied as well as dissatisfied with their performance. They were also more likely to mention the age of other persons with whom they competed, such as the seventy-two-year-old runner who complained that his age division, sixty and over, was too inclusive, especially since there were a "bunch of hot dogs" in their sixties.

A large body of research demonstrates that people prefer to compare themselves to similar others (e.g., Feldman & Ruble 1981; Miller 1982; Suls, Gaes, & Gastorf 1979). Comparison with similar others provides the most information about competence level (Goethals & Darley 1977), as well as probable outcomes of direct competition in one's age division (Suls et al. 1979). Wood (in press) has argued, on the other hand, that people prefer dissimilar targets when the dimension of comparison is an attribute that is desirable and personally important, since that enables individuals to feel unique and superior to others. We found evidence of comparison to both similar and dissimilar others. The competitors cited as stimulating higher performance were described as similar in age and as younger 77 percent and 18 percent of the time, respectively. Similarly, when competitive results were cited as a satisfaction of the last race, the competitors were described as similar in age and younger 75 percent and 25 percent of the time. The comment of a forty-seven-year-old woman exemplifies the particular satisfaction older runners experienced when they beat younger ones: "It felt good to be gray and in good shape. I passed youngsters while I was running uphill."

The literature provides only indirect evidence regarding age norms as evaluative standards. The work of Taylor and Wood (Taylor, Wood, & Lichtman 1983; Wood 1987; Wood, Taylor, & Lichtman 1985) has documented the importance of "manufactured normative standards of comparison." In this study, women cancer patients and their spouses essentially fabricated norms of adjustment that were highly enhancing to themselves. Similarly, research on consensus estimates (Alicke 1985; Campbell 1986; Goethals 1986) has shown that when an attribute is an admirable one, such as athletic performance, individuals tend to underestimate the achievements of others relative to themselves. In a similar way, the stereotype of older people as frail, physically limited individuals serves to emphasize the unique superiority of older competitive runners.

An emphasis on age norms may have a particular functional utility for older people. First, from an attributional point of view, there are some advantages to competing with youth. Since older persons consider age to be an inhibiting factor in running performance (as evidenced by the importance of age as a factor in unsatisfactory performance), comparisons with younger persons are essentially nondiagnostic of low ability (Goethals & Darley 1977; Trope 1986). Low ability can be discounted as a cause of doing worse than a younger person, since age provides a plausible alternative explanation. The augmentation principle, on the other hand, suggests that a performance that is equal to or better than that of a younger person is indicative of very high ability (Goethals & Darley 1977). The outcome of an attributional analysis based on age norms may be even more enhancing to an older runner since it focuses on the inhibiting factor of age to the exclusion of possible facilitating factors such as amount of race experience, knowledge of the course, or time available for training.

Second, the use of normative standards means that there is rarely any hard evidence regarding actual consensus behavior. Thus, self-enhancing comparison with a normative standard is less likely to be proven wrong than is comparison with a specific other.

A third advantage of normative comparison is that it eliminates some of the socially awkward aspects of comparison with specific others. Both inferior and superior positions can be cause for embarrassment, to the extent that people will go to some lengths to avoid social comparison (Brickman & Bulman 1977). By focusing on age norms, older adults are buffered from feelings of embarrassment when they are slower than "youngsters." In addition, they can attribute greater capabilities to themselves by referring to past accomplishments (Ross & Conway 1986), which are likely to be less threatening to younger competitors than a current rivalry (Tesser 1980).

A fourth advantage is that the use of a normative standard makes these individuals doubly distinctive. They are distinctive not only as elders among runners but as runners among their peers. This unique status may be a source of considerable pride (Alicke 1985; Campbell 1986), as evidenced by one sixty-five-year-old runner who returned his questionnaire along with a magazine article about himself! One particularly intriguing passage from this article included normative comparisons with both younger and same-age nonrunners: "It doesn't escape him that he is both the nemesis and role model for his peers and those approaching their masters years. Many friends his age have 'given up' and accepted the sentence of a sedentary life. 'I've got the body of a 35-year-old and the heart of a teenager,' Walzer smiles" (Sell 1985).

Finally, there is a particular pride associated with being a model for others, and as exceptions to age norms, older athletes serve as models for younger ones. People identify with the successes of similar others who are older (Brickman & Bulman 1977), particularly if the attribute is a distinctive one (Miller et al. 1987). When asked to describe those whose presence enhances performance, a twenty-five-year-old woman replied, "Older folks, and women who have kids are back to running. They're my role models." Fourteen of the fifteen runners who said that the example of others was a source of personal inspiration specifically cited older runners. At least some older runners are conscious of the status conferred on them by age. A fifty-three-year-old man called us to task: "It seemed to me your questions overlook other important motivations for older runners: To preserve or enhance physical appearance; *to be held in esteem by younger people* who are not in as good a shape; to defuse anxieties of work, reduce tension, etc." (italics added).

In retrospect, we must agree. Although competition with agemates became increasingly important with age, as we predicted, our original conceptualization probably underestimated the importance of enhancing comparisons based on age norms. As a result of our increased appreciation for the importance of normative standards based on age, we are currently reevaluating some of our earlier work with children.

PERCEIVED COMPETENCE IN PRESCHOOL CHILDREN

Like adults at the other extreme of the age continuum, younger children find age to be a highly salient and distinctive attribute (McGuire & McGuire 1987). Whereas older runners may be gratified by the fact that just about anything they do vastly exceeds the norm, the high perceived competence of young children may be based on norms that tell them they will eventually be able to do just about anything older children do.

Unless a preschool child lives in a very isolated area, he or she will have many opportunities to observe the greater skills of schoolchildren as they swim at the beach or bicycle and skateboard down the street. Older children can read and often pass on their own knowledge of games by explicitly teaching the younger ones. Preschoolers, similarly, often guide toddlers, who also differ obviously from them in skill level. Parents entertain their children with photographs and stories about how the youngsters learned milestone skills like walking, thus reinforcing children's conceptions of themselves as prodigious learners.

Consequently, the momentary failings of a young child may be of little concern, since he or she can look forward to inheriting eventually the successes of older children. Successes that children can anticipate as their own may well heighten their self-perceptions of competence. Higgins and Parsons (1983) have argued that the social world of preschool children and their own experience with very rapid skill development lead them to conceptualize ability as an unstable attribute. They cite data showing that preschoolers, unlike older children, base performance expectancies not on past performance or on their attributions for that performance but on their expectations that they *will learn* how to do the task.

What we are proposing is that self-assessment in the preschool child has elements of both social and temporal comparison. Self-awareness of previous and future progress is heightened by observing consistent age-related differences in the behavior of others. With this perspective, social comparison among young children may be directed at evaluating *when* one should, or is likely to, acquire a particular skill rather than determining underlying competence. As the following example suggests, age norms are not taken lightly by young children. A six-year-old, hearing a four-and-a-half-year-old say she could ride bikes, responded indignantly, "She *cannot.* She's only in preschool!" Age norms can also help children save face when confronted with failure. A child who was being taunted for her inability to read responded, "Come on, I'm only in kindergarten." While writing this chapter, one of the authors recalled an articulation problem she had as a youngster: she would say "lellow" rather than "yellow." She was unconcerned, convinced that she would have no problem when she reached the exalted age of six, a prediction that was tested and confirmed on the morning of that birthday.

Thus, we suggest that children's beliefs about their skills deserve greater scrutiny. Research has shown that eight-year-old children will make reasonable inferences regarding social norms, based on observed frequencies with which groups exhibit particular behaviors (Perry & Bussey 1979). The ability of younger children to make similar inferences has not been tested, although indirect evidence comes from differences in the speech preschoolers use when talking to younger children (Shatz & Gelman 1973). Evidently, preschoolers expect linguistic competence to be associated with age. Brody suggests that children have well-established age expectancies and systematically adjust their behavior when interacting with younger children (Brody, Graziano, & Musser 1983; Brody, Stoneman, & MacKinnon 1982). By focusing on age norms, young children, like older runners, may shield themselves from disappointment. That focus also enables both groups to feel a special satisfaction when their accomplishments exceed age norms. The daughter of one of the authors was very proud that she could ride her bike without training wheels in *kindergarten,* a skill that was somewhat unusual among her agemates.

If our analysis is correct, we must ask why children lose a developmental perspective, and the attendant buffer against failure, during the primary grades. Higgins and Parsons (1983) suggest that the age stratification of school classrooms may stimulate greater attention to individual differences between agemates. As rate of maturation slows, comparative differences come to be seen as indicative of underlying competence. These changes in social environment may decrease the developmental perspective of children and their parents. One-room schools, where same-age peers are an exception, would not be expected to show this pattern. In such a situation, we would predict that comparative information seeking would be less common than in age-stratified classrooms (Frey & Ruble 1985), but also would be less threatening, since comparisons could be interpreted as referring to age differences in performance rather than individual differences in competence. Other social experiences, such as having closely spaced siblings (Tesser 1980) or attending an age-stratified preschool might be expected to hasten the onset of social comparison of underlying competence.

The ability to create realistic goals in an activity despite declines in performance capabilities extends the idea of mastery orientation in a new direction and gives new meaning to the word *persistence*. In youngsters, we define *mastery* as the ability to regroup after failure and to devise new strategies to reach the goals. This is reasonable, since children are rarely presented with, or allowed to continue in, situations that are ultimately impossible (psychological experiments excepted). Adults, on the other hand, often attempt to achieve what ultimately *may* be impossible—e.g., maintaining physical capabilities for thirty years without decline, eliminating the federal deficit, obtaining international peace, etc. Thus, the ability to assess and reassess probability of success and the flexibility to create alternative, satisfying goals may be more important factors in achievement motivation of adults than in children.

INDIVIDUAL DIFFERENCES IN ADJUSTMENT AND PARENTS' COMPARISON CRITERIA

The older runners in our study were, in effect, all success stories—they were still running and enjoying the activity. The dramatic decline in the numbers of older runners, far beyond expected mortality rates, suggests that many of the younger runners will not persist into their sixties.[3] Although we have argued that flexibility in self-evaluative standards may be the key to continued success, our self-selected sample of older persons greatly limits our analysis of individual differences. In order to examine individual differences in comparison standards, we turned our attention to a population whose continued efforts are less easily abandoned—parents. In this way, we could have a population with a less restricted range in which to study the relation between comparison standards and satisfaction.

We suspected that the self-evaluation process utilized by parents would differ from that of runners in one significant respect. Self-evaluation of parenting skills is likely to be largely determined by the behavior of another. Since perceived competence as a parent rests heavily on the behavior of the child (Deutsch et al., in press), we looked at comparisons parents made regarding their children's behavior as well as their own. The behavior of the child can be thought of as an outcome measure of parenting ability, a measure that is particularly informative for parents since their performance is difficult to evaluate on its own (Bandura 1982).

Parents of special needs children are an especially interesting group in which to study the processes of evaluation, for the expected standards of development do not provide them with positive information. They, like older runners, need to be flexible in selecting evaluative standards that maintain their sense of competence. We sought insight into the kinds of comparisons that served as important yardsticks for these parents. In real-life situations involving trauma, comparisons with less fortunate or less competent others are more common than are comparisons with others of similar or more well endowed circumstances (Taylor et al. 1983; Wood et al. 1985). Thus, we expected that most social comparisons would involve exemplars with more severe conditions rather than with normal or less impaired youngsters. We expected temporal comparisons to show a similar enhancing bias, emphasizing absolute improvements over time.

We (Frey & Ruble 1985) as well as others (McGuire & McGuire 1981, 1987; Taylor et al. 1983) have argued that spontaneous comments are more likely to indicate issues of central importance to the speaker than those elicited by an interviewer. We therefore focused on spontaneous comparisons made during an interview conducted with twenty-five pairs of parents, part of a longitudinal study of fifty families with special needs

3. The age differences are, of course, confounded by cohort differences. Thus, predictions about future cohorts are highly speculative.

children (Frey et al. 1988). The children in these families ranged in age from 3.2 years to 10.2 (M = 6.5 years). Down's syndrome was the most common disability (40 percent), followed by cerebral palsy (16 percent). The ninety-minute interview included questions about timing of the original diagnosis, parents' past and present feelings about the diagnosis, expectations and concerns about the future, impact of the disability on the marriage and sibling relations, the extent of family support, and factors seen by the parents as assisting or inhabiting their adjustment to having a child with special needs. Responses made in a comparative format were coded after the interview. No attempts were made to compare the spontaneous comments of mothers and fathers, since they often took turns acting as "spokesperson," with the other nodding agreement but not commenting personally.

Our predictions that enhancing comparisons would predominate were clearly confirmed. Of the twenty-five couples, 60 percent (fifteen) made only enhancing comparisons, 20 percent (five) made only deprecating comparisons, 12 percent (three) made both, and 8 percent (two) made no comparisons (X^2 (3) = 17.08, $p < .01$). Thus, the majority of parents evidenced the flexibility to shift this standard of evaluation from typical age norms to more enhancing criteria.

Although most of the interview questions referred to the parents' experience, children were the predominant focus of evaluative comparisons. Comparative comments about the child were made by 92 percent (twenty-three) of the couples, and only 12 percent (three) made self-referent comparisons. The disparity in the numbers of parent- and child-focused comparisons may indicate that the most valued measure of parental competence is considered to be the behavior of the child.[4] It may also reflect a preference for less overt ways of presenting self-congratulatory information (Ruble & Frey 1987; Schofield 1981). Certainly it is socially more acceptable for parents to indulge themselves with enthusiastic accounts of a child's competence than of their own.

Social Comparison with Other Children

As predicted, a substantial proportion, 40 percent (ten), of our parent pairs spontaneously compared their child's condition to a more severe

4. Perhaps that explains the complaints one hears from teachers that many parents are satisfied only with feedback that imparts comparative information about their child. As the first hard evidence most parents have about the outcome of some six years of effort, report cards may represent self-evaluation for the parents as well as evaluation of the child.

one. Comparisons were made to prototypical groups of others along selected dimensions (e.g., "children with degenerative diseases") rather than to specific persons (Taylor et al. 1983; Wood et al. 1985). Interestingly, the self-consoling nature of these comparisons was evident to the parents. Eight of the ten made this type of comparison when asked about factors that helped them adjust to having a child with special needs. For example, the mother of a six-year-old with a highly uncertain prognosis said, "Everyday I think about how it would be if my children had leukemia or cancer, and I couldn't do anything about it. I always think things could be much worse, so if things could be worse, they can't be that bad."

An unexpectedly large proportion of the parents, 28 percent, made spontaneous upward comparisons to normal children or those with less severe conditions. Some of these comparisons were of an objective nature: "She's not one of the higher-functioning Down's." Others expressed their inability to utilize standards other than normal progress. The mother of a five-year-old girl with Down's syndrome gestured toward her normal daughter and remarked, "It's hard not to compare her to this bright, attractive, gifted, eager-to-please little girl."

As with downward comparisons, the majority of upward comparisons occurred when inquiries were made about parental adjustment. Upward comparisons, however, were cited as factors *hindering* adjustment. Unlike previous findings that show spontaneous upward comparison to be quite rare (Wood et al. 1985), the focus of these comparisons is not the self. It may be more socially acceptable to lament the situation of one's child than of oneself, since the latter may be viewed as indulging in self-pity (Wood et al. 1985). It is also possible that upward comparisons were more common in our sample because they had high informational value. Most of the upward comparisons were made to normal children, suggesting the importance of age norms as a comparative standard. Although parents of special children cannot base expectations for their child on chronological age, knowledge of the child's behavioral age equivalent is very important for predicting present and future probability of success. When parents were specifically asked to estimate their child's level of functioning, all responded in terms of age level: "As far as motor skills, she's two, two and a half. In social skills, she's more like a four-year-old." Thus, age norms were highly salient criteria for parents of special needs children.

Comparison with Expected Progress. Since all these parents could point to some improvement in their child's behavior, we expected to hear spontaneous temporal comparisons about that progress. We found, however, that evaluation of the child's progress took a slightly different form, with comparisons made between the initial prognosis and current skill level. Spontaneous comments of 36 percent (nine) of the couples indicated that their child's progress had far exceeded low expectations formed at the time of diagnosis. In the judgment of the interviewer, these were made with an emotional intensity lacking in other comparisons. As one mother reported, some six years after the attending physician had given her child a very poor prognosis, "He made me *so* angry. I was determined to defy his predictions. Last summer when he went back [to the same hospital] for tests, I thought about going to see him just to make him eat his words."

Eight of the nine couples cited misinformation provided by health-care professionals as the primary source for what they now felt were inappropriately low expectations. With retrospective accounts, we can make no conclusions regarding the accuracy of the parents' recall or original processing of the earlier prognoses. Parents may have been particularly receptive to negative information at diagnosis, a time when the child's condition is perceived as most serious (Marteau & Johnston 1986). Subsequent positive evaluations made by parents may be based on comparisons between current perceptions of the child's condition and those formed at diagnosis. It has also been noted that recall is biased toward confirming subjects' expectations of behavior change over time (Ross & Conway 1986). Nevertheless, whether they were accurate or not, parents evidenced a special triumph as they recounted dire predictions made for their children: "Look at her. And they said she'd never walk!"

In laboratory studies, satisfaction with performance is based on both absolute performance level and difference between attainment and initial expectancies (Bandura 1982; Shrauger 1975). When children markedly exceed expectations, the implications for parent competence are enhancing on three counts. First, it suggests that the parents must be unusually skilled in the care and management of their children to have succeeded against all odds. Second, the success attests to the persistence and devotion of parents, who refused to slacken their efforts, despite having ample cause for discouragement. Third, the success validates the persistence, demonstrating that parents were ultimately more knowledgeable than the "expert" who made the low prognosis.

Comments made by parents supported our belief that a child's progress is a potent source of perceived competence for parents. Seven respondents used words similar to those of the mother of an eight-year-old:

"I've come to see that I'm the expert as far as my child is concerned. No one else knows her needs as well as I do." These parents had adopted the image of themselves as experts to the extent that their own evaluations of educators and health-care professionals were based on the extent to which these personnel consulted and deferred to the parent's (usually the mother's) judgment. This may be an unusually clear example of how information inconsistent with the self-concept is discredited by questioning the credibility of the source (Shrauger 1975). Furthermore, all the families who complained of earlier inaccurate information had by now selected a physician who accorded the mother expert status.

Parental Adjustment and Comparative Strategy. Participants also completed questionnaires designed to measure family and individual adjustment. Parents who made more enhancing comparisons reflecting either their child's advantages relative to others or their child's higher than expected progress reported fewer psychiatric symptoms (p's $< .05$) on the Brief Symptom Inventory (Derogatis & Spencer 1982). Fathers were less anxious and less depressed, and reported fewer psychosomatic symptoms; mothers were less hostile. As indicated by the Ways of Coping Scale (Vitaliano et al. 1985), more enhancing comparisons were associated with less avoidance of disability-related problems and less wishful thinking (p's $< .05$) on the part of fathers. Although coping style in mothers was not related to spontaneous comparisons, mothers related their *ability* to cope as higher when more enhancing comparisons were made during the interview ($p < .01$).

As measured by the relationship dimension of the Family Environment Scale (Moos & Moos 1981), fathers perceived the family relationship to be closer and less conflictual when enhancing comparisons were made more frequently ($p < .05$). The association for mothers was in the same direction, although it was not significant. Mothers and fathers also reported their happiness in marriage (as measured by the Locke-Wallace Scale, 1959) to be higher when enhancing comparisons were made more frequently and when deprecating comparisons were made less frequently (p's $< .05$).

It is noteworthy that the child's actual level of functioning, either in an absolute sense or relative to age norms, was not related to the tendency of parents to make enhancing or deprecating comparisons. In the eyes of the parents, even the most disabled children had done very well compared to someone, or to some earlier expectation.

The study illustrates that enhancing comparisons are indicative of healthy personal functioning and satisfaction in family relationships. This is congruent with the hypothesis that self-enhancing comparisons and evaluative strategies are important for maintaining self-esteem and psychological health, although we cannot rule out the possibility that the selectivity evidenced in spontaneous comparisons is due to a habitual response orientation characteristic of adaptive and maladaptive families.

CONCLUSIONS

In our research with runners and parents of special needs children, we have argued that individuals typically select performance comparisons that buffer themselves from failure and enhance their sense of competence. Comparisons that stress the individuals' unique contribution to a successful outcome are particularly rewarding. Thus, older runners may see themselves as bucking social norms about aging as well as the physical constraints of age. Parents may see themselves as bucking incompetent doctors and insensitive educational systems as well as the limitations of their child's disability.

Individuals high in self-esteem tend to engage in self-enhancing evaluation when their self-concepts are threatened (Crocker et al. 1987). Both of our subject populations were likely to be facing some threats to self-esteem. The literature on special populations has demonstrated the self-blame and feelings of unworthiness that often accompany (at least for a while) the birth of a congenitally impaired child (e.g., Cummings 1976; Emde & Brown 1978). As for older runners, it would be surprising if the loss of a youthful appearance and vigor were not threatening in a society that values those attributes highly. Consistent with Crocker et al. (1987), we found downward comparison to be characteristic of well-adjusted, but not poorly adjusted parents. Focusing on the threat these populations may feel, however, may underestimate the prevalence of enhancing biases in the population at large. Nondepressed college students, for example, consistently enhance their self-descriptions relative to others (Alloy & Ahrens 1987; Tabachnik, Crocker, & Alloy 1983).

A strategic choice of self-evaluative criteria does not mean that diagnostic information is necessarily avoided, although most research on self-assessment and self-enhancement have placed comparative information seeking in conflict with enhancement goals. Outside the laboratory, self-assessment and self-enhancement may be compatible or even complementary processes (Brickman & Bulman 1977; Taylor et al. 1983). Trope (1986) argues, for example, that accurate self-assessment is necessary if the individual is to make choices that ensure enhancing future performance feedback. Furthermore, the selection of a strategic evaluative standard implies that the selection is based on some prior assessment of the greatest likelihood of receiving enhancing feedback.

In our studies, there was no evidence that individuals had avoided diagnostic information; all runners knew their most recent race times and parents were knowledgeable regarding their child's actual level of functioning. After all, individuals lacking such information would have difficulty predicting future performance and opportunities for satisfaction. Selectivity is more evident in the choice of goals and attendant forms of comparative evaluation. Since a sense of mastery and ultimately the motivation to persist in an activity depend on obtaining some measure of success, the likelihood of focusing on particular comparative goals will vary according to the likelihood of success. As our data suggest, goals in any activity shift during the life span, and those shifts lead to shifts in the selection and weighting of comparative information (Bandura & Cervone 1986).

Although lab studies often focus on determining the relative weight of enhancement and assessment goals, our analysis suggests that a more important question may be whether the individual can adopt a flexible approach to self-evaluation. It may be that the ability to shift standards of performance is intrinsic to healthy functioning across the life span. Such shifts may enable individuals to confront emotionally the possibility of future decline and to plan accordingly. Furthermore, decisions have to be reevaluated at a later date. To hold onto one's earlier perspective too rigidly may exacerbate feelings of inadequacy. As Bandura (1982) points out, achievement in the real world sometimes requires so much effort that people choose not to exceed or even repeat their former accomplishments. In that case, new goals must be developed, as well as new standards that allow the individual to feel that the new goals are worthy of effort and enthusiasm.

By discussing the utility of flexible standards so glibly, we are in danger of suggesting that it is an easy process. Our work suggests that readjustment of expectations can be highly traumatic. The parents we interviewed were able to look back on their children's progress with satisfaction only after extended and often discouraging effort. Many parents reported that they were more appreciative of the gains their child made because they took so long and were not guaranteed. The importance that athletes of all ages place on personal improvement suggests that adoption of another perspective can be difficult. A forty-nine-year-old man responded to the question, "What could you do now that would give you the most satisfaction as a runner?" by writing, "Get younger!" He appended a note to the questionnaire: "Getting older does not equal faster; that's something I'm having difficulty with right now."

CHAPTER 8

Cognitive Strategies, Coping, and Perceptions of Competence

JULIE K. NOREM
AND NANCY CANTOR

From the past several years of research, it has become increasingly clear that motivation and performance involve far more than a simple manifestation of inherent capacity or ability. Our understanding of intelligence has progressed from a focus on relatively undifferentiated IQ scores to an emphasis on the development of more specific skills and abilities (Sternberg 1984). In a parallel manner, our conceptualization of motivation has shifted from an emphasis on stable motive levels to concentration on individuals' beliefs about their own abilities, the particular requirements of different tasks, and the implications of good or bad performance for aspects of the self-concept (Bandura 1977; Harter 1983; Markus & Nurius 1986; Weiner 1982).

Of particular relevance here is the increasingly sophisticated understanding of the multiple components of self-esteem and perceived competence in different life domains (Harter 1985a), and the increased role accorded to subjective assessments of competence in controlling performance (Bandura 1986)—even when those assessments conflict with standardized measures of ability or performance history (e.g., Paulhus &

We are pleased to acknowledge the technical assistance of Nancy G. Exelby, and the comments of Charles Carver, Leslie Clark, Carol Dweck, Christopher A. Langston, Hazel Markus, Christopher Peterson, Carolin Showers, and Sabrina Zirkel. This research was supported in part by Grants #BNS84–11778 (Cantor & Korn), and BNS#87–18467 (Cantor & Norem) from the National Science Foundation.

beliefs about competence, beliefs about tasks, motivation for
:, and actual performance. Specifically, our research uses the
ognitive strategies to describe the coherent patterns of ap-
ning, retrospection, and effort that translate an individual's
liefs into action (Bruner, Goodnow, & Austin 1956; Showers
985). Strategies, such as self-handicapping, defensive pessi-
epressive self-focus, constitute characteristic ways that indi-
reach desired end states and avoid undesirable outcomes in
sk settings. Strategic thinking involves a more or less explicit
self—past, present, and possible; the task as it is now and as it
fore or might become; and on the regulation of effort, feel-
ughts, as performance unfolds and outcomes become appar-
es represent individuals' attempts to gain mastery and thus to
l" of the self and of the task.

IVATION TO ACTION: COGNITIVE BRIDGES

work on motivation, researchers examined the expectations
ormulated in particular situations in order to connect mo-
n (MacCorquodale & Meehl 1953; Tolman 1955). Following
in and his colleagues on "level of aspiration" (Lewin 1948;
1944), attention was directed toward the situationally specific
dividuals set for themselves. As Atkinson writes, expectations
y[ed] to carry the burden of the meaning of the situation"

s studies attest to the importance of expectations as "carriers
' in performance situations (Carver, Blaney & Scheier 1979;
6). With few exceptions, the available data strongly suggest
expectations are related to positive outcomes, and negative
to negative outcomes (Atkinson 1964; Baumeister, Hamil-
1985; Dweck 1986; Mischel 1973; Phillips 1984). In addition,
her cognitive variables have emerged to help carry and to
urden" of meaning.

y and a sense of personal control appear to be intricately
pectations (Bandura 1977, 1982, 1986). Judgments of self-
task domain, for example, do not always correspond to
pinion or derive in any obvious way from prior performance
fact, mismatches of both sorts have been observed (e.g., see
amson, 1982, on "illusions of control," and Phillips, 1984, on

Martin 1987; Phillips 1984). Accom
and complexity of perceived comp
more varied dimensions of task co
goals for a single task.

Individuals with objectively cor
example, may appraise achievemen
(e.g., Norem 1987), so that functi
"tasks." Frequently these variation
ferent abstract beliefs about the natu
a fixed entity or a malleable proce
manifest in different goals for the ta
goals), and in different reactions
Dweck 1988; Nicholls 1984a).

These two lines of thought about
in recent work on possible selves—
to be gained, avoided, embraced, c
(Markus, Cross, & Wurf, this volu
possible-selves perspective adds a t
ceived competence and incompete
himself back in the past, and into
construction of task-specific possible
of efficacy (and inefficacy) in similar
opportunities and risks for the self
about current feelings or mood stat
system signals a shift in the literatur

One way of understanding this sl
on the *processes* by which motivation
performance (Cantor & Norem, in
has noted, a great deal can interced
action capacity, on the one hand, an
on the other. We are all prone to "d
obstacles to self-completion or self-
1985; Steele 1988), and sometimes e
tiveness of a "mindlessly" embraced
ner 1985). These perturbations in th
and intentions, and subsequent actio
to any simple account of the origins

In this chapter, we hope to illustr
illuminate one aspect of this complex

ships amon
performanc
concept of
praisal, pla
goals and b
& Cantor 1
mism, and
viduals try t
particular ta
focus on the
has been be
ings, and th
ent. Strateg
"take contr

FROM MO

Early on in
individuals
tives to acti
work by Le
Lewin et al.
goals that in
were "emp
(1957, 616)

Numero
of meaning
Feather 19
that positiv
expectation
ton, & Tice
however, o
clarify the "

Self-effica
related to e
efficacy in
consensual
records—i
Alloy & Ab

Martin 1987; Phillips 1984). Accompanying recognition of the centrality and complexity of perceived competence is a complementary focus on more varied dimensions of task construal and the influence of multiple goals for a single task.

Individuals with objectively comparable performance histories, for example, may appraise achievement situations in radically different ways (e.g., Norem 1987), so that functionally they are working on different "tasks." Frequently these variations in task construal are linked to different abstract beliefs about the nature of intelligence (e.g., intelligence as a fixed entity or a malleable process) (Dweck 1986). These beliefs are manifest in different goals for the task (e.g., performance versus learning goals), and in different reactions to performance setbacks (Elliott & Dweck 1988; Nicholls 1984a).

These two lines of thought about self- and task-construal are combined in recent work on possible selves—individuals' conceptions of end states to be gained, avoided, embraced, or discarded, in specific task contexts (Markus, Cross, & Wurf, this volume; Markus & Nurius 1986). The possible-selves perspective adds a temporal-dynamic dimension to perceived competence and incompetence—as if the person is projecting himself back in the past, and into the future. One can envision the construction of task-specific possible selves from highly specific memories of efficacy (and inefficacy) in similar past contexts, from beliefs about the opportunities and risks for the self presented by a task, and from input about current feelings or mood state. This dynamic portrait of the self-system signals a shift in the literature.

One way of understanding this shift in emphasis is in terms of a focus on the *processes* by which motivation and ability are manifested in actual performance (Cantor & Norem, in press; Norem 1987). As Kuhl (1985) has noted, a great deal can intercede between a person's intentions and action capacity, on the one hand, and observed performance outcomes, on the other. We are all prone to "degenerated intentions," frustrated by obstacles to self-completion or self-affirmation (Gollwitzer & Wicklund 1985; Steele 1988), and sometimes even pleasantly surprised by the effectiveness of a "mindlessly" embraced strategy or action (Vallacher & Wegner 1985). These perturbations in the relationship between beliefs, goals, and intentions, and subsequent actions and reactions, present a challenge to any simple account of the origins of performance.

In this chapter, we hope to illustrate how a focus on *process* can help to illuminate one aspect of this complex self-regulatory picture: the relationships among beliefs about competence, beliefs about tasks, motivation for performance, and actual performance. Specifically, our research uses the concept of *cognitive strategies* to describe the coherent patterns of appraisal, planning, retrospection, and effort that translate an individual's goals and beliefs into action (Bruner, Goodnow, & Austin 1956; Showers & Cantor 1985). Strategies, such as self-handicapping, defensive pessimism, and depressive self-focus, constitute characteristic ways that individuals try to reach desired end states and avoid undesirable outcomes in particular task settings. Strategic thinking involves a more or less explicit focus on the self—past, present, and possible; the task as it is now and as it has been before or might become; and on the regulation of effort, feelings, and thoughts, as performance unfolds and outcomes become apparent. Strategies represent individuals' attempts to gain mastery and thus to "take control" of the self and of the task.

FROM MOTIVATION TO ACTION: COGNITIVE BRIDGES

Early on in work on motivation, researchers examined the expectations individuals formulated in particular situations in order to connect motives to action (MacCorquodale & Meehl 1953; Tolman 1955). Following work by Lewin and his colleagues on "level of aspiration" (Lewin 1948; Lewin et al. 1944), attention was directed toward the situationally specific goals that individuals set for themselves. As Atkinson writes, expectations were "employ[ed] to carry the burden of the meaning of the situation" (1957, 616).

Numerous studies attest to the importance of expectations as "carriers of meaning" in performance situations (Carver, Blaney & Scheier 1979; Feather 1966). With few exceptions, the available data strongly suggest that positive expectations are related to positive outcomes, and negative expectations to negative outcomes (Atkinson 1964; Baumeister, Hamilton, & Tice 1985; Dweck 1986; Mischel 1973; Phillips 1984). In addition, however, other cognitive variables have emerged to help carry and to clarify the "burden" of meaning.

Self-efficacy and a sense of personal control appear to be intricately related to expectations (Bandura 1977, 1982, 1986). Judgments of self-efficacy in a task domain, for example, do not always correspond to consensual opinion or derive in any obvious way from prior performance records—in fact, mismatches of both sorts have been observed (e.g., see Alloy & Abramson, 1982, on "illusions of control," and Phillips, 1984, on "illusions of incompetence"). High self-efficacy and self-esteem, however, are related to greater persistence, less anxiety, and greater effort after failure (Bandura, Adams, & Beyer 1977; Dweck & Gilliard 1975).

The conjunction of expectations and efficacy/control as cognitive bridges between motivation and action is particularly helpful in illuminating the conditions under which negative expectations do *not* lead to negative outcomes. For example, when negative outcomes can be construed as possible yet avoidable, confronting them beforehand may strengthen resolve and motivate increased effort (Carver & Scheier 1986; Ickes et al. 1982; Wortman et al. 1976). Reflecting extensively on these negative possibilities may allow one to work through anxiety and formulate effective contingency plans (Showers 1986). These examples are especially important in that they emphasize the possibility of working to *gain* control—as opposed simply to *being* in control or not.

EXPECTATIONS AND STRATEGIES

Cognitive strategies address the traditional problem of connecting motivation and action (Kuhl & Beckmann 1985). Looking at strategies allows us to account for the uniqueness of individual approaches to particular situations by incorporating the interpretations people make of situations as they form performance expectations and assess their sense of control. Research on the strategy of *defensive pessimism* provides further evidence that negative expectations need not lead to negative outcomes and that individuals have the potential to increase their feelings of control as they work at tasks. Individuals using this strategy, even when they have experienced success in the past, set defensively low expectations and feel anxious and out of control before their performance on a task (Norem & Cantor 1986a, 1986b). However, they are not debilitated by their pessimistic outlook: their low expectations do not become self-fulfilling prophecies, nor do they appear to withdraw effort from achievement tasks (cf. Wine 1971). Instead, these individuals do better on laboratory achievement tasks to the extent that they are able to confront their anxiety in advance, focus on negative expectations, and plan ahead for negative outcomes. Furthermore, defensive pessimism subjects seem "protected" by use of the strategy—at least insofar as they were no less satisfied than optimistic subjects, yet did not resort to the face-saving attributional maneuvers found in the latter group when they failed.

In contrast to the negative emphasis of defensive pessimism, the *op-*

timistic strategy begins with positive expectations that are in line with good past performances and ends with post hoc attributions designed to preserve or bolster self-esteem. Thus, individuals using the optimistic strategy are apt to deny responsibility for poor outcomes and claim control over successful outcomes.

Defensive pessimism and optimism as cognitive strategies are conceptually distinct from pessimism and optimism as more general orientations or dispositions. The latter conception implies generalization of a positive or negative outlook *across* domains, as well as being associated with a distinction between nondepressed and depressed individuals, and those who are high versus low in generalized self-esteem (Scheier, Weintraub & Carver 1986). In contrast, the strategies of optimism and defensive pessimism refer to specific processes of setting expectations *within* a particular task domain—in this case, when working on academic/achievement tasks—and encompass other dimensions of construal, as well as reactions to performance within the domain.

The distinction between strategy and disposition highlights two features of defensive pessimism. First, individuals using that strategy set low expectations when anticipating future performance, *even though* they acknowledge having done well in the past. This contrasts with the realistic pessimism of someone who has performed poorly in the past and with the pessimism characteristic of depressives who may discount past successes.

Second, the pessimism of those using the strategy effectively is a "confined" one: people using the strategy in one domain do not necessarily construe other domains in the same negative light (Norem 1987). Results from two large-scale tests show that the correlation between the social and academic versions of the defensive pessimism prescreening questionnaire hover about a modest, but significant .30 (Norem & Cantor 1986a, 1986b; Showers 1986). This is precisely the correlation obtained between the two versions of the questionnaire administered to an honors college population. Clearly there is some overlap between use of defensive pessimism or optimism in one domain and its use in another, but that overlap is far from complete. This point is further supported by the data reviewed below.

COGNITIVE STRATEGIES IN A LIFE TRANSITION

The experimental research on defensive pessimism referred to above strongly supports the contention that subjects using this strategy are able to manage their anxiety about achievement tasks and motivate themselves to perform well. These studies also illustrate the usefulness of the concept of cognitive strategies in tying together several variables important to understanding achievement situations; they include expectations about performance, anxiety and feelings of control prior to the task, persistence on the task, actual performance, and reactions to performance feedback (Dweck 1986). The pattern of relationships among these variables is different for optimists and defensive pessimists; nevertheless, there is coherence to those relationships within each group.

Laboratory research showed that different individuals *can* use each of these strategies effectively in achievement situations. The obvious next question is whether people actually *do* use either of these strategies in real-life achievement contexts. Accordingly, we set out to study these strategies in the context of the transition from high school to college among a group of honors college students at the University of Michigan (see Cantor et al., 1987, for details of the full study). Over the course of their first three years in college, groups of students completed a variety of self-report questionnaires, an experience-sampling study, a social event study, two in-depth interviews, and a telephone survey concerning health outcomes.

We will first focus our discussion here on the two strikingly different cognitive strategies of optimism and defensive pessimism used by these academically accomplished students during their first year in college. We hope to show that the strategies these individuals employ make sense of the ways they marshal perceptions of themselves and their tasks.

The next step will be to contrast the academic performance of these two groups during their first and second years in college with that of a group of students with equivalent backgrounds, who do not use either optimism or pessimism consistently within the academic domain. The latter students—while hardly failing at their academic tasks—seem to work to master a different set of tasks as they adjust to college life. Keeping this in mind, we can also make sense of the ways in which their construals relate to their eventual performance and affect their investment in academic and social tasks.

As we look at changes in the relative standing of these groups over the course of three years, we will demonstrate three related points (1) understanding strategies requires that we consider both the content of the knowledge individuals bring to bear (e.g., positive or negative beliefs about ability) and the ways in which that knowledge is used; (2) the strategies individuals use, and the ways those strategies may change over time, reveal considerable potential for individuals actively to take control of difficult tasks and work toward mastery—even in the face of initial confusion or negative appraisal; and (3) looking at the strategies individuals use in relation to specific task domains highlights the potential effectiveness and drawbacks of different strategies and the importance of considering strategy-task fit. As tasks change over time, so might the appropriateness of previous strategies.

STRATEGIC APPROACHES TO ACHIEVEMENT

We asked 127 honors college students to complete an optimism–defensive pessimism prescreening questionnaire as part of a set of questionnaires administered during their first semester. The prescreening was a nine-item, face-valid questionnaire (Norem & Cantor 1986a). Subjects indicated the extent to which each item was characteristic of them. Another question asked subjects to indicate the extent to which they believed they had done well in the past. Subjects in the bottom and top thirds (for defensive pessimism and optimism, respectively) of the distribution of answers were selected as representative of each strategy group, providing that they strongly endorsed the item about positive past experience. (Again this was done in order to select for *defensively* pessimistic subjects.) In our sample, 34 students were categorized as defensive pessimists and 43 as optimists in academic situations. The remaining 50 students, about whom more will be said below, were considered aschematic with respect to these strategies.

The results from the data we collected converged strongly with those from experimental data. There was no significant difference between the two strategy groups in high school performance, and both groups continued to do well their first term in college. There were other differences in their interpretations of and reactions to the academic task domain, however. Defensive pessimists initially appraised their achievement tasks significantly more negatively than optimists. Though they performed as well and were just as satisfied as the optimists, the pessimists felt significantly more anxious, significantly more absorbed, and significantly less in control of their academic tasks than the optimists. It is important to note, however, that the pessimists' negativity was confined to the academic domain: they appraised the social domain as positively as the optimists and did not report more global life stress (Cohen et al. 1983).

The patterns of cognitive activity and the strategic value of the activity were distinctive for each strategy group (Cantor et al. 1987). In addition to their greater negativity in construing achievement tasks, pessimists reported more mismatches between their ideal and actual "student" self-concepts (Higgins et al. 1985). For pessimists, however, academic self-ideal discrepancy was *positively* related to subsequent performance (GPA). (There were no differences between the groups in amount of social self-ideal discrepancy.) The mean amount of reflective planning about academic tasks was not different for the two groups, but more planning was associated with *better* performance for the pessimist, and *worse* performance for the optimists. Interestingly, relative lack of control and greater anxiety did not impair performance for the pessimists, though the extent to which they found academic tasks personally rewarding was positively related to GPA. There was no such relationship for optimists.

During their first year in college, then, both optimists and defensive pessimists were performing quite well, but their cognitive paths to academic success looked very different. Further results from an experience-sampling study indicate that each group's preferred strategy also had somewhat different implications for their choice of activities, social network, and emotional experience or "terrain" during this transition.

In the spring of their freshman year, six optimists and eight pessimists were among twenty-four participants in an experience-sampling study of the honors students' activity, social interactions, and emotional life (Cantor & Norem, in press; Norem 1987). Students in the study carried electronic pagers for ten consecutive days, responding with extensive activity-and-emotion reports to five randomly timed beeps during the day. Several key differences between the strategy groups emerged from these data.

Congruent with our argument that pessimism can function as a domain-specific strategy, defensive pessimists enjoyed socializing as much as the optimists and spent equivalent amounts of time doing so. Striking differences were apparent, however, in the emotional profiles of the two groups when they were in academic situations. The pessimists felt significantly less in control, more stress, more challenge, and less enjoyment when studying or in class than did the optimists. In line with our characterization of defensive pessimism as a preparatory strategy, these differences were most marked when the pessimists were preparing for upcoming academic events.

As a function of their increased pessimism in academic situations relative to social situations, the pessimists had a relatively rocky emotional life. Optimists, in contrast, emerged with a much more even-keeled emotional portrait. This was especially true with respect to feelings of control, which were significantly more variable for pessimists than for optimists.

The results, based on multiple reports per subject from real-life experience, provide quite compelling support for the domain specificity of defensive pessimism and for our descriptions of the dynamics of both strategies. They also point to important points of contrast between using optimism or defensive pessimism, on the one hand, and being *aschematic* in the achievement domain, on the other.

THE ASCHEMATICS AND "UNSTRATEGIC" CONSTRUAL

The relationships among task construal, self-ideal discrepancy, reflectivity, feelings of control, and performance were far from straightforward for subjects using defensive pessimism and optimism. Knowing an individual's preferred strategy, however, did begin to make sense of those relationships and the ways in which the individuals used their knowledge about themselves and their tasks. The question remained, of course, of how we were to understand those relationships for the subjects who were neither consistently negative nor consistently positive in their construal of academic tasks. The difficulty with this group of subjects, whom we have called aschematics, was that some aspects of their task construal resembled the pessimists', and some the optimists'.

Aschematics were significantly less absorbed and anxious than the pessimists, but they also felt significantly less responsible and in control than the optimists. They were somewhat less reflective about their academic tasks, but not significantly so, and they had *fewer* mismatches between their academic actual and ideal selves than the optimists and pessimists. These latter two variables, however, simply did not relate to GPA performance for the aschematics. Both feeling in control and finding academic tasks rewarding were positively related to performance for the aschematics.

In terms of actual performance, the aschematics did not achieve quite as high a GPA as the pessimists and optimists, but the difference during the first semester was not significant. During their second semester, 29 percent of the aschematics' activity reports from the experience-sampling study involved academic activity, compared to 38 percent and 35 percent for optimists and defensive pessimists. More important, these aschematics ($N = 10$) were significantly more lonely and angry in virtually every situation than the two strategy groups, and they reported experiencing significantly more conflict (Norem 1987).

When one examines the aschematics' reports of their feelings of control, the profile that emerges is different from that of either the optimists or the defensive pessimists. Congruent with their construal of academic tasks during their first semester, they felt considerably less in control than the optimists when reporting on-line via the beepers. *Unlike* the pessimists, however, they did not seem to *take control* as they worked on their academic tasks, and their level of control was consistently low across academic and social situations. This was especially significant in that low control was associated with poorer performance for aschematics, whereas pessimists did not seem to be debilitated when they felt out of control—perhaps because one focus of their strategy was on working through their anxiety so that they could feel in control.

Overall these results seem to suggest that the aschematics were somewhat less invested in their academic tasks than were the members of the two strategy groups, and that they may have been at risk for poorer performance relative to optimists and defensive pessimists. This interpretation was supported by data collected during the students' second semester of their second year in the honors program. By this time, the aschematics enjoyed their academic tasks significantly less than the other groups and were performing significantly more poorly on GPA.

At this point consideration of the specific tasks individuals were working on at a given time became especially important, as did the issue of *fit* between strategies and tasks (Norem 1989). Our argument is that the construals and use of self- and task-knowledge were especially *strategic* for the optimist and defensive pessimist subjects, because they were each using strategies that were well designed to deal with their unique construal of academic tasks. That is, the defensive pessimist faced the achievement domain with a considerable amount of anxiety *and* the belief that academic tasks were important and absorbing. Even though the defensive pessimists may have felt anxious about achievement tasks, they also clearly valued and enjoyed doing them well. The defensive pessimist strategy was designed admirably for "solving" achievement tasks formulated in precisely this way.

The achievement task faced by the optimists was constructed somewhat differently, however. These individuals were much less *absorbed* in achievement tasks and were concerned with doing well, but did not feel particularly anxious about their performance. Their strategy worked best when they endeavored to look on the bright side and avoid dwelling on potentially negative aspects of their tasks.

Our argument is that the appearance of floundering on the part of the aschematics, relative to the other two groups, can be understood in light of their less well articulated interpretation of academic tasks and their somewhat greater concern with interpersonal tasks. This group did not initially reap the benefits of appropriate task-strategy fit in the academic domain, because their definition of the task was not yet sufficiently clear. Another way of conveying this idea is to realize that the primary achievement task for the aschematics was to construct a workable idea of their goals within that domain.

Two sets of results provided support for this account of the aschematics. During their second year, a subsample of these students completed the Moos Family Environment Scale (FES; 1974), a ninety-item instrument composed of ten subscales used to measure subjects' perceptions of their families' values, priorities, structure, activities, rules, etc. The contrast between the perceptions of the optimists, pessimists, and aschematics was suggestive. Both the optimists and the pessimists perceived their families as significantly more achievement-oriented than did the national norm for the scale. This fits well with their arrival, fully equipped for the achievement domain, at a very academically competitive program. In contrast to the optimists, the defensive pessimists perceived their families as providing significantly less structure for the realization of achievement goals. Though preliminary, these data suggest that though pessimists had achievement values as strong as the optimists', they may have experienced more frustrations in working toward their goals in the absence of specific structure. Thus part of their task was to structure for themselves, or take control of, their academic endeavors.

In contrast to both these groups, the aschematic subjects perceived their families as more recreation activity–oriented, and they scored somewhat lower on the independence subscale of the FES than the other two groups. This makes sense in relation to their relatively lower involvement in academic tasks *and* their consistent feelings of loneliness and anger during their first year at college. Part of their struggle to adapt to college life involved learning to be happy and productive outside the family circle. It is thus not surprising that they devoted somewhat more effort than the other two groups toward learning how to fit in comfortably during their first two years.

Further support for this picture of the aschematics' adjustment comes from data gathered in an in-depth interview during their second year (see Norem, 1987, for a detailed description). This interview focused on obtaining descriptions from the subjects of their academic and social progress since arriving at the university, their techniques or problems in becoming motivated, and difficulties they were having on either academic or interpersonal tasks. These interviews were videotaped, and the tapes were coded, incorporating ideas from several perspectives on coping and problem-solving strategies and styles.

The results suggested that the more the aschematics used others' interpretations of tasks and tried to match their understanding of the task domains to that of prototypical or ideal others, the better they performed academically. In other words, the aschematics seemed to be somewhat confused and unsure about precisely *what* it was they were supposed to be doing. To the extent that they could accept the task definitions of others, they got along better.

It seems that, though the aschematics initially had no consistent strategy for motivating their performance in the academic domain, they were able to develop a strategy for crystallizing their tasks. This is hardly an unimportant development; after all, it is extremely difficult to come up with workable solutions to a problem before the problem itself is well defined. Once their articulation of important domains was more secure, the aschematics were well on their way to being as strategically well equipped as the other two groups.

THREE YEARS LATER

During the second semester of the students' third year at Michigan, a telephone survey was conducted by the field staff of the Institute for Social Research. The survey was designed to provide information about the ups and downs the students were encountering in their lives. They were asked about their current levels of life satisfaction and whether they were experiencing any of thirty-one psychological and physical symptoms (after Verbrugge 1980). They also reported their current GPA and answered a modified version of the Perceived Stress Scale (PSS; Cohen et al. 1983).

The results of this survey were surprising. First (and perhaps least surprising), for the first time in three years the aschematics seemed to have mastered *both* the academic and social task domains. Their GPA, social satisfaction, and PSS scores were virtually identical to those of the (still) successful optimistic subjects. They no longer reported feeling lonely, angry, or conflicted, but, rather, felt in control of their academic and social lives.

The results were less sanguine for the defensive pessimists. For the first time in three years, their GPA was lower than the other two groups', they were experiencing significantly more global life stress and more psychological symptoms, and they felt significantly less satisfied with their lives (Cantor & Norem, in press).

We have already argued that the aschematics' troubles during their first two years seemed to be largely a function of their difficulty in figuring out what they wanted to do. It thus seems plausible that their rise in fortune can be explained by assuming that most of these subjects were able to define a set of academic and social tasks that were simultaneously involving and manageable, tasks for which they were able to develop appropriate or well-fitting strategies.

In contrast, the initial fit between the defensive pessimists' strategy and their perception of academic tasks as involving, important, and rewarding (if stressful) seemed very well suited to both academic success and social satisfaction during these students' first two years. Something seemed to have happened either to their definition of those tasks or to their use of the strategy, or both, which rendered the fit between the two less functional.

Cantor and Norem (in press) have argued that emotional ups and downs of academic pessimism—as illustrated by the experience-sampling data—may take a heavy toll on well-being over time. This might be the case even though the strategy can be very effective within a restricted performance context. The continual struggle to gain control and manage anxiety may begin to water down the rewards of success and the intrinsic pleasure of the activities themselves. In addition, examination of the social networks of defensive pessimists revealed a fairly heavy reliance on a small group of close friends, who may have found their association with the pessimists' worry and anxiety trying. Thus, the pessimists' social support network may have faded over time. Indeed, it appeared that, by the third year, these side effects of defensive pessimism were taking a considerable toll.

It is difficult to tell from the current data what precisely led to the pessimists' decline relative to the other two groups. It may be that, ironically, the initial success of the strategy contributed to that decline. The defensive pessimists, after reviewing their impressive performance during their first two years, may have responded (as one might reasonably expect) by raising their expectations and standards. Indeed, it is intriguing that the pessimists at the end of their second year had the highest expectations of the three groups: they were significantly higher than the aschematics' and equivalent to the optimists'. Recalling that interference with the strategically low expectations of defensive pessimists in an experimental situation disrupted their subsequent performance (Norem & Cantor 1986b), it could be argued that these subjects interfered with their own strategy. Setting low expectations was their primary defensive maneuver for dealing with anxiety and stress. By raising their expectations, they may have simultaneously increased the pressure on themselves and decreased their arsenal of techniques for coping with that pressure. In the face of increased stress, the intrinsic reward they previously had found in their academic tasks may have been overwhelmed by anxiety.

Concurrent with their rise in expectations, the pessimists reported being even more challenged and absorbed in their academic tasks than ever and claimed to be spending a prodigious amount of time on them. Thus, the defensive pessimists may have become too involved and invested in their academic tasks. A dedication, reflectivity, and diligence that previously worked in their favor could have had unforeseen consequences for both their emotional well-being and their actual performance.

What remains unclear, and may be crucial for understanding performance during the final year in college for these subjects, is the extent to which the defensive pessimists will be able to rein in their use of the strategy. If they recognize that their strategy is getting out of control, they may be able to confine it to only those truly risky situations for which it is most appropriate (i.e., for which they can genuinely embrace strategically low expectations), thereby decrease the overall amount of stress in their lives, and recapture their enjoyment of their achievements.

The example of the aschematics should be instructive in this respect and keep us from too hastily assuming a continued downward spiral for the pessimists. They may emerge from a period of confusion and floundering, eager to pursue newly articulated (or circumscribed) tasks with renewed vigor and effectiveness. Indeed, both the initial performance of the defensive pessimists and the later performance of the aschematics vividly attest to this potential for gaining mastery.

DYNAMICS OF PERCEIVED COMPETENCE AND INCOMPETENCE

Our analyses of strategic and unstrategic reactions to academic tasks support the recent emphasis in the motivation and achievement literatures on complex and ever-shifting belief-behavior relationships. In this sample we have seen three versions of self-regulatory processes, with correspondingly variable outcomes and patterns of development over three years. The defensive pessimists came to college with a well-articulated sense of the aspects of academic tasks on which they personally needed to struggle for control. In contrast, the aschematics floundered at first and grew only slowly into a "take control" motivational stance. For these students, the first task may well have been to gain a better grasp of what their actual academic task was.

But by the third year the positions of the two groups were reversed, with the pessimists appearing to be (at least temporarily) somewhat out of control in their academic endeavors and at a disadvantage in terms of general well-being. For these students, the next task may be to recapture the constructive intensity of their earlier achievement motivation, perhaps by reframing their academic tasks.

The aschematics and the defensive pessimists, then, did their motivational work at different times and in different ways, but at least they demonstrated the proclivity to take control. One can only assume that the even-keeled, confident optimists will show as much stamina and adaptive motivation if (or when) they encounter obstacles in the future (Dweck 1986). Of course, a college environment may be especially tolerant of the sorts of self-enhancing attributions and self-protective excuses that bolstered the optimists. Once these students move into the workplace, they may have to adapt their strategy to take control in new ways. It remains an open question whether the optimists' characteristic state of being in control puts them at an advantage or at risk for missing signals to adapt and change their ways (Taylor & Brown 1988).

As with most psychological phenomena, to understand these dynamics of motivation and performance we must follow individuals in and out of qualitatively different life experiences. We suspect that it will become increasingly evident that no one set of beliefs, expectations, and ideals is best for all life problems or at all times in life, in large part because each task changes too much and too frequently to be treated repeatedly or mindlessly with one solution (Langer, 1989a). Certainly the students in our study experienced these "curve balls" as they valiantly tried to attain and maintain a sense of competence and to ward off feelings of incompetence at their college life tasks. As observers we can only be impressed with their persistence and hope that it continues.

CHAPTER 9

The Role of the Self-System in Competence

HAZEL MARKUS,
SUSAN CROSS,
AND ELISSA WURF

Perceptions of one's own competence—a sense that "I am effective" or "I can do it"—are critical to individual functioning throughout life (Bandura 1986). Children develop in lockstep with their faith that they *can* accomplish various imagined undertakings (Harter 1981a; Leahy 1985). Later, well-being and successful functioning as an elderly adult are still bound up with one's feelings of competence (Atchley 1982; Gurin & Brim 1984; Kuypers & Bengston 1973). Moreover, as studies of coping with stress accrue, it is increasingly apparent that feelings of efficacy and competence are key factors in the ability to protect one's self from the effects of stress (Cohen & Edwards 1988), and perhaps even in staying healthy and preventing disease (Friedman & Booth-Kewley 1987; Kobasa 1979). What are these feelings of competence that appear to comprise nothing less than a vital life force? Where do they come from and how do they work? In exploring these questions we focus on the nature of the "I" that perceives the competence and examine the structures and processes of the self-system that are essential for creating and maintaining competence over the life span. First, we argue that felt competence is an essential aspect of actual competence and is linked to instrumental action and effective performance. Then we explore the role of the self-system in the development, maintenance, and breakdown of competence.

This research was supported by the National Science Foundation Grant BNS 84–08057. Correspondence regarding this chapter should be sent to Hazel Markus, Institute for Social Research, 426 Thompson Street, University of Michigan, Ann Arbor, MI 48106–1248.

OVERVIEW

Our central premise is that competence is mutually and reciprocally related to the self-system. It is rooted not just in one's attributes or abilities but also in the structures of the self-system that *represent* these attributes or abilities. The structures of self-knowledge that represent one's important attributes or abilities ("me" as intelligent, or lovable, or creative, or good in school) are called core self-structures, salient identities, or self-schemas (e.g., Markus 1977; Rosenberg 1965).

Competence in a domain requires *both* some ability in the domain *and* a self-schema for this ability. A self-schema involves the recognition that one has the ability and the belief that it is important or self-defining. Sometimes, the abilities and skills are present first and self-schemas are constructed from the knowledge that one possesses them. At other times, the self-structure is present first, and the abilities develop later. In this case, the self-structure that is initially present is typically a desire or an intention to possess the relevant skills as self-defining characteristics.

It is, of course, possible to have a set of abilities and to display them without actively being aware of them. Yet in most cases, the instrumental exercise of competence in a given domain requires, at a minimum, the understanding that one indeed possesses the required abilities. Such understanding is typically described as *felt* or *perceived competence.* We argue that felt competence is an essential aspect of *actual* competence. Without an explicit awareness that one possesses a given attribute, the expression of various characteristics is likely to be haphazard and not subject to systematic self-regulation and direction. Even in the face of a good performance, without a corresponding self-schema, the individual may have a psychological experience of incompetence (see Phillips & Zimmerman, this volume).

It is also possible to represent one's self as having particular attributes that one does not in fact have. When individuals do not have behavioral evidence to support their felt competence, it will either be disconfirmed and abandoned as a consequence of one's actions or will serve to organize the individual's actions so that the desired ability is eventually attained.

The Core Structures of the Self: Self-Schemas

Self-structures simultaneously summarize a particular competence or set of abilities and confer an aspect of identity. These affective/cognitive structures (in our work we have termed them *self-schemas*) are created selectively on the basis of one's experience in a given domain. They integrate representations of the self (past, present, and future) and function to organize the processing of self-relevant information in a given domain (Markus 1983; Markus & Sentis 1982; Markus & Wurf 1987).

With the development of a self-schema comes a base of knowledge about one's abilities. The individual who knows that she is "smart" or "good in school" will be enduringly sensitive and responsive to issues relevant to intelligence or school achievement, both in her own behavior and in that of others. Her expertise will include an elaborate understanding of the nature of the ability and of the strategies and situations for displaying it.

It is the self-schema—the representation and articulation of a given ability—that allows an individual to use his abilities instrumentally and to have a sense of control over them. People with a self-schema in a particular domain (schematics)—whether for an attribute, an ability, or a role in society—consider the domain to be of critical personal importance. Schematics maintain an enduring investment and commitment to their self-defining domains and have a continual need for self-validation in these areas (Wurf & Markus 1987).

Structures of the Self in the Future: Possible Selves

Structures of the self are not just passive generalizations of past actions but also claims of responsibility for one's present and future actions in a given domain. Thus, a significant component of any self-schema is one's beliefs about what is possible in a domain in the future. *Possible selves,* the future-oriented components of self-schemas, are essential for putting the self into action and are the selves we could become, would like to become, or are afraid of becoming (Markus & Nurius 1986). Possible selves are specific representations (imaginal, semantic, enactive) of one's self in the future states and circumstances that serve simultaneously to organize and energize one's actions.

As indicated in figure 9.1, possible selves are the elements of the self-system that allow one to simulate being competent in a particular domain. Such simulations not only give rise to one's feelings of competence but also marshal one's intentions and motivate one to act. Global and task-specific possible selves can thus be viewed as the carriers of competence.

Possible selves work by making the goal one's own. Cognitively and affectively, the representation of the task confronting the person and the representation of the self become one by decreasing the psychological

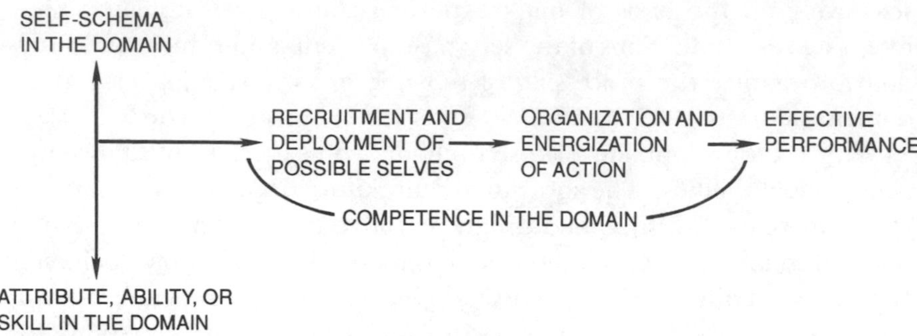

Figure 9.1. The hypothesized relationship between abilities, self-schemas, and possible selves in producing effective performance.

distance between one's current state and the desired state. Research on goal gradients (Miller 1944) indicates that animals approaching a goal box speed up because of the increased presence of goal-related cues. Similarly, individuals with a clear image of themselves in a future state (e.g., successful on a given task) will have accessible more cues relevant to that state, thus enhancing goal-related performance. The construction of possible selves allows one to experience a contingency between one's now self and one's imagined future self.

As individuals choose among actions, and as they persist in or withdraw from them, they are often guided by a sense of what is possible for them. To the extent that these possible selves are well elaborated and can be effectively summoned and deployed, they will engender feelings of competence. They will organize and energize one's ongoing actions, often affording quite precise simulations of the required performance. As a consequence, effective instrumental action and performance will be promoted and enhanced. And with effective performance comes a validation of one's sense of competence and a concomitant strengthening of identity.

An individual may construct all types of possible selves, but the further they are from the domains of one's current involvement and expertise, the less effective they will be in preparing and regulating performance. Unless possible selves are rooted in core self-structures they are likely to remain idle fantasies, because effective performance depends on a link between desires or goals and the schemas that contain the relevant procedural knowledge for realizing them (Cantor & Kihlstrom 1987).

The Self-System in Competence and Performance: How Does It Work?

How do the structures of the self-system (self-schemas and possible selves) create and carry competence? Why is it that without these structures, one will experience incompetence? As knowledge of the function of schema-like structures expands (e.g., Neisser 1985), we are able to become more specific in our hypotheses about how schemas may facilitate action. One of the most important ways in which a schema allows one to "go beyond the information given" is through the anticipation and simulation of *what* is possible in a given domain. The ability to simulate (conceptualize, feel, image) specific futures is thus a powerful consequence of becoming *schematic* in a given domain; this is one of the key mechanisms by which the self-system creates and sustains competence. Imagery and mental practice for future attainments prepares one for the actual performance.

The psychological literature contains a variety of studies on the general effects of anticipation and simulation on performance: they probe how imagining a desired future state influences current performance. Overall they suggest that anticipation has beneficial effects on current performance. With respect to making decisions about the future, for example, Kahneman and Tversky (1982) suggest that people run mental simulations by constructing scenarios of alternative outcomes. The ease with which a particular event can be simulated is used to evaluate the likelihood of realizing that event. Similarly, Anderson (1983) and his colleagues (Anderson, Lepper, & Ross 1980) have suggested that the scripts that come most easily to mind are those that will be relied on most heavily in making decisions about the future and that imagining one's self in a behavioral script markedly influences one's expectations about carrying out the behavior. Further, such images influence not only one's expectations but also *actual* behavior. Thus, Gregory, Cialdini, and Carpenter (1982) found that many more people who imagined themselves with cable television subscribed to it than did those who simply listened to a persuasive message about its virtues. And Sherman and Anderson (in press) found that psychotherapy patients who imagined themselves returning for at least four sessions were less likely to drop out than did those who did not engage in this imagery.

Similarly, an earlier but neglected literature on the beneficial effects of mental practice shows clearly that mental practice (the symbolic rehearsal of physical activity in the *absence* of any gross muscular movements) is often associated with improved task performance (for reviews, see MacKay 1981; Richardson 1967a, 1967b). Richardson (1967a) in his review found that mental practice improved performance in ring tossing, juggling, tennis, card sorting, digit substitution, muscular endurance, and mirror drawing. Consistent with these studies are statements from athletes about how they prepare for a performance. Greg Louganis, the Olympic champion high diver, described how he envisions every feature of an upcoming dive, mentally rotating his body through time and space. Similarly, champion skier Jean-Claude Killy reported that he prepares for an event by mentally reproducing an upcoming ski run while sitting in a chair. The time on a stopwatch he allotted to mentally rehearse a given run was within fractions of a second of the time it actually took. These examples reveal the precision with which anticipated events can be constructed and simulated by an expert.

Despite a diversity of intriguing anecdotes and empirical findings, there is no compelling theory of *why* anticipation of the future or mental practice should work to enhance actual performance. Recent work, however, is suggestive. For example, Nigro (1983) found that making imaginary throws of darts or beanbags substantially improved actual throwing performance. Subjects reported somewhat different experiences as a result of their mental practice: some saw the dart in flight, some visualized their own bodies in motion, and some had very little visual imagery but were able to experience kinesthetic feelings. In this type of mental simulation there is a rehearsal not just of the required movements but of the coordination of perception with movement. In Neisser's (1985) terms, there is a coordination of perceptual schema with action schema. Similarly, Finke (1980) shows that visual imagery shares portions of the visual perceptual cycle, such that an individual who imagines reading a book shows a pattern of perceptual activity similar to that of someone actually reading a book (and a different pattern from someone imagining a ship on a horizon). This work implies a coherence among perception, imagery, and action that is only now beginning to be understood (see Volpert 1985). Coherence would, of course, be especially beneficial when the anticipated performance is physical in nature. Yet, even if it is *mental* performance that is anticipated, the anticipation may still serve to organize and energize future actions.

We suggest that the development of global possible selves related to competence in a specific domain (e.g., "a good student" possible self) will enable the construction or retrieval of related, but more focused, task-relevant possible selves (e.g., "me successfully completing this anagram task"). Motivated, intentional, or willful actions will occasion a temporary reorganization of the working self-concept. The working self-concept is the array of self-relevant representations that are currently accessible (see Markus & Kunda 1986; Markus & Nurius 1986). When performance is effective, this functional self-concept will be dominated by task-relevant possible selves, and relevant negative or feared selves will be suppressed so that they will not interfere with task performance.

When the working self-concept is configured of positive possibility, it is these senses, images, and conceptions that will regulate individuals' actions. This means that individuals will be extremely self-focused (cf. Carver & Scheier 1982; Klinger 1975), yet focused on future selves rather than on current selves. Further, they will be focused not on their current state but on actions instrumental for achieving the desired goal (cf. Kuhl & Beckmann 1985). That all the individual's actions are bound and driven by the accessible possible selves should have significant consequences.

First, experiencing a desired possible self should create a positive emotional state, and the desire to maintain or enhance this state should be generally arousing or energizing. Second, information processing should be biased in favor of stimuli that are consistent with the desired possible self. Moreover, imagery will be specific and focused on the desired end state and how to realize it. For example, a person preparing to write a class paper will focus on the specific activities that will achieve this goal: "me going to the third floor of the library, photocopying articles, checking out books, staying home tonight," etc.

By envisioning or partially enacting anticipated possible selves, individuals may also be able to recruit or construct some kinesthetic representations of the self in the future. For example, tennis players thinking of a coming match often anticipate various strokes by very slight muscle tensions and micromovements (Horowitz 1979). Ach (1910, as quoted by Kuhl & Beckmann 1985), in fact, postulated "a subjective moment of volition" which gave rise to sensations in various parts of the body of the type that may actually occur during performance.

Though the interplay of various representations of the self in the future—visual, auditory, kinesthetic—a plan of action is created. The individual becomes committed to this plan, partly because other actions now seem less accessible and partly because many of the scripts and schemas that will produce the anticipated outcomes are already off and running. Such activity may create a sense of competence, efficacy, or control, and simultaneously promote effective instrumental action.

We can also speculate that a keenly experienced possible self may function to focus or coordinate some aspects of the autonomic, neural, or sensorimotor systems and thus further prepare the person for action. In contrast, the presence of negative or conflicting possible selves may disrupt the synchronous functioning of these systems. (For further discussion of related ideas, see McGuigan 1978).

Why a Need for Competence?

The links between the self-system and competence sketched above help us understand why individuals have what White (1959) called a need for effectance, or a need to exercise and extend one's capabilities. Others have labeled this urge a need for competence (Harter 1978), self-determination (Angyal 1941; Deci & Ryan 1980), personal causation (deCharms 1968), and control (Glass & Singer 1972). This need grows out of an even more basic need to know that one exists, to have a sense of who one is and how one is different from others. Validating one's self-defining generalizations through one's actions provides this assurance both to one's self and to others. Expressing one's competencies provides evidence that one exists; thus competence is reciprocally bound with the nature of the self-system.

The exercise of one's competencies in the service of maintaining an identity is in most cases not an effortful or even conscious activity, and it is inherently pleasurable because it validates one's identities. When so engaged, individuals are most likely to experience what is commonly labeled "intrinsic motivation"—a sense that "I" am engaging in this activity because "I" want to (e.g., Deci & Ryan 1980). The shape of the "I" at any point depends on the nature of one's self-defining structures.

It is through one's actions that one develops the self-system, or identities and it is through actions that these identities are maintained. If one's identities include "mother, psychologist, jogger, nuclear freeze advocate, friend, overweight, creative, caring person," then these identities must be validated by one's actions. Individuals can lay claim to their identities only if they behave accordingly. In this view, the individual does not discover a true self, but rather brings it into existence. Sartre (1958) claimed that those who cannot construct a self will experience the existential dread—they will perceive the self as nothingness. When individuals fail to develop a set of self-defining schemas, as in the case when the environment does not afford sufficient self-definitional opportunities, they will experience an unstable and diffuse identity as well as a sense of general incompetence. Similarly, crises in identity will occur when one's self-defining competencies are challenged, threatened, or not allowed expression.

Perceived Competence: Reality or Illusion?

From the perspective outlined here, it follows that most of the time when one has a sense of competence, one *will be competent* (or be on the way to becoming competent), at least relative to one's self without this feeling. And conversely when one feels incompetent, one *will be incompetent.* Some current treatments of the power of felt competence and related phenomena, such as perceived control, effectance, mastery, or optimism, analyze these experienced states primarily as "illusions" with little objective basis. Thus Taylor and Brown (1987) cite numerous studies showing that most people believe that they are more skilled, more in control, and more likely to experience good outcomes than other people.

Our view, however, is that felt competence should not be formulated as an illusion. With respect to the actor's construction of reality, there is no illusion. When a person experiences a sense of competence, it is typically carried and maintained by a set of self-relevant internal structures that can facilitate competent performance in a given domain. What may appear to an observer as an unfounded optimistic belief that one is competent can actually create competence by selectively directing attention, efforts, and energies toward the desired action, and away from inconsistent or contradictory thoughts, feelings, and actions. With the preparation that the creation of specific task-relevant possible selves affords come well-grounded feelings of efficacy, mastery, and optimism about the impending performance. Individuals will thus experience not *illusions* of competence but *actual* competence. Felt competence, then, is not a cognitive product that can be separated from actual competence. Instead, it is an integral aspect of competence.

COMPETENCE THROUGH THE LIFE COURSE

The Development of Self-Structures and Competence

Why do some people develop the stable structures of the self required for competence and others do not? Competence may develop *either* from a person having a particular ability and then building a self-structure around it *or* from a person developing a self-structure and then using it to motivate the acquisition of the actual ability. In either case, the role of the social environment is crucial to development.

In the first case, individuals start to develop competence because they have a particular ability. In order to develop a self-schema, the person must both attend to this ability and make internal, stable attributions for relevant performances. Individuals may come to notice an ability because others label it for them or because they contrast their own performance with that of others. A "good at school" schema, for example, may originate with one's own observation that one has an easier time solving problems or writing reports than other students, from comments made by parents, or from the fact that the teacher always singles one's paper out for praise. In particular, *distinctive* characteristics are the most likely to be noticed both by others and by the self, and it is around these that self-schemas are likely to develop.

Whether this distinctiveness is noticed depends heavily on the nature of the person's immediate social environment. All individuals have a wide variety of attributes, and those in the environment (including the individuals themselves) can attend to only a subset of these. In the most obvious case, people are likely to develop a self-schema in a particular domain if they possess some attribute that is relatively unusual. The research of McGuire (e.g., McGuire 1984; McGuire & McGuire 1982) shows that people are most likely to describe themselves spontaneously in terms of those features that make them distinctive in a given social environment. When a characteristic is unusual relative to the population as a whole, or when a person is part of a local environment in which a characteristic stands out, over time this characteristic should become the basis of an enduring self-structure. Thus, a person who is *unusually* musically talented should, if given opportunities to make music, eventually develop a self-schema for this aspect of self. Yet even a person who has only average musical talent, relative to the larger population, should be inclined to develop a concept of the self as musical *if* she grows up in an environment where everyone else is tone deaf.

A second critical issue in developing a self-schema is how the person explains or attributes his distinctive abilities. In order to develop a self-schema, the person must make internal and stable attributions for his distinctive performances. Self-schemas entail a belief that the person is responsible for his own behavior (Markus 1983). If external attributions are made for distinctive performances, the person may fail to develop a self-structure around his ability. For example, if a child's peers suggest that she won first place in the science fair only because of help from her physicist father, she will have a hard time believing she herself has any scientific ability (even if the project was her idea and her father helped only a little).

Similarly, although the belief that effort can make a difference in performance is highly adaptive, particularly after failure (Bandura 1986; Dweck 1986), the belief that one's successful performance is due *only* to effort can be very detrimental to the development of self-conceptions of ability (Nicholls 1984a). Thus, Deaux (1976) reports that girls are socialized to believe their successes are due to effort; boys are socialized to attribute success to ability. And conversely, girls explain their failures as due to lack of ability, while boys are encouraged to attribute failure to lack of effort. This differential pattern of socialization suggests that girls will often fail to develop schemas for being talented and will be especially prone to developing negative self-schemas that imply a lack of talent. Similar results are reported by Phillips and Zimmerman (this volume), who find that because of overly negative self-perceptions girls are particularly likely to underestimate their true abilities and to suffer deficiencies in motivation and coping.

In general, the person who has a special ability that is positively valued and who makes internal, stable attributions for successful performance is likely to develop a positive self-schema in that domain. Similarly, a person who possesses a troublesome or negatively valued characteristic (e.g., low ability in some area or a disliked physical characteristic) and makes internal, stable attributions for this is likely to develop a negative self-schema around that attribute. Harter (1985a), for example, reports that low self-worth children are those who are distinctive in important domains: they do poorly in their schoolwork or are not socially accepted. And further, she finds that these children make non-self-serving attributions: they take as much responsibility for their failures as for their successes, and they attribute their successes to external circumstances. Such patterns of noticing and attributing one's abilities mediate self-schema development. Once formed, these positive or negative self-schemas for ability work in tandem with the ability itself to create actual competence or incompetence.

The individuals in one's immediate social environment also influence the development of one's self-structures even in the absence of any distinctive attribute. First, these important others determine what attributes are valued. In some environments, athletic skills are valued; in others, being creative is of critical import. Through direct and indirect feedback, the person may be encouraged to develop and validate particular possible selves that reflect these values. For example, if a teacher tells a child she is artistically talented, she may develop an idea of herself as creative even if she is merely average in ability. But this belief can lead to the child engaging in behaviors (enrolling in art classes, practicing drawing) that in effect make her more creative. In general, the research on the self-fulfilling prophecy (Jussim 1986; Miller & Turnbull 1986) and on reflected appraisals (Shrauger & Schoeneman 1979) suggests that people frequently come to see themselves as others see them. The more consistent and the longer term such evaluations are, the more likely the person is to adopt the others' perspective on the self, coming to value (or devalue) and emphasize those attributes or abilities that others value (or devalue).

The social environment also sets the standards that determine whether a person is said to possess an attribute and whether or not the person believes he can meet these standards. Some parents, for example, socialize their children to believe either that ability is a fixed entity that one has or doesn't have or that abilities are achievable through hard work (Dweck 1986). Which theory one subscribes to can have drastic consequences for effort, persistence, and self-evaluations of achievements. For example, Leggett (1985) found that girls are more likely than boys to subscribe to the idea that intelligence is a stable entity; and consistent with this belief, a study by Licht and Dweck (1984) shows that girls are more likely to show decreased performance after initial failure or confusion than are boys. Improvement and fundamental self-change are more possible for people with an "incremental" theory of their abilities. They should have a plethora of well-developed, future possible selves to guide their efforts. But people who subscribe to an "entity" theory are limited to displaying who and what they already are; they are present- rather than future-oriented, and fail to develop and strive for achievable possible selves.

Maintenance of Competence across the Life Span

Once individuals develop stable structures of the self in a particular domain, it is important to continually verify and affirm them. This strengthens both one's sense of felt competence and one's identity. Thus, throughout the life span, the individual must continue to perceive and develop existing or new skills in a domain, to form a self-schema concerning them, and to recruit and deploy possible selves that direct action.

As with the development of competence, the social environment is of critical importance to maintaining competence. To the extent that the social environment remains stable, it should be relatively easy to maintain one's competencies and self-definitions in particular domains, assuming that the abilities that gave rise to the structures of the self in the first place remain fairly stable.

When analyzing development across the life span, it is obvious that formative, age-graded changes in the social environment may decrease after early adulthood (Baltes, Reese, & Lipsett 1980; Duncan & Morgan 1980; Gurin & Brim 1984). The twenties and thirties are typically marked by the completion of one's education, commitment to a career, marriage, and parenthood. These life tasks provide the impetus and structure for the development and maintenance of many specific competencies. In succeeding decades, however, the individual usually faces fewer major life changes. Moreover, by middle age people have had time to choose the environments and situations that reflect their competencies (Costa & McCrae 1980; Mischel 1973; Wachtel 1973). Thus, competencies may tend to remain relatively stable unless or until the individual experiences a major life event.

Even then, however, competence may well be maintained because threats to it can be buffered by secure jobs, families, and social structures (Atchley 1982; Gurin & Brim 1984). In fact, situations, friends, jobs, and spouses may have been chosen to reflect and reinforce one's competencies. The man who is schematic for being able to fix things may have chosen a career in engineering. The woman who developed a self-schema of being gregarious and good with people may have chosen a real estate career where she could employ these skills. By their forties many people appear to be settled into life-styles that allow them to affirm their identities and simultaneously experience a sense of competence and general self-worth (Gurin & Brim 1984).

Maintenance of Competence through Specialization. The adult development literature suggests that older adults may strengthen their identity and competence not by proliferating domains of involvement, as do younger adults, but by specializing in a very few important domains (Baltes 1987; Lowenthal, Thurnher, & Chiroboga 1975). Thus it may be important for the thirty-year-old to see himself as effectively accomplishing career goals, being adept at social relationships, keeping up with younger men on the basketball court, and staying abreast of world events. Older adults, in contrast, appear to have fewer and different types of self-structures. The antecedents and the psychological meaning of this tendency to narrow the basis of one's identity remain to be specified, however.

With development, the bases of self-definition and competence not only are more narrowly defined but appear to involve a shift from outward-oriented or physical abilities to inward abilities, characteristics, or "wisdom" (Baltes 1987; Dixon & Baltes 1986; Lowenthal, Thurnher, & Chiroboga 1975; Neugarten 1964). With waning physical abilities, retirement, and perhaps a more restricted social life, the older person may define herself primarily as "a kind person," "an independent person," a "loving grandmother," or "someone who knows how to get things done" (Cross & Markus, in press).

From the perspective of the self-system there are several ways to understand this specialization. It may result from a casting off of self-schemas in those domains in which abilities have started to decline or are no longer affirmed by society or are seen as not age-appropriate. Alternatively, specialization may involve a new representation and new organization of one's abilities. Thus, elements of a "good parent" self-schema may be combined with elements of a "talented and effective in my profession" self-schema to create an "effective at caring for people" self-schema. Such a schema may be useful in regulating the actions of a person who has retired and now works as a hospital volunteer. Such restructuring may involve relabeling one's previous abilities or coming to understand them anew, or it can also involve the development of new attributes.

The choice of domains for identity specialization and restructuring may depend on whether the person can develop and elaborate relevant possible selves. The fifty-year-old who can't construct the possible self of being a student will not pursue further education. In a study by Cross and Markus (in press), respondents aged eighteen to eighty-four were asked to list their possible selves and answer several questions about the most important ones. The number of possible selves, both positive and negative, decreased with age, reflecting a narrowing or specialization in self-definition. In interpreting these results, one might argue that today's young people are likely to claim more possible selves simply because they have more opportunities available to them. Yet, when respondents were asked what actions they had taken to bring about their hoped-for possible selves, or to prevent their feared selves, the number of actions undertaken increased with each older cohort. Thus the young person who perceives that anything is yet possible (Breytspraak, 1984) may develop many possible selves, but if the social environment fails to support them or the requisite skills fail to develop, many of these possible selves may be abandoned. Thus, as people age, they can maintain competence by investing more of themselves into fewer domains.

Maintenance of Competence through Life Review. Self-schemas may also be used to revise the individual's past, thus conveying a sense of ongoing competence. Situations or actions that are inconsistent with well-developed self-schemas are likely to be ignored or selectively forgotten (Hastie 1981; Markus 1980). Self-schemas may foster a selective reinterpretation and reorganization of the past that is consistent with one's present self-conception (Greenwald 1980; Ross & Conway 1986).

People who engage in a life review are most likely to view their lives as consistent or congruent (Butler 1963; Cohler 1982; Lewis 1971). A belief in the consistency of one's life serves to reaffirm important self-schemas and also provides a sense of mastery over one's life (Gurin & Brim 1984; Kuypers & Bengston 1973). Costa and Kastenbaum (1967) find, in fact, that centenarians who undertake a life review are most likely to also have hopes and plans for the future. A life review guided by important self-schemas will allow people to "remember" earlier aspirations as supportive of current accomplishments and to diminish threats to the self and to felt competence from current unattained or unrealistic goals (Atchley 1982; Marshall 1980; Thurnher 1974; Weinstein 1980). Well-developed structures of the self provide a framework within which individuals are able to integrate their past, present, and future actions and to imbue them with meaning (see Whitbourne 1985).

Maintenance of Competence in the Face of Challenge. Critical life events—the loss of a spouse, unemployment, the sudden onset of disease—can shatter or cripple even the most stable self-systems and call into question the most well-grounded competencies. Research on coping and adjustment indicates that the ability to anticipate or simulate negative life events is a crucial factor in how the event is handled (Albrecht & Gift 1975; Sears 1981; Brim & Ryff 1980; Hultsch & Plemons 1979; Rosow 1973). When the death of a spouse or the end of a career is expected or "on time" (Neugarten 1968), a person is likely to have developed a set of possible selves for coping with "me as a widow" or "me as no longer a teacher."

Consistent with this idea, Ryff and Dunn (1983) found that events that occurred atypically *early* in life resulted in *reduced* self-efficacy, and events that occurred atypically *late* in life resulted in *increased* self-efficacy.

Gurin and Brim (1984) suggest that the enhanced efficacy of those experiencing "late" events may be due to increased resources for handling the event, but Neugarten (1970) says it may be a result of anticipation and preparation for the event. Anticipation may aid the coping process by allowing individuals to develop positive possible selves that offset the feared selves that derive from anticipated negative outcomes. A study by Markus, Porter, and Nurius (1986), in fact, suggests that those individuals who believe themselves to be coping effectively with a life crisis report a wide variety of very positive possible selves, which appear to function as resources that can be recruited by the individual to construct different and more comforting worlds.

Self-structures and perceptions of competence may also be challenged by failure or disappointment. What of the aspiring model who gains twenty pounds; the assistant professor who fails to get tenure; the university baseball star who is passed over by the major leagues? In these cases, having a self-schema for the domain will require that the person struggle to maintain the self-perception despite the failure. The threat of incompetence in such a domain is a threat to one's identity.

Individuals whose self-structure is threatened may attempt to make a self-serving attribution for the failure, explaining it away as due to external, unstable, and/or uncontrollable circumstances (Bradley 1978; Snyder 1979). Thus, the assistant professor can note that none of his predecessors in the past ten years has gotten tenure, and blame his failure on departmental policy. A second technique is to make downward social comparisons, looking for others who have done even less well. Hochschild (1973) examined this type of social comparison among older women in an age-concentrated apartment building and found what he labeled a "poor-dear hierarchy": women bolstered their sense of worth by comparing themselves to others who were worse off in terms of health or social support. Other strategies for handling a threat to the self may involve denying or ignoring the importance of the threat. Finally, individuals may attempt to affirm themselves in other important domains (Steele 1988).

Although people maintain an arsenal of self-defense strategies, only some will be suitable for challenges to centrally self-defining domains. Thus, simply leaving the field and concentrating one's efforts in a different domain (Tesser 1986; Wicklund & Gollwitzer 1982) will often not be an option. Domain switching, compensatory self-inflation, or self-affirmation techniques ("I may not have a job, but I ran a marathon") will probably be the strategy of last resort when a core aspect of the self is involved (Greenberg & Pyszczynski 1985; Steele 1988).

The Breakdown of Self-Structures and Competence

Once a person has a well-elaborated self-schema in a particular domain, it is likely that he or she will go to great lengths to preserve it. When challenges to one's self-defining structures and felt competencies cannot be countered through one of the processes specified above, a breakdown of competence can be expected. Once again, the nature of the social environment is critical. For example, downward social comparison is an important mechanism for maintaining competence. Yet with the loss of roles that accompanies retirement or widowhood may also come a loss of appropriate reference groups (Rosow 1973). As a result, many older people may be forced to compare themselves inappropriately to younger people (Bengston 1973; Kuypers & Bengston 1973). In addition, without reference groups to provide norms and standards, the aging person may be unable to develop new positive self-structures, including hoped for possible selves.

Stereotypes of the elderly present still more threats to self-definition of older persons. The elderly person is often seen as helpless, passive, and nonsocial (Rodin & Langer 1980), and old age is often viewed as the worst time of life (Bortner & Hultsch 1972; Chiroboga 1978). Rodin and Langer (1980) found that behavior that is seen as normal for a middle-aged person may be viewed negatively in an elderly person. As Atchley (1982) noted, the older person may be better able to discount the occasional threat to the self, yet a prolonged threat, such as these negative stereotypes pose, may weaken the old person's ability to defend the self. In addition, when friends and relatives hold these negative stereotypes, few of the elderly person's abilities or strengths will be acknowledged or encouraged. Instead, friends, relatives, and others may treat the elderly person as if her or she were incompetent and childlike. Taking away responsibility from the elderly person or opportunities to be independent or in control (Rodin & Langer 1980) may lead the person to become dependent and passive. Thus, the stereotypes will become self-fulfilling prophecies (Cooper & Goethals 1981; Kuypers & Bengston 1973; Schulz & Hanusa 1980).

Stereotypes of the elderly may also encourage them to explain their

Wurf & Markus (1983) found that negative self-schemas function essentially like positive self-schemas. They help a person attend to, organize, and remember schema-relevant information in a given domain.

Once an individual has a self-schema for shyness, for example, she will read and interpret her social experience according to the generalizations provided by her self-schema. One might wonder, then, why individuals develop negative self-schemas. Why don't they simply discount or selectively avoid such self-relevant negativity? But some inabilities are difficult to ignore and must eventually be confronted. Still others, however, might just as well be ignored or interpreted in more positive ways. To explain the apparent paradox, Wurf (1987) has shown that negative self-schemas develop when individuals desire to change and become different. By becoming schematic in a given domain, individuals may develop an impressive expertise about what elicits and maintains their undesired qualities and what they can do to change. Negative self-schemas may be an indication that one intends systematically to alter one's behavior until the incompetence is overcome. They are a signal that "I know what I am not and I know what I would like to be." Such negative self-schemas may thus be important markers of anticipated self-concept change.

CONCLUDING COMMENTS

The goal of this chapter was to explore the relationship between competence and the self-system across the life span. We have argued that self-definition depends on the nature of one's competencies and that an essential aspect of competence in any domain is the explicit cognitive representation of the competence. Specifically, an individual's abilities cannot be manifested and purposefully used unless they are represented in explicit self-schemas. These include a thorough understanding of the nature of the corresponding abilities and an articulation of the strategies for exercising them.

An obvious question is how the approach sketched here relates to other similar approaches. Our view is one of several that stress the importance of self-relevant thoughts in motivation, anxiety, and performance (see Schwarzer, 1986, for a discussion of these ideas). The knowledge of a contingency between one's abilities or attributes and various outcomes is a central component of most cognitive theories of motivation and actions (Bandura 1977; Heckhausen 1977; Kuhl & Beckmann 1985). Our contribution is to examine how self-relevant structures may function to produce competence, and how beliefs or expectancies about the self (Bandura 1986; Carver & Scheier 1982) may have powerful effects on behavior.

The self-referent thoughts that are implicated in competence are not simply abstract beliefs about one's ability to do what needs to be done. The critical component of these beliefs is the individual's representation of *herself* or *himself* approaching and realizing the outcome. This representation allows the individual to simulate the anticipated performance—to build a bridge between the current state and the desired outcome. The more elaborate the possible selves that can be deployed in preparation for a performance, the better the performance, since many of the routines required for the performance will already be engaged through the process of anticipation and simulation. Self-structures, particularly possible selves, can thus be seen as the carriers of competence, without which one's abilities cannot be effectively utilized.

The specific self-relevant representation of competence is important because it is the basis of one's self-definition. Deploying one's abilities confirms one's existence. Without explicit self-knowledge of one's abilities, one will experience both incompetence and an unstable, diffuse identity. In this approach, we assume an even stronger interdependence between competence and the self-system than does Harter (1985a), who argues that competence is an important dimension of self-esteem.

The investigation of the links between competence and the self-system leads to important unanswered questions. Why, for example, are some individuals able to sustain threats to their abilities and attributes, and others cannot? Are differences in appraisal and coping with threat best understood in terms of differences in abilities or in individuals' self-representational structures? How do the dynamic structures of the self that embody felt competence control action? Finally, is it possible to create competence or to help individuals become competent? Answering these questions will further the goal of understanding the nature and extent of the self-system's role in creating, fostering, and maintaining competence.

PART THREE

CLINICAL PERSPECTIVES

CHAPTER 10

Interpersonal Relationships and the Experience of Perceived Efficacy

CARRIE E. SCHAFFER
AND SIDNEY J. BLATT

This chapter explores the ways in which interpersonal relationships serve as the foundation for the development of a sense of self and perceived efficacy. One's perceived efficacy reflects beliefs about the success of one's action and is part of a fundamental sense of the self as cohesive and integrated. A cohesive sense of the self derives from interpersonal relationships, especially from early experiences in the caring relationship, but is then augmented by later experiences in other intimate relationships.

Interpersonal relationships provide both the physiological and psychological regulating mechanisms necessary for the development of self-experience. Ongoing relationships continue to serve a variety of functions, but gradually, as the individual matures, he or she becomes increasingly able to achieve a great deal of self-regulation by the internalization of aspects of transactions initially experienced in caring relationships. Our understanding of the development of a sense of self can be explicated by integrating the clinical-theoretical formulations of three different approaches to be discussed in this chapter.

THE INFANT'S NEED FOR RELATEDNESS: THE CONTRIBUTIONS OF OBJECT RELATIONS THEORY

Many theoretical formulations discussing the impact of the caring relationship on psychological development view the child as the passive recipient of the parents' care. Psychoanalytic theory, for example, recognized the importance of the mother-infant relationship in personality development, but emphasized its role primarily in terms of the mother providing the infant relief from states of tension. These theorists stressed that the infant's development was influenced by the physical ministrations of the care giver, but little emphasis was placed on the psychological importance of these interpersonal experiences. Early attachment to the care giver was viewed as gratifying primitive drive states, reducing tension, and providing protection (Bowlby 1971).

More recently, formulations stress that the infant is an active agent in this relationship. Observation of infants in institutions (e.g., Spitz 1946; Provence & Lipton 1962) and the research on the early relationship between neonate and mother (e.g., Harlow & Harlow 1966), however, indicate that the mother provides much more than feeding; she also provides warmth, tactile experiences, and a wide range of other stimulation essential for the infant's growth and development. Rat pups, for example, attempt to maintain proximity to their mothers, and following separation, even an anesthetized mother reduces the pups' vocalizations of separation distress (Hofer 1987). These patterns of response, documented in kittens, puppies, monkeys, and human infants, are consistent with the formulations of the British object relations theorists (Winnicott, Guntrip, Balint, Fairbairn, Kahn) who propose that the infant is primarily "object seeking"; in other words, the psychological aspects of interpersonal relatedness are crucial to the infant's development (Sutherland 1980).

The importance of the early infant–care giver relationship lies in its capacity to allow the infant a state of what Winnicott called "going on being," or enabling the infant to take for granted the continuity of his or her existence. The mother, through a process of identification with her infant, recognizes and prevents possible impingements that would interfere with this sense of continuity and threaten the unity of the ego and the survival of the self. In the safety of the care-giving relationship, the infant exists without having to deal constantly with external impingements and thus has the opportunity to experience his or her own impulses and sensations. These impulses are experienced as personal, and they form the basis for the emergence of the infant's awareness of affective experiences and the ability to reflect on them—to have a sense of self (Blatt 1983). The mother also enables the infant to experience a sense of separateness and thereby develop a sense of self, in the overall context of relatedness (Winnicott 1956, 1958, 1960). Furthermore, the mother's recognition and fulfillment of the infant's needs provide the context in which the undifferentiated urges of the infant become initially organized (Loewald 1960), giving the infant an initial sense of his or her existence. The stable secure relationship with the mother provides the child with a sense of being (Erlich & Blatt 1985) and the "sense of assured stable selfhood" that forms the basis of "spontaneous, creative activity" (Guntrip 1971, 120). This healthy state also provides the infant the opportunity to experience his or her own acts as efficacious, thereby contributing to further definition of a sense of self.

Caring relationships that fail to provide a secure basis from which the child can begin to develop a sense of stable selfhood force the child to find alternate, less constructive ways of creating a sense of self. Some individuals develop compensatory mechanisms to define the self through forced, driven action and others replace spontaneity with imitation (Erlich & Blatt 1985). Still others become apathetic, uninvolved, and withdrawn. In each of these situations, the maternal relationship has failed to provide the infant with adequate experiences of affection and consistent caring such that the infant has to create an artificial (or false) sense of relatedness (Guntrip 1971; Winnicott 1960).

Early experiences of a continued sense of being that emerge from feelings of relatedness with the mother are an essential basis for psychological development. A caring relationship that also enables the infant to feel held and valued psychologically enables the infant to feel that his or her spontaneous gestures are accepted and understood by the mother. A sense of self begins to form out of the organization provided by the mother's constructive response to her infant's spontaneous expressions of needs. These gestures become a form of communication, facilitating the infant's development of the capacity to use symbols (Winnicott 1960).[1]

The mother's understanding of and response to the infant's gestures as a shareable and perceivable communication leads not only to the infant's

1. It is the extent to which a mother is able to accept her child's own gestures, rather than encourage gestures that she herself desires, that leads to the child's recognition of his or her own sense of identity (Khan 1972). Just as the socioculturally available modes of communication and expression both form and limit the adults' experience and expression of self, the parent's response to the child's spontaneous gestures may either facilitate or inhibit the emergence of the child's identity. When the care giver's vision of the child's future can be influenced by the child's emerging capacities (rather than the mother's own desires), a wider range of experience and expression is open to the child.

development of the capacity for symbolization but also to the infant's awareness that experiences can be communicated to and shared by another; the infant learns that experiences of others, though unique to them, bear a relation to one's own experiences. This experience of the world as an environment of interpersonal communication helps the infant to attend to and utilize his or her own feelings. This sense of reliance on one's own feelings enhances the individual's capacity increasingly to differentiate one's own feelings, to share them with others, and to understand and appreciate the feelings of others. Feelings of efficacy emerge from interpersonal relatedness and an appreciation of the value of personal subjective experiences, and this utilization of affective experiences becomes increasingly more differentiated, integrated, and subtle with subsequent development.

Individuals differ widely in the confidence with which they rely on their perceptions of interpersonal experiences and their ability to appreciate affects both within themselves and in the experiences of others. Differences among individuals in the capacity to engage in reciprocal interpersonal experiences derive from the early experiences of the care giver's abilities to create a mutually meaningful and shared reality with the infant, initially on a physiological level and subsequently enriched by symbolic and psychological dimensions. The mother who is able to recognize the meaning of her infant's gestures and to share in her infant's affective states creates a trusting relationship in which the spontaneous expression of feelings is associated with the experience of being understood.

If the mother is relatively unable to acknowledge the infant's experiences and transform his or her gestures into occasions of mutual and shared understanding, the child struggles to achieve a compensatory sense of relatedness with the mother by negating some of his or her own feelings (Kohut & Wolf 1978; Miller 1981). Without an appreciation of and capacity to reflect on one's own affective experiences, there is a limited capacity to understand the feelings of others and to establish close and intimate relationships in which experiences are mutually created and shared. The child avoids interpersonal interactions and struggles to establish and preserve a limited sense of selfhood independent of the support normally provided by constructive relationships. Frequently the child feels an inexplicable lack of congruence between his or her experiences and an understanding of the experiences of others.

Without early experience of mutually shared, reciprocal relationships, one's sense of self-efficacy is severely compromised. One retains one's original experiences of having little or no effect on the world and continues to withdraw in order to defend oneself in the face of a potentially unresponsive world that might continue to negate one's unique existence. Thus, the development of a sense of efficacy is related to the degree to which the mother enables the child to feel understood and accepted and the degree to which the child experiences that he or she has a unique impact on the ways in which the mother responds to the child's needs. The findings of Sroufe (1983) on the relations between early infant-mother attachment behavior and ratings of self-esteem and interpersonal skills at age four support this view. These formulations are also consistent with retrospective accounts of adolescents and young adults that suggest that the sense of efficacy is related to parent-child relationships in which parents are described as responsive, nurturant, supportive, nonpunitive, and nonjudgmental.

Empirical Data: Relations between Parental Qualities and Efficacy

In an effort to study empirically our hypothesis that efficacy grows out of a parent-child relationship characterized by nurturance, support, and acceptance, we examined the relations between particular qualities of parental descriptions written by college students and their experiences of perceived efficacy. Using a system developed to evaluate parental descriptions (Blatt et al. 1988), students' descriptions of their mothers and their fathers were rated on three factors: benevolence, striving, and punitiveness. Additionally, we administered the Depressive Experiences Questionnaire (DEQ; Blatt, D'Afflitti, & Quinlan 1979) in order to assess perceived efficacy. The DEQ, a sixty-six-item rating scale assesses three components of the phenomenological experience of depression: affiliation/dependency, achievement/self-criticism, and perceived efficacy.

In the first of two samples of male and female college students, Blatt et al. (1979) found that students' sense of perceived efficacy was significantly correlated with the degrees to which they described their mothers as benevolent and as striving. The degree to which the mother was described as punitive was unrelated to perceived efficacy. The qualities of benevolence, striving, and punitiveness ascribed to the father were uncorrelated with perceived efficacy. These findings suggest that it is the relationship with the primary care giver that is central in the development of a sense of efficacy. As the responsibility for early care giving shifts and men assume increasing responsibility for this function, we would expect to see efficacy more clearly correlated with descriptions of the father.

These findings were replicated in a second sample of college students (Blatt, Quinlan, & Bers, in preparation), who were also administered the Parker Bonding Instrument (PBI; Parker, Tupling, & Brown 1979) which yields factor scores for the perception of one's parents as caring and as protective. The data from this sample essentially paralleled the findings from sample 1, but for males only. Efficacy was significantly related to descriptions of mother as benevolent and as striving. In additional, efficacy was inversely related to the description of mother as punitive. Again, there were no relationships between perceived efficacy and descriptions of fathers in males. The relationship between efficacy and descriptions of mothers for females, however, were nonsignificant. In fact, ratings of efficacy in females were significantly correlated with descriptions of fathers as punitive. It is unclear why these relationships differed as a function of gender.

These findings were supported by the results with the PBI. Ratings of perceived efficacy correlated significantly with ratings of caring in both mother and father for males but not for females. A two-way ANOVA (caring × protectiveness) on perceived efficacy revealed significant main effects for caring in females' descriptions of their mothers and for males' descriptions of both their mothers and their fathers. Protection, however, yielded no significant main effect or significant interaction with caring in relation to perceived efficacy.

Employing a slightly different methodology, Homann and Blatt (1988) asked college students to write descriptions not of their parents but of their relationship with each parent. The DEQ was used to measure perceived efficacy. Results indicated a significant correlation between perceived efficacy and one's sense of security in the males' relationship to their mothers. Consistent with findings mentioned earlier, these results were not found in females. The "sense of security" factor comprised ratings of affection, respect, and ability to confide in the parent, and descriptions of the parents as idealized, communicative, reasonable, and available in a relationship characterized by low anger and frustration in which the individual felt a sense of effectance.

In summary, the relationship with a caring and benevolent mother seems to be a crucial experience in the formation of a sense of efficacy. A responsive mother facilitates the emergence of a sense of self and feelings of efficacy in a variety of ways. The mother-infant relationship provides physiological and affective regulation, both of which contribute to the development of perceived efficacy. The emergence of a sense of an integrated self and perceived efficacy derives from the interaction of both the physiological and the psychological components of early attachment.

INTERPERSONAL FACTORS IN PHYSIOLOGICAL REGULATION

One of the important functions of the early infant-mother relationship is its provision of physiological homeostasis. When the mother provides the presence required for the infant to obtain an optimal level of regulation, the infant experiences a sense of control and feelings of safety. Additionally, the infant's communications facilitate the mother's ability to satisfy the infant's physiological needs, leading to the infant's establishment of a sense of efficacy. The loss or impairment of this important relationship with the mother leads to the deregulation of physiological and psychological homeostasis (Hofer 1984), and the child experiences a sense of helplessness and a loss of control. Perhaps it is these early experiences of global, stable, and internal expectations of uncontrollability that lead to the sense of helplessness and inefficacy associated with learned helplessness seen in some types of depression (Abramson, Seligman & Teasdale 1978).

The effects of interpersonal transactions on physiological states have been increasingly explored over the past fifteen years. Singer (1974), for example, found that small variations in experimental procedures and mannerisms of experimenters significantly altered physiological and psychological measurements. Variations in the degree to which the subject became involved with the examiner were paralleled by changes in cardiovascular response, blood pressure, and adrenocorticosteroid levels. Lynch (1977), discussing the effects of loneliness and interpersonal isolation on disease, reported that divorced, widowed, and single men die from a wide range of illnesses at a rate two to three times higher than married men. The lack of intimate interpersonal relatedness affects both momentary and tonic physiological states. Similarly, relationships may serve a physiologically reparative function, such as that seen in the account by Lynch of a comatose fifty-four-year-old man whose heartbeat changed abruptly when a nurse held his hand.

Autonomic arousal patterns (heart rate and skin temperature) can be altered by instructing trained subjects to display facial expressions associated with particular affects (Ekman, Levenson, & Friesen 1983). Thirty-six-hour-old infants have been found to be able to discriminate and imitate facial expressions of happiness, sadness, and surprise (Field et al. 1982). Taken together, these findings suggest that facial mirroring produces parallel physiological states in the mother and infant. It also suggests that alteration of the infant's physiological state may occur in response to changes in the mother and vice versa. Within an intimate relationship, individuals are capable of subtle facial discriminations and imitations, possibly even at birth. This type of intuitive, empathic communication may offer the infant the opportunity early in development to share the mother's physiological state. This has been demonstrated in adults by Greenblatt et al. (cited by Lynch 1977), who demonstrated a concordance between the heart rate of patients and therapists over the course of many sessions, with concordance most pronounced during times that the therapist felt he or she had communicated most effectively.

Recent evidence suggests that for primates, periodic and regularly occurring social interactions serve as cues that entrain circadian pacemakers in the hypothalamus to function on twenty-four-hour biological cycles. If not entrained, these pacemakers run freely on twenty-five-hour cycles and separate homeostatic functions grow out of phase from one another (Moore-Ede, Sulzman, & Fuller 1982). For instance, Wever (1970, 1979) found that subjects isolated in rooms from all environmental cues entrained to a twenty-four-hour rhythm in response to a bell which was rung to signal urine sample collection; twenty-four-hour lighting cycles were insufficient for entrainment. Wever concluded that the bell was sufficient for entrainment in that it served to symbolize social interaction (urine collection).

Hofer (1984) points out that many of the untoward effects of maternal separation, sensory deprivation, and bereavement (decreased weight and body temperature; endocrine, sleep, and cardiac changes; anxiety, etc.) may derive from a deregulation of homeostatic functions normally served by relationships. Subjects in situations of separation, deprivation, and/or loss "are suffering from withdrawal of patterns of sensorimotor stimulation that had been exerting an imperceptible regulating action on the subjects' minds and on their internal biologic systems" (191). Hofer (1987) concludes that the synchronous and reciprocal interactions studied in humans are present in biologically less evolved and simpler behavioral systems and suggests that we are genetically predisposed to establish relationships that serve these functions.

Although these studies demonstrate that relatedness has both general and specific effects on the physiological functions of each participant, they have not examined the specificity of effect of particular components of interpersonal transactions on these physiological functions. The numerous physiological effects associated with relatedness are assumed to be mediated by the unified experience of engagement. In fact, it is often assumed that the physiological concomitants of loss are secondary to its psychological effect. The recent work of Hofer (1984) on the effects of separation in rat pups has found that the various changes that result from loss are a composite of independent processes and only appear to be a unified pattern of change because they are simultaneously activated when separation occurs. Indications of independent processes are seen, for example, in the fact that though heart rate and oxygen consumption of two-week-old rat pups are regulated by the interaction with mother during feeding, the pup's activity level is regulated specifically by maternal body warmth. The pup's biologic regulation is partially delegated to the mother, even when the pup is old enough to survive on its own.

It is important to stress that this is a reciprocal process because the pup's behavior also contributes to the physiological regulation of the mother. Feeding cycles, for example, which are embedded in sleep cycles, require the pup to suck quietly during two thirds of the nursing cycle so that the mother may enter the slow-wave sleep required for milk letdown. Thus, in order for the pup to receive milk, it must facilitate the mother's ability to carry out her biologic potential (Hofer 1987).

Such experiences of mutual regulation in humans are likely among the first in which the infant learns the congruence between his or her own actions and the environment's response. If the interaction goes well, the infant has a very early experience of self as efficacious. Among the infant's initial experiences are learning that he or she can achieve homeostatic regulation by affecting the care giver and thus participating in physiological regulation. This physiological regulation provides an initial sense of order that is later enhanced by the symbolic aspects of the relationship that provide order; both the physiological and psychological experience of order guard against the helplessness that leads to feelings of inefficacy.

RELATIONSHIPS PROVIDE ORDER AND REGULATION OF SELF-EXPERIENCES

An essential feature of the care giver–infant relationship is the creation of order, organization, and harmony (Basch 1975). This organizing function protects infants from experiences of anxiety and helplessness that might lead to their feeling unable to control their internal state and/or external environment resulting in perceived inefficacy. The mother-infant relationship provides a sense of order through physiological regulation, and these physiological components of the dyadic transaction establish the prototype for experiencing the psychologically organizing aspects of the relationship.

As discussed by Behrends and Blatt (1985), the mother's heartbeat provides an intrauterine, rhythmically organized environment which is disrupted at birth and leaves a "permanent, neurologically encoded trace which serves as the prototype for all later anxiety, the essence of which is the threat of impending disorder. Viewed in this manner, what the mother-infant relationship provides is the re-establishment of a fundamental order. By empathically and reliably attuning herself to her infant's signals, the mother conveys an ordering rhythmicity which somewhat replicates the predictable rhythmicity of the womb" (18–19). The importance of the reestablishment of the rhythmicity of the intrauterine environment has been associated with the finding that women are more likely to hold infants left of the mid-sternal line (thus, closer to the heart) as compared to how they hold a package (Sperber & Weiland 1973). Additionally, Salk (1973) found that an electronically amplified maternal heartbeat in a nursery significantly decreases neonatal crying.

Although initially the mother's heartbeat itself helps restore the original intrauterine rhythm, her steady and reliable care-taking functions also become associated with the ordering experience of the intrauterine heartbeat. The orderly interpersonal transaction of mother and infant complements the regulatory effects of their physiological relatedness. The mother's ability to integrate and create order out of the infant's potentially overwhelming tensions and excitations engenders a "background of safety" which is phenomenologically opposite to anxiety (Sandler 1960). The mother's ordering capacity guards against anxiety by providing the infant with the experience of modulating and integrating excitatory stimulation. The lack of a relationship that provides organization results in experiences of traumatic anxiety and eventually the dissolution of a cohesive sense of self. Infants and children denied the opportunity to merge with their parents' calmness and omnipotence experience a limited capacity for self-soothing. Since anxiety cannot be regulated, the world is experienced as dangerous (Kohut & Wolf 1978) and the individual feels a lack of efficacy. In extreme cases, stereotypy and immobility create a sense of order as compensation for the failure to experience order in the interpersonal transaction with the mother. When others can be relied upon to offer calmness and order, the resulting stability and organization serve as a buffer against extreme sensitivity to experiences of failure and disappointment and help modulate one's self-esteem.

DEVELOPMENTAL PSYCHOLOGY ON THE EMERGENCE OF A SENSE OF SELF AND PERCEIVED EFFICACY

Just as the care giver's provision of organization through physiological regulation contributes to the infant's feelings of cohesiveness, security, and efficacy, the sense of shared meaning provided by the care giver's understanding responses also contributes to the infant's feelings of integrity and efficacy. As with physiological components of the relationship, affective transactions with the mother provide the infant with three important aspects of relatedness that bear directly on the development of a sense of efficacy: (1) experiences of order and organization that guard against helplessness, (2) participation in a bidirectional relationship in which one's experiences can be shared and have an effect on others, and (3) the experience of self-regulation which occurs as one increasingly is able to internalize the functions provided by the mother.

Stern's (1985) research on affect attunement between mother and child demonstrates clearly the importance of the accurate correspondence of the shape, timing, and intensity of the child's and mother's gestures for the development of the sense of communion and communication. These correspondences often occur across sensory modalities indicating an affective matching or attunement rather than simple imitation. For instance, the intensity and duration of the child's voice may be matched by features of the mother's body movement. When the mother matches the intensity, timing, and shape of the infant's excitement, the child continues to attend to the activity at hand. When a mother is instructed to mismatch intentionally the child's affective expression, the child stops what he or she is doing and facially expresses a need for clarification. Stern concludes that the experience of communion derived from affect attunement helps the infant realize that internal feeling states can be shared with others. Importantly, feeling states to which the mother is not attuned are experienced in isolation by the infant and will not contribute to the development of shared affective experiences.

The experience of communion and affect attunement with the mother not only enables the child to learn that affective experiences can be shared, but also that one has the capacity to influence one's interpersonal world, thus deriving a sense of efficacy. Tronick and Gianino (1986) found that moments of well-coordinated and poorly coordinated mother-infant interactions normally alternate, with poorly coordinated interactions occurring about 70 percent of the time. Of these poorly attuned interactions, however, 34 percent are spontaneously corrected. When mothers were intentionally unresponsive and unemotional toward their infants, those infants who were more accustomed to naturally occurring reparations attempted more vigorously to get the mother to respond by directing a greater number of signals to her as compared with infants less accustomed to naturally occurring reparations. The researchers concluded that infants who normally experience a relatively higher level of natural reparations "had the clearest representation of the interaction as reparable and of themselves as effective" (8). Infants who normally experienced fewer repairs after misattunements turned away in sadness and distress, and seemed to feel ineffective in interpersonal reparations. Tronick and Gianino believe that these responses develop over time and become pervasive and generalized self-sustaining regulatory styles.

Similarly, Bettes (in press) has shown that a depressed mother's slow response to her infant's needs interferes with the infant experiencing the contingencies between his or her gestures and mother's response. This interference creates a dissociation between the child's gesture and the mother's reaction such that the mother's behavior is no longer experienced as a "response." What is lost is not the receipt of necessary supplies as much as the confirmation of oneself as a person-in-relationship.

These studies suggest that in experiences of affect attunement with the mother, infants learn how to regulate both their own internal emotional state and their relationship with the external world. The attainment of regulation emerges out of a mutually reciprocal dyadic regulatory system with the care giver in which the "caretaker responses serve as an external segment of the infant's regulatory capacities" (Tronick & Gianino 1986, 7). The infant participates in obtaining this aid by indicating an optimal level of stimulation to the mother and thus derives a sense of efficacy when the optimal level of stimulation is achieved through the joint effort of both members of the dyad.

Specifically, the mimetic musculature of the face at birth is relatively developed and allows the newborn to express an optimal level of stimulation (Tomkins 1962). By three to five months of age, the gaze of the infant exerts major control over the "level and amount of social stimulation" that the infant finds as optimal (Stern 1985, 21). Gaze behavior serves both to distance and to reinitiate contact with the mother. At a later age, motor coordination (i.e., walking away and returning) serves these same regulatory functions. Thus, the mother's success at meeting the infant's needs is partly related to the infant's capacity to communicate need to the care taker. These affective attunements parallel the physiological processes of regulation described earlier, such as milk let-down, in that both require reciprocity between mother and infant and are bidirectional. Once again, we stress that a sense of self and self-efficacy emerge from early experiences of a balance between being adequately cared for by and having an impact on the care giver.

Parallel to the physiological constituents of the mother-infant relationship, affective attunements provide infants with the opportunity to experience a sense of continuity and to become aware of their own feelings. Additionally, affective congruence facilitates experiences of being understood and understanding the feelings of others. Through infants' participation in creating experiences of attunement, they become aware of their capacity to regulate a relationship with another and thus achieve regulation of the self. These experiences, paralleled on the physiological level, serve to form and enhance the infant's and child's experience of efficacy. Engagement in relationships that provide a stable base for shared physiological and psychological regulation provide a supportive format for participation in self-regulation and, later, for the capacity to assume these functions for oneself through internalization of aspects of important relationships. One's capacity to assume the functions one previously depended on others to provide occurs through the development of increasingly complex internalizations of aspects of significant need-gratifying relationships in one's life (Behrends & Blatt 1985). These internalizations promote the development of a sense of autonomy, but in the context of relatedness, and result in increased feelings of efficacy.

THE ROLE OF INTERNALIZED OBJECT REPRESENTATIONS

We now turn our attention from the effects of proximal mutual interpersonal relatedness to the role of mental representations in the development of psychological and physiological aspects of self-experience and feelings of efficacy. Mental representations are the result of internalization of gratifying experiences. As Behrends and Blatt have written, "Internalization refers to those processes whereby individuals recover lost or disrupted, regulatory, gratifying interactions with others, which may have been either real or fantasied, by appropriating those interactions, transforming them into their own enduring, self-generated functions and characteristics" (1985, 22). This formulation of internalization stresses the subject's role as a transformer of experience, as does Schafer's (1968). It emphasizes that it is relationships rather than objects that are internalized (Loewald 1960, 1970) and that these internalizations may be of real or imagined relationships. It is the experience of relatedness rather than its actuality that is internalized.

It is likely that early internalizations occur initially around sensorimotor experiences of reestablishing homeostatic equilibrium and over time become more complex and symbolic (Blatt 1974). To the extent that the early attachment figure was reliable in meeting the infant's needs, these early representations will give rise to the belief that homeostatic disruptions will be corrected and thus lead to a sense of security (Pipp & Harmon 1987). The internalization of satisfying sensorimotor experiences provides the impetus for the individual to assume the functions that had been previously provided by the care giver, leading to a sense of independence and efficacy (Behrends & Blatt 1985). Erikson considers the first social achievement to be the capacity to allow the mother out of sight because "she has become an inner certainty as well as an external predictability" (1950, 247).

The extent to which people utilize mental representations of significant others for psychological and physiological homeostasis is suggested by the finding that illusions and hallucinations occur in 12 to 40 percent of bereaved individuals (Rees 1975) and in a significant number of participants in sensory deprivation studies (Heron 1961). When the usual sources of environmental and human stimulation are lost, mental representations of relationships replace interactions and help restore a sense of personal integration. These representations allow individuals to experience temporary separations without the profoundly disruptive behavioral and physiological changes frequently associated with early separation, sensory deprivation, or bereavement. Just as Hofer demonstrated that separate physiological responses are specifically mediated by particular aspects of the mother-infant relationship, he also contended that particular aspects of mental representations may be specifically related to particular biologic responses and that during early stages of mourning, revisions of representations of the lost person result in a "dissolution of their associative link to biologic systems, so that the internal representation gradually ceases to be an effective regulator" (1984, 193).

These formulations suggest that the extent to which one is able to call forth complex, multidimensional, symbolic representations of significant others should predict the capacity for psychological and physiological self-regulation. Since efficacy derives in part from the achievement of these forms of regulation, the complexity of internalized representations of relationships with significant others should also correspond with feelings of perceived efficacy. Impairments in the capacity for object representation might therefore be associated with the need for proximal interactions to serve these functions and may lead to the depression, helplessness, or feelings of inefficacy that occur in bereavement or sensory deprivation (Blatt 1974; Freud 1917; Klein 1934).

Because of this impairment in representation, individuals experiencing depression struggle to maintain contact with other people who might gratify their needs. Depression can be expressed in the need to maintain direct, physical, sensory need-gratifying contact with another or in the need to win the love of others through achievement. Because of the failure to establish adequate levels of representation, depressed individuals' sense of well-being depends on someone else actually fulfilling their needs. Lacking the internalized capacity to provide for themselves the satisfactions derived from these relationships, they also lack a sense of efficacy. Additionally, individuals may suffer with feelings of inefficacy because they have internalized certain negative aspects of the care giver's character. For example, internalization of the attitudes of a mother who feels inadequate may lead to similar feelings in the child.

The relations between efficacy and the complexity of the mental representations of important others have been studied in both nonclinical and clinical samples. Blatt et al. (1979) studied the relations among depression, efficacy, and impairments in the development of mental representations. Parental descriptions, the Depressive Experiences Questionnaire, and the Zung Self-Rating Scale (1965) for depression were collected from college students. Using the system for scoring parental descriptions described earlier, the researchers obtained the conceptual level of parental representations for each subject. Conceptual level reflects the degree of differentiation, complexity, and integration in descriptions ranging from sensorimotor-preoperational to concrete-perceptual to external iconic to internal iconic to conceptual. As hypothesized, higher conceptual levels of parental representations were associated both with lower levels of depression as measured by the Zung and with higher scores on perceived efficacy as measured by the DEQ, supporting the hypothesis that the complexity of internalized need-gratifying relationships is related to a sense of efficacy.

In a study by Blatt and Marcus (in preparation) the relations between particular features of responses depicting human forms on the Rorschach and efficacy as measured by the DEQ were explored in a group of twenty-nine adolescents and young adults hospitalized in a long-term inpatient treatment facility. Ratings of perceived efficacy were significantly correlated with the degree to which full human figures are seen on the Rorschach as accurately perceived, well articulated, and engaged in appropriate and constructive actions and interactions.

Taken together, these studies suggest that the capacity to represent humans in complex and integrated ways and to maintain complex and diversified representations of parents is associated with a sense of perceived efficacy and relatively lower levels of depression. These data affirm the formulation that the development of enduring internalized representations of need-gratifying others is a necessity for psychological well-being.

SUMMARY

The main points of this chapter may be summarized as follows: (1) Interpersonal relationships form the foundation for the individual's development of a sense of self and perceived efficacy. (2) In the early relationship with care givers, infants come to know themselves by being given the opportunity to experience their unique impulses and sensations and being encouraged to express themselves spontaneously. (3) The mother's caring and understanding responses instill in the infant the sense that his or her actions are understandable by others and that they have an impact on the other's responses. Out of these experiences emerge the initial perceptions of self as efficacious. (4) The physiological regulations that take place between mother and infant allow the infant to achieve equilibrium and stability; a sense of efficacy derives from the infant's facilitation of the mother's ability to satisfy the child's physiological needs. (5) Parallel to the processes that occur during these physiological regulations, feelings of efficacy derive also from experiences of affective attunement between mother and infant. (6) Physiological and psychological regulation lead to feelings of order and control that guard against experiences of helplessness, anxiety, and perceived inefficacy. (7) Over the course of development, internalized aspects of the care-giving relationship allow individuals to increasingly assume the functions originally provided by the care giver. Although relationships are essential throughout life, one's sense of efficacy is enhanced by being able to achieve self-regulation. (8) The experience of efficacy in self-regulation generalizes to the feeling that one will be efficacious in other endeavors. (9) Impairments in the capacity to maintain physiological/psychological homeostasis because of undependable relationships and/or internalizations have a variety of consequences including an impaired sense of self and perceived efficacy. (10) Feelings of inefficacy may result in (a) attempts to use "action" to compensate for a clear and confident sense of who one "is," (b) experiences of depression centered around a sense of failure in relatedness and/or self-definition, and (c) the development of various types of compensatory mechanisms to cope with these developmental disturbances.

CHAPTER 11

Success and Success Inhibition

DAVID W. KRUEGER

This chapter concerns some developmental and psychodynamic issues that can facilitate or impede ambition and effectiveness or competence. The discussion is offered as a step in an evolving understanding of the many dynamic forces that impinge on the individual's unique developmental process. My focus is on internal factors, although I recognize that many external forces—biological, social, and environmental, among others—are components of the matrix that is incorporated internally.

The chapter explores the most basic human motivation—effectiveness—and influences impinging on it over developmental time, as well as some pathological manifestations of its arrested or conflicted development and some therapeutic implications. I stress the importance of developmental building blocks and unconscious motivation and the ways in which they affect or determine conscious processes and events. The motivation for mastery and the experience of effectiveness (or more broadly, competence) has been demonstrated as existing from earliest infancy (Beebe & Demos 1985; Emde 1983; Greenspan 1981; Krueger 1989; Lichtenberg 1985; White 1959, 1963) and extending throughout development in changing form.

My intrapsychic focus and developmentally informed perspective derives from my clinical work in psychotherapy and psychoanalysis, psychological and psychoanalytic developmental studies, and direct observational studies.

ON THE PSYCHOLOGY OF WORK

Childhood Play as a Precursor to Work

The relationship of play in childhood to later adult functioning is important. Play serves as the basis for developing interpersonal skills and the ability to interact with others socially as well as an internalized belief in mastery of tasks. Work has its origins in the efforts of early childhood: children learn, through play, mastery of themselves and their environment. Erikson (1964) emphasizes competence as a virtue developed in childhood which "characterizes what eventually becomes workmanship."

Children play for the conscious pleasure of it—because play is fun. In part, the fun lies in their experience of mastery. Thus Piaget (1965) called play "functional pleasure," and White (1963) said it is the "feeling of doing something, of being active or effective, of having an influence on something." Murphy (1962) observed different responses in children who, from birth, did things for themselves as opposed to having another do it. She observed that children's capacity to enjoy themselves and their activity was closely connected to a sense of triumph: "I can do it." The satisfying feeling of "bliss" in being the passive recipient of efforts by another is distinguished from the joy of triumph and mastery in oneself and one's activities—a satisfaction that is particularly associated with play and work. The experience of positive mastery and triumph is a gratifying exchange with one's environment, and leads to further eagerness and motivation to respond to the environment as well as to the optimistic expectation of future mastery.

One function of play can be found in the process of the mastery and management of anxiety through fantasy. Traumatic experiences of the past or present, anticipated traumas, and internal conflicts are reproduced in play. This attempt to master conflict or trauma in an active rather than passive way is the essence of a variety of coping styles. Sublimation and symbolization develop as the ego functions in part by the use of play as a developmental process of dealing with instinctual and affiliative needs. Fantasy and play act as safety valves that can spare more open conflict with people and the environment (Sarnoff 1976).

Play provides the opportunity for the child to develop mastery over a traumatic event by repeating the event until it becomes detoxified and mastered. A child, after returning from a visit to the doctor or the hospital, may play-act visiting the doctor until his or her anxiety is assuaged. Moreover, when abstract thinking is established, even an anticipatory mastery may be perfected through playing. Playing can also be used to repeat gratifying experiences for recapitulated enjoyment. Play, then, is a natural mechanism for mastering the child's world as well as anxiety-provoking experiences in everyday life.

If, however, the arena of playing is constricted by internal conflict or sex-role stereotypes, or because of parental pathology, later adult work might be compromised as well as the analogues of childhood play: mastery of the environment, a sense of competence, and the ability to cope with and manage stress, which solidifies ego strength.

Work Inhibition in Children and Adolescents

Work can satisfy a variety of psychological needs. Among the more important is its function in the consolidation of self-image and identity. It is a source of gratification and an expression of ambition and creativity. It expresses values and beliefs, fosters self-validation, serves defensive functions, and offers relief of guilt or escape from other life stresses (Nadelson & Notman 1981). Work can also be seen as a sublimation of aggressive impulses, as the product of the urge to mastery. Formulations about work must consider all types from many points of view.

The capacity to work involves more than simply symptom-free functioning for both adults and children. Although intrapsychic conflicts may compromise the capacity to play and work, the absence of such conflicts is not a sufficient factor for pleasurable and effective work and play for the adult (Sarnoff 1976).

Halpern (1964) has demonstrated the correlation between psychodynamic and cultural determinants of work inhibitions in children and adolescents and work inhibition in adults. Most often the symptom of work inhibition in children and adolescents is manifested in poor academic performance. Developmental arrest compromising autonomy and self-regulation may be a precursor to work inhibition in adults. The success of childhood work life is related to the degree of separateness and individuality in the development of the child as distinct intrapsychically from his or her parents. The increasing exploration, the triumph of skill, the demand for privacy, and the selection of goals are components of this individuation and the child's sense of separateness from parents.

If one or both parents are excessively controlling and center activity around themselves and their needs, however, the child must either comply or use extreme measures to attain distinctness. These children may experience their parents as overinvolved in a controlling way, as if the parents were threatened by their children's separateness. The children may then refuse to achieve in school or work in an attempt to define a boundary between themselves and their parents; it may be the only way they can carve out their own area of autonomy. These children make an irrefutable statement to their parents that they are not an extension of them or their desires. In extreme cases, a child may feel that almost every accomplishment is in the service of his or her parents. Thus, inhibition of achievement (or other behaviors that are negativistic and self-defeating) is the result of the child's adaptive attempt to be autonomous.

Emotional separation is a further prerequisite to developing the capacity to make independent decisions about oneself and one's future, as well as establishing intimate relationships with others. A gradual, stepwise, and phase-appropriate diminution of the parents' involvement with the child is concomitant with an increase in the child's autonomy. When parents react to the child's natural moves toward independence as though the child were abandoning or competing with them, the child may feel insecure about normal growth processes and experience extreme or pathological levels of separation anxiety. One symptom of separation anxiety is school phobia. This anxiety may be manifested as an upset stomach or some other illness which abates only when the child and mother are reunited. But the child's avoidance of school to ward off anxiety at leaving the mother is only part of the problem; the other part is the mother who disallows autonomy and exerts a subtle, often conscious, regressive pull on the child in an effort to deal with her own anxiety.

Ideals and Identification

The answer to the question "What is successful work?" is as unique as each person. Generally speaking, there are several kinds of success in life. One lies in the development of warm and intimate relationships with both men and women. Another involves the development of skill and/or professional expertise. Yet another kind of success is productivity in the home as a parent.

For example, parents may want their daughters to be independent and successful, yet may unwittingly give them signals to the contrary, emphasizing from an early age the importance of marrying and pleasing a husband. If the child manifests expansiveness and potency, the parents may see them as destructive forces. To respond, rather than initiate, may be deemed more appropriate by the parents. One young woman who came for treatment was soon to graduate with a business degree. She was in a great deal of anguish about her ambivalence in wanting to be independent and have a career, yet fearing to leave home and function autonomously. Because she had not finished a final project required for her degree, she might have to postpone graduating. Although her parents apparently encouraged her and were proud of her accomplishments, they also indicated that "of course, if you can't make it or find a job, you can always stay here and we'll take care of you." This young woman did not have the benefit of parents who encouraged her autonomy.

Certain personality traits are often regarded as gender-linked, some affecting only men, others only women. The stereotypic limitations on ambition in women have their counterpart in constrictions on sensitivity, emotional expression, and empathy in men. In families where it is not unmasculine for a boy or man to develop and express warmth, tenderness, and emotion, however, femininity is also not at stake with the development of ambition in a girl or woman (Krueger 1984).

The family background of a man is related to his attitudes toward women as well. To the degree that the gender-linkage of traits has been previously established, a man may have difficulty accepting, acknowledging, and supporting a woman's ambition. When threatened by a woman's assertiveness and quest for independence, he may react with defensiveness: withdrawal, criticism, aggressiveness, or depreciation of her desirability as a sexual partner.

Gender-linkage of personality traits by a family (or later, a therapist) disallows empathic understanding of each individual's personal goals (Krueger 1984). The ability to recognize the individual's point of view and the flexibility psychologically to perceive a wide range of viewpoints and ideals are important to escape gender stereotypes. Individual goals outside stereotypic domains can then be pursued more freely—for example, by the woman who desires to pursue a military career rather than become a successful mother.

ACHIEVEMENT INHIBITION

I will summarize in this section from my earlier work *Success and the Fear of Success in Women* (1984) aspects of the ways in which fear of ambition and achievement is presented clinically.

Success and achievement, in whatever context they are defined, are the fullest expression of mastery. Mastery is a broad concept, referring to a functional synthesis of intrapsychic sublimation and organization with external goal-oriented tasks. The failure of any of the components of internal or external mastery, or of successfully and appropriately coupling the two, can result in failure of achievement.

Someone who has success inhibition may work diligently while success or a completed achievement seems to be at a safe distance, but as the goal is approached he or she may become anxious and sabotage efforts at successfully achieving the goal or, just after achieving it, may depreciate it or fail to enjoy it. The manifestations of success inhibition represent a common outcome of different developmental difficulties. There is, however, no reliable relationship between a certain manifestation of success phobia and a specific underlying pathology.

Avoidance of Completions

The final step to accomplishment may be phobically avoided. Anxiety may reach a crescendo just before the culmination of a task, only to be calmed by a withdrawal from the final completion. The graduate student may lack a few lines on the last paragraph of a Ph.D. dissertation and decide to abandon it or become an interminable or perpetual student, thereby postponing success. One may fear to be discovered as a phony when taking final examinations. More may be planned than can possibly be achieved, in order to forestall completion and success.

The path to success may be barred early, before success can possibly be achieved. The student may forget to register or take an entrance exam. A job applicant may come late or antagonize an interviewer. The fear of success may also be whispered in the everyday "choke" or "clutch" situation: becoming so anxious on examinations that function is impaired, for example, or being unable to polish off an opponent at tennis. Major developmental achievements, such as taking an important position, getting promoted, graduating, or even marrying may often be sabotaged at the final step. Most often these conflicts represent unconscious issues, which are incomprehensible intellectually. That they are unconscious, emotional, and often seemingly illogical explains why self-help books or intellectual explanations are frustratingly inadequate.

As long as there is no appreciable success, one can work toward a goal relatively unambivalently. If and when success becomes imminent, anxiety manifests itself and the near-success is replaced with a mandate to avoid it. Feeling oneself to be the object of criticism or inadequate to live up to expectations, one may then abandon a long-cherished goal and perhaps substitute alternate goals. To recognize this success inhibition one may have to recognize it as a fear of failing, or a fear of rejection or humiliation. One man indicated that he had never reached his full capacity because he had never stayed with a company as consultant for more than eighteen months. As soon as he was on a job for that length of time, he began feeling anxious: people around him had witnessed his total expertise, he thought, and he no longer had anything to teach them. He became preoccupied with the fear that his "incapability and inadequacy" would become evident. He would then begin to feel he was the subject of criticism and increased scrutiny, since he was not absolutely certain he knew more than anyone working with him. His failure internally to acknowledge his expertise propelled him continually to avoid any anticipated exposure of inadequacy.

A related type of inhibition exists in individuals who can never allow themselves to function at fullest capacity. These individuals protect themselves from fear of criticism or of failing with a built-in excuse: "If I had really given it my all, I would have succeeded." The fear of making a mistake may further create inhibitions based on the expectation of criticism for any performance that is perceived as less than perfect. The narcissistic individual who requires constant or immediate feedback or applause may also find completion of successful endeavors difficult. Sustained effort is often stalled without external admiration on an ongoing basis.

A characterological resolution to this conflict about success may be the belief that staying in the background guarantees safety; one will not then reveal supposed inadequacies. The fear of being discovered to be an impostor or of having bluffed one's way along is a common element in success phobia. The person reasons that with greater success will come a potentially harder fall. Being viewed by others as highly competent often is coupled with the internal feeling of being incompetent, inadequate, or an impostor. The rationalized lowering of one's ambition is the stepping back from the anxiety-provoking success situations. With this step backward, however, may come depression in reaction to the loss of one's goals in conjunction with the loss of self-esteem.

Erosion of Successful Accomplishment

Some well-known characters in literature unexpectedly fall ill just when a deeply rooted wish comes to fulfillment, as if they could not endure their own success. Shakespeare's Lady Macbeth and Ibsen's Rebecca West suffer grave illnesses almost immediately following the knowledge that a major wish fulfillment is actually at hand; in this way they destroy all enjoyment of their success.

Self-defeating behavior may erode performance, motivation, or completion of a task. Money, prestige, or achievement may be destroyed or depreciated. The sabotage of work-related efforts may manifest itself in efforts to sabotage the work itself: making errors, having accidents, being chronically late, procrastinating. A self-defeating attitude was exemplified by the patient who stated, "Whenever I do something really well and someone acknowledges or compliments me, I have to point out something that is not good—a criticism or flaw. It has the quality of undoing whatever I do." Another woman stated, "If I get a compliment about how I look, I think to myself, 'Well, if you saw me without my makeup, you wouldn't think I was so pretty.'" Whenever she looked in the mirror, rather than seeing what was actually a model's face featured in cosmetics advertisements, she focused entirely on her one "flaw"—an almost imperceptible freckle. Her feelings about herself were negative, despite ample contrary evidence. She disallowed any intimate relationships because she feared that eventually she would be rejected when someone found out what she was really like. Presupposing an eventual rejection, she engineered many.

A promotion or advancement may be met with depression or anxiety, which may be disruptive enough to prevent maximum or even adequate functioning in the new job. Some people have experienced major depressions in response to a significant corporate advancement.

Success can be downplayed through several defensive maneuvers. The accomplishment may be disavowed, attributed to an "accident," "luck," or "circumstances" rather than to motivation and work. The individual may convince herself that she fooled anyone who feels she is really intelligent. One woman felt that she was mistakenly admitted to medical school because of an error by the admissions committee.

A fear of failure is the opposite side of the same coin: it is a rationalized fear of success, made consciously understandable. Almost all the people whom I have seen with some form of success inhibition have tried to explain (to themselves) their difficulty on this basis. The consequences are identical: to avoid completion of an effort, to retreat from competition and divert success, or, upon successful completion of a task, to withdraw, depreciate, or erode the accomplishment. The diversion from success may even give the appearance of indolence or laziness.

Ambition without Goal-Setting

One way people may avoid success is by not setting goals or by establishing goals that are vague or undefined. This strategy ensures that goals will never be reached, thereby avoiding the assumed consequences of success. Or a person may profess a belief in luck and destiny to disavow pursuit of goal-directed accomplishment. A patient stated, "If I do something well, it's because of luck or it just happened, and if I fail at something, it's my fault." This inconsistency characterizes the dilemma caused by an internal inhibition to success. A belief in predetermination, fate, or God's will may be the rationalized disavowal of one's own efforts to achieve. This cover for responsibility for one's efforts and goals disparages recognition of accomplishment and the full enjoyment of mastery.

Another way of avoiding success is to set more goals than one can possibly accomplish, thereby ensuring that none will be reached or successfully completed. Often ambitious feelings can be very intense, yet coupled with goals passively achieved. For example, after achieving a highly specialized or technical degree and skill, one may hope to be pursued and "discovered" by an employer in order to receive the perfect position. After obtaining a specialized degree in the science field, one young woman told of her fantasy that potential employers would find out about her skills and accomplishments and tailor-make a job for her. Her failure to take realistic steps to acquaint potential employers with her expertise left her disappointed when nothing happened.

This combination of ambition coupled with passivity is an example of how ambition can remain unfulfilled when conscious and unconscious goals oppose one another. Grandiose goals and expectations of achievement, even a sense that one is entitled to achieve, reflect the magical thinking of early childhood in which one becomes a prince or princess overnight, movie stars are discovered at the corner drugstore, and the four-year-old is thrust into a bases-loaded, bottom-of-the-ninth batting position to hit a home run and win the series.

With an understanding of the various clinical manifestations of success inhibition, we can now trace their origins in specific developmental phases.

DEVELOPMENTAL STAGES OF EFFECTIVENESS

An important question in looking at internal issues is that of developmental diagnosis, which asks the question: where in developmental time is the nucleus of the current arrest or conflict? It is imperative as a therapist to understand the developmental issues with which the patient is struggling in order to be able empathically to understand the level, intensity, and content of conflicts that preclude the realization of one's full potential, whether for internal comfort, happiness, relatedness with others, sense of self, or successful achievement.

Separation-Individuation Origins

The individuals with earliest developmental conflict unconsciously equate success with creating a breach in a dyadic bond with the mother. An anticipation of retaliation from the mother in earliest childhood becomes a fear of severance of the relationship and of abandonment by her. With individuals whose conflicts are in this developmental area, success reverberates with the first steps to autonomy and independence which occur in the separation-individuation phase between two and three years of age. If there have been difficulties in this phase of development, there is extreme anxiety associated with steps toward autonomy, the loss of the child's belief in omnipotence, and concern about the emotional availability of the parents.

Following the achievement of success, an individual may feel depressed and depleted, and retreat into a withdrawn state. Success is unconsciously equated at one level with the withdrawal of the mother, who leaves if success and autonomy are achieved. Historically, the mother, unable to accept loss of the child, dissuades her or him from taking a step toward self-sufficiency by threatening emotional separation. When the resultant state of aloneness and abandonment is experienced, a rapprochement with the mother is effected, and the mother is once more warm and responsive. In addition, the child may experience a fear of becoming angry, which would destroy the continuity of the relationship with the mother, since anger poses an even greater threat of the mother's retaliatory abandonment.

In extreme cases, parents can criticize and belittle the child's attempts at mastery and acquisition of skills and thus cripple his or her crucial development of both mastery and self-expression. The environment then becomes a source of terror. Being afraid of various aspects of living—being afraid to drive, swim, or succeed in a vocational endeavor—may create such a need for adjustment to them that much of the joy of living is lost.

Origins in Pathological Narcissism

A particular type of work inhibition is produced in someone with narcissistic tendencies who is preoccupied with the risk of failure. Any performance includes the possibility of making a mistake, which is equated with being flawed. Situations in which these individuals are not certain they can succeed, and succeed from the outset, are avoided. Unrealistically high expectations and ambitions are coupled with self-reproach, sometimes bitter, for failing to live up to these standards. These individuals may pursue ambitions up to a certain point, only to back down just before the moment of real testing. They may withdraw an application to a prestigious school just before being "turned down," or fail to complete papers or dissertations, or not take examinations. Most often, a sudden and puzzling disappearance of interest occurs in what had seemed to be an engrossing pursuit.

The interest of such individuals in their chosen endeavors seems to be characterized more by ideas of some narcissistic gain—having an illustrious career or being admired—than by the satisfaction of functioning in the job itself. They therefore view their difficulties as evidence of some grievous basic defect in their makeup which they feel powerless to remedy. They may also resent any discomfort, such as experiencing difficulties in a task, and respond with rage, feeling that something unfair is occurring. Any difficulty or discomfort particularly undermines their motivation for attempting to surmount their difficulties, because they feel more or less consciously that they should not be expected to put up with such problems. They appeal to fate, await outside intervention, or seek tricks that will make the difficulty disappear. When magic is not effective, and when others do not respond in exactly the desired way—almost as an extension of the individual—a narcissistic rage may follow.

These individuals may come to treatment full of doubts about their capacity, convinced that they lack some central feature necessary for success. In academic life or in work, they feel they have fooled people or gained positions fraudulently.

Oedipal Origins

A seed is planted in childhood for a particular view of competitiveness and work with others. This seed—the oedipal situation—is present in everyone. But only in a soil of parental pathology and climate of failed empathic attunement will it grow to become a conflictual issue and express itself in inhibitions. The conditions may be provided by the mother, who may compete with her daughter, feeling threatened by the girl's capability or attractiveness; or the father may respond in a somewhat seductive manner, making the actualization of the wish to attract him dangerously close, necessitating an anxiety-laden retreat. The father may feel competitive himself, if his sense of manliness is threatened by the emerging competence of his young daughter or son. Alienation between parents such that the child can win the parent of the opposite sex away from the other parent by taking sides intensifies the oedipal dilemma. This situation may arise when one or both parents are narcissistic, when attempts at individuation are stifled by parents, or when a parent is psychologically or physically absent through death, divorce, or prolonged separation.

Physical intimidation by parents or siblings reinforces the unconscious equation of success with aggression. The desire, usually unconscious, for victory over a powerful rival or intimidator generates both guilt and the fear of an equally violent retaliation. The result is an inhibition or withholding of aggression. The inhibition of aggression may then be generalized to assertion. Or, if success is achieved, guilt may require suffering or some penance, thus initiating masochistic or self-sabotaging efforts. A further step in the generalization of this conflict is that any subsequent competition, identified unconsciously with the original rivalry of childhood, is inhibited. Inhibition of aggression undermines self-confidence, esteem, and effectiveness, and may result in a chronic sense of inadequacy.

Assertion becomes unconsciously equated with success, and may be defended by a passivity in which the object of success-striving is abandoned, distorted, or substituted. The basic wish is not to fail, but failing before a final step of success may be equated unconsciously with passivity and safety; thus one is spared the dangerous consequences of self-assertion. The central conflict is the fear to be and to act as a full-fledged man or woman, because the powerful parent of the same sex is seen as a prohibitive threatening force. The later derivative, success-related anxiety may entail expectation of catastrophe if one is self-assertive. The final step to the successful completion of a task, then, evokes the symptoms of anxiety by strong unconscious forces, and anxiety ultimately gains control. Fear and guilt are thus incurred, not because of inferior ability, but because of an assumption that superior performance would result in in a "taboo" victory. Performance must then be sabotaged directly or, if the performance is completed, depreciated as inconsequential. Failure, the result of such rationalization, is caused not by innate ability but by an inhibition by fear, since success is unconsciously perceived as aggressive and competitive. A whisper of this fear of success can be found in one's difficulty accepting either the outcome or the significance of performance.

An intrinsic resolution of dealing with aggression, if aggression does not fit one's ideal or is enmeshed with conflict, is to defend against the aggression by seeing oneself as inadequate or ineffective. This defensive position becomes a basic assumption which is then enacted to confirm and validate a supposed sense of inadequacy.

A common perception of the assertiveness often required for successful achievement is that when one person succeeds another fails or is beaten. This may be the predominant conflict for some individuals, when a major component of one's ideal is that of being caring and giving to others. When enmeshed in oedipal conflict, the thrill of victory assumes the defeat of an opponent. One woman attorney put it succinctly: "Childhood seemed like a series of win-or-lose situations. It always seemed that if I would win, someone else would lose or suffer. It wasn't necessarily physical warfare, but a series of win-or-lose situations of bitter sarcasm to reduce myself or others to tears. I realize that when I win in a legal situation in court now, I feel bad and pity the opponent." Thus the thrill of success is leavened by an imagined opponent's agony of defeat. A legitimate arena for the enactment of this conflict was found in the woman's choice of a legal career.

A promotion involving money, status, or other success may be unconsciously tantamount to an oedipal victory. If the success is heir to a significant unresolved oedipal conflict, the unwelcome accompaniment may be guilt about competence and a fear of retaliation ("losing everything I've gained"; "paying for it in other ways") or of abandonment ("being envied but all alone with my success"). To ensure safety from such unconscious expectations, the desired goal may be relinquished. Accompanying that surrender may be the erosion of a self-image of competence and assuredness.

The opposite side of the same coin of developmental arrest or conflict is driven, compulsive work. Since its manifestation is so different, it will be described separately.

WORK COMPULSIONS

Work compulsion, closely related to work inhibition, manifests as its opposite. The work addict, or workaholic, is incessantly driven, relentlessly active. Inactivity or any activity other than work engenders guilt or anxiety about inadequacy and self-worth. The compulsion to work acts as a defense against such underlying concerns as inadequacy, guilt, invalidation, and worthlessness.

Like the mythical Sisyphus, who endlessly pushed a huge rock to the top of a hill, only to have it roll down again, the person with work compulsion cannot rest. Work that is passionate, long, and hard, and that brings satisfaction is not the same as work addiction. It is only when the person cannot do without work to maintain comfort or a sense of worth that he or she is addicted.

In a psychoanalytic study of work compulsion, Kramer (1977) describes its underlying patterns which include impostorous feelings, struggles in relation to authority figures, a need for recognition and fame, and a continuing sense of inadequacy. Work can become a means to withdraw from relationships, to manipulate relationships by limiting one's availability, or to moderate relationships that are overstimulating sexually or aggressively. The wish for admiration is a profound underpinning for many work compulsions. Immersion in work may be a compulsive attempt to reverse feelings of diminished self-esteem. Enslaved by the drive to prove oneself powerful and adequate, the individual constantly turns his or her attention and energy to new sources of attainment, acquisition, and relentless striving. Even when seeming to attain what is most sought after, the compulsive worker is still dissatisfied.

If confirmation and approval by admiring parents in response to the child's achievements were not part of his or her experience, the child may acquire an intense, driven ambition to get approval and admiration from as many sources and in as great a quantity as possible. This unrelenting ambition, the driven need for approval and validation, is the basis for some work compulsions. Even remarkable successes are not permanently gratifying. Each accomplishment may be followed by a letdown or depression, as if the goal were the pursuit of more challenge rather than an accomplishment itself. When the goal is completed, excitement diminishes quickly. As soon as the echoes of the applause die, the person feels empty and seeks new sources of external admiration through accomplishment.

For the individual with narcissistic pathology, work may become a central organizer, a means to self-validation. One woman described the meaning of work to her: "My work reassures me. When I feel overwhelmed, I turn to my work, which I know well, and I feel calmed. I became an achiever because it's something I could do that would exist in time and space and become objectively real. It gives me pats on the back." She further described how she used work for continuity and stability; when there was any disruption in her life, she became even more immersed in work to reestablish internal order. She didn't remember her parents ever holding her or calming her. When she became upset as a child, she would retreat to her room furiously to engage in (what was to her, then) work.

Very few of these individuals may be seen in treatment, however, as they are often considered successful by themselves and others, and receive substantial gain from their achievement—as long as accomplishment is on an ascending scale. When a goal is reached, it is often experienced as a kind of deprivation: love can no longer be earned by performing well. So reaching a desired goal is not actually satisfying. Reaching a goal, much like leisure time or vacations, only adds to the feeling of unworthiness, nonproductivity, and guilt. The personal tragedy of a successful, hardworking, and aggressive person of this type is the unremitting drive to escape from even the mere perception of guilt or inadequacy. There must always be a challenge and a conquest. The basic scenario perpetuates itself, unless examined therapeutically, throughout life. Although the names of the characters change, the same psyche is writing the script with its recurrent themes.

C H A P T E R 1 2

Perceived Fraudulence as a Dimension of Perceived Incompetence

J O H N K O L L I G I A N, J R.

In his Norton Lectures, Lionel Trilling (1971) inadvertently makes reference to the experience of perceived fraudulence when he discusses historically the cognate ideals of sincerity and authenticity and observes that the cultural awareness of the "inauthenticity of human experience" is a recent and contemporary phenomenon. Trilling underscores its importance when he suggests that sincerity involves the effort of being honest and loyal for the purpose of avoiding falseness to others, whereas authenticity refers to the process of knowing and making "genuineness" judgments about one's own self as an end in itself. In this spirit, perceived fraudulence, or impostorous thoughts and feelings, seems recently to have been rediscovered and documented in the personality literature as a real psychological experience of individuals, an experience with usually distressing and often maladaptive consequences (e.g., Clance & Imes 1978; Gediman 1985; Harvey & Katz 1985; Kolligian & Sternberg 1989). That is, buried in the hearts and minds of many high-achieving individuals is the private sense of being an impostor or a fraud.

For instance, Clance and Imes (1978) coined the term *impostor phenomenon* to describe an internal experience of intellectual phoniness that ap-

I am indebted to Julie B. Sincoff for many stimulating conversations that greatly helped in the formulation and preparation of this chapter, as well as for her many insightful comments on earlier drafts. I am grateful to Robert J. Sternberg for his important contributions to the work presented here and his helpful comments on an earlier draft. I also would like to thank Edward Zigler and Jerome L. Singer for their thoughtful suggestions and careful reading of an earlier draft.

pears especially prevalent and intense among certain high-achieving adults. Alternatively, Gediman (1985, 1986) believes the concept of perceived imposture or authenticity should be viewed in the context of a continuum or spectrum: at one extreme is the "true" impostor who assumes multiple false identities in order to deceive deliberately and, at the other, is the self-perceived impostor who tends to feel fraudulent and inauthentic when, to the objective observer, he or she is not. Thus, both extremes encompass self-perceptions; the continuum is the underlying "reality" upon which these perceptions are based.

Conrad (1975), similarly, distinguishes between the extremes of this continuum by outlining the "neurotic" and "delinquent" impostors. The neurotic impostor is one who *feels* like an impostor, but by most objective accounts is not; the person may be a physician, lawyer, or the head of an organization, but feels that he or she is fooling everyone. In contrast, the delinquent, or true, impostor attains status by assuming false identities, by lying, stealing, or pretending to have achieved something that he or she has not achieved. Conrad considers the person who feels like an impostor to have essentially the same syndrome as the impostor who actually assumes a false identity. In reviewing a case, Conrad implies that specialness, perceived atypicality, and the use of flattery, charm, or personality all play major roles in the interpersonal operations of both forms of imposture (see Gottdiener 1982).

This chapter takes a new look at the notion of perceived fraudulence by viewing it as a particular manifestation of perceived incompetence. Perceived incompetence—a term that will be used interchangeably with low perceived competence—refers to an individual's negative perceptions or low ability judgments of self that are, at least in part, inaccurate. Perceived fraudulence here will be embedded in the context of the phenomenologically more generalized experience of perceived incompetence. A central point is that authenticity concerns and fraudulent ideation in a variety of domains represent important, yet often overlooked and understudied, aspects of individuals' more general self-referential perceptions and judgments of competence.

THE EXPERIENCE OF PERCEIVED FRAUDULENCE

Historical Perspectives

The phenomenon of imposture is not without its historical and conceptual antecedents in psychoanalytic theorizing and writing over the course of the century. Interestingly, the literature has documented a small number of clinical case studies of impostors—instances of the phenomenon of a real impostor or a liar. The purpose of these clinical investigations has been to understand the intrapsychic dynamics that incline an individual toward making overt falsifications or highly implausible claims about his or her identity, status, position, and accomplishments (Chasseguet-Smirgel 1985; Finkelstein 1974; Greenacre 1958a). Although these writings focus on the personality of the deliberately deceiving individual, they lay the clinical foundations for, and suggest some common features to, investigations into a related personality style or subjective experience characterized by an individual's self-perception of fraudulence in the absence of objective evidence.

Several interrelated characteristics or personality tendencies emerge from a brief review of the case studies of real impostors. They incline to mimicry and imitating gestures, excessive use of charm, and exaggerations—leading to their self-enhancement, perfectionistic ideation, and acute audience sensitivity. For instance, Greenacre (1958a, 1958b) outlined a detailed portrait of impostors' mental functioning and development, highlighting their problems of identity and pathological narcissism. In addition, she focused on three sets of symptom constellations: the persistence of family romance fantasies; a disturbed sense of reality and identity—i.e., a clear impostorous role and a poorly defined identity; and a lack of principles around the use of reality testing and normally introjected or internalized values. Greenacre also suggests that these symptom constellations contribute to the development of an early underlying cause of the impostor's narcissistic problem—parents' admiration of his or her heightened use of mimicry and gestures in imitating adult behaviors. These parents showed great interest in the way in which their child copied adult behaviors and language, and Greenacre implies that this interest may have, in part, reinforced later impostorous behaviors. Finkelstein (1974) also underscores the necessity of considerable talents for acting and mimicry in order to deceive one's audience effectively, although it is acknowledged that there is much evidence suggesting that such abilities are also characteristic of socially competent individuals (e.g., Levine & Redlich 1960; Zigler, Levine, & Gould 1967).

Related to their polished acting abilities is the impostors' excessive use of ingratiating personality and charm in their interactions with others. For instance, in one of the earliest clinical papers on impostors, Abraham (1925) reported his encounters with an impostor who had an uncanny ability to seduce, captivate, and eventually manipulate people for his own purposes—not unlike many reports of the "charming" psychopath. Finkelstein (1974) commented that the impostor is usually successful, at least for a while, in charming an audience into believing the veracity of most of his or her deceptions.

Many clinical writers have focused on the characterological basis of this seduction by outlining those tendencies that may motivate an individual to lie and deceive others about his or her identity. Finkelstein (1974) and Deutsch (1955) believe that impostorous tendencies derive from needs for narcissistic self-enhancement in defense against feelings of worthlessness, emptiness, and defectiveness. The discrepancy between the person one is supposed to be and the person one actually is becomes too vast to reconcile. Thus, the impostor assumes completely false identities because he must hide from himself and from everyone else the inadequacies of his actual self. In a sense, the antics and behaviors of the real impostor may be viewed as a form of decompensation or a defense against psychological disturbances ranging from self-critical feelings to severe depression (Blatt 1974; Blatt & Shichman 1983; Zigler & Glick 1984, 1988).

Another common characteristic of real impostors is that of perfectionistic tendencies. In a case presentation, Finkelstein (1974) discussed the importance of parental expectations in encouraging perfectionistic appearances and strivings. Indeed, the struggle to present oneself in a particular manner requires a high degree of skill, self-monitoring, and perfectionism. For instance, Kaplan (1984) discusses imposture as an adolescent experience in males[1] whose development parallels eating disorders in females: adolescent boys set out to prove themselves not through a method of self-starvation but through a "pursuit of perfection." Accordingly, Kaplan believes the male impostor is a person who assumes a false identity for the sole purpose of deceiving others; imposture flourishes during the closing stages of puberty as the young man attempts to reconcile the inadequate person he supposes himself to be with the exalted masculine ideal conveyed to him during childhood. The male impostor knows that he is not the person he pretends to be, but he feels that he must be some person greater or more magnificent than are the ordinary mortals he sets out to deceive. Thus, his shaky identity is held together by the false images he imposes on his audience.

By focusing on the audience—fooling authorities and thereby expos-

1. It should be noted that although Kaplan (1984) acknowledges the existence of different forms and varying degrees of imposture, she believes that all "full-fledged impostors" are male.

ing their weaknesses—impostors draw attention away from themselves and onto the imperfections of others. Accordingly, a fourth feature of real impostors is their acute awareness of their audience; this awareness, of course, may vary in intensity from mild audience anxiety to more severe paranoid ideation (Gediman 1985; Meissner 1978). Indeed, impostors' sensitivity to the "art of illusion"—particularly with respect to their ability to discover what their audience is ready and eager to believe—distinguishes them from the ordinary braggart who offends an audience by a disregard for its feelings (Finkelstein 1974). More recently, Gottdiener (1982) viewed the phenomenology of the impostor from a social or "interpersonal" perspective. Imposture is seen as a result of the influence of collusive partners on an individual; impostors are masters of flattery and of appearing empathetic, especially when such qualities impress their audiences (Gediman 1985). Indeed, Greenacre (1958a) goes so far as to suggest that fraudulent individuals were successful only because many others were inclined to believe in their authenticity. In sum, this overview highlights several common, narcissistic themes in the phenomenon of real imposture—early mimicry skills, charm, exaggeration and self-enhancement, perfectionism, and audience awareness. Interestingly, variations on these themes also seem to play a role in recent conceptualizations of perceived fraudulence.

Perceived Fraudulence: A Review of Recent Research

Clance and Imes (1978) first identified the impostor phenomenon as a prevalent experience among high-achieving women—viewing the self-perpetuating nature of perceived fraudulence in terms of sex differences in the attribution process. They concluded that, unlike men, who are more likely to view success as attributable to a quality inherent in themselves, women are more likely to project the source of success outward to an external cause (e.g., luck) or to a temporary internal quality (e.g., effort), a source they do not equate with inherent ability.

Clance and Imes also observed several types of behavior that tend to maintain perceived fraudulence. Individuals may express extreme diligence and high levels of effort in their pursuits, making it relatively easy for them to attribute their success to the fact that they worked so hard; they may also actually engage in minor intellectual inauthenticity (e.g., by choosing at times not to reveal their real ideas or opinions) or use their charm and perceptiveness to win the approval of superiors. Although this investigation is important in that it highlights the self-deprecating way in which some individuals actually make attributions about their abilities and competencies, its labeling of perceived fraudulence as an exclusively female experience is questionable, for it relied entirely on unstructured personal interviews as a method of data collection and remains highly speculative and anecdotal on the specific causal mechanisms of the experience.

In the first empirical investigation of perceived fraudulence, Imes (1979) examined its relationship to sex-role orientation in high-achieving men and women. She hypothesized that subjects high in fraudulent self-perceptions would (1) frequently attribute success to luck, (2) be highly sensitive to others' expectations of them, (3) be perceived as being well-liked by others, and (4) give impressions of possessing strong intellectual ability. Imes found that a close relationship exists between these four fraudulence-related dimensions and subjects high in femininity and androgyny. These results, then, were consistent with Clance and Imes's (1978) previous suggestion that perceived fraudulence tends to be a female experience. It is noteworthy that, although Imes combined four features into a composite "impostor" variable, she did not independently assess whether subjects high on her composite are more inclined to feel fraudulent than are those low on her composite. Thus, this impostor variable raises serious questions about whether Imes's study is actually perceived fraudulence or simply a study of certain attributional and interpersonal styles that are presumed to be fraudulence-related.

In a doctoral dissertation, Harvey (1981) developed and cross-validated a fourteen-item Impostor Phenomenon Scale (IPS). Using the IPS with an extreme-groups procedure, Harvey found that high-achieving students reporting high levels of fraudulent feelings on her scale attributed significantly more of their scholastic successes to their interpersonal assets (e.g., charm, personal appeal) than did those scoring low on her scale, a pattern consistent with the previous theoretical formulations of Clance and Imes. She also found marginally significant correlations between perceived fraudulence scores and high self-monitoring and low self-esteem. The construct validity of the IPS, however, remains questionable and in need of further empirical investigation. For instance, Edwards et al. (1987) found an undesirably low level of internal reliability for the full-scale IPS (alpha = .34). Their results revealed that, when the IPS was factor-analyzed, the factor subscales (i.e., impostor, unworthiness, inadequacy) had considerably higher alpha scores than did the total scale. Finally, other studies have related the IPS as possessing, at best, moderate levels of internal reliability, with alpha coefficients in the .60s and .70s (Harvey 1981; Kolligian & Sternberg 1989).

Topping (1983) also attempted to establish the construct validity of the IPS. She administered it to university faculty members and found that men had a significantly higher mean IPS score than did women. This finding is contrary to the clinical formulation of Clance and Imes (1978), indicating that additional research is warranted to confirm the relationship between perceived fraudulence and gender. In addition, Topping found that perceived fraudulence was positively related to trait anxiety. She hypothesized that the relationship between the two may be due in part to a triggering of anxiety responses by recognition that one is creating a false impression and the perception that one is, therefore, at risk of being exposed as an impostor. Admittedly, it is also possible for anxiety to precede feelings of fraudulence, or for anxiety and fraudulent feelings to be correlates of a third common variable, such as actual deception or guilt over manipulation.

Finally, it should be noted that these researchers have adopted, for the most part, atheoretical conceptions with respect to the etiology and development of perceived fraudulence. Both Clance (1985) and Harvey (Harvey & Katz 1985) have written popular self-help books that discuss fraudulent self-perceptions in terms of a global personality phenomenon. The existing research studies offer little evidence in support of such a conceptualization of fraudulence. Indeed, it is noteworthy that the term *perceived fraudulence* more accurately captures the technical meaning of the experience than do other terms commonly used in the preceding studies—such as *impostor phenomenon* or *impostor syndrome*. These general terms seem to suggest that the experience should be viewed as a pervasive mental illness or global personality disorder—a position that does not seem to be supported in the literature.

TOWARD A CONCEPTUALIZATION OF PERCEIVED FRAUDULENCE

An Initial Conceptualization

My conceptualization is based on research I conducted in collaboration with Robert J. Sternberg. It is important to note that our conception of perceived fraudulence involves studying the experience as a normal personality trait, as opposed to a situationally induced feeling or thought. It is acknowledged, however, that the particulars of situations and the environments in which the fraudulent thoughts and feelings are evoked represent important constraints on the expression of the experience. Moreover, consistent with this conceptualization, perceived fraudulence is viewed not as a pervasive syndrome or phenomenon but as a specific self-perception, or self-referential ideation with both cognitive and affective components, that is best characterized in the context of a normative continuum of experienced intensity.

There are, no doubt, many possible paths through which perceived fraudulence may develop and then be expressed. But we can speculate that perceived fraudulence may evolve through (1) an initial defective or incompetent view of the self, (2) an intolerance for this defective or negative self, (3) a perceived need for maneuvers that protect the self against the negative thinking of self and others, leading to both fraudulent actions and self-perceptions, and (4) additional negative thoughts and feelings about the self—now because of both incompetence *and* fraudulence (Kohut 1971, 1977, 1984).

Expanding on this developmental sequence, aspects of the self are seen as somehow incompetent or defective (Kohut 1984). This is a critical part of the experience of perceived fraudulence: with the self viewed as incompetent and overrated by others, one is therefore unworthy of any successes one attains. Admittedly, the potential reasons for this initial self-perception are manifold. A depressive self-schema or orientation may play a role in that such an outlook may characterize an inability to internalize positive events and lead to a proclivity to discount achievements. These individuals may be characterized, then, as setting very high standards for, and being highly critical of, themselves and their performance in a variety of situations.

Furthermore, this view of the self is intolerable. Individuals do not want to see themselves in a negative light—just as they do not want others to view them negatively. This distaste is especially acute, given the high achievement orientation of these individuals and the significant perceived disparity between how competent these individuals think they are and how competent they believe others think they are. It is not necessarily the existence of this disparity that is so crucial in the experience of perceived fraudulence as much as it is one's negative or anxious reaction to the perceived disparity. An important part of perceived fraudulence, therefore, is that of anxiety, typically in reaction to impending potentially negative outcomes or the threat of social exposure.

Ultimately, these individuals perceive themselves as (and may even act) fraudulent through any one of a number of maneuvers. High self-monitoring seems to be an important part of perceived fraudulence in that it sensitizes one to the impact of one's behaviors on others and serves as a way of coping with incompetent thoughts and feelings (Snyder 1987); it also acts as a set of maneuvers or overt behaviors through which these individuals "mislead" others into believing the authenticity of their "fraudulent" performances. In a sense, their awareness of their impression-management skills may in part lead them to attribute successes or positive outcomes to the sophisticated nature of these skills rather than to their own inherent intellectual abilities or talents. Finally, the cycle of negative thoughts and feelings about the self is now exacerbated because of the existence of self-perceptions of fraudulence as well as incompetence.

Consider, however, that perceived fraudulence may take one of two forms. First, it may involve thoughts and feelings of fraudulence and subsequent exposure fears or anxiety with respect to the domains in which the individual feels fraudulent. Individuals may be overtly egocentric or exhibit a form of cognitive paranoia with respect to the belief that others are as concerned with their thoughts and behaviors as they themselves are—they may perceive themselves as playing a more central role in other individuals' thoughts and actions than the situation dictates (Zigler & Glick 1984, 1988). Second, it may involve experiencing only fraudulent thoughts and feelings—irrespective of any fear about being exposed as fraudulent. Although it seems likely that the two experiences go together, whether they actually do or not is still an empirical question.

A Study of Perceived Fraudulence

In accordance with the conceptualization outlined above, Sternberg and I conducted a three-part study of perceived fraudulence (1989). These experiments were designed to accomplish two objectives: (1) to investigate the properties of an extended perceived fraudulence scale and thus serve as a first stage in its validation as a new self-report inventory and (2) to explore the relationships between perceived fraudulence, as measured by this new scale, and several other constructs hypothesized to play an important role in a dispositional analysis of the experience in college-age adults. An individual's proneness to fraudulent thoughts and feelings, we postulated, would result from complex interactions among several personality variables.

In experiment 1, undergraduate students completed a battery of questionnaires that assessed the relationships between perceived fraudulence and achievement pressures, attribution-processing style, depressive symptoms, social anxiety, egocentricity, self-consciousness, self-image disparity, and self-esteem. The Perceived Fraudulence Scale (PFS), a new measure constructed for the study, and the Harvey Impostor Phenomenon Scale (Harvey 1981) were used to assess perceived fraudulence. We found that perceived fraudulence correlated positively and at significant levels with achievement pressures, negative attributions for successes, depression, social anxiety, egocentricity, public self-consciousness, and real-ideal self-image disparities; also as predicted, perceived fraudulence correlated negatively with self-esteem. Multiple-regression analyses demonstrated that social anxiety, self-critical aspects of depressive feelings, and achievement pressures were the best predictors of perceived fraudulence.

Experiment 2 was designed to investigate two questions that experiment 1 raised but did not definitively answer. For example, how can researchers be sure that those individuals who score highly on self-reports of fraudulence actually perceive themselves as frauds in other situations, real or imagined? This question addresses the possibility that, because of the demands on individuals' self-awareness, the private nature of the experience, and the limitations of questionnaires in assessing such private experiences, perceived fraudulence may not be identified adequately via self-report alone. Accordingly, experiment 2 also included thought-listing and interview components. It was expected that the inclusion of these two components would assist in the identification of individuals experiencing fraudulent cognitions and feelings; strong correlations among different measures of the same construct (i.e., perceived fraudulence) would contribute toward the convergent validation of existing psychometric measures.

In addition to including these new components, the Perceived Fraudulence Scale that was administered in experiment 1 was revised for experiment 2 in order to assess both more directly and more accurately the experience of perceived fraudulence. Specifically, in order to distinguish more clearly between socially anxious and fraudulent ideation, a revision of the PFS with additional "fraudulent" items and fewer "nonfraudulent," anxiety-oriented items was administered. Because of their theoretical relations to perceived fraudulence, subjects' self-monitoring and daydreaming styles were also assessed. Of course, it should be noted that we tapped subjects' perceptions of their own self-monitoring skills, not their actual self-monitoring behaviors, although Snyder (1987) has evidence suggesting that the two are highly related.

Thus, in experiment 2, undergraduate students completed questionnaires that investigated the relationships among perceived fraudulence, achievement pressures, depressive symptoms, social anxiety, self-esteem, self-monitoring, and daydreaming styles. As predicted, perceived fraudulence correlated positively and at significant levels with achievement pressures, depression, social anxiety, negative self-esteem, high self-monitoring, and dysphoric daydreaming. A principal-components factor analysis of the PFS revealed that it is composed of two factors: one assesses directly feelings of inauthenticity or fraudulence, whereas the other assesses subjects' self-critical or self-deprecating feelings. This factor structure was replicated in experiment 3.

Experiments 1 and 2 demonstrated the reliability and the convergent validity of the PFS. Subjects' scores on a thought-listing exercise and semistructured interview designed to assess fraudulent self-perceptions and ideation confirmed the scale's convergent validity. The thought-listing exercise was designed to tap subjects' thoughts in response to their imagined involvement in various situations. This converging-operations approach showed that subjects who scored high on the PFS also reported more spontaneous fraudulent self-perceptions in response to the thought-listing exercise and interview than did subjects who scored in the low range of the PFS. In addition, multiple-regression analyses again served to underscore common themes in the general experience of perceived fraudulence—namely, a combination of self-critical and depressive tendencies, social anxiety, and achievement pressures; this regression model accounted for 76 percent of the variance in subjects' scores on the PFS. Stepwise-regression analyses also indicated that subjects' scores on measures of dysphoric daydreaming patterns, self-monitoring skills, depression, and achievement pressures predicted their scores on the feelings of inauthenticity or fraudulence factor of the PFS; this model accounted for 63 percent of the variance in subjects' factor scores. Thus, young adults who see themselves as frauds, compared with young adults who do not, are especially likely to criticize themselves and to monitor closely the impressions they make on significant individuals, they are also likely to be socially anxious, to exhibit depressive symptoms, and to feel pressured to achieve by peers, teachers, and family members.

Given the close relations among perceived fraudulence, social anxiety, and depression, experiment 3 was conducted to demonstrate the discriminant validity of the PFS. Undergraduate students completed the scale along with two depression scales and two social-evaluative anxiety scales.

The results revealed that although perceived fraudulence is related to social-evaluative anxiety and depression, it is also distinct from these two more global affects.

A Revised Model of Perceived Fraudulence

Before considering the relation between perceived fraudulence and perceived incompetence, I will present a model of perceived fraudulence that resulted from our research. We found that perceived fraudulence is best characterized by a combination of fraudulent ideation and feelings, depressive tendencies, self-criticism, social-evaluative anxiety, strong pressures to excel and achieve, and high self-monitoring skills. There are, no doubt, several ways to account for these results. One possible way is that fraudulent individuals are, by nature, highly critical of themselves, and because of their self-criticism, they are anxious about the prospect of others evaluating their work. Still, they feel strong pressures to achieve and excel in their work. Their own self-critical thoughts may contribute to their fear that others are concerned with, and will ultimately detect, the flaws they have detected in themselves. To reduce the possibility of exposure and minimize their anxiety, they closely monitor their behavior and the impressions they make on others. In turn, their self-monitoring behaviors may exacerbate their fraudulent self-perceptions. They feel and acknowledge that their acting or pretending ability not only has been protective for them but has mislead others into overestimating their abilities. In sum, these individuals believe that if they did not monitor their behavior so closely, they would not perform so well. Their self-critical feelings, and their unwillingness to attribute their successful performance to their own inherent abilities, lead to depressive symptoms.

Like subjective feelings of inadequacy or hopelessness, feelings of fraudulence may be viewed as another symptom or even a specialized form of general perceived incompetence—with accompanying depressive affect and anxiety. The transformation of more general perceptions of incompetence into perceptions of fraudulence may be facilitated through these individuals' heightened self-conscious attention to others and to themselves, as evidenced by high self-monitoring and impression-management skills. Heightened self-monitoring skills have been hypothesized as a potentially important discriminating variable of the experiences of perceived incompetence and perceived fraudulence (Kolligian & Sternberg 1989). This conceptualization, of course, does not consider the role of certain situational factors, such as the novelty of one's environment or task and the skills of one's referent groups, in evoking incompetent and fraudulent self-perceptions (Edwards et al. 1987; Kolligian & Sternberg 1989; Langer 1979). Additional research and causal modeling techniques are required to test the relative influence of the many personality variables and situational factors that are hypothesized in this chapter as important to the expression of perceived fraudulence.

RELATIONS AMONG PERCEIVED FRAUDULENCE, PERCEIVED INCOMPETENCE, AND OTHER NEGATIVE SELF-PERCEPTIONS

Selective Review of Theory and Research on Perceived Competence and Incompetence

The Self and Perceived Competence. The self-concept has been a beleaguered construct in the psychological literature over the years, plagued by many unresolved definitional and assessment issues (Greenwald & Pratkanis 1984; Kihlstrom & Cantor 1984; Wylie 1974, 1979). Indeed, in the literature on the self, the terms *self-theory, self-esteem, self-concept, self-perception, self-competence, self-evaluation, self-efficacy,* and *self-worth* are often used interchangeably—even though theorists and researchers frequently are talking about different notions of concepts, however slight the difference (Harter 1985a). Theorists and researchers have not been explicit about their precise working definitions of these terms, leading to much confusion about what aspects of the self are being studied. Indeed, the terms *perceived competence* and *perceived incompetence* may be looked upon as yet another variation on this confusing theme. As Cauce (1987) correctly notes, "Finding cogent operational definitions for these self-evaluative constructs has proven a difficult task" (287).

In many writings on the topic, Harter (1982, 1983, 1985a, 1986b) and her colleagues have been instrumental in "reviving the self as a legitimate psychological construct" and in carefully determining the role of the dimension of competence as a dimension of the self. Harter (1982, 1985a) seems to view competence as one of several dimensions that constitutes our overall sense of self and self-worth. She sees the notion of perceived competence, more specifically, as referring to an individual's self-judgments of competence and ability, particularly with respect to certain specific domains or content areas. What ultimately goes into the formula in determining the nature of these judgments is another matter, of course. Indeed, low self-perceptions of competence can arise through very different combinations of personality dispositions, life experiences, and general mechanisms; furthermore, these combinations may differ depending on the age or developmental level of the individual, as well as on domains in which incompetence is perceived. Thus, I will not try to come up with a definitive formula for the child or adult with low self-esteem; rather, I will selectively highlight some work most relevant to the relations between perceived incompetence and fraudulence.

In understanding what determines the level of an individual's self-worth, Harter (1985a) makes a strong case for the inadequacy of perceived competence in telling the whole "self" story. Clearly, the impact and meaning of a perceived-competence judgment for a child or adult ultimately depends on how critical it is for the individual to succeed in a given domain. Without entering into the ongoing debate on the many ways in which the self-system may be structured, I think it is nevertheless clear that both the *accuracy* and the *value* or importance of one's self-perceptions of competence play major roles in one's more general sense of worth and related achievement behaviors.

Harter (1985a), indeed, has isolated three groups of children: those who overrate their competence, relative to the teacher's judgment; those who underrate their competence, relative to the teacher's judgment; and those whose ratings are congruent with the teacher's judgment. Bierer (1982) found that both underraters and overraters selected easier tasks to perform than did accurate raters. Thus, the accuracy of one's competence judgments seems to be a major determinant of actual achievement-oriented cognitions and behaviors.

Moreover, Harter (1985a) has explored other factors that need to be taken into account in understanding overall self-worth. Two others include the affects attached to these judgments and the degree of control that one experiences over successful and unsuccessful outcomes. The importance of one's judgments may often be assessed through an understanding of the level of one's affective responses to the judgments. Similarly, the extent to which one has a sense of control over and feels causally responsible for successes, failures, and attributes of the self may often determine perceptions of self-worth (Harter & Connell 1984).

For instance, in discussing his notion of self-efficacy or, more specifically, perceived inefficacy, Bandura (1981, 1982) points out the relation between self-affects and one's sense of control when he comments that pride and self-satisfaction are not derived from a view that one's performances are heavily dependent on external factors. Harter (1983, 1985a,

1986b) has isolated a pattern of control beliefs, characterized by greater internality for failure than for success and a propensity to ascribe failures to internal rather than to external causes, that is endorsed most consistently by children with low perceived and actual cognitive competence (Phillips 1984; Seligman 1975; see also Weisz, 1986, and Weisz et al., 1987, for related discussions of perceived control and depression in children and adolescents). This work provides a basis for hypothesizing that individuals with low perceived competence will suffer motivational deficits and tend to avoid challenging endeavors.

Motivation and Perceived Competence. Dweck (1986) points out that it has long been realized that factors other than ability influence whether children seek or avoid challenges and when they use and develop their skills effectively. Dweck and her colleagues have viewed perceived competence as a function of goals, or two classes of goal orientation—performance and learning (e.g., Dweck 1986; Dweck & Elliott 1983). A performance goal focuses children on ability; this focus, however, risks making their confidence in their ability fragile, as even the mere exertion of effort calls these children's ability into question. Performance goals require that children's confidence in their current ability remain high if they are to choose appropriately challenging tasks and pursue them in effective ways. Alternatively, a learning goal focuses children on effort as a means of utilizing, activating, or increasing their ability, as well as of surmounting obstacles. Thus, although children adhering to different goal orientations may not differ in intellectual ability, these patterns can have profound effects on cognitive and motivational performance. Differences among implicit theories of goal orientation or competence—rather than any actual differences in competence—seem to guide children's motivational patterns and influence achievement behaviors. Dweck comments that, for children with performance goals, being a high-achieving student and knowing one has done well in the past does not appear to translate into high confidence in one's abilities when faced with future challenges or current difficulties.

If there is a sizable population of high achievers with maladaptive motivational patterns, then how do some of these children still end up as high achievers (Dweck 1986; Phillips 1984, 1987)? Dweck (1986) deals with this question directly by pointing out that grade school may not provide tasks for these high achievers that are difficult enough to create failures; to make matters worse, these students also have the choice of not pursuing a given subject area if they think it may be difficult. For these reasons, maladaptive patterns may not yet come into play. It may be that only in subsequent school years will these maladaptive tendencies have their impact on achievement, when children with these patterns must perform tasks posing real difficulties. This explanation still does not completely explain the existence of adolescents and adults who, despite adhering to maladaptive motivational patterns and negative self-schemas, still are high achievers. Preliminary evidence suggests that adults who are high in perceived fraudulence do not demonstrate the same decrements in achievement behaviors (Kolligian & Sternberg 1989). It is possible that—like individuals susceptible to fraudulent self-perceptions—those with low perceived competence may exhibit heightened self-conscious attention to others' views of them. In this way, individuals with low perceived competence may work hard to impress others and to maintain high achievement strivings in order that significant others will remain unaware of their perceived deficiencies. Of course, many who perceive themselves as incompetent are actually very competent and will succeed on some tasks by virtue of their abilities. Clearly, research is still needed to determine the factors that compete with negative self-perceptions to enable bright individuals with low perceived competence to sustain their academic striving over time.

For some individuals, perceived incompetence has been associated with impaired problem solving (Dweck & Goetz 1978), dysfunctional inferences about achievement outcomes (Nicholls 1979a), attenuated achievement goals (Bandura & Dweck 1985; Dweck 1986), behavior problems (Blechman et al. 1985), and depression (Blechman et al. 1986). Indeed, both Phillips (1984) and Harter suggests that—in addition to the level of self-perceived competence—the accuracy of one's perceived competence is of great importance for learning, achievement, and adjustment (see also Connell & Ilardi 1987). For instance, Phillips has conducted an investigation of the achievement orientations of high-achieving children who held low academic self-concepts, or the "illusion of incompetence." Her work is important in that it represents one of the few direct investigations of the experience of perceived incompetence in children and suggests many directions for future work in this area. In addition, this work, along with the findings of Harter, Dweck, and their colleagues, suggest some possible commonalities between competence-related and fraudulence-related perceptions.

In brief, Phillips (1984) studied a group of high-achieving elementary-age children who failed to acquire positive academic perceptions of competence; of particular interest were comparisons between the achievement orientations of highly capable children who adopted erroneous perceptions of incompetence and their intellectual peers who accurately viewed themselves as highly competent. The children's subjective appraisals of their abilities significantly influenced their achievement orientations in two major ways. First, the low-perceived-competence children, in contrast to their more confident peers, set less demanding achievement standards for themselves, adopted lower expectancies for academic success, and perceived their teachers as expecting less of them. Thus, children with fragile self-perceptions appear to adopt a self-protective strategy; they become adept at avoiding critical feedback of their abilities by, for example, minimizing their effort and failing to persist in their schoolwork.

Second, the low-perceived-competence children were more likely to attribute positive outcomes to external, uncontrollable factors and to attribute negative outcomes to internal factors than were their more confident peers. In addition, their teachers characterized low-perceived-competence children as introverted, self-blaming, and reticent. These two findings strongly suggest that they are so sensitive to critical feedback that even isolated instances of failure loom large in their attributions and subsequent self-evaluations of competence. As with the children who hold performance goals as discussed by Dweck (1986), the psychological cost of failure appears especially great for students whose sense of self is heavily invested in their academic performance.

Low-perceived-competence children's tendency to interpret errors as indicative of insufficient ability—rather than as being due to amount of effort or external circumstances—is similar to that of learned-helpless children (Seligman et al. 1984), fraudulent young adults (Kolligian & Sternberg 1989), and depressed adults (Abramson, Seligman, & Teasdale 1978; Seligman 1975). Thus, attributing one's failures to personal deficiencies of an internal, enduring, and generalized nature—and one's successes to external, brief, and specific factors—constitutes salient features of perceived incompetence in children, as well as perceived fraudulence and depressive experiences in adults. In two clinical investigations, Blechman and her colleagues found that children with low perceived academic and social competence experienced the most frequent and most serious behavior problems (Blechman et al. 1985) and were most prone to be depressed (Blechman et al. 1986). Despite the highly suggestive nature of these findings, these researchers were unable to support definitively the behavioral causal formulation that incompetence precedes depression.

In light of this work, however, acquiring an understanding of the processes that might perpetuate self-disparagement among individuals with low academic or social competence remains a chief task for researchers in this area. Social comparisons—like favorable comparisons with low achievers (Brown 1979) or unfavorable comparisons with high achievers (Harter 1986b; Ruble 1983)—represent a process that can lead to negative self-evaluations (Phillips 1984, 1987). Situations in which "risky" social comparison processes are most operative include those with relatively novel task demands or with new or different referent groups: environments that offer new problems or different peer groups present an opportunity for new types of social comparisons. Thus, individuals may be more at risk of making unfair comparisons to other, possibly more capable or more experienced, peers when presented with a novel situation or environment (e.g., beginning a new school year or a new job).

Harter (1986b) has explored the use of social comparison among special groups of children, such as mentally retarded and learning-disabled students. She found that learning-disabled pupils tend to compare their academic performance with that of regular classroom peers, resulting in significantly lower perceptions of competence for these children as compared to nondisabled children. Although these self-perceptions are accurate—they *are* less competent than the nondisabled children—their self-esteem would benefit from comparisons with less able peers. In contrast, mentally retarded pupils tend to compare themselves to their mentally retarded peers, resulting in perceived-competence judgments that are less harsh than the judgments of learning-disabled students. The important point is that primary referent groups matter: identifying the individuals to whom one is comparing the self is of great importance in competence-related perceptions. It is risky if one chooses to compare oneself to more gifted individuals. As Bandura (1982) comments, "Even the mere sight of a formidable looking opponent instills lower self-percepts of efficacy than does one who looks less impressive" (142).

In a recent study, Phillips (1987) found that parents of low-perceived-competence children viewed their children's abilities more negatively than did parents of average- and high-perceived-competence children. She also found that low-perceived-competence children believed their parents viewed them as less smart; they also felt more pressured by their parents than did the high and average groups. As previously mentioned, individuals experiencing fraudulent self-perceptions also reported high levels of pressure to excel and achieve from a composite of parents, teachers, and peers (Kolligian & Sternberg 1989). These studies point up the benefits of considering variations in perceived and actual competence in relation to important socialization contexts and agents. As Cooley (1964[1902]) aptly suggested, others can often be the looking glass to ourselves. If an individual, for whatever reason, is predisposed to pick up any negative feedback from these significant others, then the person is clearly vulnerable to self-perceptions of incompetence and possibly to self-perceptions of fraudulence.

Placing Perceived Incompetence and Perceived Fraudulence in Perspective

Rorer and Widiger (1983) have complained that personality literature reviews "appear to be disparate conglomerations rather than cumulative or conclusive integrations" (432). Indeed, a recent review of the literature by Singer and Kolligian (1987) confirmed this and other authors' (e.g., Watson & Clark 1984; Wolfe et al. 1987) belief that segregated literatures have developed around a number of personality constructs and measures that, despite dissimilar names, conceptually overlap and statistically intercorrelate so highly that they may be the same constructs under different names. Specifically, there is a high degree of conceptual closeness and similarity among many of the personality constructs discussed in this chapter and other constructs not commonly associated with perceived incompetence or perceived fraudulence.

There is a notable similarity between preliminary descriptions of perceived fraudulence and traditional descriptions of success-fearing personalities (or the "fear of success" experience). For instance, Canavan-Gumpert, Garner, and Gumpert (1978) have defined success-fearing persons as having the following four traits: (1) a low and unstable self-esteem, (2) a preoccupation with being evaluated and with competitive implications of performance, (3) a tendency to repudiate their competence by citing external factors such as luck or the help of others to explain their accomplishments, and (4) a tendency to become anxious in the face of impending or imminent success and to sabotage the success, usually by doing something to prevent its occurrence. In a similar fashion, research has demonstrated that perceived fraudulence is associated with low self-esteem, a preoccupation with evaluation and performance, and a tendency self-critically to repudiate or derogate one's competence (Kolligian & Sternberg 1989). Indeed, the self-punitiveness of perceived fraudulence may be likened to the self-sabotaging behavior of success-fearing personalities (Canavan-Gumpert et al. 1978; Krueger 1984). Self-punitive or self-critical tendencies may be a central mechanism or mediating construct in the etiology, development, and maintenance of perceived incompetence and fraudulence, in addition to other forms of psychopathology, such as depression.

The importance of self-punitiveness or self-criticism in psychopathology has been confirmed by numerous theorists and researchers. For instance, (Blatt (1974) and his colleagues Blatt, D'Affliti, & Quinlan 1976; Blatt et al. 1982) have attempted to differentiate among the many states that have been labeled depression. In doing so, Blatt et al. (1976) have underscored a self-critical type of depression that is characterized by intense feelings of inferiority, guilt, and worthlessness as well as by a sense that one has failed to live up to certain expectations and standards. Furthermore, Carver and Ganellen (1983) have proposed that achievement pressures, self-deprecatory judgments, and generalization of negative judgments all come together in self-punitive, depressed individuals. It should be acknowledged that variations of these components have been discussed previously in terms of both perceived fraudulence and perceived competence—and now as aspects of self-punitiveness. Each of these components of a self-punitive style also seems descriptive of important aspects of perceived incompetence and perceived fraudulence.

Self-punitiveness may be best conceptualized as a central "at risk" dimension for a host of disorders, ranging from perceived incompetence and fraudulence to depression (Blechman et al. 1986; Rehm 1977; Zigler & Glick 1986; Zuroff & Mongrain 1987), eating disorders (Garner, Olmstead, & Polivy 1983), and forms of chronic self-destructiveness (Kelley et al. 1985). The mediational role of self-punitiveness suggests the utility of the construct as a vehicle for drawing together disparate phenomenon and differentially labeled concepts.

Perceived fraudulence may also be conceptualized as a subset of "negative affectivity" (Watson & Clark 1984; Wolfe et al. 1987); that is, perceived fraudulence may be seen as a specialized manifestation of more general tendencies of a negative outlook or worldview. Watson and Clark (1984) have described negative affectivity as a disposition to experience aversive emotional states. It reflects the tendency to be distressed, upset, and have a negative view of oneself, while dwelling upon and magnifying one's mistakes, frustrations, and disappointments. This dimension is strikingly similar to many other constructs—for instance, negative attribution style (Abramson, Seligman, & Teasdale 1978), depressive self-schema (Hammen, Marks, deMayo, & Mayol 1985; Hammen, Marks, Mayol, & deMayo 1985), pessimistic self-preoccupation (Strack et al. 1985), characterological self-blame (Janoff-Bulman 1979), and perfectionism (Burns 1980; Hewitt & Dyck 1986; Hollender 1978)—not to mention the related constellation of self-punitive or self-critical tendencies already discussed as characteristics of individuals experiencing perceived fraudulence.

Perceived fraudulence, then, may be viewed as one possible manifestation of subjective personality tendencies toward negative affectivity or pessimistic self-preoccupation and as a product of a sophisticated interaction between an individual's personality style and certain situational characteristics. Most researchers, however, have not fully appreciated the extent to which many constructs and their measurement instruments are related and intercorrelated (Nicholls, Licht, & Pearl 1982; Watson & Clark 1984). In order for future researchers to make meaningful distinctions among a host of related, yet subtly distinctive, constructs—such as perceived fraudulence, fear of success, and negative affectivity—we must be attentive to, and explicitly state, the specific similarities and differences of these related constructs as both the conceptual and the measurement levels at all phases in the development and validation of personality constructs (Lazarus et al. 1985; Nicholls, Licht, & Pearl 1982). As Watson and Clark (1984) put it, "As the story goes, when one can see the whole elephant, a clearer and more accurate conception of the animal emerges" (484).

A Developmental Context: Some Final Thoughts on Perceived Fraudulence

Etiology in Childhood. Until more research is conducted on the experience of perceived fraudulence, our understanding of its etiology remains highly speculative. One focus for further research concerns the question of how an individual's relationships with parents in childhood may influence the predisposition to experience fraudulent self-perceptions. For instance, Phillips (1987) has investigated the role of parental socialization patterns on children with self-perceptions of incompetence. Also, as previously mentioned, psychoanalytic clinical reports have highlighted the role of parents' encouragement of their child's imitative and mimicry behaviors in the etiology of fraudulence. In their study of perceived fraudulence among successful women, Clance and Imes (1978) observed two patterns of impostorous family dynamics. Some women were brought up in families that directly or indirectly underscored their nonacademic attributes (e.g., sensitivity, sociability) and, at the same time, deemphasized their intellectual abilities, whereas other women were brought up in families that believed they were infallible, perfect children and were thus indiscriminately praised for their achievements. According to Clance and Imes, both types of families encouraged these women's discounting or distrust of their successes.

Perhaps Blatt's (1974) analysis of the family antecedents of self-critical tendencies offers the most theoretically grounded discussion of differential vulnerability to perceived fraudulence (see McCranie & Bass 1984). It is possible that parents at risk of rearing self-critical children use methods of controlling their child that are predominantly negative; they exhibit elements of strictness combined with inconsistent expressions of love and affection, thus reflecting conditional acceptance (McCranie & Bass 1984). Both parents demand achievement and success as conditions of acceptance, with the child reacting by striving to win their approval through performance (Blatt et al. 1979). Intense self-criticism may reflect the internalization of parental aspirations and criticisms. This pattern is paralleled by research indicating that perceived incompetence in children (Phillips 1984, 1987) and perceived fraudulence in young adults (Kolligian & Sternberg 1989) is associated with high levels of perceived parental pressures to achieve. Theory and research suggest that parents who stress achievement strivings and press for the rapid attainment of their child's developmental milestones (or who, at least, are perceived by their child as doing so) are at risk of socializing the critical self-evaluations that are so characteristic of incompetent or fraudulent self-perceptions (Elkind 1981; Ladd & Price 1986; Phillips 1987). Of course, these findings, however suggestive, require further empirical investigation.

Etiology in Adolescence. Although the struggle with self-related issues is ongoing at all life stages, it is perhaps most problematic during adolescence; self-criticisms and other negative feelings are most severe and widespread during this period (Rosenberg 1985). Leahy (1985) has suggested that one of the major "clinical costs of development" from childhood to adolescence is a greater vulnerability for self-critical attributions because of burgeoning social-cognitive skills, including the acquisition and refinement of role-taking skills. With increasing awareness of the self as an object of others' thoughts and feelings, adolescents may feel more transparent, become more self-conscious, and even begin attempts to prevent others from knowing certain "true" aspects of themselves that they believe may not measure up to the values established by others (Elkind 1967, 1976; Elkind & Bowen 1979). This sense of self-transparency may also contribute to a concern that others will see both their flaws and their subsequent anxiety, leading others to reject them (Leahy 1985). Whereas younger adolescents may reveal an inability to recognize or accept conflicts and gaps between notions of self and others, older adolescents may reveal an inability to recognize or accept internal conflicts and incongruence between various aspects of the self (Ullman 1987).

One way to view the development of perceived fraudulence during adolescence may be as a response to shifting self-identity or role differentiation. Erikson (1950, 1959, 1968) has stressed the importance of a sense of unity or harmony among one's self-conceptions for the establishment of stable ego identity. Yet, a consequence of the emergence of a distinction between public and private aspects of the self is that performances by the public self, which are socially rewarded, may not be viewed by the adolescent as reflective of the private self; thus, these performances are at risk of not being internalized (Leahy 1985). For the adolescent, this kind of role integration becomes a primary developmental task and involves many roles and identities, such as social, sexual, familial, ideological, and occupational (Harter, 1985a). The focus here is on potential clashes, or lack of integration, among the multiple roles—the self within the academic setting, the self within the family setting, and the self within the peer culture. Although most of us present different sides of ourselves in different contexts—depending upon the demands of the situation, our personal goals, and our intentions—some individuals may be especially critical of themselves for their awareness of having shifted from the self in one role to the self in another (Kihlstrom 1987; Kihlstrom & Cantor 1984). It is possible that insight into the dynamics of such role conflicts may shed light on why certain individuals are at risk for experiencing perceived fraudulence and others are not. However, evidence for individuals' vulnerabilities to perceived fraudulence as a function of individual differences in multiple self-identity or role tolerance has not yet been investigated empirically.

In all likelihood, it is the older child, adolescent, or adult who has the ability to perceive the different attributes, roles, or possible selves (Markus & Nurius 1986; Ogilvie 1987) as somehow inconsistent and as not united by a superordinate self. Again, an appreciation for these inconsistencies among different sides of ourselves goes beyond the identification or cognitive recognition of contradiction in that intrapsychic conflict is actually experienced—with negative consequences such as low self-esteem. Thus, the adolescent is bothered by these contradictory self-perceptions, whereas the younger child is not. This fact may support the notion that, whereas low perceived competence can occur in many domains across the life cycle, perceived fraudulence may be a more specialized experience requiring the heightened self-consciousness or "imaginary audience" (Elkind 1985; Lapsley 1985; Lapsley & Murphy 1985; Lapsley & Rice 1988) that usually emerges in adolescence, as well as an advanced appreciation for inconsistencies in one's thoughts, feelings, and behaviors. A significant achievement of adolescence and young adulthood, therefore, may represent the ability to conceive of, and accept, a view of oneself that is diverse and multifaceted—without feeling inauthentic or fake (Markus & Nurius 1986).

SUMMARY

This chapter has reviewed perceived fraudulence by viewing it within the context of the more generalized experience of perceived incompetence, thus charting the course of potential relations between incompetent and fraudulent self-perceptions. Clinical studies highlighted several common themes in the phenomenon of "real" fraudulence—namely, early mimicry skills, charm, exaggerated self-enhancement, perfectionism, and audience awareness; variations of these themes also played a role in recent conceptualizations of perceived fraudulence. A review of the recent literature on perceived fraudulence underscored the self-deprecating ways in which some individuals actually make attributions about their abilities and competencies; however, most existing research studies offered little support for some theorists' conceptualization of perceived fraudulence as a global personality style. My conceptualization of, and research on, perceived fraudulence showed that the experience involves an interplay among several personality variables—namely, fraudulent or inauthentic ideation, self-critical thinking, social anxiety, and self-monitoring skills. A selective review of the literature on perceived incompetence (or low perceived competence) revealed that self-punitive or self-critical tendencies may be a central feature of the etiology, development, and maintenance of both perceived incompetence and perceived fraudulence. Finally, differential vulnerability to perceived fraudulence in childhood was discussed as a product of early family dynamics and socialization patterns. The expression of perceived fraudulence in adolescence—a period in which self-criticisms and negative self-perceptions may be most severe—was viewed, in part, as a "developmental cost" resulting from a burgeoning self-consciousness and a maladaptive responses to shifting multiple-role identities. A central objective of this chapter has been to underscore how authenticity concerns and fraudulent ideation in a variety of domains represent important, yet often overlooked and understudied, aspects of individuals' more general self-referential perceptions and judgments of competence.

CHAPTER 13

The Development of Self-System Vulnerabilities: Social and Cognitive Factors in Developmental Psychopathology

MARLENE M. MORETTI AND E. TORY HIGGINS

The development of the self has attracted the attention of clinicians for well over a century (Basch 1983; Bowlby 1971, 1975; Erikson 1950; A. Freud 1946; Horney 1950). Several changes have occurred during this time in the types of assumptions adopted by theoreticians and researchers investigating the development of the self-system. First, contemporary models tend to recognize the self as an independent psychological structure that directs and controls behavior (Bowlby 1971; Erikson 1950; Sullivan 1953) rather than simply as a mediator between primitive id impulses and reality demands (Freud 1923). Second, researchers have become increasingly sensitive to the primary importance of attachment needs and interpersonal relations in the development of the self (Aber & Allen 1987; Ainsworth 1982; Ainsworth et al. 1978; Bowlby 1971, 1975; Easterbrooks & Goldberg 1984; Main & Weston 1981; Matas, Arend, & Sroufe 1978), and the gratification of biological needs and impulses now

This research was partially supported by a Social Sciences and Research Council of Canada Fellowship to the first author and Grant MH39429 from the National Institute of Mental Health to the second author. This chapter was initiated while the second author was a Fellow at the Center for Advanced Study in the Behavioral Sciences. The support provided by the John D. and Catherine T. MacArthur Foundation and by the Alfred P. Sloan Foundation is deeply appreciated. We would like to thank Robbie Case, Robin Wells, and Erik Woody for their thoughtful comments while this chapter was prepared.

tends to be viewed as secondary. Finally, contemporary theorists place greater emphasis on the importance of the relation between developing cognitive abilities and the emergence of the self-system than did early theorists (Cicchetti & Rizley 1981; Harter 1983; Kegan 1982; Loevinger 1976).

We believe that an adequate model of self-development should permit researchers and clinicians to make predictions about the types of quantitative and qualitative shifts in children's self-evaluative and self-regulatory patterns at different ages (and levels of cognitive development), as well as predictions about the types of emotional and behavioral difficulties they might encounter from infancy to late adolescence. In this chapter we consider the interaction between cognitive development and parental socialization practices in the development of self-evaluative and self-regulatory processes as they relate to self-system vulnerabilities in particular.

SELF-DISCREPANCY THEORY I: A MODEL OF SELF-SYSTEM VULNERABILITY IN ADULTS

When individuals evaluate themselves or their performances, they can draw on numerous types of standards and guides during the self-evaluative process (see Higgins, Strauman, & Klein, 1986, and Higgins & Moretti, 1988, for a review of standards and issues of normative standard utilization). The basic premise of self-discrepancy theory is that different self-state representations act as important guides for self-evaluation (Higgins 1987; Higgins, in press, b). Individuals may evaluate their actual selves (the attributes they believe they actually possess) in relation to either their ideal-self (the hopes or wishes they believe someone holds for them) or their ought-self (the duties and obligations they believe someone holds for them). Within each of these self-domains, individuals can view their performance either from their own perspective or from the standpoint of a significant other. Combining across these two dimensions of the self (domains × standpoints) yields four potentially different self-state representations that individuals may adopt as self-evaluative standards or guides: ideal-own, ideal-other, ought-own, and ought-other.

Self-discrepancy theory predicts that when the attributes of the actual-self are perceived as highly discrepant from the attributes of the ideal-self, individuals will view themselves as unable to attain their own important aspirations (ideal-own) or to fulfill the hopes and desires that others hold for them (ideal-other). This negative psychological situation, which represents the absence of positive outcomes, is associated with feelings of disappointment, dissatisfaction (ideal-own), or embarrassment (ideal-other). In contrast, when the attributes of the actual-self are perceived as highly discrepant from the attributes of the ought-self, individuals will perceive themselves as having violated important duties and obligations prescribed by themselves (ought-own) or prescribed by others (ought-other), which is associated with punishment. This negative psychological state, which represents the (anticipated) presence of negative outcomes, is associated with feelings of guilt and worthlessness (ought-own) or fear and apprehension (ought-other). Predictions based on this model are supported by the observations of past theorists (e.g., Adler 1964; Cooley 1964[1902]; James 1948[1890]; Rogers 1961) as well as from the results of a number of empirical studies (see Higgins 1987; in press, b).

In the first empirical test of the self-discrepancy model, the unique relations of actual-ideal discrepancy to dejection-related emotions and of actual-ought discrepancy to agitation-related emotions were examined. Higgins, Klein, and Strauman (1985) had subjects record attributes that characterized their actual-self, how they ideally wished they could be (ideal-self:own perspective), and how they felt they should or ought to be (ought-self : own perspective). Subjects also recorded the attributes they believed significant others ideally wished they possessed or that significant others thought they should possess. Self-descriptive attributes were provided entirely by the subject ensuring the personal relevance of each attribute; at no point were subjects asked to consider or judge the relations between self-states for the presence of discrepancy. Hence, subjects did not need to be aware of the self-discrepancies they possessed.

As predicted, the results of the Higgins et al. (1985) study indicated that subjects characterized by higher levels of self-discrepancy were more likely to suffer from psychological distress. Partial correlational analyses also revealed that the particular type of self-discrepancy an individual possessed was related to the type of psychological discomfort he or she experienced: actual-ideal discrepancy was more closely associated with dejection-related emotions (e.g., dissatisfaction, shame, feeling blue) than with agitation-related emotions (e.g., guilt, panic, fear), and actual-ought discrepancy was more closely related to agitation-related emotions than to dejection-related emotions.

The concordant relation of self-discrepancies to psychological discomfort was also assessed by Higgins, Bond, Klein, and Strauman (1986). Subjects were asked to imagine either a positive event (received an A in a course; just spent an evening with someone they had long admired) or a negative event (received a D; a lover had just left them). Ideal-discrepancy subjects who imagined a negative event experienced greater dejection and demonstrated more psychomotor retardation (reduced writing speed) than did either ideal-discrepancy subjects who imagined a positive event or ought-discrepancy subjects who imagined a negative event. In contrast, ought-discrepancy subjects who imagined a negative event experienced greater agitation and psychomotor excitation (increased writing speed) than did either ought-discrepancy subjects who imagined a positive event or ideal-discrepancy subjects who imagined a negative event.

The type of self-discrepancy possessed by an individual also appears to be predictive of the extent and type of psychological discomfort the person is likely to experience in the future. Higgins, Klein, and Strauman (1987) assessed the relation between actual-ideal and actual-ought self-discrepancy and depressive and anxiety symptoms at a two-month followup. As predicted, actual-ideal discrepancy was a better predictor of depressive symptoms at follow-up than was actual-ought discrepancy, and actual-ought discrepancy was a better predictor of anxiety symptoms than was actual-ideal discrepancy. Strauman and Higgins (in press) have found similar results using a latent-variable analysis to assess the relation of self-discrepancy and symptoms of depression and anxiety at a one-month followup. Again, results supported the unique relation of actual-ideal discrepancy to symptoms of depression and of actual-ought discrepancy to symptoms of social anxiety.

Not only have self-discrepancies been found to be concurrently and predictively related to the types of psychological distress individuals experience, but when individuals possess more than one type of self-discrepancy the type of emotional distress they experience at a particular time is a function of the *accessibility* (i.e., the readiness with which constructs are accessed during processing) of specific self-discrepancies. Higgins et al. (1986) measured subjects' self-discrepancies four to six weeks prior to "priming" discrepancies (increasing the accessibility of discrepancies) by asking them to describe either the type of person they believed their parents would ideally like them to be (ideal-priming) or the type of person they believed their parents felt they should be (ought-priming). Subjects high in both types of discrepancy experienced greater dejection-related emotions when exposed to the ideal-discrepancy priming, and greater agitation-related emotions when exposed to the ought-discrepancy priming.

Further studies have indicated that activating a specific self-attribute that is a structural component of a self-discrepancy is sufficient to activate the negative psychological situation represented by the discrepancy. Strauman (1987) and his colleagues (Strauman & Higgins 1987) primed self-discrepancies by asking subjects to complete sentences about *others* who possessed particular personality attributes. When subjects completed sentences that included a self-discrepant attribute that they themselves possessed they experienced increased emotional distress. The type of distress was specifically related to the type of self-discrepancy made accessible by the priming procedure: subjects completing sentences that contained ideal self-discrepancies experienced increased dejection-related emotions, decreased galvanic skin response (GSR) and decreased verbal output, whereas subjects completing sentences that contained ought self-discrepancies experienced increased agitation, increased GSR, and increased verbal output (Strauman & Higgins 1987, study 1). This effect could be produced only by priming self-attributes that were discrepant with a self-guide (Strauman & Higgins, in press, study 2). Similar results have been found in a clinical sample of depressed and social phobic clinical patients (Strauman 1987).

This research suggests that the psychological importance of any actual-self attribute is clearly understood only within the context of its relation with self-evaluative guides. If this is true, self-concept measures based solely on ratings of the actual-self should not be as strongly related to the affective consequences of self-evaluation than should measures of actual-self/self-guide discrepancy. In a recent study that examined this question, Moretti and Higgins (in press) assessed the contribution of self-discrepancy in predicting self-esteem beyond actual-self ratings. As predicted, actual-ideal discrepancy was strongly related to self-esteem even when the contribution of actual-self ratings was statistically removed. In contrast, the relationship of actual-self ratings to self-esteem was not significant when the contribution of actual-ideal discrepancy was statistically removed. Moreover, the mere presence of negative actual-self attributes did not predict low self-esteem; only negative actual-self attributes that were discrepant from the ideal self-guide were associated with low self-esteem. Similarly, the mere presence of positive actual-self attributes did not predict high self-esteem; only positive actual-self attributes that were not discrepant from the ideal self-guide were so related.

The most compelling evidence for the limited importance of actual-self attributes alone in predicting psychological distress has recently been reported by Van Hook and Higgins (1988). Based on the assumption that discrepancies between self-state representations have negative psychological consequences, regardless of whether this discrepancy occurs between the actual-self and a self-guide or between two self-guides, Van Hook and Higgins predicted that (1) conflict between two self-guides would be associated with higher levels of psychological discomfort independent of the relation of these self-guides to the actual-self, and (2) self-guide : self-guide conflict would be associated with feeling confused and unsure of oneself and one's goals, and with being distractible and rebellious. As predicted, self-guide : self-guide conflict was associated with feelings of confusion, uncertainty, distractibility, and rebelliousness. This finding was independent of the relation between the actual-self and self-guides and other psychological symptoms reported by the subjects (e.g., dejection-related or agitation-related emotions).

Why is it that individuals who possess self-discrepancies are highly vulnerable to experiencing psychological discomfort? One possibility has to do with the nature of individuals' outcome-contingency beliefs concerning the consequences of failing to meet the guides they hold for themselves or the guides they believe others wish they would meet or think they ought to meet. If individuals strongly believe that failing to meet others' hopes and wishes or duties and obligations for them will lead to a loss or withdrawal of love or rejection and punishment, they will be extremely vulnerable to negative emotional experiences when they perceive that they have failed to meet these standards. Preliminary research supports the prediction that outcome-contingency beliefs are important in determining the psychological consequences of self-discrepancy. In one study (Higgins, Klein, & Strauman 1987), subjects with high levels of actual-ideal discrepancy who strongly believed that their failure to live up to parental hopes and wishes was associated with negative consequences (e.g., abandonment) reported higher levels of chronic depression than did subjects with high actual-ideal discrepancy who did not endorse this belief. The presence of high actual-ideal discrepancy in combination with high ideal-outcome contingency beliefs was not related to increased levels of anxiety symptoms. In contrast, subjects with high levels of actual-ought discrepancy who strongly believed that their failure to live up to the duties and obligations prescribed by their parents was associated with negative consequences (e.g., rejection) reported higher levels of chronic anxiety and fear than did subjects with high actual-ought discrepancy who did not endorse this belief. The presence of actual-ought discrepancy in combination with high ought-outcome contingency beliefs was not related to increased levels of depressive symptoms.

The results of a follow-up study by Higgins and Tykocinsky (see Higgins, in press, b) corroborated earlier findings by showing that subjects who strongly believed that failing to meet their parents' ideals would lead to the loss of positive outcomes reported greater levels of depression than did subjects who did not endorse this belief. In contrast, subjects who strongly believed that failing to meet the duties or obligations prescribed by their parents would lead to the presence of negative outcomes reported greater levels of anxiety and agitation than did subjects who did not endorse this belief.

The results of these studies underscore the importance of the self-system in determining vulnerability to psychological distress. Not only is the psychological significance of actual-self attributes determined by the relation of these attributes to the self-guides, but the relation of self-guides to each other also has important psychological implications. In addition, preliminary research on outcome-contingency beliefs suggests that the psychological importance of self-discrepancy depends on its conjunction with strong beliefs about the negative consequences of possessing the discrepancy.

Self-discrepancy theory might offer some important insights into the *development* of vulnerable self-systems. Research evaluating the relation of beliefs about the consequences of failing to meet parental guides is suggestive in this respect. Although the results of this research are obviously limited because of their retrospective nature, they do suggest that the study of self-system development must address not only the issue of the emerging self-concept and the development of different self-state representations but also the development of outcome-contingency beliefs.

SELF-DISCREPANCY THEORY II: A DEVELOPMENTAL MODEL OF SELF-SYSTEM VULNERABILITY

Two factors are important in the development of outcome-contingency beliefs and self-discrepancies. First, we must consider developmental changes in the child's ability to form complex mental representations. For a child to develop contingency beliefs about others' responses to their behaviors or attributes they must be able to represent the relation between features of their behavior and the responses of others to them. As their ability for complex mental representations increases, children become increasingly able to consider their own features in relation to standards or guides they believe others hold for them. They are also able to represent complex outcome-contingencies about others' responses to their features and to experience discrepancies within the self-system.

The second factor we need to consider is the impact of parental socialization practices on the development of the self-system. These practices determine both the *extent* to which guides are available and accessible to the child and the *relation* of these guides to the child's self-features (whether the child's features are congruent with or discrepant from parental guides for them).

The Development of Mental Representational Capacity

Developmental shifts in mental representational capacity have been well documented by researchers (Case 1985; Fischer 1980; Selman 1980). Changes in the child's capacity to represent mentally the relation between events might well produce qualitative shifts in self-system development. In the following section, we outline five levels of development in mental representational capacity and the implications of these cognitive shifts for changes in the self-system (see Higgins, in press, a, for a fuller discussion of these developmental changes). The description of these levels of cognitive development draws heavily from Case's (1985) analysis of intellectual development. Each level of development represents a qualitative shift in the child's cognitive capacity to represent the relation between events with increasing complexity.

Level 1: Early Sensorimotor Development. The capacity of the infant to experience positive and negative affective states and to detect features of the environment that correspond to these emotional states is important for survival (Case 1985). This is not to imply that infants possess the capacity to encode and represent the relation between features of the environment and their own affective states, but rather that they are capable of differentiating positive and negative features of the environment. Their ability to differentiate environmental features in this manner and affectively respond to them has obvious implications for the communication of their needs to caretakers.

At this early level of development, infants have the capacity to experience the presence or absence of positive events as well as that of negative events. Whereas the presence of positive events such as feeding or cuddling is associated with feelings of satisfaction or happiness (Case 1988; Sroufe 1984), the absence of positive events such as the inability to find a sought-after object or a change from mother's affectionate play to her withholding communication is associated with sadness, disappointment, and frustration/anger (e.g., Campos & Barrett 1984; Kagan 1984; Sroufe 1984; Trevarthen 1984). Similarly, the presence of negative events such as hunger, punishment, or exposure to unexpected or noxious persons is associated with feelings of distress and fear (e.g., Emde 1984; Kagan 1984), whereas the absence of negative events such as removing the child from noxious stimulation is associated with feelings of security and contentedness (Case 1988; Sroufe 1984). These four psychological events may be experienced in relation to the gratification (or lack thereof) of both interpersonal needs and biological needs (Case 1988; Sroufe 1984).

Even though infants at this level are able to anticipate positive or negative events, they have not yet represented the occurrence of these events in relation to some behavior or feature of themselves, so that experiences at this age will not necessarily affect their subsequent experiences and evaluations of themselves. This does not mean, however, that infants suffer psychological distress associated with negative events to a lesser extent than do older children or adults who relate these events to themselves. Nor does it imply that this level of development is unimportant for later self-development. To the extent that infants anticipate either the absence of positive events or the presence of negative events, they might withdraw or respond negatively to the approaches of others and hence provoke negative rather than positive responses. If this is the case, negative interpersonal events are more likely to occur in the future and will be related to the self when children have reached a level of cognitive maturity to be able to do so.

Level 2: Late Sensorimotor and Early Interrelational Development. At around age eighteen months to two years, the child's ability to mentally represent events shifts dramatically with the emergence of symbolic representational abilities (Bruner 1964; Case 1985; Fischer 1980; Piaget 1951; Werner & Kaplan 1963) and the ability to consider *bidirectional* relations between objects. Hence, children are able schematically to represent the relation between two objects and to use this representation to direct their behavior toward a desired outcome (Case 1985). Children are now capable of representing the relation between themselves or their actions and the responses of another individual. In other words, children are now able to perceive their actions as objects or events that are separate from others (self-as-object) and elicit particular types of responses from others (other-as-object). For example, at this level young children understand that when they smile, their mother smiles and speaks. They are also able to represent the psychological impact of others' responses to them (e.g., feelings of happiness, sadness, fear) in this representational sequence.

Hence, they can consider even more complex representations such as the relation between their behavior (e.g., smiling, making faces) and the response of another individual (e.g., mother's smiling, cuddling) that then results in their experience of a particular psychological situation (e.g., happiness).

The development of the capacity to represent complex relations is important to the development of the self-system. The ability to represent the impact of a particular self-feature (attribute) on the responses of another individual permits the child to represent *self-other contingencies.* In children at this early level of development self-other contingencies consist of representations between the children's behavior or actions rather than their self traits (see level 3) and the responses of other individuals (Harter 1983, 1986a; Rosenberg 1979). Since children can now represent both the relation between their behavior and the response of another person and the impact of the other person's response on their own psychological state, they are now sensitive to monitoring their behavior and are motivated to consider self-other contingencies so as to ensure the presence of positive psychological events and avoid the presence of negative ones. Even though children's representations of self-other contingencies are rather concrete and behavioral at this time, these representations are *early precursors of self-evaluative guides* and are used by children for *self-regulation.* Thus, at this level they become sensitive to others' responses to themselves and this phenomenon is the *precursor of the self-evaluative process.* Although these two developments in the self-system are rudimentary, they are the central factors that lead to the development of the self-system and, in some cases, to the development of self-discrepancies.

Level 3: Late Interrelational and Early Dimensional Development. During the period of development between the ages of four and six, children undergo yet another important shift in cognitive functioning. Whereas prior to this level of development, they have difficulty viewing the world and themselves from a perspective other than their own, they are now able to adopt the inferred viewpoints of others in considering events, including their own behaviors and actions. The development of *perspective-taking* or role-taking ability that occurs with the shift from "egocentric" to "nonegocentric" cognitive functioning has been well documented (see Case 1985; Feffer 1970; Fischer 1980; Higgins 1981; Piaget 1965) and has important implications for understanding the development of the self-system.

Perspective-taking ability can be defined in terms of the capacity to (1) prevent one's own immediate reactions to a target from intruding on one's judgment about a target person (self or other), and (2) *simultaneously* consider several events and the impact of these events on others independent of one's own experiences (see Case 1985; Higgins 1981). Once children develop the capacity for perspective-taking, they begin to make inferences not only about the experiences of others in relation to a particular event but also about others' opinions and evaluations of their behaviors and actions. Since children are now capable of simultaneously representing their own behavior and the inferred values or preferences of others, they can compare these two perspectives and evaluate the extent to which they are discrepant. In other words, children are now capable of *self-regulation* and *self-evaluation* in terms of a *standard or guide for their features that is associated with the inferred viewpoint or perspective of another individual.* For example, children are now able to understand that it is the discrepancy between their behavior (e.g., playing aggressively with playmates) and the behavior desired by their mother (e.g., playing cooperatively with playmates) that underlies the association between their behavior, their mother's response (e.g., separating the child from playmates), and the negative psychological situation that is associated with her response (e.g., sadness or fear of punishment). These cognitive developments increase children's ability and motivation to monitor their behavior in terms of significant standards associated with the inferred perspectives or viewpoints of others.

At this level, children are also able to compare their behavior to other standards that are important for self-evaluation. For example, they now begin to compare their performances to the performances of others (social comparison standard) or to their performance in the past (autobiographical standard) when evaluating themselves (see Ruble & Rholes 1981; Shantz 1983). In general, children develop a greater interest and motivation in self-evaluation and in monitoring their behavior against any number of self-evaluative standards.

In addition to these changes, children also undergo a shift in the nature of their self-representations and now begin to consider patterns and consistencies in their behavior and to view themselves in more stable behavioral terms (see Harter 1983, 1986a; Rosenberg 1979). They begin to form traitlike descriptions of themselves which are concrete and behaviorally based. For example, children may begin to describe themselves as good or poor at sports, or as good or poor at school. Even though the organization of self-descriptive attributes is simple rather than complex, these self-descriptions are the rudimentary foundations of the self-concept (Harter 1983, 1986a; Rosenberg 1979).

The implications of these cognitive changes for self-regulation and self-evaluation are profound. Since children now possess the cognitive capacity to regulate and evaluate themselves with reference to the inferred viewpoints of others, and they are motivated to do so, they become vulnerable to experiencing discrepancy between their own actual behaviors or attributes and those they believe others wish they would or feel they should possess. They are likely to feel humiliated and sad if they believe they have not behaved as others wish, and they are likely to feel fear or even a form of guilt that is associated with the anticipation of punishment if they believe they have not behaved as others think they should.

Not only are children more vulnerable to a wider range of negative psychological experiences, but since they now possess more stable, organized self-descriptions, the evaluations they make of themselves are more likely to have lasting implications. In addition, children at this level of cognitive development need not engage in discrepant behaviors in order to experience the psychological distress associated with self-discrepancy since simply being exposed to a stimulus that reminds them of a discrepant self-attribute (e.g., observing another child's behavior that reminds them of one of their own attributes that is discrepant from parental standards) is sufficient to produce discomfort. Thus, the range of events that might lead a child to experience psychological distress are increased substantially at this level of development.

Level 4: Late Dimensional Development. Between the ages of nine and eleven years, children develop the ability to make relative judgments about themselves and others that take into consideration rankings on two dimensions simultaneously. For example, in evaluating the ability of other children to play baseball, children at this level are able to consider (1) the age of another child and (2) the amount of effort the child exerted in playing the game in coming to a conclusion about the relative ability of the child to play baseball (see Case 1985). The ability to represent these complex relationships allows them to make attributions of causality for themselves and others.

This shift in cognitive ability means that children are now able to compare their own performance across situations and time, and in comparison to others, and thus can make dispositional and traitlike judgments about themselves and others (Rholes & Ruble 1984). As a result, children are more likely to describe themselves using abstract, dispositional attributes rather than behavioral terms. At this level of development, then, children can tell others about what type of person they are (referring to dispositional characteristics and abilities) in addition to describing the behaviors they engage in. Moreover, their inferences of how others view them are now more likely to be organized in terms of generalized traits rather than behaviors. For example, they can also describe what personality characteristics they believe their parents would ideally wish them to possess or feel they should possess.

These changes in their cognitive representation of the self are associated with changes in self-evaluation and potential difficulties in self-regulation. Since the self is now represented in more general and global terms, children are more likely to make general self-evaluations when they compare themselves to the inferred viewpoint or perspective that others hold for them. Note that children continue to feel motivated to regulate and evaluate themselves in terms of others' standards for them in order to ensure the presence of positive psychological outcomes and to avoid negative ones. If children experience discrepancy between themselves and the standards they believe others hold, the task of altering themselves to reduce the discrepancy becomes more problematic because now the discrepancies may reflect dispositional characteristics. That is, it is no longer a question of children changing only *what they do* but also *who they are* in order to meet parental standards. Hence, children at this level might be vulnerable to feelings of *helplessness and hopelessness* in addition to dejection and/or agitation-related feelings associated with different types of self-discrepancy.

Children at this level of development are also beginning to consider other perspectives on themselves, such as that of their peers. The ability to consider multiple perspectives on the self and to represent the self in terms of dispositional or traitlike features may also coincide with the emergence of children's *own* perspective on themselves, depending on their culture's emphasis on such an independent, personal perspective. Children at this level may begin to consider the relationship between their actual-self and how they would ideally like to be (ideal-self : own perspective) or feel they should be (ought-self : own perspective). Their consideration of multiple perspectives on the self might result in greater vulnerability to perceptions of discrepancy. The perception of discrepancy in and of itself does not necessarily lead to psychological distress unless the child believes that negative consequences are associated with the state of discrepancy (a negative outcome-contingency belief); however, the fact that the child can now consider multiple perspectives on the self heightens the probability that he or she will perceive the self as discrepant from some viewpoint or standard that is psychologically significant.

Level 5: Vectorial Development. The final shift in cognitive development we will consider occurs during early adolescence (ages thirteen to sixteen). This level of development is marked by the adolescent's ability *simultaneously* to consider several perspectives on the same object (Case 1985; Fischer 1980; Inhelder & Piaget 1958; Selman & Byrne 1974). At this level, information about several distinct traits can be integrated and abstractions drawn about personality types. Consequently, representations of the self from one's own perspective and the perspective of others are now likely to contain highly interconnected information about personality or identity (Harter 1983).

One potential effect of this shift is an increase in the adolescent's vulnerability to overgeneralized self-evaluations. Adolescents' perception of a discrepancy between their actual-self and a self-guide might lead them to make very global negative self-evaluations similar to the negatively distorted views of the self found in individuals suffering from depression (e.g., Beck 1967, 1976; Seligman, Abramson, et al. 1979).

This shift has further implications for the process of self-evaluation and self-regulation. At this level, adolescents can simultaneously consider the relation of the actual-self to *several* self-guides, and the relation of self-guides to each other. In addition, they are able to represent the relation between a target person's attributes and the responses of multiple persons to those attributes (e.g., father is not critical of himself for drinking, but mother berates him for his behavior) and to compare these relations to their own system of self-evaluation and self-regulation.

The ability to consider oneself from many perspectives simultaneously could lead to a more elaborated and differentiated view of the self and could have positive consequences (see Linville 1985), but it brings with it many risks for psychological distress. For example, an adolescent might feel agitated and apprehensive by failing to live up to the duties and obligations prescribed by his parents (e.g., getting high grades, not staying out late; abiding by rules and regulations prescribed by schools and society), but feel happy and satisfied by being the type of person he believes his peers wish him to be (e.g., having little regard for rules, regulations, and formalities at school and in society). The conflict between these two self-guides might lead to feelings of conflict, confusion, and rebelliousness.

When individuals experience conflict between two or more self-guides, they are likely to experience difficulties in self-regulation and self-evaluation. Positive self-perceptions and feelings result from evaluating oneself in relation to one self-guide, but negative self-perceptions and feelings result from another self-guide. Thus, adolescents are likely to experience considerable fluctuations in self-perception and mood over short periods of time. They may also be confused, indecisive, and uncertain about their behavior and plans for the future because they fluctuate in deciding which self-guide they will use for self-evaluation and self-regulation. When they adopt one self-guide, they might feel rebellious because they are rejecting another. As previously noted, the findings of Van Hook and Higgins (1988) are consistent with these predictions.

The phenomenon of self-guide : self-guide conflict clearly captures the struggle and challenge of adolescence as described by Blos (1961) and Erikson (1959). Adolescents are faced with a multitude of ways to evaluate and regulate their behavior, and they need to consider, compare, and work through the conflict between alternative self-guides to achieve a personal resolution. During this process, they are vulnerable to many different types of negative psychological experiences: discrepancy between actual- and ideal-self representations that may lead to feelings of dejection; discrepancy between actual- and the ought-self representations that may lead to feelings of agitation; and discrepancy between different self-guides that may lead to feelings of confusion, indecision, and rebelliousness. The psychological strain of this period may lead some individuals to avoid the crisis of personal integration and prematurely adopt a set of self-guides that has been transferred to them from their parents and other significant individuals (i.e., identity foreclosure) or to avoid the crisis and commitment to self-guides altogether (i.e., identity diffusion). Others may enter an extended period of crisis in which they experience difficulty committing themselves to personal self-guides (i.e., identity moratorium). For the adolescent who enters this period with sufficient psychological resources and support, however, it marks a period of crisis that can lead to personal commitment to self-guides and maturity (i.e., identity achievement; Erikson 1959).

PARENTAL SOCIALIZATION OF SELF-OTHER CONTINGENCY AND SELF-GUIDES

Thus far we have considered the development of the child's cognitive ability to represent complex relations and events, and the implications of these cognitive shifts for understanding changes in the representation of the self. We will now consider the effects of different socialization practices on the child's acquisition of self-guides and self-evaluative and self-regulatory processes (see also Higgins 1987, in press, a).

The Acquisition of Self-Other Contingency Knowledge and Self-Guides

The acquisition of self-guides for self-evaluation and self-regulation depends on children's understanding of the relation between their behaviors and parental responses. To the extent that children are not exposed to sufficient information about this relation, they will have difficulty evaluating and regulating their behavior. In our view, their acquisition of self-other contingency knowledge depends on the same types of factors that determine their acquisition of knowledge in general (see also Higgins, in press, a).

Children are more likely to acquire self-other contingency knowledge when (1) parents *frequently* expose their children to information about the relation between their behavior and the parent's response, (2) the relation between their behavior and parental responses is demonstrated *consistently,* (3) parents present information about the relation between the child's behavior and parental responses *clearly* and under conditions that draw attention to this relation, and (4) it is communicated by persons who are *significant* to the child (the response of this individual to the child is emotionally and motivationally important).

Strong self-guides are likely to be easily retrieved from memory (highly accessible) when they are well-integrated and clear (coherent) and emotionally and motivationally significant (relevant). (See Higgins & King, 1981, for a discussion of the factors that contribute to knowledge availability and accessibility.) For example, for children whose attempts at independence have been frequently, consistently, and clearly responded to by their parents with punishment, the parental self-guide that they should be dependent rather than independent will be easily and clearly retrieved from memory when they engage in or consider independent behavior, and this information will precipitate feelings of agitation and apprehension that they will be motivated to avoid. In contrast, when self-other contingency information has not been communicated frequently, consistently, with clarity, or by significant individuals, children may have difficulty predicting the responses of others to their behavior and forming self-guides for self-evaluation and self-regulation. For example, a child whose demands for attention are sometimes met with acceptance and other times with rejection may have difficulty ascertaining what aspects of herself are acceptable and unacceptable and forming a clear self-guide for behavioral evaluation and regulation.

Although research to date has not directly investigated the effects of these particular socialization factors on self-regulation in children, related features have been examined that permit a comparison between our analysis and the literature. The perspective we have outlined suggests that when children are exposed to socialization practices that encourage the development of strong self-guides, they will be more likely to demonstrate prosocial, nonaggressive, obedient behavior, and high levels of behavioral regulation. Consistent with this prediction, previous research indicates that when parents demonstrate high involvement and demandingness in their socialization practices (i.e., high frequency and consistency), children are more likely to display obedient and nonaggressive behavior (Maccoby & Martin 1983). In addition, when parents adjust their communication to children's attentional level and explain policies, use induction, or explicitly teach contingencies (i.e., high level of clarity), children are more likely to demonstrate social responsibility and independence in self-regulation (Baldwin 1955; Lewin, Lippitt, & White 1939; Maccoby & Martin 1983). Finally, when parents' communications of their expectations are accompanied by strong expressions of affect (i.e., high salience/clarity and significance), children are more likely to show prosocial, obedient behavior.

In contrast, when children are exposed to socialization practices that do not encourage the development of strong self-guides, we predict that they will have difficulties in behavioral regulation. There is considerable evidence to support this view. For example, the infrequent use of control techniques by parents has been associated with low levels of compliance and behavior problems (Maccoby & Martin 1983). Parental socialization practices that fail to communicate expectations frequently and consistently are associated with increased levels of aggression, disobedience, and lack of self-control in children. In addition, the failure of parents to communicate their expectations at an appropriate level for the child has been associated with poor self-control and behavioral difficulties (Patterson 1982).

The Acquisition of Types of Self-Other Contingency Knowledge and Self-Guides

Parental socialization practices can also influence the *type* of self-guides that children adopt. According to self-discrepancy theory (Higgins 1987, in press, b), different types of self-guides are related to different types of psychological situations. The development of self-guides and self-discrepancies rests upon (1) whether parents are oriented toward identifying and responding to the child's features that *match* or *do not match* their guides for the child, and (2) whether parents are oriented toward positive outcomes (absent or present) for their child or toward negative outcomes (absent or present) for their child (for a fuller discussion, see Higgins, in press, a). Four "pure" types of parenting orientation associated with children acquiring strong self-guides are described below (see table 13.1).

TABLE 13.1 Relation of Parents' Guides for Children and Parents' Contingency Orientation to Children's Psychological Development under Strong Self-Guide Acquisition Conditions

Parent's guides for children	Ideal[a]	Ought[b]	Ideal	Ought
Parent's contingency orientation	Matches	Matches	Mismatches	Mismatches
Psychological outcome for child	Presence of positive	Absence of negative	Absence of positive	Presence of negative
Development of self-discrepancies	Congruency between actual-self and ideal self-guide	Congruency between actual-self and ought self-guide	Discrepancy between actual-self and ideal self-guide	Discrepancy between actual-self and ought self-guide
Emotional consequences	Low emotional distress—satisfaction, happiness	Low emotional distress—security, relaxation	High emotional distress—dejection, disappointment	High emotional distress—agitation, apprehension

a. Parents' hopes and wishes for the child
b. Parents' duties and obligations prescribed for the child

Parents' Contingency Orientations 1 and 2: Child-Parent Match. If parents are oriented toward identifying and responding to their child's features that are *concordant* with their *hopes and wishes* for the child (1) or with the *duties and obligations* they have prescribed for the child (2), their relationship with their child is likely to be dominated by the *presence of positive outcomes and/or the absence of negative outcomes.* When parents perceive that their child's features are concordant with their hopes and wishes for their child (the child is behaving in a way they had ideally wished for), they are likely to feel satisfied and to communicate this to their child. The parents' perception of a match between their child's features and their hopes and wishes for their child is associated with the *presence of positive outcomes.* When parents perceive that their child's behavior and attributes are concordant with the duties and obligations they have prescribed for the child (their child is behaving in the way they feel he or she should), they are likely to feel relaxed and secure about their child and to communicate these feelings. The parents' perception of a match between their child's features and the duties and obligations they have prescribed for their child is associated with the *absence of negative outcomes* for the child.

A socialization orientation that highlights the concordance of the child's features with parental ideal guides frequently, consistently, and with clarity and significance is likely to result in the child's acquisition of *strong ideal self-guides,* and one that highlights the concordance of the child's features with parental ought guides is likely to result in the child's acquisition of *strong ought self-guides.* Children exposed to these conditions are likely to develop a self-concept characterized by concordance rather than discrepancy between self-state representations. Nonetheless, children will be motivated to meet their parents' guides to ensure the continued presence of positive outcomes or absence of negative outcomes. It is likely that the perception of self-concordance is associated with a more positive emotional state than is the perception of self-discrepancy.

Some parents' socialization orientation is characterized by infrequent, inconsistent, and ambiguous attention to their child's behaviors and attributes that match their guides for their child (e.g., the permissive parent). Children exposed to this style of parental socialization may have difficulty establishing firm self-guides and identifying those self-attributes that are highly praised by others. They may view themselves somewhat positively and expect others to respond positively, albeit inconsistently, to them, but they may have difficulty in establishing a firm sense of self and regulating their behavior in relation to self-guides.

Parents' Contingency Orientations 3 and 4: Child-Parent Mismatch. If parents are oriented toward identifying and responding to their child's features that are *discrepant* from their *hopes and wishes* for the child (3), or from the *duties and obligations* they have prescribed (4), their relationship with their child is likely to be dominated by the absence of positive outcomes and/or the presence of negative outcomes. When parents perceive that their child's features are discrepant from their hopes and wishes for their child, they are likely to feel disappointed and dissatisfied, and they may communicate these feelings to the child by withdrawing their support and acceptance. The parents' perception of a *mismatch* may be associated with the *absence of positive outcomes* for the child. When parents perceive that their child's features are discrepant from the duties and obligations they have prescribed, they are likely to criticize, reprimand, or punish the child. The parent's perception of a *mismatch* may be associated with the *presence of negative outcomes* for the child.

A socialization orientation that highlights the discrepancy between the child's features and parental ideal guides frequently, consistently, and with clarity and significance is likely to result in the child's acquisition of *strong ideal self-guides;* a socialization orientation that highlights the discrepancy between the child's features and parental ought guides is likely to result in the child's acquisition of *strong ought self-guides.* Since both socialization orientations focus on the mismatch between the child's features and parental guides, children exposed to these conditions are likely to develop a self-concept characterized by discrepancy rather than concordance between self-state representations. They will be motivated to meet parental guides in order to reduce the negative psychological state associated with the perception of self-discrepancy—i.e., to reduce feelings of disappointing others and feelings of embarrassment that are associated with actual-ideal discrepancy, or to reduce feelings of agitation, apprehension, and fear that are associated with actual-ought discrepancy.

When parents' socialization orientation is characterized by infrequent, inconsistent, and vague attention to their child's features that are discrepant from their guides (e.g., the inconsistently punitive parent), children may have difficulty establishing firm self-guides and identifying those self-attributes that are unacceptable to others. They may view themselves somewhat negatively, expect others to abandon, reject, criticize, or punish them, and have difficulty in self-regulation.

It is important to recognize that these descriptions are simplified prototypes of socialization orientations. Most parents probably employ a mixture of these characteristics in parenting and may vary in their parenting orientation across time, circumstances, and types of behavior enacted by the child.

MENTAL REPRESENTATION CAPACITY × PARENTAL SOCIALIZATION PRACTICES: IMPLICATIONS FOR SELF-SYSTEM VULNERABILITIES

In this final section we consider the *interaction* between children's developing capacity for representational thought and parental socialization practices. We approach this task by describing the predicted sequence of self-development from representational levels 1–5 for each prototype of parental socialization practices. We also consider the variation in self-development that may occur for each of these prototypes under strong and weak self-guide acquisition conditions.

Parents' Contingency Orientations I and 2: Child-Parent Match

Infants whose parents' socialization orientation focuses on the match between the infant's behaviors and their guides for the infant are likely to experience the presence of positive outcomes and the absence of negative outcomes. This orientation toward the infant seems more likely to occur when parents have realistically appraised the infant's needs and abilities and have adjusted their expectations for the infant in accordance with this appraisal. Infants exposed to this type of socialization orientation are likely to develop trust rather than mistrust (Erikson 1963) of their caretakers and the environment, and are likely to approach rather than avoid new experiences and activities. Upon entering the second level of cognitive development (late sensorimotor and early interrelational development), young children begin to understand that many of their behaviors produce responses from their parents that in turn lead to feelings of happiness, security, and contentment. These self-other contingency representations permit the children to regulate their behavior to ensure the presence of positive outcomes or the absence of negative outcomes.

It is not until level 3 that children understand that the relation between their own behavior and their parents' responses to them is mediated by their parents' evaluation of the behavior in relation to their parents' standards for them. At this level children can adopt the perspective of their mother or father on their own behavior and understand their parents' responses to them as a function of this perspective. Children exposed to a parental orientation that focuses on the match between their behavior and the parents' guides for them are likely to experience themselves positively when adopting the perspective of their parents and to feel that their parents are satisfied with them. These self-perceptions become increasingly consolidated and traitlike as children move through levels 4 and 5 of cognitive development. They come to view themselves as possessing positive stable personality characteristics which elicit positive responses from others. Such children know which self-characteristics result in either the presence of positive responses or the absence of negative responses from others, and they are able to regulate their behavior to ensure both. Upon entering adolescence, they are able to evaluate themselves from numerous perspectives without experiencing intense feelings of dejection or agitation because they already possess a stable and positive view of themselves. The evaluation of themselves that occurs in adolescence is not intensely threatening, and hence they do not avoid this process nor are they overwhelmed by it.

Although research to date has not examined the impact of parenting styles on child development as a function of the child capacity for mental representation, descriptions of parenting styles that promote self-confidence and social competence are consistent with our description of a socialization orientation that focuses on the match between parental standards and child characteristics. In general, warm, consistent, and responsive parenting is associated with greater social competence in children (Baumrind 1967, 1971; Bryant & Crockenberg 1980; Spivack, Platt, & Schure 1976). Cole and Rehm (1986) found that mothers of psychologically healthy children were twice as likely to reward their child's task performance with expressions of positive affect than were mothers of depressed children. Children experiencing low levels of depression and distress also perceive their families as more cohesive, positive, and supportive than do children experiencing depressive symptoms (Asarnow, Carlson, & Guthrie 1987; Jaenicke et al. 1987).

The picture of self-development for the child exposed to socialization practices that focus on the match between the child's behavior and parental guides, but do so infrequently, inconsistently, vaguely, and with little significance, may be quite different. As an infant, the child also experiences the presence of positive outcomes and the absence of negative outcomes, but these events seem to occur randomly. Hence, the infant is unsure of when and how to approach other individuals and new experiences. Such children may experience difficulty acquiring self-other contingency knowledge during level 2 of cognitive development because it is not clear which behaviors or self-features lead to the presence of positive or the absence of negative responses from their parents, and they have difficulty regulating their behavior. During level 3, these children again experience difficulty because they do not possess sufficient information to form perspectives on how others view their behavior. The lack of adequate information about the impact of their features on others' responses to them makes it difficult for them to consolidate a stable self-concept during levels 4 and 5 of cognitive development. Since others' responses to them have never been strongly related to their own behavior, they may fail to understand their impact on others. They approach adolescence with an inadequate representation of themselves, and with little sensitivity to how others view them. They may feel that their behavior, and more fundamentally their "self," is simply insignificant. Their lack of development of a firm sense of self may also lead them to experience difficulties in determining self-other boundaries. With little firm basis from which to compare their own self-view with alternative perspectives of themselves, the probability of adequate adjustments to early adulthood is compromised for these young adults.

Our description of a parental socialization orientation that is positive but bears no relation to a child's behavioral variation is similar to descriptions of parenting styles of children and adolescents who experience difficulty in establishing a stable sense of self (Guidano 1987). In such cases, parents have been described as attempting to provide an image of a perfectly happy family environment and they appear dedicated to their child's welfare. Guidano speculates that this parenting orientation stems from the parents' intense need for positive confirmation of themselves and their inability to tolerate negative feelings in their relationship with their child. As a consequence, children are unable to establish clear boundaries between themselves and their parents, a characteristic often noted in the families of patients suffering from eating disorders (Minuchin, Rosman, & Baker 1978).

Parents' Contingency Orientations 3 and 4: Child-Parent Mismatch

When parents' socialization orientation to their child highlights the mismatches between their guides for the child and the child's behavior, the child is likely to experience negative psychological consequences that include the absence of positive outcomes and/or the presence of negative outcomes. This socialization orientation may be adopted for many reasons. First, some parents might experience difficulty in realistically appraising their child's behavioral repertoire and adjusting their expectancies in accordance with this appraisal. The parents' inability realistically to appraise and adjust their expectations for their child increases the likelihood that their interactions with the child will be dominated by the mismatch between their expectancies and the child's behavior. Second, some infants might be more prone temperamentally to produce behavior that does not match parental expectations. For example, infants characterized by withdrawn or timid behavioral predispositions might be more likely than more sociable infants to elicit a socialization orientation from parents that emphasizes the mismatch between child behavior and parental guides. Kagan and his colleagues (1984) have indeed observed that mothers of behaviorally inhibited children are more likely to try to change their child's behavior than are mothers of sociable children. These two factors—parents' capacity to adjust their expectancies for their child and the child's temperamental predisposition—interact to influence the socialization orientation adopted by parents (Rubin & Lollis, in press). Finally, the parents' own emotional problems could produce a mismatch orientation to their child. For example, a depressed mother who is preoccupied with her own concerns and suffering from general motivational deficits might withdraw from her child.

Infants exposed to a mismatch socialization orientation might have difficulty establishing trust in their caretakers because they either fail to elicit positive parental responses or elicit negative parental responses. Without a sense of trust in their environment, these children may avoid new experiences and activities (Erikson 1963). On the one hand, a lack of positive parental responses may produce a lack of positive emotional experiences for the child (e.g., dejection), or on the other, the presence of negative parental responses may produce negative emotional experiences for the child (e.g., fear, apprehension).

When children enter the second level of development, they begin to represent self-other contingencies between their behaviors and parental responses. They are likely to perceive the lack of positive parental responses and/or the presence of negative parental responses as related to their behavior and they may attempt to monitor their behavior to avoid both of these negative psychological situations. Such children might appear excessively inhibited or avoidant. The lack of positive parental responses might also lead to feelings of dysphoria in the child while the presence of negative parental responses might lead to feelings of fear, agitation, and apprehension. Hence, even though children at this early level of development might not express some features of depression found in older children or adults (negative self-referent cognitions, expressions of low self-esteem), it is possible that they could experience some affective and behavioral symptoms of depression and/or anxiety.

At level 3 of development, children begin to realize that the relation between their own behavior and parental responses is mediated by their parents' evaluations of the behavior in relation to the parents' standards for them. Children at this level also form the rudiments of a self-concept based on their observations of their own behavioral patterns and their parents' responses to them. These developmental changes may produce a shift in the types of symptoms experienced and expressed by children exposed to a mismatch socialization orientation.

First, the capacity of young children to infer the guides their parents hold for them and to compare their behavior to these guides furthers their capacity to monitor their behavior to prevent negative psychological outcomes. Hence, children exposed to a mismatch socialization orientation might exhibit even greater vigilance and inhibition than at earlier levels of development. Second, because children exposed to a mismatch socialization orientation are likely to experience discrepancy when they compare their behavior to their parents' guides for them, they are highly vulnerable to feelings of shame and humiliation when they perceive they are a disappointment to their parents, and/or to feelings of fear and, to some extent, guilt when they perceive they are failing to fulfill the duties and obligations prescribed by their parents. Finally, children exposed to a mismatch socialization orientation are likely to begin to make highly negative self-evaluations about themselves based on the discrepant relation between their behavior and parents' standards for them. These negative inferences about the self increase in stability and cohesiveness with further development. At this point, then, one would expect children exposed to a mismatch socialization orientation to express a fuller range of depression and anxiety symptoms including both new negative affective states (e.g., shame) and negative self-cognitions.

The consolidation of self-concept is a central feature of development in levels 4 and 5. Children now begin to make dispositional inferences about themselves and others. Children who have been consistently exposed to a mismatch socialization orientation are likely to view themselves as possessing stable negative personality characteristics that elicit either disappointment and/or hostility and anger from others. Not surprisingly, this self-perception is likely to lead to increasing inhibition and avoidance. However, the use of avoidance strategies to reduce the likelihood of negative psychological situations (the absence of positive outcomes or the presence of negative outcomes) may actually increase the interpersonal problems that the child is motivated to avoid.

Upon entering adolescence, children exposed to a mismatch socialization orientation are likely to appear highly inhibited and/or avoidant and may express a full range of depressive and/or anxiety symptoms that includes global negative self-regard and feelings of hopelessness. Attempts to evaluate themselves from the perspective of peers or other significant individuals might precipitate intense feelings of dejection and/or agitation. Hence, the consolidation of identity during adolescence is likely to be experienced as painful and overwhelming.

Our proposal that a mismatch parental socialization orientation is likely to produce feelings of dejection, agitation, and low self-worth in children is supported by research indicating that harsh and rejecting parental practices are associated with feelings of low self-worth and social incompetence in offspring (Aber & Allen 1987; Jaenicke et al. 1987). There is also evidence that the higher risk for depressive illness and anxiety disorder in the offspring of depressed parents and anxiety-disordered parents (Billings & Moos 1983; Hammen, Adrian, et al. 1987; Turner, Beidel, & Costello 1987; Weissman et al. 1987) is mediated by quality of parent-child interactions. To date, researchers have found that depressed mothers are less positive in their interactions with their children (Mills et al. 1984) and make more unsuccessful attempts to restrict their child's behavior than nondepressed mothers (Sameroff, Barocas, & Seifer 1982). The tendency of depressed mothers to lack warmth and to be more resentful and hostile in their interactions with their children has been shown to be predictive of higher rates of psychiatric disorder in their offspring (Weissman, Paykel, & Klerman 1972; Weissman & Paykel 1974). Researchers have yet to examine the consequences of socialization practices associated with parental depression on self-development as a function of the child's growing capacity for mental representation. Other researchers, however, agree with our prediction that such parental practices are likely to lead to the development of a negative and vulnerable self-system representation (Cassidy 1988; Guidano 1987).

The picture of self-development for children exposed to parental socialization practices that focus on the mismatch between the children's features and parental guides infrequently, inconsistently, and without clarity or significance may be quite different. Like children exposed to a consistent mismatch, these children also experience the absence of positive and/or the presence of negative parental responses. These responses appear to occur randomly, however. Hence, the children experience difficulty establishing a sense of predictability in their environment. The failure of parents to communicate their standards consistently results in their children's inability to establish clear self-other contingency representations during level 2 of development. This type of socialization orientation might engender feelings of apathy because the children's attempts to regulate their behavior to avoid negative psychological events are futile.

At level 3 of development, children possess the representational capacity to understand that parental responses to their behavior are mediated by the relation of their behavior to their parents' guides for them. However, children exposed to a low-consistency mismatch orientation experience difficulty identifying precisely which self-features provoke negative parental responses. These children might suffer from an extreme sense of helplessness and diffuse anxiety; they are not able to predict parental responses and cannot exert control over their environment by modifying their own behavior. They are also vulnerable to feelings of dejection and agitation associated with the absence of positive and the presence of negative parental responses, respectively.

Such children are likely to enter adolescence experiencing diffuse symptoms of depression and anxiety. Without a clear representation of the relation between their behavior and others' responses they might experience difficulty regulating their behavior which in turn could produce behavioral disorders (e.g., delinquency). Their socialization history has led them to expect that others will respond negatively to them, and consequently their negative expectancies in interpersonal relationships could cause them to withdraw from or negatively react to social situations. This interpersonal style in turn could elicit the abandonment or rejection they anticipate. For this child, adolescence is likely to be volatile and difficult.

Research to date provides some support of the relation between rejecting, harsh, and inconsistent parenting and psychopathology in children (e.g., Egeland & Sroufe 1981). Although this research has yet to examine the relation between parental practices and child psychopathology as a function of the development of capacity for mental representation, results indirectly support our proposal that this socialization orientation results in general negative experiences and difficulties in behavioral regulation. For example, the most common disorders found in the offspring of depressed parents are affective disorder and attention-deficit disorder (Biederman et al. 1987; Orvaschel et al. 1981; Orvaschel, Walsh-Allis, & Ye 1988). Although researchers have several explanations for the higher risk of affective disorders in this population, they are at a loss to explain the higher rates of attention deficit disorder that also occur. One possibility is that while children who are at risk only for affective disorder have been exposed to *consistent* mismatch socialization practices, the offspring who are at risk for attention deficit disorder have been exposed to *inconsistent* mismatch socialization practices. Such children would experience difficulty in behavioral regulation, a central feature of attention deficit disorder. This analysis is congruent with the finding that many children with attention deficit disorder have depressed mothers who are inconsistent, punitive, and rejecting (Weismann, Paykel, & Klerman 1972).

CONCLUDING REMARKS

This chapter has presented a preliminary model of the development of emotional vulnerabilities related to the development of the self-system. It has a number of distinctive features: the model (1) considers how developmental changes in cognitive capacity influence the development of self-guides (self-regulatory and self-evaluative standards) rather than just the development of the self-concept; (2) explicates the *dual role of self-guides* in development—their role in both self-regulation and self-evaluation; (3) describes the underlying characteristics of parent-child interaction that determine children's acquisition of strong self-guides; (4) distinguishes between *types* of self-guides that are used in self-regulation and self-evaluation; (5) describes how the etiology of different types of self-guides is related to different types of psychological situations produced by different types of parent-child interaction; and (6) makes predictions about the development of distinct emotional vulnerabilities as a function of *specific interactions* between developmental differences in cognitive capacity and individual differences in parent-child interaction.

This chapter has focused on the development of self-guides, which are valued end states that people are motivated to meet. For a fuller understanding of the development of self-system vulnerabilities, it would be necessary to consider as well the effects of both developmental changes in cognitive capacity and individual differences in socialization on the development of *means* for attaining these valued end states—from social problem-solving procedures to coping strategies to defense mechanisms. Indeed, it may be that it is the complex interrelation between type of preferred end state (including emotional end state) and type of preferred means to attain it that underlies the perplexing variety of disorders from which people suffer.

CHAPTER 14

Conclusion: Reflections on Nonability Determinants of Competence

ALBERT BANDURA

Recent years have witnessed major changes in the conception of human ability and competence. Competence is not a fixed property that one does or does not have in one's behavioral repertoire. Rather, it involves a generative capability in which cognitive, social, and behavioral skills must be organized and effectively orchestrated to serve innumerable purposes. There is a marked difference between possessing knowledge and skills and being able to use them well under diverse circumstances, many of which contain ambiguous, unpredictable, and stressful elements.

A capability is only as good as its execution. People often fail to perform optimally even though they know full well what to do and possess the requisite skills. This is because self-referent thought mediates the translation of knowledge and abilities into skilled performance. Among the different facets of self-referent thought, none is more central or pervasive than beliefs regarding personal capabilities. Because of their substantial impact on motivation, affective arousal, and thought processes, self-beliefs of capability partly govern the level of performance attainments. Thus, with the same set of skills people may perform poorly, adequately, or extraordinarily depending on their self-beliefs of efficacy.

Preparation of this commentary was facilitated by Public Health Research Grant MH-5162-25 from the National Institute of Mental Health and a grant from the MacArthur Foundation. Some of the organizing conceptions presented in this commentary are drawn from the book, *Social Foundations of Thought and Action: A Social Cognitive Theory* (Englewood Cliffs, N.J.: Prentice-Hall, 1986).

MEDIATING MECHANISMS

The research reviewed in this volume has added greatly to our understanding of the centrality of perceived competence in sociocognitive functioning. Some progress has also been made in delineating the processes by which beliefs of personal capabilities affect psychological well-being and performance attainments. Several features of the experimental methodology employed in research conducted within the framework of self-efficacy theory are well suited for clarifying mediating mechanisms. Self-beliefs of efficacy are measured in terms of designated domains of functioning. Because of their greater relevance, domain-linked appraisals of self-efficacy generally have higher explanatory and predictive power than do nondescript omnibus measures (Bandura 1988c). Analyses of the causal contribution of self-efficacy beliefs to behavior test the postulated dual linkage in the causal process—external influences are related to the efficacy mediator which is, in turn, related to action. The efficacy-action link is corroborated by microlevel relations between particular self-percepts of efficacy and corresponding action, or by macrolevel relations between aggregated self-percepts of efficacy and aggregated behavior. Perceived self-efficacy is systemically varied rather than merely correlated, which removes ambiguity about the direction of causality. The impact of self-efficacy beliefs is assessed in relation to diverse outcomes including cognitive, affective, and behavioral functioning.

Perceived self-efficacy is concerned with people's beliefs in their capabilities to mobilize the motivation, cognitive resources, and courses of action needed to exercise control over task demands. Perceived competence is similarly concerned with judgments of personal capabilities. Self-beliefs of efficacy affect action through several intervening processes, which are reviewed next. Some of these processes, such as affective arousal and cognitive activities, are of considerable interest in their own right, rather than merely as intervening influencers of action.

Motivational Processes

People's self-beliefs of efficacy determine how much effort they will exert in an endeavor, and how long they will persevere in the face of obstacles. The stronger the belief in their capabilities, the greater and more persistent are their efforts (Bandura 1988a). When faced with difficulties, people who have self-doubts about their capabilities slacken their efforts or abort their attempts prematurely and settle for mediocre solutions, whereas those who have a strong belief in their capabilities exert greater effort to master the challenge (Bandura & Cervone 1983, 1986; Cervone & Peake 1986; Jacobs, Prentice-Dunn, & Rogers 1984; Weinberg, Gould, & Jackson 1979). Strong perseverance usually pays off in performance accomplishments.

There is a growing body of evidence that human attainments and positive well-being require an optimistic sense of personal efficacy (Bandura 1986). This is because ordinary social realities are strewn with difficulties—impediments, failures, setbacks, frustrations, inequities. People must have a robust sense of personal efficacy to sustain the perseverant effort needed to succeed. Self-doubts can set in fast after some failures or reverses. The important matter is not the self-doubt, which is a natural immediate reaction, but the speed of recovery of perceived self-efficacy. Some people quickly recover their self-assurance; others lose faith in their capabilities. Because the acquisition of knowledge and competencies usually requires sustained effort in the face of difficulties, it is resiliency of self-belief that counts.

In his delightful book *Rejection,* White (1982) provides vivid testimony that the striking characteristic of people who have achieved eminence in their fields is an inextinguishable sense of efficacy and a firm belief in the worth of what they are doing. This resilient self-belief system enabled them to override repeated early rejections of their work. A robust sense of personal efficacy provides the needed staying power.

Many of our literary classics brought their authors repeated rejections. The novelist Saroyan accumulated several thousand rejections before he had his first piece published. James Joyce's *The Dubliners* was rejected by twenty-two publishers. Gertrude Stein continued to submit poems to editors for about twenty years before one was finally accepted. Now that's invincible self-efficacy. Over a dozen publishers rejected a manuscript by e.e. cummings. When he finally got it published the dedication, printed in upper case, read: *With no thanks to* . . . followed by the long list of publishers who had rejected his offering.

Early rejection is the rule rather than the exception in other creative endeavors. The impressionists had to arrange their own art exhibitions because their works were routinely rejected by the Paris Salon. Van Gogh sold only one painting during his life. The musical works of most renowned composers were initially greeted with derision. Stravinsky was run out of town by an enraged audience and critics when he first served them the *Rite of Spring.* Many other composers suffered the same fate, especially in the early phases of their career. The work of the brilliant architect Frank Lloyd Wright was widely rejected during much of his career.

To turn to more familiar examples, Hollywood initially rejected the incomparable Fred Astaire for being only "a balding, skinny actor who can dance a little." Decca Records turned down a recording contract with the Beatles with the evaluation, "We don't like their sound. Groups of guitars are on their way out." Whoever issued that pronouncement must cringe at the sight of a guitar.

It is not uncommon for authors of scientific classics to experience repeated initial rejection of their work, often with hostile embellishments if it is too discordant with what is in vogue. Scientists often reject theories and technologies that are ahead of their time. Because of the cold reception given to most innovations, the time between conception and technical realization typically spans several decades.

The findings of laboratory investigations are in accord with these records of human triumphs regarding the centrality of the motivational effects of self-beliefs of efficacy in human attainments. It takes a resilient sense of efficacy to override the numerous impediments to significant accomplishments.

Affective Processes

People's beliefs in their capabilities affect how much stress and depression they experience in threatening or taxing situations, as well as their level of motivation. Such emotional reactions can affect action both directly and indirectly by altering the quality and course of thinking. Threat is not a fixed property of situational events, nor does appraisal of the likelihood of aversive happenings rely solely on reading external signs of danger or safety. Rather, threat is a relational property concerning the match between perceived coping capabilities and potentially aversive aspects of the environment.

People who believe they can exercise control over potential threats do not conjure up apprehensive cognitions and, therefore, are not perturbed by them. But those who believe they cannot manage potential threats experience high levels of stress. They judge themselves as highly vulnerable and view many aspects of their environment as fraught with danger (Ozer & Bandura in press). They tend to dwell on their coping deficiencies. Through such inefficacious thought they distress themselves and constrain and impair their level of functioning (Bandura 1988b, 1988e; Lazarus & Folkman 1984; Meichenbaum 1977; Sarason 1975).

That perceived coping efficacy operates as a cognitive mediator of anxiety has been tested by creating different levels of perceived coping efficacy and relating them at a microlevel to different manifestations of anxiety. Perceived coping inefficacy is accompanied by high levels of subjective distress, autonomic arousal (Bandura, Reese, & Adams 1982), and plasma catecholamine secretion (Bandura et al. 1985). The combined results from the different manifestations of anxiety are consistent in showing that anxiety and stress reactions are low when people cope with tasks in their perceived self-efficacy range. Self-doubts produce substantial increases in subjective distress and physiological arousal. After perceived coping efficacy is strengthened to the maximal level, coping with the previously intimidating tasks no longer elicits differential physiological arousal. Perceived self-inefficacy in exercising control over stressors also activates endogenous opioid systems (Bandura et al. 1988), which enables people to handle stressful situations with some relief from physical aversiveness.

Anxiety arousal in situations involving some risks is affected not only by perceived coping efficacy but also by perceived self-efficacy in controlling dysfunctional apprehensive cognitions. The exercise of control over one's own consciousness is summed up well in the proverb: "*You cannot prevent the birds of worry and care from flying over your head. But you can stop them from building a nest in your head.*"

The influential role played by thought control efficacy in anxiety arousal is corroborated in research examining the different properties of perturbing cognitions and their correlates. The results show that it is not the extent of frightful cognitions per se that accounts for anxiety arousal but rather the strength of perceived self-efficacy to control their escalation or perseveration (Kent 1987; Kent & Gibbons 1987). Thus, the incidence of frightful cognitions is unrelated to anxiety level when variations in perceived thought control efficacy are controlled for, whereas perceived thought control efficacy is strongly related to anxiety level when extent of frightful cognitions is controlled. Analysis of the aversiveness of obsessional ruminations provides further support for efficacious thought control as a key factor in the regulation of cognitively generated arousal (Salkovskis & Harrison 1984). It is not the sheer frequency of intrusive cognitions but rather the perceived inefficacy to turn them off that is the major source of distress.

Perceived self-inefficacy to fulfill desired goals that affect evaluation of self-worth and to secure things that bring satisfaction to one's life also create depression (Bandura 1988a; Cutrona & Troutman 1986; Holahan & Holahan 1987a, 1987b; Kanfer & Zeiss 1983). When the perceived self-inefficacy involves social relationships, it can induce depression both directly and indirectly by curtailing the cultivation of interpersonal relationships that can provide satisfactions and buffer the effects of chronic daily stressors (Holahan & Holahan 1987a). Depressive rumination not only impairs ability to initiate and sustain adaptive activities but further diminishes perceptions of personal efficacy (Kavanagh & Bower 1985; West, Berry, & Powlishta 1988).

Cognitive Processes

Self-beliefs of efficacy affect thought patterns that may be self-aiding or self-hindering. These cognitive effects take various forms. Much human behavior, being purposive, is regulated by forethought embodying cognized goals. Personal goal setting is influenced by self-appraisal of capabilities. The stronger the perceived self-efficacy, the higher the goals people set for themselves and the firmer their commitment to them (Bandura & Wood 1989; Locke et al. 1984; Taylor et al. 1984). Challenging goals raise the level of motivation and performance attainments (Locke et al. 1981; Mento, Steel, & Karren 1987).

Many activities involve judgmental processes that enable people to predict and control events in probabilistic environments. Discernment of the predictive rules requires effective cognitive processing of multidimensional information that contains ambiguities and uncertainties. Predictive factors are usually related probabilistically, rather than invariably, to future events which leaves some degree of uncertainty. Moreover, events are typically multidetermined The fact that the same predictor may contribute to different effects and the same effect may have multiple predictors introduces ambiguity as to what is likely to lead to what.

In ferreting out predictive rules people must draw on their state of knowledge to generate hypotheses about predictive factors, to weight and integrate them into composite rules, to test their judgments against outcome information, and to remember which notions they had tested and how well they had worked. It requires a strong sense of efficacy to remain task-oriented in the face of judgmental failures. Indeed, people who believe strongly in their problem-solving capabilities remain highly efficient in their analytic thinking in complex decision-making situations

(Bandura & Wood 1989; Wood & Bandura 1989). Those who are plagued by self-doubts are erratic in their analytic thinking. Quality of analytic thinking, in turn, affects performance accomplishments.

Self-efficacy beliefs usually affect cognitive functioning through the joint influence of motivational and information-processing operations. This is illustrated in research designed to explain variation in memory performance. The stronger people's beliefs in their memory capacities, the more time they devote to cognitive processing of memory tasks which, in turn, enhances their memory performances (Berry 1987).

A major function of thought is to enable people to predict the occurrence of events and to create the means of exercising control over those that affect their daily life. As alluded to earlier, people's perceptions of their efficacy influence the types of anticipatory scenarios they construct and reiterate. The highly self-efficacious visualize success scenarios that provide positive guides for performance, whereas those who judge themselves as inefficacious are more inclined to visualize failure scenarios which undermine performance by dwelling on how things will go wrong. Numerous studies have shown that cognitive reiteration of scenarios in which individuals visualize themselves executing activities skillfully enhances subsequent performance (Bandura 1986; Corbin 1972; Feltz & Landers 1983; Kazdin 1978). Perceived self-efficacy and cognitive enactment affect each other bidirectionally. A high sense of efficacy fosters cognitive constructions of effective actions and cognitive reiteration of efficacious courses of action strengthens self-percepts of efficacy (Bandura & Adams 1977; Kazdin 1978).

In their analysis of the role of self-systems in competence, Markus, Cross, and Wurf posit cognized possible selves as the guidance system for competence. Possible selves that are well-articulated help to organize behavior and energize it in pursuit of selected goals. Self-systems serve this function well when they contain the relevant plans and procedural strategies for realizing desired futures. Ill-defined possible selves remain but idle fantasies. The nonprescriptiveness of indefinite selves is captured well in Lily Tomlin's portrayal of a character named Chrissy, who never quite manages to get her act together. Self-reflection on her unrealized ambitions leads her to an incontestable insight: "All my life I've always wanted to *be* somebody. But I see now I should have been more specific."

Markus and her colleagues regard anticipatory cognitive simulation as the key mechanism by which self-systems get translated into behavioral competence. The evidence cited earlier corroborates that cognitive rehearsal of efficacious actions enhances performance. The authors consider processes by which cognitive simulation might produce its effects. On the assumption that perception, imagery, and action have parallel structural properties, cognitive simulation presumably coordinates perceptual and action schematas.

Perceptual processes play a major role in the acquisition of conceptions of skilled actions (Carroll & Bandura 1988). But the production of appropriate behavior is concerned more with conception-action coordination because, in most instances, actions are structured by conceptions rather than by perceptions of events. If structural similarities led to automatic translation of cognitive schemata into action schemata, the development of behavioral proficiency would be an easy matter. In actuality, it is usually a long arduous process, especially where complex skills are involved. An interpretation in terms of cross-modal coordination of perceptual and action schematas leaves unexplained the transformational production mechanism by which cognition is converted into proficient action.

One solution that has been proposed for the transformation problem relies on a dual knowledge system—declarative knowledge and procedural knowledge (Anderson 1980). Procedural knowledge provides production systems which embody decision rules for solving tasks. Construing the acquisition of competence in terms of factual and procedural knowledge is well suited for cognitive problem solving where solutions are cognitively generated and either no actions are involved or they are trivially simple. One must distinguish between knowledge and behavioral skills, however. Activities requiring the construction and adept execution of complex actions call for additional mechanisms to get from knowledge structures to proficient action. Procedural knowledge and cognitive skills are necessary but insufficient for competent performance. A novice given complete information on how to ski and a set of procedural rules, and then launched from a mountain top would most likely end up in the intensive care unit of the local infirmary. Procedural knowledge alone will not convert an awkward retiring person into a demonstrative adept one.

In social cognitive theory (Bandura 1986), the mechanism for transforming thought into action operates through a conception-matching process. Conceptual representations of efficacious actions are formed on the basis of knowledge gained through observational learning, inferences from the outcomes of enactive experiences, and innovative cognitive syntheses of preexisting knowledge. These conceptions then serve as guides for response production and as internal standards for response correction. Conceptions are rarely transformed into appropriate performance without error on the first attempt. Skilled performances are usually achieved by repeated corrective adjustments in conception matching during behavior production (Carroll & Bandura 1985, 1987). Monitored physical enactment provides the vehicle for converting conception to skilled action. The feedback accompanying the enactment provides the information for detecting and correcting mismatches between conception and action. The behavior is thus modified based on the comparative information to achieve a close match between conception and action. The amount of overt enactment needed to correct mismatches depends on the complexity of the activity, the informativeness and timing of the feedback information, and the exent to which the requisite subskills have already been developed.

Selection Processes

Thus far the discussion has centered on efficacy-related processes that enable people to create beneficial environments and to exercise control over them. Judgments of personal efficacy also affect choice of activities and selection of environments. People tend to avoid activities and situations they believe exceed their coping capabilities, but they readily undertake challenging activities and pick social environments they judge themselves capable of handling. The social influences operating in the selected environments can set the direction of personal development by the competencies, values, and interests they cultivate (Bandura 1986; Snyder 1987).

The power of self-efficacy beliefs to affect the course of life paths through choice-related processes is most clearly revealed in studies of career decision making and career development (Betz & Hackett 1986; Lent & Hackett 1987). The more efficacious people judge themselves to be, the wider the range of career options they consider appropriate and the better they prepare themselves educationally for different occupational pursuits. Self-limitation of career development arises more from perceived self-inefficacy than from actual inability. By constricting choice behavior that can cultivate interests and competencies, self-disbeliefs create their own validation.

MULTIFACETED NATURE OF COMPETENCE AND ITS SOCIAL LABELING

Like other human activities, the judgment of competence is influenced by properties of the behavior and social-labeling processes. Some of the judgmental factors are grounded in the behavior, but many are extraneous to it and may be quite subjective. Sternberg shows that, although there is some consensus in the types of behaviors that one considers indicative of intellectual competence, children, laypersons, and academics differ in the relative weight they give to such things as social adeptness, verbal facility, inquisitiveness, problem-solving skill, and abstract reasoning in their prototypic view of intellectual competence. Langer and Park identify contextual factors that influence the ascription of competence or incompetence to given performances.

A judgment of competence is, by definition, a social construction. No performances ever appear with indwelling labels of competence affixed to them. Although much emphasis is placed on how factors extraneous to behavior can influence how it is labeled, one should not lose sight of the fact that certain properties of behavior can essentially dictate the social construal. In activities in which consequences are inherently linked to quality of performance, nature renders a forceful verdict, regardless of what others may think. Thus, for example, an earnest sailor who, through extraordinary ineptness, manages to frequently sink expensive sailboats in fine working order under optimal sailing conditions does not leave much leeway for socially redeeming labeling. He might be labeled as precompetent according to the taxonomy of competence proposed by Langer and Park. But since there is room for improvement in virtually every endeavor, the rechristening of objectively defective performances as precompetence would essentially eliminate the construct of incompetence from the psychological lexicon.

The social labeling of competence is more than a semantic issue. It serves social functions, beneficially in some applications and detrimentally in others. Societies use competence labeling so as not to place the welfare of people in the hands of those who perform in objectively defective ways. Air travelers demand a reliable system for gauging competence and are not about to climb aboard airliners piloted by precompetent pilots backed up by precompetent navigators. Unfortunately, competence labeling is also often misused for purposes of social control. In such instances, disputes arise over the indexes of competence that are used to justify such practices.

Sternberg's review clarifies some aspects of how variations in socialization practices cultivate different intellectual skills. They may involve practical problem-solving ability, skill in analytic reasoning, or interpersonal competence. People may prefer to use their intellectual capabilities creatively, administratively, or evaluatively. If skills happen to match situational priorities and demands, the persons are viewed as intellectually competent, whereas mismatches foster ascriptions of incompetence. Discontinuities over time in which forms or styles of intelligence are valued can socially transform competence into incompetence or vice versa. One saving grace is that there exist many routes to success so that those who are fortunate in matching their intellectual styles and skills to what is socially valued enjoy a measure of self-efficacy and self-esteem.

THE ORIGINS AND DEVELOPMENTAL SOURCES OF PERCEIVED COMPETENCE

Infants' experiences with their environment provide the initial basis for developing a sense of causal agency. However, newborns' immobility and limited means of action upon the physical and social environment restrict their domain of influence. The initial experiences that contribute to development of a sense of personal agency are tied to infants' ability to control the sensory stimulation from manipulable objects and the attentive behavior of those around them. Infants behave in certain ways, and certain things happen. Shaking a rattle produces predictable sounds, energetic kicks shake their cribs, and screams bring adults.

Realization of causal agency requires both self-observation and recognition that one's actions are part of oneself (Bandura 1986). By repeatedly observing that environmental events occur with action, but not in its absence, infants learn about contingent relations between actions and effects. Repeated experiences of efficacy in influencing events fosters development of a sense of causal agency and efficacious actions (Finkelstein & Ramey 1977; Ramey & Finkelstein 1978). Development of a sense of personal agency requires more than simply producing effects by actions. Those actions must be perceived as part of oneself. The self becomes differentiated from others through differential experience. Thus, if self-action causes pain sensations, whereas seeing similar actions by others does not, one's own activity becomes distinct from that of all others. Infants acquire a sense of personal agency when they begin to perceive environmental events as being personally controlled—a growing realization that they can make events occur.

During the initial months of life, the exercise of influence over the physical environment may contribute more to the development of a child's sense of causal agency than does influence over the social environment (Gunnar 1980). This is because manipulating physical objects produces quick, predictable, and easily observable effects, thus facilitating perception of personal agency in infants whose attentional and representational capabilities are limited. In contrast, causal agency is more difficult to discern in noisier social contingencies, where actions have variable social effects and some of them occur independently of what the infants are doing. With the development of representational capabilities, however, infants can begin to learn from probabilistic and more distal outcomes flowing from actions. Before long, the exercise of control over the social environment begins to play an important role in the early development of a sense of personal agency.

Efficacy experiences in the exercise of personal control are central to the early development of social and cognitive competence. Parents who are responsive to their infants' communicative behavior, who provide an enriched physical environment, and who permit freedom of movement for exploration have infants who are relatively accelerated in their social and cognitive development (Ainsworth & Bell 1974; Yarrow, Rubenstein, & Pedersen 1975). During the course of development infants and parents operate as reciprocal interactants. Parental responsiveness increases competence, and infant capabilities elicit greater parental responsiveness (Bradley, Caldwell, & Elardo 1979). In their chapter in this volume, Schaffer and Blatt underscore the importance of mutuality and the exercise of influence in social and affective transactions in the development of a robust sense of efficacy.

Children have to develop, appraise, and test their capabilities in broadening areas of functioning with increasing age. The initial efficacy experiences are centered in the family, but as the growing child's social world rapidly expands, experiences with peers contribute importantly to children's development and self-knowledge of their capabilities. It is in the context of peer interactions that social comparison processes come strongly into play. Each period of development brings with it new challenges for coping efficacy. As adolescents approach the demands of adulthood, they must master new competencies and the ways of the adult society. The ease with which the transition from childhood to adulthood is made depends, in no small measure, on the assurance in one's capabilities built up through prior mastery experiences. In young adulthood people have to learn to cope with many new demands arising from lasting relationships, parenthood, and careers. As in earlier mastery tasks, a firm sense of self-efficacy is an important personal resource in the attainment of further competencies and success.

People's beliefs in their efficacy can be enhanced in four principal ways (Bandura 1986). The most effective way of developing a strong sense of efficacy is through *mastery experiences*. Performance successes build a sense of personal efficacy; failures create self-doubts. If people experience only easy successes they come to expect quick results and are easily discouraged by failure. A resilient sense of efficacy requires experience in overcoming obstacles through perseverant effort. Some setbacks and difficulties in human pursuits, therefore, serve a useful purpose in teaching that success usually requires sustained effort. After people have become convinced they have what is takes to succeed, they persevere in the face of adversity and quickly rebound from setbacks.

The second way of strengthening self-beliefs of efficacy is by *modeling*. The models in people's lives serve as sources of interest, inspiration, and skills. Ready access to able models fosters competencies that strengthen beliefs in one's capabilities. People partly judge their capabilities in comparison with the achievements of others. Seeing people similar to oneself succeed by sustained effort raises observers' beliefs about their own efficacy. By the same token, negative modeling can be an undermining influence. The failures of similar others can instill self-doubts about one's own efficacy to master similar activities.

Social persuasion is a third way of strengthening people's beliefs that they possess the capabilities to achieve what they seek. Social support and realistic encouragements that lead people to exert greater effort increase their chances of success. Skilled efficacy builders do more than simply convey positive appraisals. In addition to cultivating people's beliefs in their capabilities, they structure situations for them in ways that bring success and avoid placing them prematurely in situations where they are likely to experience repeated failure. To ensure progress in personal development, success is measured in terms of self-improvement rather than by triumphs over others.

People also rely partly on *judgments of their bodily states* in assessing their efficacy. They read their stress and tension as signs of personal vulnerability to deficient performance. In activities involving strength and stamina, they use somatic information as indicators of physical capacity or limitations. The fourth way of modifying self-beliefs of efficacy is to enhance physical status, reduce stress levels, or alter how people interpret their bodily states.

Krueger approaches the origins of a sense of personal effectiveness from a psychoanalytic perspective. In this view, perceived effectiveness originates in mastery of traumatic events, especially in symbolic play. The exercise of control over potential threats can contribute to a sense of personal efficacy (Bandura 1988b; Williams 1987). As previously noted, however, the development of perceived efficacy relies on diverse sources of social influence, most of which function as positive enhancers of personal efficacy rather than operate through intrapsychic conflicts over tabooed impulses.

Krueger devotes considerable attention to phobic avoidance of success. He regards fear of success as arising from fear of maternal abandonment for independent behavior and oedipal competitiveness with narcissistic parents. Because successful performance would result in tabooed victory, success is sabotaged or deprecated. Self-sabotaging of success is also said to be motivated by fear of exposure of inadequacy. Considering that repeated failures conspicuously exhibit one's inadequacy, Krueger does not explain how behaving inadequately avoids exposure of inadequacy.

Krueger relies on material produced in psychotherapeutic sessions as the main source of support for the suppositions regarding the causes of human failings. There are several limitations to this approach that arise from both the causal structure of the theory and the validity of the method of verification. Although psychoanalytic theory postulates a sweeping psychic determinism, the causal dependencies between psychic dynamics and human behavior are too loosely formulated to be easily testable. The inner dynamics not only can produce any variety of effects but can show up in opposite forms of behavior as well. For example, Krueger interprets children's school failures as efforts to create individuating boundaries between themselves and overcontrolling parents. Scholastic failures can have many causes. Children may view themselves as individuated but simply rebel against high parental pressures for scholastic achievement (Brehm 1966). Educational efforts are often debilitated by anxious self-preoccupation about the adverse consequences of scholastic failure (Sarason 1975; Wine 1980). Studies that measure alternative causative factors are needed to decide between rival interpretations of scholastic failure in terms of interpersonal boundary seeking, psychological reactance, self-debilitating preoccupation, or some other psychological process. There are, of course, countless pushy parents who have high-achieving children. Scholastic failure does not characterize the children of some of the most overcontrolling and overprotective parents (Levy 1943). Clearly, the issue of scholastic performance is more complex than simply children individuating themselves by fouling up in school.

The interview method of verification also leaves much to be desired. In a scholarly analysis of the foundations of psychoanalytic theory, Grünbaum (1984) seriously questions the evidential value of clinical data produced in psychotherapeutic sessions on the ground that such data are too tainted by the therapist's suggestive influence. As Marmor (1962), among others, has noted, each psychodynamic approach has its own favorite set of inner causes. The presupposed determinants can be readily confirmed in self-validating interviews because the therapist makes suggestive interpretations and selectively rewards clients' accounts that are consistent with the therapist's views (Murray 1956; Truax 1966). Thus, advocates of differing theoretical orientations repeatedly discover their chosen motivators at work but rarely find evidence for the motivators emphasized by proponents of competing viewpoints. The types of causal dependencies that Krueger has proposed for aborted or failed human efforts clearly require more stringent empirical scrutiny.

PERCEIVED COMPETENCE AND SELF-WORTH

Harter's chapter on the origins and functions of self-worth addresses important questions but raises a number of conceptual and methodological issues. In the literature, the terms *perceived competence* and *self-esteem* or *self-worth* are often used interchangeably as though they represent the same phenomenon. In fact, they encompass different things. Perceived competence is concerned with judgments of personal capabilities, whereas self-esteem or self-worth is concerned with the degree to which one likes or dislikes oneself. Judgments of self-worth and of self-capability have no fixed relation. Individuals may regard themselves as highly efficacious in an activity from which they derive no pride (e.g., a skilled forecloser of mortgages of families that have fallen on hard times) or may judge themselves inefficacious at an activity without suffering a loss of self-worth (e.g., inept skater). However, in many of the activities people pursue, they cultivate capabilities in what gives them a sense of self-worth. If empirical analyses are confined to activities in which people invest their sense of self-worth, this will inflate correlations because domains of functioning where people judge themselves inefficacious but could not care less are simply ignored.

In Harter's conceptual scheme, judgments of self-worth and of personal competence seem to represent levels of generality within the same phenomenon. Self-worth is said to be global and perceived competence is domain-specific. Global self-worth is treated as an emergent property that is more than the sum of the domain-specific parts. Its assessment is disembodied from particular domains of functioning that may contribute in varying degrees to one's sense of self-pride or self-dislike. That is, persons are asked how much they like or dislike themselves without any regard as to what they like or dislike about themselves. Measurement of self-worth noncontextually and perceived competence specifically presumably integrates unidimensional and multidimensional perspectives on the self-concept.

As noted earlier, judgments of self-worth and personal competence represent different phenomena rather than part-whole relations within the same phenomenon. Moreover, self-worth is no less multidimensional than is perceived competence. The following section is devoted to a more detailed consideration of the issue of multidimensionality.

OMNIBUS VERSUS DOMAIN-LINKED ASSESSMENTS

Psychological theories have traditionally approached the assessment of personal attributes and states in terms of omnibus tests. Such measures include a fixed set of items, many of which may have little relevance to the domain of functioning being analyzed. Moreover, in an effort to serve varied predictive purposes across diverse domains of functioning and ages the items have to be cast in a general form. The more general the items, the greater is the burden on respondents to define what is being asked of them. It is unrealistic to expect omnibus tests to predict with much accuracy how people will function in different domains under diverse circumstances. Indeed, in comparative studies, domain-linked measures of personal capability typically predict changes in functioning better than do general measures (Bandura 1988c).

Use of domain-linked scales does not mean that there is no generality to perceived capability. If different classes of activities require similar functions and subskills, one would expect some generality in judgments of competence. Even if different activity domains are not subserved by common subskills, some generality of perceived competence can occur if development of competencies is socially structured so that the cultivation of skills in dissimilar domains covaries. Commonality of subskills and covariation of development will yield generality. Multidomain measures reveal the patterning and degree of generality of people's sense of personal competence. Some may judge themselves highly efficacious across a wide range of domains of functioning, others may judge themselves as inefficacious in most domains, and many may judge themselves relatively efficacious in domains in which they have cultivated their competences, moderately efficacious in domains in which they are somewhat less conversant, and inefficacious in domains comprising activities for which they lack talent. One can derive degree of generality from multidomain scales, but one cannot extract the patterning of perceived personal efficacy from conglomerate omnibus tests.

In adopting the multidimensional approach in the assessment of perceived competence, Harter does justice to the variegated nature of self-beliefs. I am puzzled, however, by why physical appearance is included as a facet of perceived competence. Physical appearance is a feature, not a capability. Another issue concerns the level of multidimensionality. As people continue to develop their competencies through selective pursuits, their perceptions of their capabilities become more differentiated. One can increase the explanatory and predictive power of measures of perceived competence by appropriate differentiations within major activity domains. Consider perceived scholastic competence as an example. High school students will vary, often widely, in the degree to which they consider themselves competent in mathematics, physical sciences, linguistic capabilities, social sciences, and the humanities. When asked in Harter's test of perceived competence to judge their scholastic competency by rating whether they are "good at schoolwork," they have to engage in subjective weighting and aggregation across subject matters to come up with a single judgment. Because the patterning of perceived scholastic efficacy across different "schoolwork" is likely to vary from student to student, similar overall judgments may mean different things. General items linked to an assemblage of activities within a broad class are an improvement over omnibus measures disembodied from definite activities and contextual factors, but indefinite multidimensionality still sacrifices explanatory and predictive power. Microanalytic approaches linking particularized indexes of perceived competence to distinct domains of sociocognitive functioning are better suited to clarify how self-beliefs affect human thought, affect, and action. Large-scale efforts to identify causal structures usually include a sizable set of possible determinants. When subjects' time and patience are limited, investigators seek brief omnibus measures for each of many different things. Networks of relationships obtained with suboptimal measures may underestimate or misrepresent the causal contribution of given factors.

SOURCES AND MULTIDIMENSIONALITY OF SELF-ESTEEM

One can distinguish different sources of self-esteem or self-worthiness (Bandura 1986). It can stem from evaluations based on competence or on possession of attributes that have been culturally invested with positive or negative value. In self-esteem arising from competence, people derive self-pride from fulfilling their standards of merit. When they meet or surpass valued standards they experience self-satisfaction, but when they fail to measure up to their standards of merit they are displeased with themselves.

Other people frequently voice evaluations reflecting their likes and dislikes of particular attributes rather than in response to evident competencies. Such social judgments can influence how the recipients evaluate their self-worthiness. Moreover, people are often criticized or deprecated when they fail to live up to the ideals or aspirational standards of others. The role played by personal competence and social evaluation in the development of self-esteem receives support from the studies of Coopersmith (1967). He found that children who exhibited high self-esteem had parents who were accepting, who set explicit attainable standards, and who provided considerable support and latitude to acquire competencies that could serve them well in their pursuits.

Cultural stereotyping is another way in which social judgments affect perceptions of self-worth. People are cast into valued or devalued groups on the basis of their ethnic background, race, sex, or physical characteristics. Those who possess socially disparaged attributes, and who accept the stereotyped evaluations of others, will hold themselves in low regard despite their talents. Persons combining limited competencies, exacting standards, and disparaged attributes are the ones most likely to harbor a pervasive sense of worthlessness.

The different sources of self-devaluation call for different corrective measures. Self-devaluation rooted in incompetence requires cultivation of talents. Those who suffer from self-disparagement because they judge themselves harshly against excessively high standards become more self-accepting after they are helped to adopt more realistic standards of achievement (Rehm 1982). Self-devaluation resulting from belittling social evaluations requires new social experiences that affirm one's self-worth. Self-devaluation stemming from discriminatory disparagement of attributes requires modeling and rewarding a sense of pride regarding those attributes. Efforts by minorities to instill pride in racial characteristics (e.g., "Black is beautiful") illustrate this approach. When self-devaluation arises from multiple sources, multiple corrective measures are needed as, for example, fostering pride in one's characteristics and also cultivating competencies that instill a high and resilient sense of personal efficacy.

Self-worth is multidimensional as is perceived competence. For example, some students derive self-satisfaction from their academic accomplishments but devalue themselves in social or athletic domains. Those who invest themselves heavily in athletic pursuits may be self-approving in athletics but self-discontented in academic activities. Hard-driving executives may value themselves in their vocational pursuits but devalue themselves as parents. Domain-linked measures of self-esteem reveal the patterning of human self-esteem and areas of vulnerability to self-disparagement.

A global measure of self-worth, as used in the research reported by Harter, may obscure the origins of self-worth or yield anomalous findings. For example, physical appearance emerges as a surprisingly large contributor to global self-worth, regardless of whether the samples include children ($r = -.66$), college students ($r = -.80$), or adults ($r = -.61$). Having just returned from a spirited meeting with graduate students who were hardly fastidiously groomed, I find it difficult to believe that their sense of self-worth springs more from how they judge their looks than from how they judge their intellectual competencies. If, indeed, self-worth were so heavily rooted in physical appearances, then beauticians, haberdashers, and plastic surgeons hold the major key to self-esteem. The role left for psychologists in this route to self-worth would be as alterers of standards of beauty.

IMPACT OF CONCEPTIONS OF ABILITY AND PERCEIVED CONTROLLABILITY ON UTILIZATION OF COGNITIVE SKILLS

Sternberg and his colleagues find that people use their conceptions of ability in judging their own intellectual competency and the competency of others. Conceptions of ability affect not only social judgment but also how effectively people use the cognitive skills they possess. Recent research has identified two major conceptions of ability to which people subscribe (M. Bandura & Dweck 1988; Dweck & Elliott 1983). In one perspective, they construe ability as an *incremental skill* that can be continually enhanced by acquiring knowledge and perfecting one's competencies. People with this conception adopt a learning goal. They seek challenging tasks that provide opportunities to expand their knowledge and competencies. Errors are regarded as a natural, instructive part of an acquisition process. They judge capabilities more in terms of personal improvement than in comparisons with the achievement of others.

In the contrasting perspective, ability is construed as a more or less *fixed entity*. Because performance level is regarded as diagnostic of intellectual capacity, errors and deficient performances carry personal and social evaluative threats. Therefore, people adopting the entity view tend to pursue performance goals of demonstrating their competence. They prefer tasks that minimize errors and permit ready display of intellectual proficiency at the expense of expanding their knowledge and learning new skills. High effort, which is often required to develop competencies in complex activities, also poses evaluative threats because high effort is taken as indicative of low ability. An entity conception of ability is less conducive to effective management of failure than is the view of ability as an incremental skill (Elliott & Dweck 1988).

According to social cognitive theory (Bandura 1986, 1988a), self-regulation of motivation and performance attainments is governed by several self-regulatory mechanisms operating in concert. They include affective self-evaluation, perceived self-efficacy for goal attainment, and personal goal setting. The conception of ability with which people approach complex activities can have a substantial impact on these self-regulatory influences. Substandard performances are likely to carry markedly different diagnostic implications depending on whether ability is construed as an acquirable skill or as a relatively stable entity. When performances are viewed as skill acquisition in which one learns from mistakes, perceived self-efficacy is unlikely to be adversely affected by substandard performances. This is because errors become a normative part of any acquisition process rather than indicators of basic personal deficiencies. In contrast, when performances are construed as diagnostic of underlying cognitive capability, frequent experience of substandard performances can take a heavy toll on perceived self-efficacy.

That conceptions of ability strongly affect the self-regulatory mechanisms governing complex decision making is revealed in a study by Wood and Bandura (1989). Much of the research on human decision making examines single trial judgments in static environments (Beach, Barnes, & Christensen-Szalanski 1986; Hogarth 1981). Judgments under such conditions may not provide a sufficient basis for developing either descriptive or normative models of decision making in dynamic naturalistic environments which entail learning and motivational mechanisms. In such environments, decision makers must weigh and integrate a wide array of information from diverse sources. Decisions must be made during a continual flow of activity under time constraints. Moreover, many of the decisional rules for exercising control over dynamic environments must be learned through exploratory experiences in the course of managing the ongoing organizational activities under conditions of uncertainty and social pressure.

It requires a strong sense of efficacy to deploy one's cognitive resources optimally and to remain task-oriented in the face of repeated difficulties and failures as one attempts to ferret out relevant information, construct options, and test and revise one's knowledge based on results of decisional actions. People with a low sense of efficacy easily fall apart under these types of conditions. Those who judge themselves inefficacious in coping with environmental demands tend to become more self-diagnostic than task-diagnostic (M. Bandura & Dweck 1988). Such self-referent intrusive thinking creates stress and undermines effective use of capabilities by diverting attention away from how best to proceed to concerns over personal deficiencies and possible adverse outcomes.

We examined the psychological effects of different conceptions of ability on the cognitive functioning of highly talented business school graduates as they managed a simulated organization. In executing their decision-making activities they had to match individuals to organizational subfunctions and to use goals, instructive feedback, and social incentives in optimal ways to achieve organizational levels of performance that were difficult to fulfill. They performed the managerial task over a series of trials under instated conceptions of ability as either an acquirable skill that is improvable with practice or a basic intellectual entity reflecting underlying cognitive capacities. They received feedback on how well their group performed relative to the challenging standard of organizational attainment. At several points in the managerial simulation, the managers' perceived managerial self-efficacy and the goals they sought to achieve were assessed. The adequacy of their analytic strategies for discovering managerial rules and the level of organizational performance they achieved were also measured.

The impact of the different conceptions of ability on self-regulatory mechanisms governing the utilization skills and performance accomplishments may be seen in figure 14.1. Managers who were led to construe

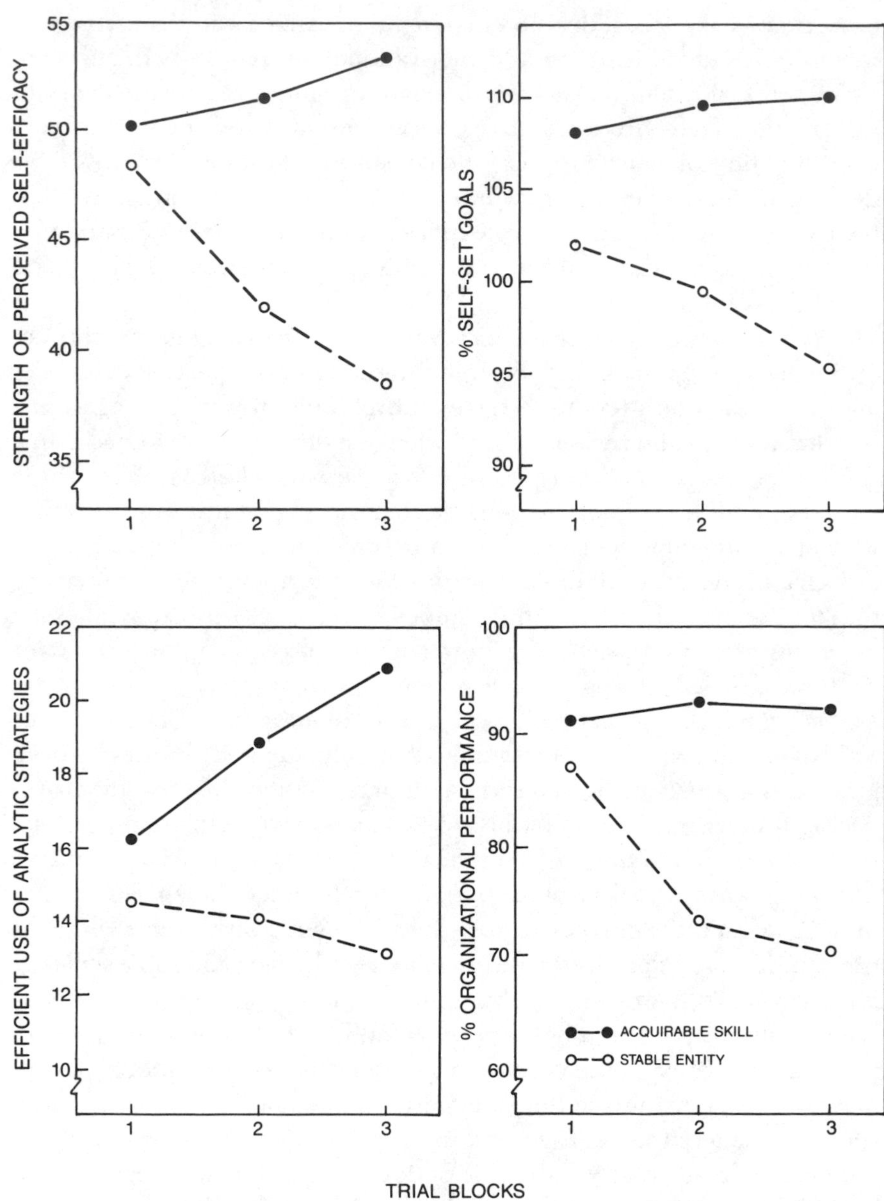

Figure 14.1. Changes in perceived managerial self-efficacy, the performance goals set for the organization relative to the preset standard, effective analytic strategies, and achieved level of organizational performance across blocks of trials under acquirable skill and entity conceptions of capability. Each trial block comprises six different production orders (Wood & Bandura 1989).

decision-making ability as reflecting basic cognitive capacities were beset by increasing doubts about their managerial efficacy as they encountered problems. They became more and more erratic in their decisional activities, they lowered their organizational aspirations, and they achieved progressively less with the organization they were managing. In marked contrast, induced construal of ability as an acquirable skill fostered a highly resilient sense of personal efficacy. Even though assigned taxing goals that eluded them, they remained steadfast in their perceived managerial self-efficacy, they continued to set themselves challenging organizational goals, and they used analytic strategies in efficient ways that aided discovery of optimal managerial decision rules. Such a self-efficacious orientation, which is well suited for handling adversity, pays off in uniformly high organizational attainments. In path analyses, perceived self-efficacy exerts a direct effect on organizational performance and an indirect effect through its influence on analytic strategies. Personal goals also affect organizational performance through the mediation of analytic strategies.

Induced differential conceptions of ability bias how similar substandard performances at the outset are cognitively processed. Construal of substandard attainments as indicants of personal deficiencies gradually creates an inefficacious self-schema in the particular domain of functioning, whereas construal of substandard attainments as instructive guides for enhancing personal competencies fosters an efficacious self-schema. Such evolving self-beliefs further bias cognitive processing of outcome information and promote actions that create confirmatory behavioral evidence for them. This produces an exacerbation cycle of motivational and performance effects.

There are two aspects to the exercise of control that are especially relevant to belief systems that can alter how effectively personal skills are put to use (Bandura 1986; Gurin & Brim 1984). The first concerns the level of self-efficacy to effect changes by productive use of capabilities and enlistment of effort. This constitutes the personal side of the transactional control process. The second aspect concerns the changeableness or controllability of the environment. This facet represents the level of system constraints and opportunity structures to exercise personal efficacy. Human behavior is, of course, governed by perceptions of personal efficacy and social environments rather than simply by their objective properties. Thus, individuals who believe themselves to be inefficacious are likely to effect little change even in environments that provide many opportunities. Conversely, those who have a strong sense of efficacy, through ingenuity and perseverance, figure out ways of exercising some measure of control in environments containing limited opportunities and many constraints.

In the transactions of everyday life, beliefs regarding self-efficacy and environmental controllability are not divorced from experiential realities. Rather, they are products of reciprocal causation (Bandura 1986). Thus, when people believe the environment is controllable on matters of import to them, they are strongly motivated to exercise fully their personal efficacy, which enhances the likelihood of success. Experiences of success, in turn, provide behavioral validation of personal efficacy and environmental controllability. If people approach situations as largely uncontrollable, they are likely to exercise their efficacy weakly and abortively, which breeds failure experiences. Over time, failures take an increasing toll on perceived self-efficacy and beliefs about how much environmental control is possible.

Organizational simulation research underscores the influential impact of perceived controllability on the self-regulatory factors governing decision making that can enhance or impede group attainments (Bandura & Wood 1989). People who managed a simulated organization under a cognitive set that organizations are not easily changeable quickly lost faith in their managerial capabilities even when performance standards were within easy reach and they lowered their sights for the organization (figure 14.2). Those who operated under a cognitive set that organizations are controllable displayed a resilient sense of managerial efficacy, set themselves increasingly challenging goals, and used good analytic thinking for discovering effective managerial rules. They exhibited high resiliency of self-efficacy even in the face of numerous recurrent difficulties. The divergent changes in these self-regulatory factors were accompanied by large differences in organizational attainments.

Path analyses reveal that, when initially faced with managing a complex unfamiliar environment, managers relied heavily on performance information in judging their efficacy and setting their personal goals. But, as they began to form a self-schema concerning their efficacy through further experience, the performance system was powered more extensively and intricately by self-conceptions of efficacy (figure 14.3). Perceived self-efficacy influenced performance both directly and through its strong effects on personal goal setting. Personal goals, in turn, enhanced organizational attainments directly and via the mediation of analytic strategies.

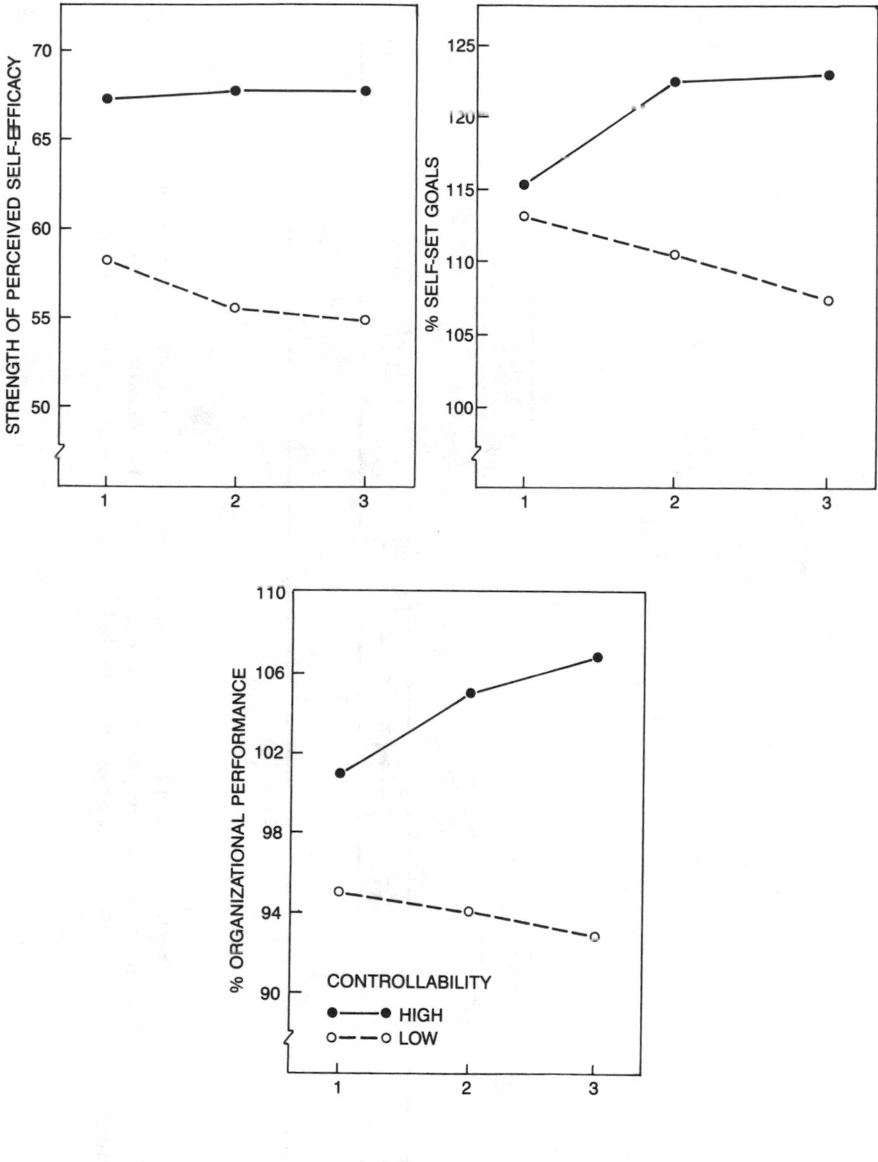

Figure 14.2. Changes in strength of perceived managerial self-efficacy, the performance goals set for the organization, and level of organizational performance for managers who operated under a cognitive set that organizations are controllable or difficult to control. Each trial block comprises six different production orders (Bandura & Wood 1989).

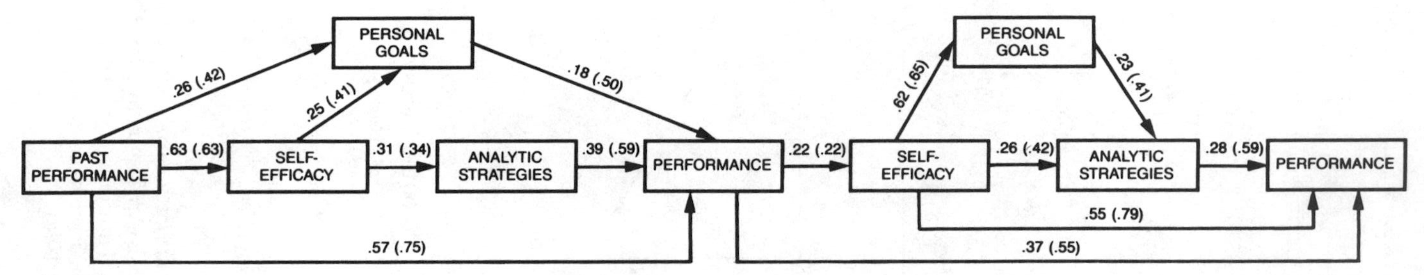

Figure 14.3. Path analysis of causal structures. The initial numbers on the paths of influence are the significant standardized path coefficients (*ps* < .05); the numbers in parentheses are the zero-order correlations. The network of relations on the left half of the figure are for the initial managerial efforts, and those on the right half are for later managerial efforts (Wood & Bandura 1989).

The findings of these studies show that a strong belief in one's personal efficacy and in the modifiability of the environment pays off in psychological well-being and personal accomplishments. The speed with which efficacy-undermining cognitive sets impair the cognitive functioning of bright graduates with managerial experience attests to the power of belief systems over capability.

DIFFERENTIAL FUNCTION OF PREPARATORY AND PERFORMANCE JUDGMENTS OF COMPETENCE

Norem and Cantor present the seemingly paradoxical notion that negative thinking spawns good performances. They find that some people use pessimistic expectations as a strategy to motivate themselves and to cushion the blows of failure. The anticipatory pessimism is conceptualized as a domain-linked strategy rather than a global personality trait. These findings appear to fly in the face of a large body of evidence that negative thinking typically impairs performance attainments. One would not prescribe that people approach tasks with strong disbelief in their capabilities and anticipate the futility of their efforts as the way to promote success. A solution to the apparent paradox may lie in a temporal qualifier regarding the functional properties of self-doubt.

Self-efficacy theory distinguishes between the effects of strength of self-beliefs of efficacy during acquisition phases of an endeavor and during exercise of established skills (Bandura 1986). In approaching learning tasks, people who perceive themselves to be highly self-efficacious in the undertaking have little incentive to invest much preparatory effort in it. For example, students who greatly underestimate the difficulty of academic course demands and remain blissfully free of self-doubt are more likely to party than to hit the books to master the subject matter. As Confucian wisdom warns regarding preparatory self-appraisal, "Too much confidence has deceived many a one." Salomon (1984) provides some evidence bearing on this issue. He found that children's high perceived self-efficacy as a learner is associated with a high investment of cognitive effort and better learning from instructional media children consider difficult, but with less investment of effort and poorer learning from media they believe to be easy. Thus, some uncertainty can benefit preparation.

In applying skills already acquired, a strong belief in one's efficacy is essential to mobilize and sustain the effort needed to succeed on difficult tasks, which is hard to achieve if one is doubt-ridden. One cannot execute well what one knows while wrestling with self-doubt. In short, self-doubt creates the impetus for acquiring knowledge and skills, but it hinders adept use of preexisting skills.

The social manipulation of preparatory and performance efficacy is a standard procedure in athletic activities. To motivate players to improve suspect skills and competitive strategies in preparation for upcoming contests, coaches inflate the capabilities of their opponents and downgrade those of their own team. Bravado self-appraisals are frowned upon. But at the time of the contest, coaches attempt to instill a strong sense of efficacy to get the players to perform at their best. Teams strive hard to overpower their opponents at the beginning of a contest to convince them that their worst doubts are warranted. Coaches try to sustain self-efficacious thinking in the face of difficulties that can shake a team's belief that the extra effort is worthwhile.

Instances in which optimistic anticipations were rudely dashed remain highly salient in people's thinking. It is not uncommon for them to invoke anticipatory pessimism as a superstitious means of exercising cognitive control over untoward outcomes. We know from Langer's (1975) research that rituals that are completely irrelevant to what will happen are viewed as providing some measure of control over outcomes entirely determined by chance. The longitudinal study by Norem and Cantor excluded negative thinking that impairs performance by confining the study to academically gifted students. Most likely, their anticipatory pessimism reflects superstitious thinking rather than genuine self-disbelief that they lack the capability to succeed. If carried too far, however, preparatory negative thinking can turn into a stressor and debilitor rather than a motivator. Norem and Cantor report that academic pessimistic thinking eventually takes a heavy toll on psychosocial functioning. Those who strive to forestall incessant anticipated misfortunes demand much of themselves, drive themselves hard, distress themselves, constrict their social life, gain little satisfaction from their activities, and begin to undermine their accomplishments. Optimists fare much better in psychosocial well-being and academic accomplishments.

VERIDICALITY OF SELF-APPRAISAL: SELF-AIDING OR SELF-LIMITING?

It is widely believed that misjudgment produces dysfunction. Certainly, gross miscalculation can get one into trouble. But optimistic self-appraisals of capability that are not unduly disparate from what is possible can be advantageous, whereas veridical judgments can be self-limiting. When people err in their self-appraisal they tend to overestimate their capabilities, which is a benefit rather than a cognitive failing to be eradicated. If self-efficacy beliefs always reflected only what people can do routinely, they would rarely fail but they would not mount the extra effort needed to surpass their ordinary performances.

Evidence suggests that it is often the so-called normals who are distorters of reality. But they distort in the positive direction. Anxious and depressed people have been compared in their skills and their self-beliefs with those who are unburdened by such problems. The findings show that the groups differ little in their actual skills, whereas they differ substantially in their beliefs about their efficacy. People who are socially anxious are often just as socially skilled as the more sociable ones. But socially active people judge themselves as much more adept (Glasgow & Arkowitz 1975).

Depressed persons usually display realistic self-appraisals of their social competencies. The nondepressed view themselves as much more adroit then they really are. As depressed people improve in treatment, they show the self-enhancing biases that characterize the nondepressed (Lewinsohn et al. 1980). In laboratory situations where people's actions do not affect outcomes, the depressed are quite realistic in judging they lack control. The nondepressed believe they are exercising a good deal of control in such situations (Alloy & Abramson 1979). After nondepressed people are made temporarily depressed they become realistic in judging their personal control. When depressed people are made to feel happy they overestimate the extent to which they exercise control (Alloy, Abramson, & Viscusi 1981). Thus, the depressed appear as realists, the nondepressed as confident illusionists.

Social reformers strongly believe that they can mobilize the collective effort needed to achieve social change (Bandura 1986; Muller 1979). Although their beliefs and the collective sense of efficacy they instill in others are rarely fully realized, they sustain reform efforts that achieve lesser, but important, gains. Were social reformers to be entirely realistic about the prospects of transforming social systems, they would either forgo the endeavor or fall easy victim to discouragement. Realists may adapt well to existing realities, but those with a tenacious self-efficacy are likely to change adverse realities.

The emerging evidence indicates that the successful, the innovative, the sociable, the nonanxious, the nondespondent, and the social reformers take an optimistic view of their personal efficacy to exercise influence over events that affect their lives. If not unrealistically exaggerated, such self-beliefs foster personal and social accomplishments.

In their informative review, Phillips and Zimmerman identify some of the determinants and developmental changes in the self-appraisal patterns of able students who either underestimate or overestimate their capabilities or display veridical judgment. The research of Collins (1982) shows that perceptions of personal efficacy often diverge from actual ability at all levels of ability. Moreover, perceived self-efficacy affects how well children use their capabilities. Collins selected children who judged themselves to be of high or low mathematical capability at each of three levels of mathematical ability. They were then given difficult problems to solve. Mathematical ability contributed to mathematical performance. But within each level of mathematical ability, children who regarded themselves as efficacious discarded faulty strategies more quickly, solved more problems (figure 14.4), chose to rework more of those they had failed, and did so more accurately. Level of interest in mathematics was significantly related to perceived self-efficacy but not to actual ability. Thus, children may perform poorly because they lack the ability or, if they possess the ability, because they lack the perceived efficacy to make good use of their talents.

Phillips and Zimmerman report striking developmental sex differences in disparity between ability and perceived competence. Whereas boys tend to inflate their sense of competence, girls generally disparage their capabilities. These differential patterns of self-appraisal have their origins in parental gender-linked beliefs regarding their children's capabilities. Parents judge school to be more difficult for daughters than for sons even though they do not differ in actual achievement. Girls perceive their mothers as having lower academic expectations and less stringent achievement standards for them than for boys. Adoption of feminine gender-role identity is also associated with underestimation of capabilities.

Students' beliefs in their efficacy can profoundly affect the direction of their development by influencing the career paths they follow. The choices they make in earlier years cultivate different competencies and interests and determine the occupational options that can be realistically considered. It is now well documented that students' beliefs in their efficacy govern their career decision making and career development (Betz & Hackett 1986; Lent & Hackett 1987). The stronger their self-

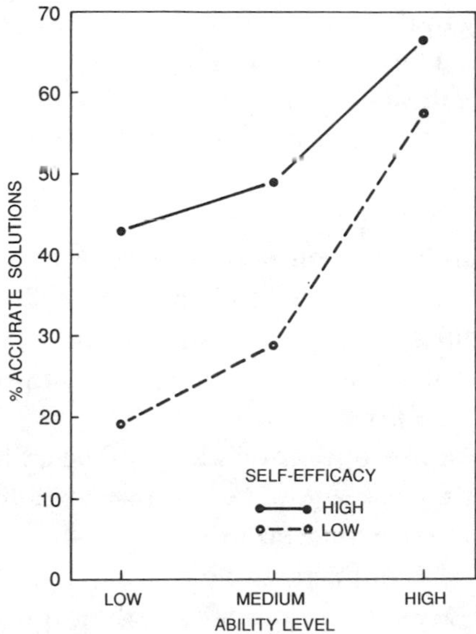

Figure 14.4. Mean levels of mathematical solutions achieved by children as a function of mathematical ability and perceived mathematical self-efficacy. Plotted from data of Collins 1982.

belief in their efficacy, the more career options they consider possible and the better they prepare themselves educationally for different pursuits. Cultural practices that convey lower achievement expectations for women, stereotypic modeling of gender roles, constraining sex typing, and dissuading opportunity structures eventually leave their mark on women's beliefs about their occupational efficacy. Female students are prone to limit their interests and range of career options by beliefs that they lack the capabilities for occupations traditionally dominated by men, even though they do not differ from male students in actual ability. The self-limitation arises from perceived inefficacy rather than from actual inability. But things may be improving. Studies of students currently coming through the school ranks reveal a smaller disparity between male and female students in their beliefs about their efficacy to pursue successfully varied careers (Post-Kammer & Smith 1985).

Computer literacy is becoming an increasingly important factor in career development and advancement. Socialization influences that breed perceived inefficacy in the use of computer tools are creating new career barriers for women. These are not easily overcome. Even at an early age, girls distrust their efficacy to program and operate computers despite instruction and the school's encouragement to acquire such skills (Miura 1987a). The lower the perceived efficacy in computer activities, the lesser the interest in acquiring computer competencies. Sex differences in perceived self-efficacy to master computer course work extend to the college level. Regardless of sex, college students lacking a sense of computer efficacy are computer avoiders. They show less interest or inclination to pursue computer course work and they see computer literary as less relevant to their future careers (Miura 1987b).

In commenting on overoptimistic self-appraisal, Phillips and Zimmerman suggest that its positive effects on achievement may reflect fear-motivated defensiveness. Children presumably drive themselves to high achievement to avoid confirming their worst fears that they are untalented impostors. Should optimism regarding one's capabilities really be cast in a mask of deceit? Even the most talented people are, from time to time, beset by self-doubts because no one ever experiences unceasing ever-rising accomplishments. Pursuit of standards that are difficult to fulfill provide challenges that sustain engrossment in activities but also bring periodic discouragements. Accomplishments that look good to others may prove self-disappointing when they fail to measure up to exacting personal standards. To add further strains on positive self-appraisals, there is no shortage of superstars to occasion humbling social comparisons. In short, self-doubts are natural reactions to inevitable failures and setbacks, but people with a resilient sense of efficacy are quick to recover belief in their capabilities.

There is reason to believe that the motivational benefits of overoptimistic self-appraisal might be more fruitfully analyzed in terms of affirmative processes than defensive ones rooted in pretending to be what one is not. This is the difference between motivation arising from an unshakable belief in oneself and from fear of being exposed as an intellectual phony. In the latter conception, human strivings become largely a matter of defensive impression management. The substantial body of evidence reviewed earlier supports the view that an optimistic sense of efficacy promotes psychological well-being and human accomplishments through advantageous processes, such as self-challenge, commitment, motivational involvement, and nonintrusive task orientation rather than through fearful self-protectiveness. Indeed, a resilient belief in one's capabilities is required to succeed in pursuits that present many obstacles.

THE PLASTICITY OF INCOMPETENCE

The work of Langer and her associates provides striking testimony for the surprising ease with which contextual and social factors can convert competence into incompetence (Langer 1979). Settings in which individuals happen to perform poorly can, in themselves, come to activate a sense of incompetence that impairs future performances in those particular contexts. The contextual activation of incompetence is well illustrated in athletic performances in which winners regularly turn into losers to weaker opponents in settings in which they have come to expect difficulties. The mere presence of a person exuding high confidence undermines observers' use of routine skills. Attending to what is strange in new tasks, rather than to what is familiar and clearly within one's range of capability, may similarly hinder effective utilization of skills. Rigid mindsets impede generative use of knowledge and established skills under changing circumstances. When people are cast in subordinate roles or are assigned inferior labels, implying limited competence, they perform activities at which they are highly skilled less well than when they do not bear the negative labels or the subordinate role designations. Offering unnecessary help can also detract from a sense of competence and thereby vitiate the execution of skills.

Mindlessness is hypothesized by Langer to underly illusory incompetence. Environmental cues suggestive of personal deficiencies are said to trigger deficient performances when routine circumstances are no longer given thoughtful consideration. Undoubtedly, some instances of deficient skill utilization reflect routinized situational control of action. Situational influences, however, may activate other processes that can also detract from effective utilization of skills. Verification of an explanatory mechanism is greatly aided if the mediating process is measured rather than simply presumed to be operating. The presumptive mediation of mindlessness could be tested by assessing whether amount of cognitive activity accounts for variations across subjects in how much their performances are undermined by situational influences suggesting personal deficiency. Degree of mindful involvement in the activities at hand could also be varied systematically and its impact on effective utilization of preexisting skills measured.

We know from other lines of research that the types of situations that produce illusory incompetence diminish perceived self-efficacy with its concomitant effects on choice behavior motivation, and self-debilitating thought. For example, the mere sight of a formidable-looking opponent instills lower self-percepts of efficacy than does one who looks less impressive (Weinberg, Yukelson, & Jackson 1980). Illusorily instated self-percepts of efficacy heighten competitive performance and resilience, whereas illusorily weakened self-percepts of efficacy debilitate competitive performance and increase vulnerability to the adverse effects of failure (Weinberg, Gould, & Jackson 1979). The more self-percepts of efficacy are diminished, the greater is the performance debilitation.

Trivial factors, such as arbitrary anchor values or sequence anchoring, that are devoid of information to affect competence nevertheless influence self-efficacy beliefs (Cervone & Peake 1986; Peake & Cervone, 1989). The illusorily instated self-beliefs of efficacy exert strong effect on level of performance motivation. Dwelling on formidable aspects of a task weakens people's belief in their efficacy but focusing on doable aspects of the same tasks raises self-judgment of capabilities (Cervone 1989). The higher the altered self-efficacy beliefs, the longer people persevere in the face of repeated failure. In these experiments, perceived self-efficacy predicts variance in motivation within treatment conditions as well as across treatments. Mediational analyses reveal that these types of external influences have no impact on motivation when variations in self-efficacy beliefs are controlled. Thus, the motivational effect of the external influences is completely mediated through changes in self-efficacy beliefs.

COGNITIVE GUIDANCE AND AUTOMATIZATION

It should be noted in passing that mindfulness is not an unmitigated virtue. It can impair the execution of skills as well as facilitate their use. Cognitive guidance plays an especially influential role in early and intermediate phases of skill development. After proficiency is attained, the skills are executed in recurring situations without requiring prior thought guides unless something goes awry. Attending to the mechanics of what one is doing after proficiency is achieved is likely to disrupt skilled performance. Partial disengagement of thought from proficient action has considerable functional value. If one had to think about the details of every skilled activity before carrying it out in recurrent situations, it would consume most of one's attentional and cognitive resources and create a monotonously dull inner life.

Human behavior is regulated by multilevel systems of control. Once proficient modes of behavior become routinized, they no longer require higher cognitive control. Their execution can be largely regulated by lower-level sensory-motor systems. However, when routinized behavior fails to produce expected results, the cognitive control system again comes into play. Both the behavior and the changing environmental circumstances are monitored to identify the source of the problem. New modes are considered and tested. Control reverts to the lower control system after an adequate mode is found and becomes the habitual way of doing things. However, automatization of skills usually entails a shift in the locus of attention from action patterns to their correlated effects rather than a total loss of consciousness of one's performance (Bandura 1986).

There are obviously substantial benefits to being able to think about other things while executing proficient skills. Routinization frees attention and thought from habitual routines for the cultivation of new competencies requiring judgment, generation of alternatives, and close monitoring of the effects of one's performances. For example, it would be a waste of cognitive resources if one had to continue to think about how to drive an automobile after one had perfected the skill. Routinization is advantageous when the ways that have been perfected are the optimal ones and remain so under a variety of circumstances. However, routinization can detract from effective functioning when people react with fixed ways in situations requiring discriminative adaptability. Langer identifies conditions under which thoughtless stereotyped reactions to superficial cues exact a toll on competent utilization of one's skills.

MAINTENANCE OF PERCEIVED COMPETENCE BY SHIFTING EVALUATIVE STANDARDS

For most activities there are no absolute indicants of level of competence. For example, the time in which a given distance is run (e.g., eight minutes) or the score obtained on a scholastic examination (e.g., 127) does not by itself indicate whether these constitute good or poor performances. When competence is not designated by an inherent outcome of performance, personal competence must be gauged in relation to some evaluative standard. The referential comparisons may take the form of normative comparison, social comparison with specific individuals, or self-comparison over time. For some regular activities, standard norms based on representative groups are used to determine one's relative standing. More often people compare themselves to particular associates in given endeavors. One's previous attainments are also used as a reference against which personal performances are judged. In the latter referential process, self-comparison supplies the measure of adequacy. Self-satisfaction is determined relationally as is judgment of competence. Reactions of self-satisfaction or self-dissatisfaction result from comparisons among three major sources of information: performance level, personal standards of merit, and the performance attainments of others (Bandura 1986).

Competence is not a static attribute. Frey and Ruble provide developmental prescripts for how to maintain a sense of competence and self-satisfaction in the face of changing capabilities. This is achieved by flexible shifting of evaluative standards depending on phase of skill development and on age-related changes in capabilities. Temporal or self-comparison is most conducive to positive self-appraisal when skills are being improved. Evidence of progressive improvement sustains a high sense of competence and provides a continuing source of self-satisfaction. However, when skill levels have stabilized or capabilities begin to wane with increasing age, self-satisfaction and perceived competence are better served by use of social comparative standards. Surpassing comparative agemates can contribute to positive self-appraisal though personal capabilities are no longer improving or may even be declining. Frey and Ruble provide evidence that evaluative strategies are, indeed, adapted to the direction of performance change in a study of older runners. They shift their evaluative standard from self-comparison to social comparison as the course of their performance changes from improvement to decline.

A word of caution is in order about overgeneralizing these findings to pursuits that are socially structured in a different manner. Runners are free to choose where and when they will compete. In addition to the exercise of control over performance situations, the contests are carefully age-graded which constrains performance comparison mainly to agemates. By contrast, in the important pursuits of everyday life, older persons have to compete with younger cohorts whether they like it or not. Young football recruits quickly supplant teammates whose skills have begun to wane. Corporate executives find younger rising superstars vying for their positions. Competitively structured systems in which one person's success is another person's loss force social comparison unless one cedes such pursuits.

Many age differences in cognitive capabilities are partly the product of cultural changes. It is not so much that older persons have declined in capability but that the younger cohorts have had the benefit of richer sources of information and experience with advanced technologies, enabling them to function at a higher level (Baltes & Labouvie 1973; Schaie 1974). Longitudinal studies reveal no universal or general decline in intellectual capabilities until the very advanced years, but in cross-sectional comparisons of different age groups the young surpass the old. Thus, older persons who weigh self-comparisons in functioning over the course of time more heavily than social comparison with younger cohorts are less likely to view themselves as declining in capabilities than if younger cohorts are used extensively in socially comparative self-appraisals.

Frey and Ruble further note that older adults who keep up their skills can maintain a high sense of competence and self-satisfaction by exploiting age norms. In such normative comparisons they come out looking superior to their agemates. This self-evaluative strategy is beneficial for those who exceed the normative age standard or for members of the mythical community of Lake Wobegon where everyone is above average. But those who have let their skills go to pot would do better to avert their gaze from normative standards unless they want to arouse self-discontent as a motivator for a program of self-reinvigoration.

Whereas Frey and Ruble prescribe normative comparison as a way of maintaining a high sense of competence and self-satisfaction, Nicholls disavows such a practice as a detrimental influence. In his view, people would do better to cease evaluating their competence and instead focus on the satisfaction and meaning they derive from their pursuits. Simpler egocentric conceptions of ability in terms of personal likelihood of success can serve this purpose better than more advanced normative conceptions of ability measured against success rates of others. Nicholls's jaundiced view of social comparison appears to stem from an exclusive focus on normative comparison. Such comparisons can certainly make the less talented miserable and wreck their sense of personal competence. As previously noted, however, social comparison can take a variety of forms and it can have beneficial as well as negative effects. Judgment of ability has considerable adaptive value. People who undertake activities without appraising their capabilities can get themselves into considerable difficulties. Some of the missteps can result in a lot of wasted effort or produce costly or irreparable harm. We shall shortly examine research showing that continuing personal attainments do not necessarily ensure self-satisfaction. This is because the strides at which activities are mastered can drastically alter self-evaluative reactions.

Most comparative self-appraisals involve particular individuals rather than group norms. This provides flexibility in the choice of comparative others and some leeway to use comparative appraisals for positive purposes. The research reported in this volume is concerned almost entirely with self-evaluation of ability through comparison with the performances of others. People also judge their capabilities on the basis of similarity in personal characteristics that are assumed to be predictive of performance capabilities (Suls & Miller 1977). The successes of models who possess similar characteristics inspire others by strengthening belief in their capabilities to succeed, lead them to try things they would otherwise shun, and bolster their staying power in the face of obstacles (Bandura 1986). But comparative self-appraisals based on faulty preconceptions concerning the relation of characteristics such as age, sex, race, and ethnic background to capability in particular domains may also lead those who are uncertain about their abilities to judge valuable pursuits to be beyond their reach when they see others with similar attributes fail.

Frey and Ruble describe a further positive function of social comparative information in which young children use the normative accomplishments of older peers as a way of neutralizing the negative impact of failure on their self-perceptions of competence. The experience of rapid skill improvement and observation of modeled proficiency by older peers leads children to view their own skill at any given time as a transitory level in a process of growth rather than as an indicant of basic capability. Anticipatory upward comparison helps to support an optimistic self-appraisal despite current performance deficiencies.

A developmental perspective on the self-appraisal of personal efficacy can have beneficial effects provided that judgments are made solely in terms of self-comparison and upward normative comparison. Unfortunately, social realities impose a third comparative factor that counteracts an exclusively developmental conception of competence. Even preschoolers are not unmindful of the speed with which their agemates acquire skills, and they are acutely aware of ability rankings (Morris & Nemcek 1982). Children judge their learning efficacy as well as their existing level of competence. Their perceptions of their learning capabilities affect how much cognitive effort they invest in instructional activities and how much they learn (Salomon 1984). Monolithic school structures in which students study the same material and teachers make frequent comparative evaluations highlight social comparative standards. Students rank themselves according to capability with high group consensus (Rosenholtz & Rosenholtz 1981). Social comparison with ones' agemates thus reinstates the diagnosticity of rate of progress and level of achievement in the judgment of personal capabilities. The less talented or ill prepared suffer the greatest losses in perceived efficacy. Moreover, their self-beliefs of efficacy are more vulnerable to the negative impact of teachers with a low sense of instructional efficacy than are those of students who believe strongly in their capabilities (Midgley, Feldlaufer, & Eccles in press).

In social cognitive theory (Bandura 1986), self-appraisal is a process in which different sources of comparative information—normative comparative, specific social comparative, and personal comparative—are weighted and integrated in formation of self-efficacy judgments and experience of self-satisfaction. Developmental changes are reflected in the relative weight given to different forms of comparative information rather than in shifts in exclusive reliance from a social-comparative standard to a self-comparative one. The relative weighting of different comparative information may vary across domains of functioning and situational circumstances.

The multidimensional influence on self-appraisal is revealed in research in which normative standards and rate of personal progress are systematically varied (Simon 1979). Students performed a cognitive task and received prearranged feedback of a decelerating pattern of improvement (improve fast initially but then taper off) or an accelerating improvement (improve slowly at first but then make large gains). They also had access to normative standards that portrayed students as performing at either the upper range or the midrange of possible attainments. The students' level of self-satisfaction was strongly influenced by both social and self-comparison. The higher the normative standards, the less self-satisfied they were with their own performance attainments. Different rates of improvement produced strikingly different patterns of self-evaluation (figure 14.5). Rapid strides occasioned rising self-satisfaction, whereas declining improvements were devalued after large initial gains had been achieved.

In the final phase, all students attained the same high performance that exceeded the normative standard. Those who surpassed the norm through accelerating improvement were highly self-approving, but those who attained the same noteworthy accomplishment through a declining rate of improvement experienced virtually no self-satisfaction. Early large success is evidently conducive to later self-dissatisfaction even though one continues to make progress. As can be seen in the right panel of figure 14.5, people who are prone to depression display even greater evaluative reactivity to their progress. They are more self-satisfied with accelerating

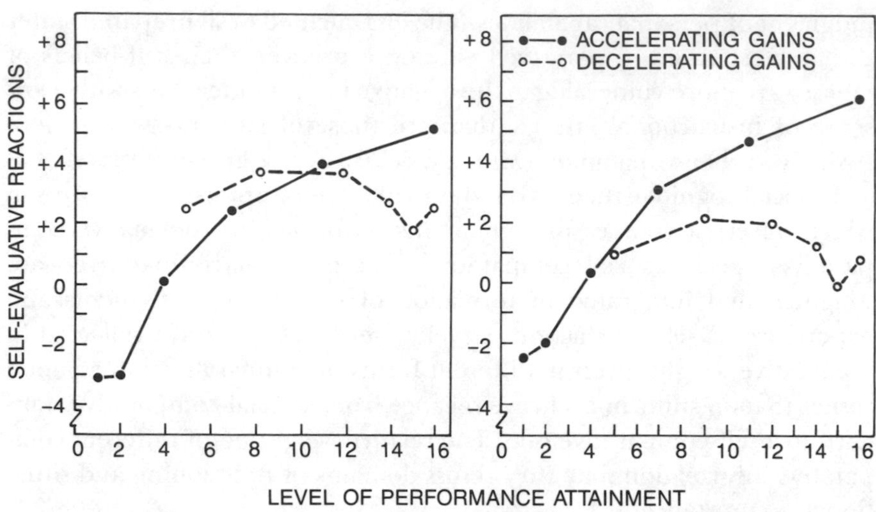

Figure 14.5. Strength of self-evaluative reactions exhibited by subjects who received feedback of a decelerating pattern of improvement (improve fast initially but then taper off) or an accelerating pattern (improve slowly at first but then make large gains). Positive numbers represent strength of self-approval; negative numbers indicate self-criticism. The graphs in the left panel are the self-evaluative reactions of normal individuals and those in the right panel are for depressed individuals. All individuals received the same performance score on the last trial (Simon, 1979).

strides, but they find even less satisfaction in modest improvements after achieving large performance attainments.

With success comes the tribulation of fulfilling not only rising personal standards but social expectations. A noted composer put it well when he remarked, "The toughest thing about success is that you've got to keep on being a success." Those who experience spectacular early successes often find themselves wrestling with self-doubts and despondency if their later work falls short of their earlier triumphs. The Nobel laureate Linus Pauling prescribed a total remedy for the woes of belittling self-comparison. When asked what one does after winning a Nobel Prize, he replied, "Change fields, of course!" The self-evaluation problem with spectacular accomplishments is by no means confined to creative endeavors. After a phenomenal long jump that shattered the existing world record by two feet, Bob Beamon avoided self-disappointment by never jumping again.

MISMATCH MECHANISMS IN HUMAN AFFECT AND MOTIVATION

Many theories of motivation and self-regulation are founded on a negative feedback control model. This type of system functions as a motivator and regulator of action through a discrepancy reduction mechanism. Perceived discrepancy between performance and a reference standard motivates action to reduce the incongruity. Discrepancy reduction clearly plays a central role in any system of self-regulation. However, in the negative feedback control system, if performance matches the standard the person does nothing. A regulatory process in which matching a standard begets inertness does not characterize human motivation.

Human self-motivation relies on both *discrepancy production* and *discrepancy reduction* (Bandura 1988a). It requires *proactive* control as well as *reactive feedback* control. People initially motivate themselves through feedforward control by setting themselves valued challenging standards that create a state of disequilibrium and then mobilizing their effort on the basis of anticipatory estimation of what it would take to reach them. After people attain the standard they have been pursuing, they generally set a higher standard for themselves. The adoption of further challenges creates new motivating discrepancies to be mastered. Similarly, surpassing a standard is more likely to raise aspiration than to lower subsequent performance to conform to the surpassed standard. Self-motivation thus involves a dual cyclic process of disequilibrating discrepancy production followed by equilibrating discrepancy reduction.

The same hierarchical dual control mechanisms operate in the construction of behavioral patterns and regulation of established ones (Bandura 1986). Foresightful conceptions and forethought guide the construction and selection of actions, and the results produced by those actions verify the adequacy of the chosen course. A system of self-regulation combining *proactive guidance* with *reactive adjustments* is best suited for adaptive functioning, especially under changing circumstances.

Moretti and Higgins present a self-discrepancy theory of self-evaluation and self-regulation in which the comparative factors include sets of attributes. They focus primarily on the affective consequences of self-discrepancies. Perceived attributes are compared against either ideal standards or standards of duty and obligation. Failure to fulfill ideal standards produces dejection when the ideals are one's own, and embarrassment when they represent the hopes that significant others hold for one. Failure to meet standards of obligation arouses feelings of guilt when the standards are self-imposed but fear when they are prescribed by others. Moretti and Higgins report several lines of evidence that provide consistent support for the hypothesized consequences of the different forms of self-discrepancy.

Several aspects of this model of self-regulation require clarification and further empirical examination. In the verification tests, subjects rate their own attributes, the standards they apply to themselves, the standards imposed on them by others, and their feeling states. Except for a few instances in which nonverbal reactions are assessed, subjects' verbal reports are the sole source of the measures for all the variables. This can inflate obtained relationships and leave ambiguities as to whether they reflect genuine causal dependencies or people's intuitive theories about how different kinds of shortcomings should make one feel.

The self-discrepancy model seems to be concerned primarily with the self-regulation of affective states. However, self-discrepancies should have motivational and behavorial effects as well, which are readily testable. For example, how are differential magnitudes of actual-ideal discrepancy reflected in level of motivation? Under conditions of low social surveillance, self-imposed ought standards should have greater restraining power over transgressive behavior than ought standards prescribed by others. What sets of conditions produce self-regulatory failures that eventuate in actual-ought discrepancies breeding guilt? Such a state of affairs appears to reflect what has been characterized as a scotch conscience—it is too weak to restrain transgressive conduct but strong enough to ensure that you do not enjoy it.

Theories of self-regulation usually include a set of subsidiary processes through which perceived discrepancies produce their effects (Bandura 1986; Carver & Scheier 1981; Kanfer 1977; Rehm 1982). Some of these subprocesses are concerned with the self-monitoring of conduct and the circumstances under which it occurs. Other subprocesses involve judgments of the conduct in terms of different patterns of referential standards, the valuation of the activity, the perceived determinants of the conduct, and self-appraisal of capabilities to fulfill given standards. A third set of subprocesses governs the nature of the evaluative self-reactions after the conduct has been judged.

Rehm's (1982) application of the discrepancy model to depressive affect illustrates the multifaceted nature of the self-regulation of affective states. With regard to self-monitoring, depressed people tend to underestimate their successes but remain acutely aware of their failures. In contrast, the nondepressed remember their successes but minimize their failures. Minimizing one's successes while accenting one's failures is a good way of driving oneself to depression. Those who are plagued by depression also display a depressogenic style of processing performance-related information. In judging the determinants of their performances, the nondepressed favor a self-enhancing bias, crediting successes to themselves and ascribing failures to situational factors. The depressed do not necessarily discount their contribution to successes, but they are quick to attribute failures to themselves. The depressed are also prone to use social-comparative information in self-belittling ways. They tend to adopt standards that exceed their perceived capabilities, whereas the nondepressed favor standards that are judged to be attainable. In the self-reactive phase of self-regulation, depressed individuals tend to be less self-rewarding for successes and more self-denying and self-punishing for failures than the nondepressed for identical performances. Self-devaluation and despondency augment each other bidirectionally.

In the Moretti and Higgins self-discrepancy model, disparity between two sets of attributes (i.e., actual-ideal or actual-ought) seems to generate dejections, embarrassments, guilts, and fears without any other intervening processes. These various affective reactions are tied to four discrete sets of discrepancies (i.e., ideal-own, ideal-other, ought-own, and ought-other). In everyday life, personal and social standards operate on behavior interactively rather than isolatedly. Different patterns of disparity between these two sets of standards will activate different emotional reactions. Consider the relation between actual-ought attributes. Transgressive conduct will produce different reactions when personal and social standards are congruent than when they are discordant. People who highly value behavior that social authorities disapprove, such as principled dissenters and nonconformists, are most likely to feel pride rather than agitation in ignoring socially prescribed demands. People commonly experience conflicts in which they are socially rewarded for behavior that violates their personal standards. If the benefits for socially accommodating behavior are highly inviting, social standards often triumph over personal ones without arousal of guilt. This is because development of a self-regulatory system does not create an invariant control mechanism within a person. Self-reactive influences do not operate unless they are activated and there are many psychological mechanisms by which moral standards can be disengaged from transgressive conduct

adopt their prescripts and modeled standards (Bandura & Walters 1959; Goslin 1969; Perry & Bussey 1984; Sears, Maccoby, & Levin 1957). According to Moretti and Higgins, if parents convey the right contingency information frequently, clearly, consistently, and forcefully, their children will adopt standards that guide them to be aspiring and dutiful. If only it were that simple. Saliency and clarity of prescripts will carry different impacts depending on whether the socializers are liked, admired, disliked, hated, seen as powerful or weak, competent or ineffectual. Socializers, of course, are embedded in a broad network of social influences that can support their efforts or give them Excedrin headaches as sources of strife. The scope of the transmission model is addressed next.

FAMILIAL AND SOCIAL TRANSMISSION MODELS

In their conception of the socialization process, Moretti and Higgins focus almost exclusively on the transmission of standards via parent-child relationships. In a provocative paper, Reiss (1965) contrasts theories based on the familial transmission model with those emphasizing transmission by broader social systems. He offers several reasons why the familial transmission model cannot adequately explain socialization processes and outcomes. Assuming, at least, a twenty-year procreation difference between generations, a long time intervenes between parents' imparting values and standards to their children and when the children can, in turn, pass on those values to their own offspring. The long time lag between succeeding descendants would produce a very slow rate of social change, whereas, in fact, extensive societywide shifts in standards and normative behavior often occur within a single generation. The marked change in sexual standards and practices and cohabitation patterns within a relatively short time span is but one recent example. The common cohabitation of unmarried couples was not occasioned by parents inculcating in their children broad-minded views regarding sexuality. Although the familial subsystem serves as an important agency of cultural transmission, standards of behavior are extensively disseminated by extrafamilial social systems. Thus, for example, racial segregation in public accommodations and infringement of voting rights were changed more rapidly by collective protest and Supreme Court decisions than by waiting for prejudiced parents to inculcate in their children more acceptant attitudes which they would display toward minority groups when they became restaurateurs and motel operators thirty or forty years later.

The adoption of values, standards, and attributes is governed by a much broader and more dynamic social reality than merely the transactions in parent-child relationships (Bandura 1986). Social learning is a continuous process in which acquired standards are elaborated and modified, and new ones are adopted. Children repeatedly observe and learn the standards and behavior patterns not only of parents but also of siblings, peers, and other adults. Moreover, the extensive symbolic modeling provided in the mass media serves as another prominent extrafamilial source of influence (Liebert & Sprafkin 1988). Hence, children's values and personal standards are likely to reflect amalgams of these diverse sources, rather than simply the familial heritage.

THE PSYCHOPATHOLOGIZING OF SELF-DOUBT

Kolligian regards perceived fraudulence as one manifestation of perceived incompetence. Many high-achieving individuals are said to perceive themselves as impostors and frauds. In psychoanalytic theorizing, from which the construct emanates, perceived fraudulence reflects a disturbed sense of reality and identity and a compensatory narcissistic self-enhancement driven by feelings of inadequacy and worthlessness. The impostorous self-enhancement is promoted through imitativeness, verbal fluency, high social skill, personal charm, and sensitivity to others' expectations. Women have never fared well in psychoanalytic theory. It, therefore, comes as no great surprise that they become the tragediennes in the pursuit of high aspirations. Psychoanalytic researchers find that "perceived fraudulence" is a predominantly female experience, especially among the high-achieving ones. So women get it coming and going. Socialization practices instill in women self-doubts about their capabilities and then their self-doubts and striving for intellectual acceptance get psychoanalytically labeled as indicants of perceived fraudulenceness. The psychopathologizing of self-doubts and the negative labeling of efforts at self-enhancement as fraudulence and impostorousness only further undermine a sense of personal efficacy and self-esteem.

Kolligian removes much of the pathologic coloring from the construct of perceived fraudulence. It becomes a self-referential ideation that has both cognitive and affective components. It evolves through an initial self-perception of incompetence to intolerance of the perceived incompetence, especially among those with high achievement strivings, to resort to fraudulent maneuvers as protection against personal and social devaluation and then to added stressful concern over acting fraudulently and threats of social exposure. People who belittle themselves and strive to excel and please others get categorized as the perceived frauds.

Labels of deceit for thoughts and feelings of inauthenticity over discrepancies between self-perceptions and social impressions can do psychological harm. The notion of impostor has already entered the pop culture with authors marketing "the impostor phenomenon" on the television circuit under catchy titles concocted by advertising wordsmiths. It is not uncommon for people who have an affinity to the pop culture to now label themselves as impostors for their fallibilities and because their self-view does not always match up to their public image. The field might be better served if self-referent thoughts and feelings of inauthenticity bore less pernicious labels.

CONCLUDING REMARKS

The contributors to this volume have given us a better sense of the origins of perceived competence and the processes by which it affects human motivation, accomplishments, and dysfunctions. The value of psychological theories is judged not only by their explanatory and predictive power but also by their operative power to effect enduring changes in human functioning. Significant progress has been made in creating ways of enhancing human functioning by empowering people with coping skills and resilient self-beliefs of capability that enable them to exercise control over events that affect their lives (Bandura 1988b, 1988c; Rodin 1986; Schunk 1984). There is much to be gained from a better understanding of how to alter self-beliefs of capability in ways that contribute to personal well-being.

REFERENCES

Aber, J. L., & Allen, J. P. (1987). Effects of maltreatment on young children's socioemotional development: An attachment theory perspective. *Developmental Psychology, 23,* 406–414.

Abraham, K. (1925). The history of an impostor in the light of psychoanalytic knowledge. *Psychoanalytic Quarterly, 4,* 570–587.

Abramson, L. Y., Seligman, M. E. P., & Teasdale, J. D. (1978). Learned helplessness in humans: Critique and reformulation. *Journal of Abnormal Psychology, 87,* 49–74.

Adler, A. (1964). *Problems of neurosis.* New York: Harper & Row.

Ainsworth, M. D. S. (1972). Attachment and dependency: A comparison. In J. L. Gerwitz (Ed.), *Attachment and dependency* (pp. 97–137). Washington, DC: Winston.

Ainsworth, M. D. S. (1979). Infant-mother attachment. *American Psychologist, 34,* 932–937.

Ainsworth, M. D. S. (1982). Attachment: Retrospect and prospect. In C. M. Parkes & J. Stevenson-Hinde (Eds.), *The place of attachment in human behavior* (pp. 3–30). New York: Basic Books.

Ainsworth, M. D. S., & Bell, S. M. (1974). Mother-infant interaction and the development of competence. In K. Connolly & J. Bruner (Eds.), *The growth of competence* (pp. 97–118). London: Academic Press.

Ainsworth, M. D. S.; Blehar, M. C.; Waters, E.; & Wall, S. (1978). *Patterns of attachment: A psychological study of the Strange Situation.* Hillsdale, NJ: Erlbaum.

Albert, R. S., & Runco, M. A. (1987). Educational and family perceptions of exceptionally gifted and gifted preadolescent boys. *Society for Research in Child Development Meetings.* Baltimore, MD.

Albert, S. (1977). Temporal comparison theory. *Psychological Review, 84,* 485–503.

Albrecht, G. L., & Gift, H. C. (1975). Adult socialization: Ambiguity and adult life crises. In N. Datan & L. H. Gensburg (Eds.), *Life span developmental psychology: Formative life crises.* New York: Academic Press.

Alessandri, S. M., & Wozniak, R. H. (1987). The child's awareness of parental beliefs concerning the child: A developmental study. *Child Development, 58,* 316–323.

Alexander, P. (1985). Gifted and nongifted students' perceptions of intelligence. *Gifted Child Quarterly, 29,* 137–143.

Alicke, M. D. (1985). Global self-evaluation as determined by the desirability and controllability of trait adjectives. *Journal of Personality and Social Psychology, 49,* 1621–1630.

Alloy, L., & Abramson, L. (1979). Judgment of contingency in depressed and nondepressed students: Sadder but wiser? *Journal of Experimental Psychology: General, 108,* 441–485.

Alloy, L., & Abramson, L. (1982). Learned helplessness, depression and the illusion of control. *Journal of Personality and Social Psychology, 42,* 1114–1126.

Alloy, L., Abramson, L., & Viscusi, D. (1981). Induced mood and the illusion of control. *Journal of Personality and Social Psychology, 41,* 1129–1140.

Alloy, L., & Ahrens, A. H. (1987). Depression and pessimism for the future: Biased use of statistically relevant information in predictions for self versus others. *Journal of Personality and Social Psychology, 52,* 366–378.

Allport, G. W. (1940). The psychologist's frame of reference. *Psychological Bulletin, 37,* 1–28.

Allport, G. W. (1955). *Becoming.* New Haven, CT: Yale University Press.

Amabile, T. M. (1979). Effects of external evaluation on artistic creativity. *Journal of Personality and Social Psychology, 37,* 221–233.

Amabile, T. M. (1982). Social psychology of creativity: A consensual assessment technique. *Journal of Personality and Social Psychology, 43,* 997–1013.

Amabile, T. M. (1983). *The social psychology of creativity.* New York: Springer-Verlag.

American Psychiatric Association. (1987). *Diagnostic and statistical manual of mental disorders* (3rd ed., revised). Washington, DC: American Psychiatric Association.

Anderson, C. A. (1983). Imagination and expectation: The effect of imagining behavioral scripts on personal intentions. *Journal of Personality and Social Psychology, 45,* 293–305.

Anderson, C. A., Lepper, M. R., & Ross, L. (1980). Perseverance of social theories: The role of explanation in the persistence of discredited information. *Journal of Personality and Social Psychology, 39,* 1037–1049.

Anderson, J. R. (1980). *Cognitive psychology and its implications.* San Francisco: Freeman.

Angyal, A. (1941). *Foundations for a science of personality.* New York: Commonwealth Fund.

Aries, P. (1962). *Centuries of childhood.* New York: Knopf.

Asarnow, J. R., Carlson, G. A., & Guthrie, D. (1987). Coping strategies, self-perceptions, hopelessness and perceived family environments in depressed and suicidal children. *Journal of Consulting and Clinical Psychology, 55,* 361–366.

Asch, S. E. (1952). *Social psychology.* Englewood Cliffs, NJ: Prentice-Hall.

Astin, H. S. (1974). Sex differences in mathematical and scientific precocity. In J. C. Stanley, D. P. Keating, & L. H. Fox (Eds.), *Mathematical talent: Discovery, description, and development* (pp. 70–86). Baltimore, MD: Johns Hopkins University Press.

Atchley, R. C. (1976). Time, roles, and self in old age. In J. F. Gubrium (Ed.), *Time, roles, and self in old age* (pp. 199–208). New York: Human Sciences Press.

Atchley, R. C. (1982). The aging self. *Psychotherapy: Theory, Research, and Practice, 19,* 388–396.

Atkinson, J. W. (1957). Motivation determinants of risk-taking behavior. *Psychological Review, 64,* 359–372.

Atkinson, J. W. (1964). *An introduction to motivation.* Princeton, NJ: Van Nostrand.

Avorn, J., & Langer, E. (1982). Induced disability in nursing home patients: A controlled trail. *Journal of American Geriatric Society, 30,* 397–400.

Baldwin, A. L. (1955). *Behavior and development in childhood.* New York: Dreyden Press.

Baltes, P. B. (1987). Theoretical propositions of life span developmental psychology: On the dynamics between growth and decline. *Developmental Psychology, 23*(5), 611–626.

Baltes, P. B., & Labouvie, G. V. (1973). Adult development of intellectual performance: Description, explanation, and modification. In C. Eisdorfer & M. P. Lawton (Eds.), *The psychology of adult development and aging* (pp. 157–219). Washington, DC: American Psychological Association.

Baltes, P. B., Reese, H. W., & Lipsett, L. P. (1980). Life span developmental psychology. *Annual Review of Psychology, 31,* 65–110.

Baltes, M., & Skinner, E. (1983). Cognitive performance deficits and hospitalization: Learned helplessness, instrumental passivity, or what? *Journal of Personality and Social Psychology, 45,* 1013–1016.

Bandura, A. (1977). Self-efficacy: Toward a unifying theory of behavioral change. *Psychological Review, 84,* 191–215.

Bandura, A. (1978). The self-system in reciprocal determinism. *American Psychologist, 33,* 344–358.

Bandura, A. (1981). Self-referent thought: The development analysis of self-efficacy. In J. H. Flavell & L. D. Ross (Eds.), *Development of social cognition* (pp. 200–239). New York: Cambridge University Press.

Bandura, A. (1982). Self-efficacy mechanism in human agency. *American Psychologist, 37*(2), 122–147.

Bandura, A. (1986). *Social foundations of thought and action: A social cognitive theory.* Englewood Cliffs, NJ: Prentice-Hall.

Bandura, A. (1988a). Self-regulation of motivation and action through goal systems. In V. Hamilton, G. H. Bower, & N. H. Frijda (Eds.), *Cognitive perspectives on emotion and motivation* (pp. 37–61). Dordrecht: Kluwer Academic Publishers.

Bandura, A. (1988b). Perceived self-efficacy: Exercise of control through self-belief. In J. P. Dauwalder, M. Perrez, & V. Hobi (Eds.), *Annual series of Euro-*

pean research in behavior therapy (Vol. 2, pp. 27–59). Lisse, Holland: Swets & Zeitlinger.

Bandura, A. (1988c). Self-efficacy mechanism in physiological activation and health-promoting behavior. In J. Madden IV, S. Matthysse, & J. Barchas (Eds.), *Adaptation, learning and affect.* New York: Raven Press.

Bandura, A. (1988d). Social cognitive theory of moral thought and action. In W. M. Kurtines & J. L. Gewirtz (Eds.), *Moral behavior and development: Advances in theory, research and applications* (Vol. 1). Hillsdale, NJ: Erlbaum.

Bandura, A. (1988e). Self-efficacy conception of anxiety. *Anxiety Research, 1,* 77–98.

Bandura, A., & Abrams, K. (1986). *Self-regulatory mechanisms in motivating, apathetic, and despondent reactions to unfulfilled standards.* Unpublished manuscript, Stanford University.

Bandura, A., & Adams, N. E. (1977). Analysis of self-efficacy theory of behavioral change. *Cognitive Therapy and Research, 1,* 287–308.

Bandura, A., Adams, N. E., & Beyer, J. (1977). Cognitive processes mediating behavioral change. *Journal of Personality and Social Psychology, 35,* 125–139.

Bandura, A., & Cervone, D. (1983). Self-evaluative and self-efficacy mechanisms governing the motivational effects of goal systems. *Journal of Personality and Social Psychology, 45,* 1017–1028.

Bandura, A., & Cervone, D. (1986). Differential engagement of self-reactive influences in cognitive motivation. *Organizational Behavior and Human Decision Processes, 38,* 92–113.

Bandura, A.; Cioffi, D.; Taylor, C. B.; & Brouillard, M. E. (1988). Perceived self-efficacy in coping with cognitive stressors and opioid activation. *Journal of Personality and Social Psychology, 55,* 479–488.

Bandura, A., Reese, L., & Adams, N. E. (1982). Microanalysis of action and fear arousal as a function of differential levels of perceived self-efficacy. *Journal of Personality and Social Psychology, 43,* 5–21.

Bandura, A.; Taylor, C. B.; Williams, S. L.; Mefford, I. N.; & Barchas, J. D. (1985). Catecholamine secretion as a function of perceived coping self-efficacy. *Journal of Consulting and Clinical Psychology, 53,* 406–414.

Bandura, A., & Walters, R. H. (1959). *Adolescent aggression.* New York: Ronald Press.

Bandura, A., & Wood, R. E. (1989). Effect of perceived controllability and performance standards on self-regulation of complex decision-making. *Journal of Personality and Social Psychology, 56,* 805–814.

Bandura, M. M., & Dweck, C. S. (1985). *Self-conceptions and motivation: Conceptions of intelligence, choice of achievement goals, and patterns of cognition, affect, and behavior.* Manuscript submitted for publication, University of Illinois.

Bandura, M. M., & Dweck, C. S. (1988). *The relationship of conceptions of intelligence and achievement goals to achievement-related cognition, affect and behavior.* Manuscript submitted for publication.

Barenboim, C. (1981). The development of person perception in childhood and adolescence: From behavioral comparisons to psychological comparisons. *Child Development, 52,* 129–144.

Basch, M. F. (1975). Toward a theory that encompasses depression: A revision of existing causal hypotheses in psychoanalysis. In E. J. Anthony & T. Benedek (Eds.), *Depression and human existence* (pp. 485–534). Boston: Little, Brown & Co.

Basch, M. F. (1983). The concept of the self: An operational definition. In B. Lee & G. G. Noam (Eds.), *Developmental approaches to the self.* New York: Plenum Press.

Baumeister, R. F. (1984). Choking under pressure: Self-consciousness and paradoxical effects of incentives on skillful performance. *Journal of Personality and Social Psychology, 46*(3), 610–620.

Baumeister, R. F., Hamilton, J. C., & Tice, D. M. (1985). Public versus private expectancy at success: Confidence booster or performance pressure. *Journal of Personality and Social Psychology, 48,* 1447–1457.

Baumrind, D. (1967). Child care practices anteceding three patterns of preschool behavior. *Genetic Psychology Monographs, 75,* 43–88.

Baumrind, D. (1971). Current patterns of parental authority. *Developmental Psychology Monographs, 4.*

Beach, L. R., Barnes, V. E., & Christensen-Szalanski, J. J. J. (1986). Beyond heuristics and biases: A contingency model of judgmental forecasting. *Journal of Forecasting, 5,* 143–157.

Beck, A. T. (1967). *Depression: Clinical experimental and theoretical aspects.* New York: Harper & Row.

Beck, A. T. (1976). *Cognitive therapy and the emotional disorders.* New York: Guilford Press.

Beebe, A., & Demos, V. (1985). *Affect and the development of the self: A new frontier.* Paper presented at the annual Self Psychological Conference, New York.

Beecher, H. K. (1956). Relationship of significance of wound to pain experience. *Journal of American Medical Association, 161,* 1609–1613.

Behrends, R. S., & Blatt, S. J. (1985). Internalization and psychological development throughout the life cycle. *Psychoanalytic Study of the Child, 40,* 11–39.

Bempechat, J. (1985). *Children's theories of intelligence: Impact and development.* Paper presented at the meeting of the Society for Research in Child Development, Toronto.

Benbow, C. P., & Minor, L. L. (1986). Mathematically talented students and achievement in the high school sciences. *American Education Research Journal, 23,* 425–436.

Benbow, C. P., & Stanley, J. C. (1980). Sex differences in mathematical ability: Fact or artifact? *Science, 210,* 1262–1264.

Bengston, V. L. (1973). *The social psychology of aging.* Indianapolis, IN: Bobbs-Merrill.

Berglas, S. (1986). *The success syndrome: Hitting bottom when you reach the top.* New York: Plenum Press.

Berglas, S., & Jones, E. (1978). Drug choice as a self-handicapping strategy in response to noncontingent success. *Journal of Personality and Social Psychology, 36,* 405–417.

Berry, J. (1984). Towards a universal psychology of cognitive competence. In

P. S. Fry (Ed.), *Changing conceptions of intelligence and intellectual functioning* (pp. 35–61). Amsterdam: North-Holland.

Berry, J. M. (1987, September 1). *A self-efficacy model of memory performance.* Paper presented at meetings of the American Psychological Association, New York.

Bettes, B. A. (in press). Maternal depression and motherese: Temporal and intonational features. *Child Development.*

Betz, N. E., & Hackett, G. (1986). Applications of self-efficacy theory to understanding career choice behavior. *Journal of Social and Clinical Psychology, 4,* 279–289.

Biederman, J.; Munir, K.; Knee, D.; Armentano, M.; Autor, S.; Waternauz, C.; & Tsaung, M. (1987). High rate of affective disorders in probands with attention deficit disorder and in their relatives: A controlled family study. *American Journal of Psychiatry, 144,* 330–333.

Bierer, B. (1982). *Behavioral and motivational correlates of children's accuracy in judging their cognitive competence.* Unpublished doctoral dissertation, University of Denver.

Billings, A. G., & Moos, R. H. (1983). Comparisons of children of depressed and nondepressed parents: A social-environmental perspective. *Journal of Abnormal Child Psychology, 11,* 463–486.

Bird, J. E. (1984). *Development of children's understanding of the concepts of "easy" and "hard" in judging task difficulty.* Paper presented at the meeting of the American Educational Research Association, New Orleans.

Blatt, S. J. (1974). Levels of object representation in anaclitic and introjective depression. *Psychoanalytic Study of the Child, 29,* 107–157.

Blatt, S. J.; Chevron, E.; Quinlan, D. M.; Schaffer, C. E.; Wein, S. J. (1988). *The assessment of qualitative and structural dimensions of object representation.* Unpublished research manual.

Blatt, S. J., D'Afflitti, J. P., & Quinlan, D. M. (1976). Experiences of depression in normal young adults. *Journal of Abnormal Psychology, 85,* 383–389.

Blatt, S. J., D'Afflitti, J. P., & Quinlan, D. M. (1979). *Depressive experiences questionnaire.* Unpublished manual.

Blatt, S. J., & Marcus, B. F. (in preparation). Concept of the object in anaclitic and introjective depression.

Blatt, S. J., Quinlan, D. M., & Bers, S. A. (in preparation). Parental caring and protection in anaclitic and introjective depression.

Blatt, S. J.; Quinlan, D. M.; Chevron, E. S.; McDonald, C.; & Zuroff, D. (1982). Dependency and self-criticism: Psychological dimensions of depression. *Journal of Consulting and Clinical Psychology, 50,* 113–124.

Blatt, S. J., & Shickman, S. (1983). Two primary configurations of psychopathology. *Psychoanalysis and Contemporary Thought, 6*(2), 187–254.

Blatt, S. J.; Wein, S. J.; Chevron, E. S.; & Quinlan, D. M. (1979). Parental representations and depression in normal young adults. *Journal of Abnormal Psychology, 88*(4), 388–397.

Blechman, E. A.; McEnroe, M. J.; Carella, E. T.; & Audette, D. P. (1986). Childhood competence and depression. *Journal of Abnormal Psychology, 95,* 223–227.

Blechman, E. A.; Tinsley, B.; Carella, E. T.; & McEnroe, M. J. (1985). Childhood competence and behavior problems. *Journal of Abnormal Psychology, 94,* 70–77.

Block, J. H. (1979). Another look at sex differentiation in the socialization behavior of mothers and fathers. In J. Sherman & F. L. Denmark (Eds.), *Psychology of women: Future direction of research.* New York: Psychological Dimensions.

Bloom, B. (1964). *Stability and change in human behavior.* New York: Wiley.

Bloom, B. (1985). *Developing talent in young people.* New York: Ballantine.

Blos, P. (1961). *On adolescence.* New York: Free Press.

Boggiano, A. K., & Ruble, D. N. (1979). Competence and the overjustification effect. *Journal of Personality and Social Psychology, 37,* 1462–1468.

Bortner, R. W., & Hultsch, D. R. (1972). Personal time perspective in adulthood. *Developmental Psychology, 7,* 98–103.

Bowlby, J. (1971). *Attachment and loss: Vol. I. Attachment.* New York: Penguin. (Original work published 1969)

Bowlby, J. (1975). *Attachment and loss: Vol. II. Separation.* New York: Penguin. (Original work published 1973)

Bowlby, J. (1980). *Attachment and loss: Vol. III. Loss, sadness, and depression.* New York: Basic Books.

Bradley, G. W. (1978). Self-serving biases in the attribution process: A reexamination of the fact or fiction question. *Journal of Personality and Social Psychology, 36,* 56–71.

Bradley, R. H., Caldwell, B. M., & Elardo, R. (1979). Home environment and cognitive development in the first two years: A cross-lagged panel analysis. *Developmental Psychology, 15,* 246–250.

Brehm, J. (1966). *A theory of psychological reactance.* New York: Academic Press.

Bretherton, I., & Beeghly, M. (1982). Talking about internal states: The acquisition of an explicit theory of mind. *Developmental Psychology, 18,* 906–921.

Breytspraak, L. M. (1984). *The development of self in later life.* Boston: Little, Brown, & Co.

Brickman, P., & Bulman, R. J. (1977). Pleasure and pain in social comparison. In J. M. Suls & R. L. Miller (Eds.), *Social comparison processes: Theoretical and empirical perspectives* (pp. 149–186). Washington, DC: Hemisphere.

Brim, O. G., Jr., & Ryff, C. D. (1980). On the properties of life events. In P. B. Baltes & O. G. Brim, Jr. (Eds.), *Life span development and behavior* (Vol. 3). New York: Academic Press.

Brody, G. H., Graziano, W. G., & Musser, L. M. (1983). Familiarity and children's behavior in same-age and mixed-age peer groups. *Developmental Psychology, 19,* 568–576.

Brody, G. H., Stoneman, Z., & MacKinnon, C. E. (1982). Role asymmetries in interaction among school-aged children, their younger siblings, and their friends. *Child Development, 53,* 1364–1370.

Broughton, J. (1980). The divided self in adolescence. *Human Development, 24,* 13–32.

Brounstein, P., & Holahan, W. (1987). *Change in self-concept and attributional pat-*

terns of gifted adolescents as a result of consensual validation. Paper presented at the annual convention of the Association for Research in Education, Washington, DC.

Brown, I. (1979). Learned helplessness through modeling: Self-efficacy and social comparison processes. In L. C. Perlmutter & R. A. Monty (Eds.), *Choice and perceived control.* Hillsdale, NJ: Erlbaum.

Brown, R. (1956). *Words and thinking.* New York: Free Press.

Bruner, J. S. (1951). Personality dynamics and the process of perceiving. In R. R. Blake & G. V. Ramsey (Eds.), *Perception: An approach to personality* (pp. 121–147). New York: Ronald Press.

Bruner, J. S. (1962). *The process of education.* Cambridge, MA: Harvard University Press.

Bruner, J. S. (1964). The course of cognitive growth. *American Psychologist, 19,* 1–15.

Bruner, J. S., Goodnow, J. J., & Austin, G. A. (1956). *A study of thinking.* New York: Wiley.

Brush, L. R. (1980). *Encouraging girls in mathematics: The problem and the solution.* Cambridge, MA: Abt Books.

Bryant, B. K., & Crockenberg, S. B. (1980). Correlates and dimensions of prosocial behavior: A study of female siblings with their mothers. *Child Development, 51,* 529–544.

Burks, B. S., Jensen, D. W., & Terman, L. M. (1930). The promise of youth. In L. Terman (Ed.), *Genetic studies of genius* (Vol. 3). Stanford, CA: Stanford University Press.

Burlingham, D., & Freud, A. (1942). *Young children in war-time.* London: Allen and Unwin. (Reprinted in A. Freud, *Infants without families: Report on the Hampstead Nurseries, 1939–1945.* New York: International Universities Press, 1973.)

Bruns, D. D. (1980). The perfectionist's script for self-defeat. *Psychology Today,* November, 34–44.

Burton, D., & Martens, R. (1986). Pinned by their own goals: An exploratory investigation into why kids drop out of wrestling. *Journal of Sport Psychology, 8,* 183–197.

Butler, R. N. (1963). Recall in retrospection. *Journal of the American Geriatrics Society, 11,* 523–529.

Butler, R. (1987). Task-involving and ego-involving properties of evaluation on interest and performance. *Journal of Educational Psychology, 79,* 474–482.

Calsyn, R. J., & Kenny, D. A. (1977). Self-concept of ability and perceived evaluation of others: Cause or effect of academic achievement? *Journal of Educational Psychology, 69,* 136–145.

Campbell, J. D. (1986). Similarity and uniqueness: The effects of attribute type, relevance, and individual differences in self-esteem and depression. *Journal of Personality and Social Psychology, 50,* 281–294.

Campos, J. J., & Barrett, K. C. (1984). Toward a new understanding of emotions and their development. In C. E. Izard, J. Kagan, & R. B. Zajonc (Eds.),

Emotions, cognition, and behavior (pp. 299–263). New York: Cambridge University Press.

Canavan-Gumpert, D., Garner, K., & Gumpert, P. (1978). *The success-fearing personality.* Lexington, MA: Heath.

Cantor, N., & Kihlstrom, K. (1987). *Personality and social intelligence.* Englewood Cliffs, NJ: Prentice-Hall.

Cantor, N., & Norem, J. K. (in press). Defensive pessimism and stress and coping. In L. Clark & E. T. Higgins (Issue Eds.), *Social Cognition,* special issue on social cognition and stress.

Cantor, N.; Norem, J. K.; Niedenthal, P. M.; Langston, C. A.; & Brower, A. M. (1987). Life tasks, self-concept ideals, and cognitive strategies in a life transition. *Journal of Personality and Social Psychology, 53*(6), 1178–1191.

Caporael, L. R., Lukaszewski, M. P., & Culbertson, G. H. (1983). Secondary baby talk: Judgments by institutionalized elderly and their caregivers. *Journal of Personality and Social Psychology, 44,* 746–754.

Carroll, W. R., & Bandura, A. (1985). Role of timing of visual monitoring and motor rehearsal in observational learning of action patterns. *Journal of Motor Behavior, 17,* 269–281.

Carroll, W. R., & Bandura, A. (1987). Translating cognition into action: The role of visual guidance in observational learning. *Journal of Motor Behavior, 19,* 385–398.

Carroll, W. R., & Bandura, A. (1988). *Representational guidance of action production in observational learning: A causal analysis.* Unpublished manuscript, Stanford University.

Carver, C. S., Blaney, P. H., & Scheier, M. F. (1979). Focus of attention, chronic expectancy, and responses to a feared stimulus. *Journal of Personality and Social Psychology, 37,* 1186–1195.

Carver, C. S., & Ganellen, R. J. (1983). Depression and components of self-punitiveness: High standards, self-criticism, and overgeneralization. *Journal of Abnormal Psychology, 92,* 330–337.

Carver, C. S., & Scheier, M. F. (1981). *Attention and self-regulation: A control-theory approach to human behavior.* New York: Springer-Verlag.

Carver, C. S., & Scheier, M. F. (1982). Control theory: A useful conceptual framework for personality-social, clinical, and health psychology. *Psychological Bulletin, 92,* 111–135.

Carver, C. S., & Scheier, M. F. (1986). A control-systems approach to the self-regulation of action. In J. Kuhl & J. Beckmann (Eds.), *Action control: From cognition to behavior.* New York: Springer-Verlag.

Case, R. (1985). *Intellectual development: Birth to adulthood.* New York: Academic Press.

Case, R. (1988). The whole child: Toward an integrated view of young children's cognitive, social, and emotional development. In A. Pellegrini (Ed.), *Psychological bases for early education.* Chichester, England: Wiley.

Casler, L. (1961). Maternal deprivation: A critical review of the literature. *Monographs of the Society for Research in Child Development, 26*(2, Serial No. 80).

Cassidy, J. (1988). Child-mother attachment and the self in six-year-olds. *Child Development, 59,* 121–134.

Cauce, A. M. (1987). School and peer competence in early adolescence: A test of domain-specific self-perceived competence. *Developmental Psychology, 23,* 287–291.

Cervone, D. (1989). Effects of envisioning future activities on self-efficacy judgments and motivation: An availability heuristic interpretation. *Cognitive Therapy and Research, 13,* 247–261.

Cervone, D., & Peake, P. K. (1986). Anchoring, efficacy, and action: The influence of judgmental heuristics on self-efficacy judgments and behavior. *Journal of Personality and Social Psychology, 50,* 492–501.

Chanowitz, B., & Langer, E. (1980). Knowing more (or less) than you can show: Understanding control through the mindlessness/mindfulness distinction. In M. E. P. Seligman & J. Garber (Eds.), *Human helplessness.* New York: Academic Press.

Chanowitz, B., & Langer, E. (1981). Premature cognitive commitments. *Journal of Personality and Social Psychology, 41,* 1051–1063.

Chasseguet-Smirgel, J. (1985). *The ego ideal: A psychoanalytic essay on the malady of the ideal.* New York: Norton.

Chen, M. J., Braithwaite, V., & Jong, T. H. (1982). Attributes of intelligent behavior: Perceived relevance and difficulty by Australian and Chinese students. *Journal of Cross-Cultural Psychology, 13,* 139–156.

Chiroboga, D. A. (1978). Evaluated time: A life course perspective. *Journal of Gerontology, 33,* 388–393.

Cicchetti, D., & Rizley, R. (1981). Developmental perspectives on the etiology, intergenerational transmission and sequelae of child maltreatment. In R. Rizley & D. Cicchetti (Eds.), *Developmental perspectives on child maltreatment* (pp. 31–55). San Francisco: Jossey-Bass.

Clance, P. R. (1985). *The impostor phenomenon.* Atlanta, GA: Peachtree.

Clance, P. R., & Imes, S. A. (1978). The impostor phenomenon in high achieving women: Dynamics and therapeutic intervention. *Psychotherapy: Theory, Research, and Practice, 15,* 241–247.

Clark, L. V. (1960). Effect of mental practice on the development of a certain motor skill. *Research Quarterly, 31,* 560–569.

Cohen, S., & Edwards, J. R. (1988). Personality characteristics as moderators of the relationship between stress and disorder. In R. W. J. Neufeld (Ed.), *Advances in the investigation of psychological stress.* New York: Wiley.

Cohen, S., Kamarick, T., & Mermelstein, R. (1983). A global measure of perceived stress. *Journal of Health and Social Behavior, 24,* 385–396.

Cohler, B. J. (1982). Personal narrative and life course. In P. B. Baltes & O. G. Brim, Jr. (Eds.), *Life span development and behavior* (Vol. 4). New York: Academic Press.

Cole, D. A., & Rehm, L. P. (1986). Family interaction patterns and childhood depression. *Journal of Abnormal Child Psychology, 14,* 297–314.

Cole, M.; Gay, J.; Glick, J.; & Sharp, D. W. (1971). *The cultural context of learning and thinking.* New York: Basic Books.

Cole, M., & Scribner, S. (1974). *Culture and thought: A psychological introduction.* New York: Wiley.

Coleman, J. S. (1961). *The adolescent society: The social life of the teenager and its impact on education.* New York: Free Press.

Collins, J. L. (1982, March). *Self-efficacy and ability in achievement behavior.* Paper presented at the annual meeting of the American Educational Research Association, New York.

Connell, J. P., & Ilardi, B. C. (1987). Self-system concomitants of discrepancies between children's and teachers' evaluations of academic competence. *Child Development, 58,* 1297–1307.

Conrad, S. (1975). Imposture as a defense. In P. Govacchini (Ed.), *Tactics and techniques in psychoanalytic theory* (Vol. 2, pp. 413–426). New York: Jason Aronson.

Cooley, C. H. (1964). *Human nature and the social order.* New York: Schocken Books. (Original work published 1902)

Cooper, J., & Goethals, G. R. (1981). The self-concept and old age. In S. B. Kiesler, J. N. Morgan, & V. K. Oppenheimer (Eds.), *Aging: Social change* (pp. 431–452). New York: Academic Press.

Coopersmith, S. (1967). *The antecedents of self-esteem.* San Francisco: Freeman.

Corbin, C. (1972). Mental practice. In W. Morgan (Ed.), *Ergogenic aids and muscular performance* (pp. 93–118). New York: Academic Press.

Costa, B. T., & McCrae, R. R. (1980). Still stable after all these years: Personality as a key to some issues in adulthood and old age. In P. B. Baltes & O. G. Brim, Jr. (Eds.), *Life span development and behavior* (Vol. 3, pp. 5–102). New York: Academic Press.

Costa, D., & Kastenbaum, R. (1967). Some aspects of memories and ambitions in centenarians. *Journal of Genetic Psychology, 110,* 3–16.

Covington, M. V., & Omelich, C. L. (1979). Are causal attributions causal? A path analysis of the cognitive model of achievement motivation. *Journal of Personality and Social Psychology, 37,* 1487–1504.

Crandall, V. C. (1969). Sex differences in expectancy of intellectual and academic reinforcement. In C. P. Smith (Ed.), *Achievement-related motives in children* (pp. 11–45). New York: Russell Sage.

Crocker, J.; Thompson, L. L.; McGraw, K. M.; & Ingerman, C. (1987). Downward comparison prejudice and evaluations of others: Effects of self-esteem and threat. *Journal of Personality and Social Psychology, 52,* 907–916.

Cross, S. E., & Markus, H. (in press). Possible selves across the life span. *Human Development.*

Cummings, S. T. (1976). The impact of child's deficiency on the father: A study of fathers of mentally retarded and of chronically ill children. *American Journal of Orthopsychiatry, 46,* 246–255.

Cutrona, C. E., & Troutman, B. R. (1986). Social support, infant temperament, and parenting self-efficacy: A mediational model of postpartum depression. *Child Development, 57,* 1507–1518.

Damon, W., & Hart, D. (1982). The development of self-understanding from infancy through adolescence. *Child Development, 53,* 841–864.

Damon, W., & Hart, D. (1986). Stability and change in children's self-understanding. *Social Cognition, 4,* 102–118.

Daurio, S. P. (1979). Acceleration vs. enrichment: A review of the literature. In W. C. George, S. J. Cohn, & J. C. Stanley (Eds.), *Educating the gifted.* Baltimore, MD: Johns Hopkins University Press.

Davidson, J. E., & Sternberg, R. J. (1984). The role of insight in intellectual giftedness. *Gifted Child Quarterly, 28,* 58–64.

Davis, R. (1967). Social influences on the aspiration tendency of older people. *Journal of Gerontology, 22,* 510–516.

Deaux, K. (1976). Sex: A perspective on the attribution process. In J. Harvey, W. Ickes, & R. Kidd (Eds.), *New directions in attribution research* (Vol. 1, pp. 335–352). Hillsdale, NJ: Erlbaum.

deCharms, R. (1968). *Personal causation.* New York: Academic Press.

Deci, E. L., & Ryan, R. M. (1980). The empirical exploration of intrinsic motivational processes. In L. Berkowitz (Ed.), *Advances in experimental social psychology* (Vol. 13, pp. 39–80). New York: Academic Press.

Deci, E. L., & Ryan, R. M. (1985). *Intrinsic motivation and self-determination in human behavior.* New York: Plenum Press.

Derogatis, L. R., & Spencer, P. M. (1982). *The brief symptom inventory.* Baltimore, MD: L. R. Derogatis.

Deutsch, F.; Ruble, D. N.; Fleming, A.; Brooks-Gunn, J.; & Stangor, C. (1988). Information seeking and maternal self-definition during the transition to motherhood. *Journal of Personality and Social Psychology, 55,* 420–431.

Deutsch, H. (1955). The impostor: Contribution to ego psychology of a type of psychopath. *Psychoanalytic Quarterly, 24,* 483–505.

Diener, C. I., & Dweck, C. S. (1980). An analysis of learned helplessness. II: The processing of success. *Journal of Personality and Social Psychology, 39,* 940–952.

Dixon, R. A., & Baltes, P. B. (1986). Toward life-span research on the functions and pragmatics of intelligence. In R. J. Sternberg & R. K. Wagner (Eds.), *Practical Intelligence: Nature and origins of competence in the everyday world* (pp. 203–235). New York: Cambridge University Press.

Duda, J. (1987). Toward a developmental theory of children's motivation in sport. *Journal of Sport Psychology, 9,* 130–145.

Duda, J. (in press). Goal perspectives and behavior in sport and exercise settings. In C. Ames & M. Maehr (Eds.), *Advances in motivation and achievement* (Vol. 6). Greenwich, CT: JAI Press.

Duncan, G. J., & Morgan, J. N. (1980). The incidence and some consequences of major life events. In G. J. Duncan & J. N. Morgan (Eds.), *Five thousand American families: Patterns of economic progress* (Vol. 8). Ann Arbor: Institute for Social Research, University of Michigan.

Duval, S., & Wicklund, R. A. (1972). *A theory of objective self-awareness.* New York: Academic Press.

Dweck, C. S. (1975). The role of expectations and attributions in the alleviation of learned helplessness. *Journal of Personality and Social Psychology, 31,* 674–685.

Dweck, C. S. (1986). Motivational processes affecting learning. *American Psychologist, 41,* 1040–1048.

Dweck, C. S., & Bempechat, J. (1983). Children's theories of intelligence: Consequences for learning. In S. G. Paris, G. M. Olson, & H. W. Stevenson (Eds.), *Learning and motivation in the classroom* (pp. 239–256). Hillsdale, NJ: Erlbaum.

Dweck, C. S., & Elliott, E. S. (1983). Achievement motivation. In P. H. Mussen (Series Ed.) & E. M. Hetherington (Vol. Ed.), *Handbook of child psychology* (4th ed., Vol. 4, pp. 643–691). New York: Wiley.

Dweck, C. S., & Gilliard, D. (1975). Expectancy statements as determinants of reactions to failure: Sex differences in persistence and expectancy change. *Journal of Personality and Social Psychology, 32,* 1077–1084.

Dweck, C. S., & Goetz, T. E. (1978). Attributions and learned helplessness. In J. H. Harvey, W. Ickes, & R. F. Kidd (Eds.), *New directions in attribution research* (Vol. 2). Hillsdale, NJ: Erlbaum.

Dweck, C. S., Goetz, T. E., & Strauss, N. L. (1980). Sex differences in learned helplessness, IV: An experimental and naturalistic study of failure generalization and its mediators. *Journal of Personality and Social Psychology, 38,* 441–452.

Dweck, C. S., & Licht, G. G. (1980). Learned helplessness and intellectual achievement. In J. Garber & M. E. P. Seligman (Eds.), *Human helplessness: Theory and applications* (pp. 197–222). New York: Academic Press.

Dweck, C. S., & Reppucci, N. D. (1973). Learned helplessness and reinforcement responsibility in children. *Journal of Personality and Social Psychology, 25,* 109–116.

Easterbrooks, M. A., & Goldberg, W. A. (1984). Toddler development in the family: Impact of father involvement and parenting characteristics. *Child Development, 55,* 740–752.

Eccles, J. (1983). Expectancies, values, and academic behaviors. In J. T. Spence (Ed.), *Achievement and achievement motives: Psychological and sociological approaches* (pp. 75–146). San Francisco: Freeman.

Eccles, J., Midgley, C., & Adler, T. F. (1984). Grade-related changes in the school environment: Effects on achievement motivation. In J. G. Nicholls (Ed.), *Advances in motivation and achievement: Vol. 3. The development of achievement motivation* (pp. 283–331). Greenwich, CT: JAI Press.

Edwards, P. W.; Zeichner, A.; Lawler, N.; & Kowalski, R. (1987). A validation study of the Harvey Impostor Phenomenon Scale. *Psychotherapy, 24,* 256–259.

Egeland, B., & Sroufe, L. A. (1981). Developmental sequelae of maltreatment in infancy. In R. Rizley & D. Cicchetti (Eds.), *Developmental perspectives on child maltreatment* (pp. 77–92). San Francisco: Jossey-Bass.

Ekman, P., Levenson, R. W., & Friesen, W. V. (1983). Autonomic nervous system activity distinguishes among emotions. *Science, 221,* 1208–1210.

Elkind, D. (1967). Egocentricism in adolescence. *Child Development, 38,* 1025–1031.

Elkind, D. (1976). Cognitive development and psychopathology: Observations on egocentrism and ego defense. In E. Schopler & R. J. Reichler (Eds.), *Psychopathology and child development: Research and treatment* (pp. 167–183). New York: Plenum Press.

Elkind, D. (1979). Growing up faster. *Psychology Today, 12,* 38–45.

Elkind, D. (1981). *The hurried child: Growing up too fast too soon.* Reading, MA: Addison-Wesley.

Elkind, D. (1985). Egocentrism redux. *Developmental Review, 5,* 218–226.

Elkind, D. (1987). Superkids and super problems. *Psychology Today,* May 1987, 60–61.

Elkind, D., & Bowen, R. (1979). Imaginary audience behavior in children and adolescents. *Developmental Psychology, 15,* 38–44.

Elliott, E. S., & Dweck, C. S. (1988). Goals: An approach to motivation and achievement. *Journal of Personality and Social Psychology, 54,* 5–12.

Emde, R. (1983). The prerepresentational self. *Psychoanalytic Study of the Child, 38,* 165–192.

Emde, R. N. (1984). Levels of meaning for infant emotions: A biosocial view. In K. R. Scherer & P. Ekman (Eds.), *Approaches to emotion* (pp. 77–107). Hillsdale, NJ: Erlbaum.

Emde, R. N., & Brown, C. (1978). Adaptation to the birth of a Down's syndrome infant. *Journal of the American Academy of Child Psychiatry, 17,* 299–323.

Entwisle, D. R., & Baker, D. P. (1983). Gender and young children's expectations for performance in arithmetic. *Developmental Psychology, 19,* 200–209.

Erikson, E. H. (1950). *Childhood and society.* New York: Norton.

Erikson, E. H. (1959). Identity and the life cycle. *Psychological Issues, I,* 18–164.

Erikson, E. H. (1963). *Childhood and society* (2nd ed.). New York: Norton.

Erikson, E. H. (1964). *Insight and responsibility.* New York: Norton.

Erikson, E. H. (1968). *Identity: Youth and crisis.* New York: Norton.

Erlich, H. S., & Blatt, S. J. (1985). Narcissism and object love: The metapsychology of experience. *Psychoanalytic Study of the Child, 40,* 57–79.

Feather, N. T. (1966). Effects of prior success and failure on expectations of success and subsequent performance. *Journal of Personality and Social Psychology, 3,* 287–298.

Feather, W. (1969). Attribution of responsibility and valence of success and failure in relation to critical confidence and task performance. *Journal of Personality and Social Psychology, 13,* 129–144.

Feffer, M. (1970). Developmental analysis of interpersonal behavior. *Psychological Review, 77,* 197–214.

Feldman, N., & Ruble, D. N. (1977). Awareness of social comparison interest and motivation: A developmental study. *Journal of Educational Psychology, 69,* 579–585.

Feldman, N., & Ruble, D. N. (1981). Social comparison strategies: Dimensions offered and options taken. *Personality and Social Psychology Bulletin, 1,* 11–16.

Feltz, D. L., & Landers, D. M. (1983). Effects of mental practice on motor skill learning and performance: A meta-analysis. *Journal of Sport Psychology, 5,* 25–57.

Fennema, E. (1974). Mathematics learning and the sexes: A review. *Journal for Research in Mathematics Education, 5,* 126–139.

Fennema, E., & Sherman, J. (1977). Sex-related differences in mathematics achievement, spatial visualization and affective factors. *American Education Research Journal, 14,* 51–71.

Fennema, E., & Sherman, J. (1978). Sex-related differences in mathematics achievement and related factors: A further study. *Journal for Research in Mathematics Education, 9,* 189–203.

Festinger, L. (1954). A theory of social comparison processes. *Human Relations, 7,* 117–140.

Field, T. M.; Woodson, R.; Greenberg, R.; & Cohen, D. (1982). Discrimination and imitation of facial expressions by neonates. *Science, 218,* 179–181.

Finke, R. A. (1980). Levels of equivalence in imagery and perception. *Psychological Review, 87,* 113–132.

Finkelstein, L. (1974). The impostor: Aspects of his development. *Psychoanalytic Quarterly, 43,* 85–114.

Finkelstein, N. W., & Ramey, C. T. (1977). Learning to control the environment in infancy. *Child Development, 48,* 806–819.

Fischer, K. W. (1980). A theory of cognitive development: The control and construction of hierarchies of skills. *Psychological Review, 87,* 477–531.

Fowler, W. (1981). Case studies of cognitive precocity: The role of exogenous and endogenous stimulation in early mental development. *Journal of Applied Developmental Psychology, 2,* 319–367.

Frankel, A., & Snyder, M. L. (1978). Poor performance following unsolvable problems: Learned helplessness or egotism? *Journal of Personality and Social Psychology, 36,* 1415–1423.

Freeman, J. (1979). *Gifted children.* Baltimore, MD: University Park Press.

Freud, A. (1946). *The psycho-analytical treatment of children.* London: Imago. (Reprinted. New York: International Universities Press, 1959.)

Freud, S. (1915). The unconscious. In J. Strachey (Ed. and Trans.), *The standard edition of the complete psychological works of Sigmund Freud* (Vol. 14, pp. 166–204). London: Hogarth Press. (Hereafter *Standard edition*)

Freud, S. (1916). Mourning and melancholia. In J. Rivière (Trans.), *The collected papers of Sigmund Freud* (Vol. 4, pp. 152–172). London: Hogarth Press. (Hereafter *Collected papers*)

Freud, S. (1917). Mourning and melancholia. In *Standard edition* (Vol. 14, pp. 243–258).

Freud, S. (1923). The ego and the id. In *Standard edition* (Vol. 19, pp. 12–66).

Freud, S. (1924). The economic problem of masochism. In *Standard edition* (Vol. 19, pp. 159–170).

Freud, S. (1933). New introductory lectures in psycho-analysis. In *Standard edition* (Vol. 22, pp. 1–182).

Freud, S. (1949). Some character types met with in psychoanalytic work. In *Collected papers* (Vol. 4, pp. 318–344).

Freud, S. (1953). On narcissism: An introduction. In *Collected papers* (Vol. 4).

Frey, K. S.; Fewell, R. R.; Vadasy, P. F.; & Greenberg, M. T. (1988). Parental adjustment and changes in child outcome among families of young handicapped children. *Topics in Early Childhood Special Education, 8*(4), 38–57.

Frey, K. S., & Ruble, D. N. (1985). What children say when the teacher is not around: Conflicting goals in social comparison and performance assessment in the classroom. *Journal of Personality and Social Psychology, 48,* 550–562.

Frey, K. S., & Ruble, D. N. (1987). What children say about classroom performance: Sex and grade differences in perceived competence. *Child Development, 58,* 1066–1078.

Frey, K. S., & Ruble, D. N. (1989). *Satisfaction in novice and experienced runners over the adult years.* Manuscript in preparation.

Friedman, H. S., & Booth-Kewley, S. (1987). The "disease-prone personality": A meta-analytic view of the construct. *American Psychologist, 42*(6), 539–555.

Fry, P. S. (1984). Teachers' conceptions of students' intelligence and intelligent functioning: A cross-sectional study of elementary, secondary, and tertiary level teachers. In P. S. Fry (Ed.), *Changing conceptions of intelligence and intellectual functioning: Current theory and research* (pp. 157–174). New York: North-Holland.

Furth, H. G. (1981). *Piaget and knowledge: Theoretical foundations* (2nd ed.). Chicago: University of Chicago Press.

Garber, J., & Seligman, M. (1980). *Human helplessness.* New York: Academic Press.

Garcia-Coll, C., Kagan, J., & Reznick, J. S. (1984). Behavioral inhibition in young children. *Child Development, 55,* 1005–1019.

Garner, D. M., Olmstead, M. P., & Polivy, J. (1983). Development and validation of a multidimensional eating disorder inventory for anorexia nervosa and bulimia. *International Journal of Eating Disorders, 2,* 15–34.

Gediman, H. K. (1985). Imposture, inauthenticity, and feeling fraudulent. *Journal of the American Psychoanalytic Association, 33,* 911–935.

Gediman, H. K. (1986). The plight of the impostorous candidate: Learning amidst the pressures and pulls of power in the institute. *Psychoanalytic Inquiry, 6,* 67–91.

Gilligan, C. (1982). *In a different voice.* Cambridge, MA: Harvard University Press.

Glasgow, R. E., & Arkowitz, H. (1975). The behavioral assessment of male and female social competence in dyadic heterosexual interactions. *Behavior Therapy, 6,* 488–498.

Glass, D. C., and Singer, J. W. (1972). *Urban stress: Experiments on noise and social stressors.* New York: Academic Press.

Goethals, G. R. (1986). Fabricating and ignoring social reality: Self-serving estimates of consensus. In J. M. Olson, C. P. Herman, & M. P. Zanna (Eds.), *Relative deprivation and social comparison: The Ontario symposium* (Vol. 4, pp. 135–158). Hillsdale, NJ: Erlbaum.

Goethals, G. R., & Darley, J. M. (1977). Social comparison theory. In J. M. Sulls, & R. L. Miller (Eds.), *Social comparison processes: Theoretical and empirical perspectives* (pp. 259–278). Washington, DC: Hemisphere.

Gollwitzer, P. M., & Wicklund, R. A. (1985). The pursuit of self-defining goals. In J. Kuhl & J. Beckmann (Eds.), *Action control from cognition to behavior.* Heidelberg: Springer-Verlag.

Goodnow, J. J. (1980). Everyday concepts of intelligence and its development. In N. Warren (Ed.), *Studies in cross-cultural psychology* (Vol. 1, pp. 191–219). New York: Academic Press.

Goslin, D. A. (Ed.). (1969). *Handbook of socialization theory and research.* Chicago: Rand McNally.

Gottdiener, A. (1982). The impostor: An interpersonal point of view. *Contemporary Psychoanalysis, 18,* 438–454.

Greenacre, P. (1958a). The impostor. *Psychoanalytic Quarterly, 27,* 359–382.

Greenacre, P. (1958b). The relation of the impostor to the artist. *Psychoanalytic Study of the Child, 13,* 521–540.

Greenberg, J., & Pyszczynski, T. (1985). Compensatory self-inflation: A response to the threat to self-regard of public failure. *Journal of Personality and Social Psychology, 49,* 273–280.

Greene, D., & Lepper, M. (1974). Effects of extrinsic rewards on children's subsequent interest. *Child Development, 45,* 1141–1145.

Greenspan, S. (1981). *Psychopathology and adaptations in infancy and earliest childhood.* New York: International Universities Press.

Greenwald, A. G. (1980). The totalitarian ego: Fabrication and revision of personal history. *American Psychologist, 35,* 603–618.

Greenwald, A. G., & Pratkanis, A. R. (1984). The self. In R. S. Wyer & T. K. Skull (Eds.), *Handbook of social cognition.* Hillsdale, NJ: Erlbaum.

Gregory, W. L., Cialdini, R. B., & Carpenter, K. M. (1982). Self-relevant scenarios as mediators of likelihood estimates and compliance: Does imagining make it so? *Journal of Personality and Social Psychology, 43,* 89–99.

Grünbaum, A. (1984). *The foundations of psychoanalysis: A philosophical critique.* Berkeley, CA: University of California Press.

Guidano, V. F. (1987). *Complexity of the self.* New York: Guilford.

Gunnar, M. R. (1980). Contingent stimulation: A review of its role in early development. In S. Levine & H. Ursin (Eds.), *Coping and health* (pp. 101–119). New York: Plenum Press.

Guntrip, H. (1971). *Psychoanalytic theory, therapy, and the self.* New York: Basic Books.

Gurin, P., & Brim, O. G., Jr. (1984). Change of self in adulthood: The example of sense of control. In P. B. Baltes & O. G. Brim, Jr. (Eds.), *Life span development and behavior* (Vol. 6, pp. 281–334). New York: Academic Press.

Halford, G. S., & Boyle, F. M. (1985). Do young children understand conservation of number? *Child Development, 56,* 165–176.

Halpern, H. (1964). Psychodynamic and cultural determinants of work inhibition in children and adolescents. *Psychological Review, 51,* 173–189.

Haltiwanger, J. (1989). *Behavioral referents of presented self-esteem in children.* Paper presented at the meeting of the Society for Research in Child Development, Kansas City, MO.

Haltiwanger, J., & Harter, S. (1988). *A behavioral measure of young children's presented self-esteem.* Unpublished manuscript, University of Denver.

Hamm, S. (1986). *Correlates of self-worth among adults in the world of work and family.* Unpublished doctoral dissertation, University of Denver.

Hammen, C.; Adrian, C.; Gordon, D.; Burge, D.; Jaenicke, C.; & Hiroto, D. (1987). Children of depressed mothers: Maternal strain and symptom predictors of dysfunction. *Journal of Abnormal Psychology, 96,* 190–198.

Hammen, C.; Marks, T.; deMayo, R.; & Mayol, A. (1985). Self-schemas and risk for depression: A prospective study. *Journal of Personality and Social Psychology, 49,* 1147–1159.

Hammen, C.; Marks, T.; Mayol, A.; & deMayo, R. (1985). Depressive self-schemas, life stress, and vulnerability to depression. *Journal of Abnormal Psychology, 94,* 308–319.

Harackiewicz, J. M., Manderlink, G., & Sansone, C. (1984). Rewarding pinball wizardry: Effects of evaluation and cue value on intrinsic interest. *Journal of Personality and Social Psychology, 47,* 287–300.

Harlow, H., & Harlow, M. (1966). Learning to love. *American Science, 54,* 244–272.

Harter, S. (1978). Effectance motivation reconsidered: Toward a developmental model. *Human Development, 21,* 34–64.

Harter, S. (1981a). A model of mastery motivation in children: Individual differences and developmental change. In W. A. Collins (Ed.), *The Minnesota symposia on child psychology* (Vol. 14, pp. 215–255). Hillsdale, NJ: Erlbaum.

Harter, S. (1981b). A new self-report scale of intrinsic versus extrinsic orientation in the classroom: Motivational and informational components. *Developmental Psychology, 17,* 300–312.

Harter, S. (1982). The perceived competence scale for children. *Child Development, 53,* 87–97.

Harter, S. (1983). Developmental perspectives on the self-system. In E. M. Hetherington (Ed.) & P. H. Mussen (Series Ed.), *Handbook of child psychology: Vol. 4. Socialization, personality and social development* (pp. 275–386). New York: Wiley.

Harter, S. (1985a). Competence as a dimension of self-evaluation: Toward a comprehensive model of self-worth. In R. Leahy (Ed.), *The development of the self* (pp. 55–118). New York: Academic Press.

Harter, S. (1985b). *The self-perception profile for children: Revision of the perceived competence scale for children.* Manual. University of Denver.

Harter, S. (1985c). *The social support scale for children.* Manual. University of Denver.

Harter, S. (1986a). Cognitive-developmental processes in the integration of concepts about emotions and the self. *Social Cognition, 4,* 119–151.

Harter, S. (1986b). Processes underlying the construct, maintenance and enhancement of the self-concept in children. In J. Suls & A. Greenwald (Eds.), *Psychological perspectives on the self* (Vol. 3). Hillsdale, NJ: Erlbaum.

Harter, S. (1987). The determinants and mediational role of global self-worth in children. In N. Eisenberg (Ed.), *Contemporary issues in developmental psychology.* New York: Wiley.

Harter, S. (1988). Developmental processes in the construction of the self. In T. D. Yawkey & J. E. Johnson (Eds.), *Integrative processes and socialization: Early to middle childhood.* Hillsdale, NJ: Erlbaum.

Harter, S., & Connell, J. P. (1984). A comparison of alternative models of the relationships between academic achievement and children's perceptions of competence, control, and motivational orientation. In J. Nicholls (Ed.), *The development of achievement-related cognitions and behaviors* (pp. 219–250). Greenwich, CT: JAI Press.

Harter, S., & Marold, D. (1986). *Risk factors in child and adolescent suicide.* Unpublished manuscript. University of Denver.

Harter, S., & Nowakowski, M. (1987a). *Dimensions of depression profile for children and adolescents.* Manual. University of Denver.

Harter, S., & Nowakowski, M. (1987b). *The relationship between self-worth and affect in children: Implications for childhood depression.* Paper presented at the meeting of the Society for Research in Child Development, Baltimore, MD.

Harter, S., & Pike, R. (1984). The pictorial perceived competence scale for young children. *Child Development, 55,* 1969–1982.

Harvey, J. C. (1981). *The impostor phenomenon: A failure to internalize success.* Unpublished doctoral dissertation, Temple University.

Harvey, J. C., Ickes, W., & Kidd, R. (1976). *New directions in attribution research* (Vol. 1). Hillsdale, NJ: Erlbaum.

Harvey, J. C., & Katz, C. (1985). *If I'm so successful, why do I feel like a fake? The impostor phenomenon.* New York: St. Martin's.

Hastie, R. (1981). Schematic principles on human memory. In T. E. Higgins, C. Herman, & M. P. Zanna (Eds.), *Social cognition: The Ontario symposium on personality and social psychology* (Vol. 1). Hillsdale, NJ: Erlbaum.

Heath, S. B. (1983). *Ways with words.* New York: Cambridge University Press.

Heckhausen, H. (1977). Achievement motivation and its constructs: A cognitive model. *Motivation and Emotion, 1,* 283–329.

Heckhausen, H. (1984). Emergent achievement behavior: Some early developments. In J. G. Nicholls (Ed.), *Advances in motivation and achievement: Vol. 3. The development of achievement motivation* (pp. 1–32). Greenwich, CT: JAI Press.

Heider, F. (1958). *The psychology of interpersonal relations.* New York: Wiley.

Heron, W. (1961). Cognitive and physiological effects of perceptual isolation. In P. Solomon, P. E. Kubzansky, P. D. Leiderman, J. H. Mendelson, R. Trumbull, & D. Wexler (Eds.), *Sensory deprivation* (pp. 6–33). Cambridge, MA: Harvard University Press.

Hewitt, P. L., & Dyck, D. G. (1986). Perfectionism, stress, and vulnerability to depression. *Cognitive Therapy and Research, 10,* 137–142.

Hewstone, M., & Ward, C. (1985). Ethnocentricism and causal attribution in southern Asia. *Journal of Personality and Social Psychology, 48,* 614–623.

Higgins, E. T. (1981). Role-taking and social judgment: Alternative developmental perspectives and processes. In J. H. Flavell & L. Ross (Eds.), *Social cognitive development: Frontiers and possible futures.* Cambridge: Cambridge University Press.

Higgins, E. T. (1987). Self-discrepancy: A theory relating self and affect. *Psychological Review, 94,* 319–340.

Higgins, E. T. (in press, a). Continuities and discontinuities in self-regulatory and self-evaluative processes: A developmental theory relating self and affect. *Journal of Personality.*

Higgins, E. T. (in press, b). Self-discrepancy theory: What patterns of self-beliefs cause people to suffer? In L. Berkowitz (Ed.), *Advances in experimental social psychology* (Vol. 22). New York: Academic Press.

Higgins, E. T.; Bond, R. N.; Klein, R.; & Strauman, T. (1986). Self-discrepancies and emotional vulnerability: How magnitude, accessibility, and type of discrepancy influence affect. *Journal of Personality and Social Psychology, 51,* 5–15.

Higgins, E. T., & King, G. (1981). Accessibility of social constructs: Information processing consequences of individual and contextual variability. In N. Cantor & J. Kihlstrom (Eds.), *Personality, cognition, and social interaction.* Hillsdale, NJ: Erlbaum.

Higgins, E. T., Klein, R., & Strauman, T. (1985). Self-concept discrepancy theory: A psychological model for distinguishing among different aspects of depression and anxiety. *Social Cognition, 3,* 51–76.

Higgins, E. T., Klein, R., & Strauman, T. (1987). Self-discrepancies: Distinguishing among self-states, self-state conflicts, and emotional vulnerabilities. In K. M. Yardley & T. M. Honess (Eds.), *Self and identity: Psychosocial perspectives* (pp. 173–186). New York: Wiley.

Higgins, E. T., & Moretti, M. M. (1988). Standard utilization and the social-evaluative process: Vulnerability to types of aberrant beliefs. In T. Oltmann (Ed.), *Delusional beliefs: Theoretical and empirical perspectives.* New York: Wiley.

Higgins, E. T., & Parsons, J. E. (1983). Social cognition and the social life of the child: Stages as subcultures. In E. T. Higgins, D. N. Ruble, & W. W. Hartup (Eds.), *Social cognition and social development: A sociocultural perspective* (pp. 15–62). New York: Cambridge University Press.

Higgins, E. T., Strauman, T., & Klein, R. (1986). Standards and the process of self-evaluation: Multiple affects from multiple stages. In R. M. Sorrention & E. T. Higgins (Eds.), *Handbook of motivation and cognition: Foundations of social behavior* (pp. 23–63). New York: Guilford Press.

Higgins, R. L., & Harris, R. N. (in press). Strategic "alcohol" use: Drinking to self-handicap. *Journal of Social and Clinical Psychology.*

Hochschild, A. R. (1973). *The unexpected community.* Englewood Cliffs, NJ: Prentice-Hall.

Hofer, M. A. (1984). Relationships as regulators: A psychobiologic perspective on bereavement. *Psychosomatic Medicine, 46*(3), 183–197.

Hofer, M. A. (1987). Early social relationships: A psychobiologist's view. *Child Development, 48*(3), 633–647.

Hoffman, M. L. (1971). Identification and conscience development. *Child Development, 42,* 1071–1082.

Hogarth, R. (1981). Beyond discrete biases: Functional and dysfunctional aspects of judgmental heuristics. *Psychological Bulletin, 90,* 197–217.

Holahan, C. K., & Holahan, C. J. (1987a). Self-efficacy, social support, and depression in aging: A longitudinal analysis. *Journal of Gerontology, 42,* 65–68.

Holahan, C. K., & Holahan, C. J. (1987b). Life stress, hassles, and self-efficacy in aging: A replication and extension. *Journal of Applied Social Psychology, 17,* 574–592.

Hollender, M. H. (1978). Perfectionism: A neglected personality trait. *Journal of Clinical Psychiatry, 29,* 210.

Hollingworth, L. S. (1931). The child of very superior intelligence as a special problem in social development. *Mental Hygiene, 15,* 3–16.

Hollingworth, L. S. (1936). Development of personality in highly intelligent children. *Yearbook of the National Elementary School Principals, 15,* 272–281.

Hollingworth, L. S. (1942). *Children above IQ 180, Stanford-Binet: Origin and development.* Yonkers, NY: World Book.

Homann, E., & Blatt, S. J. (1988). *The relationship of security of attachment to depression.* Unpublished manuscript, Yale University.

Horn, J. L. (1968). Organization of abilities and the development of intelligence. *Psychological Review, 75,* 242–259.

Horney, K. (1950). *Neurosis and human development.* New York: Norton.

Horowitz, M. J. (1979). *States of mind.* New York: Meredith.

Hultsch, D. F., & Plemons, J. K. (1979). Life events and life span development. In P. B. Baltes & O. G. Brim, Jr. (Eds.), *Life span development and behavior* (Vol. 2). New York: Academic Press.

Hunt, J. McV. (1961). *Intelligence and Experience.* New York: Ronald Press.

Hunt, J. McV. (1965). Intrinsic motivation and its role in psychological development. In D. Levine (Ed.), *Nebraska symposium on motivation* (Vol. 13). Lincoln: University of Nebraska Press.

Ickes, W.; Patterson, M. C.; Rajecki, D. W.; & Tanford, S. (1982). Behavioral and cognitive consequences of reciprocal versus compensatory responses to preinteraction expectancies. *Social Cognition, 1,* 160–190.

Imes, S. (1979). *The impostor phenomenon as a function of attribution patterns and internalized femininity/masculinity in high-achieving women and men.* Unpublished doctoral dissertation, Georgia State University.

Inhelder, B., & Piaget, J. (1958). *The growth of logical thinking from childhood to adolescence.* New York: Basic Books.

Jacobs, B., Prentice-Dunn, S., & Rogers, R. W. (1984). Understanding persistence: An interface of control theory and self-efficacy theory. *Basic and Applied Social Psychology, 5,* 333–343.

Jacobson, E. (1959). The "exceptions": An elaboration of Freud's character study. *Psychoanalytic Study of the Child, 14,* 135–154.

Jaenicke, C.; Hammen, C.; Zupan, B.; Hiroto, D.; Gordon, D.; Adrian, C.; & Burge, D. (1987). Cognitive vulnerability in children at risk for depression. *Journal of Abnormal Child Psychology, 15,* 559–572.

James, W. (1892). *Psychology: The briefer courses.* New York: Henry Holt & Co.

James, W. (1948). *Psychology.* New York: World Publishing Co. (Original work published 1890)

Janoff-Bulman, R. (1979). Characterological versus behavioral self-blame: Inquiries into depression and rape. *Journal of Personality and Social Psychology, 37,* 1798–1809.

Janos, P. M. (1983). *The psychosocial adjustment of children of very superior intellectual ability.* Unpublished doctoral dissertation, Ohio State University.

Janos, P. M. (1986). Terman's correspondence with parents of high IQ children. *Journal of Counseling and Development, 65*(4), 193–195.

Janos, P. M. (1987). 50-year follow-up of Terman's youngest college students and IQ-matched agemates. *Gifted Child Quarterly, 31,* 55–58.

Janos, P. M.; Carter, C.; Chapel, A.; Curland, M.; Cufley, R.; Daily, M.; Guilland, M.; Kehl, H.; Lu, S.; Sherry, D.; Stoloff, J.; & Wise, A. (in press). Cross-sectional study of early college entrants' self-disclosure and intimacy with same-age and older friends. *Gifted Child Quarterly.*

Janos, P. M., Fung, H., & Robinson, N. M. (1985). Self-concept, self-esteem, and peer relations among gifted children who feel "different." *Gifted Child Quarterly, 29*(2), 78–82.

Janos, P. M., & Robinson, N. M. (1985). Social and personality development. In F. D. Horowitz & M. O'Brien (Eds.), *The gifted and talented: A developmental perspective.* Washington, DC: American Psychological Foundation.

Janos, P., Sanfilippo, S., & Robinson, N. (1986). Patterns of "underachievement" in markedly accelerated university students. *Journal of Youth and Adolescence, 15*(4), 303–313.

Janos, P. M.; Shluter, D.; Lee, T.; Stoller, J.; Case, K.; Carragher, R.; Crummett, T.; King, K.; & Leu, M. (in press). The "productive shift" in science research: The publication patterns of early vs. average-age Ph.D.s in chemistry or physics. *Journal of Higher Education.*

Johnson, C. N., & Wellman, H. M. (1980). Children's developing understanding of mental verbs: Remember, know, and guess. *Child Development, 51,* 1095–1102.

Jones, A. (1987). The cornerstone: A profile of Ernestine Bayer. *American Rowing, 18,* 30–33.

Jones, E. E., & Berglas, S. (1978). Control of attributions about the self through self-handicapping strategies: The appeal of alcohol and the role of underachievement. *Personality and Social Psychology Bulletin, 4,* 200–206.

Jones, E. E.; Farina, A.; Hastorf, A.; Markus, H.; Miller, D.; & Scott, R. (1984). *Social stigma: The psychology of marked relationships.* San Francisco: Freeman.

Jung, C. (1923). *Psychological types.* New York: Harcourt, Brace.

Jussim, L. (1986). Self-fulfilling prophecies: A theoretical and integrative review. *Psychological Review, 93,* 429–445.

Kagan, J. (1984). The idea of emotion in human development. In C. E. Izard, J. Kagan, & R. B. Zajonc (Eds.), *Emotions, cognition, and behavior* (pp. 38–72). New York: Cambridge University Press.

Kagan, J.; Reznick, S.; Clarke, C.; Snidman, N.; & Garcia-Coll, C. (1984). Behavioral inhibition to the unfamiliar. *Child Development, 55,* 2212–2225.

Kahneman, D., & Tversky, A. (1982). The simulation heuristic. In D. Kaheman & A. Tversky (Eds.), *Judgment under uncertainty: Heuristics and biases.* Cambridge: Cambridge University Press.

Kanfer, F. H. (1977). The many faces of self-control, or behavior modification changes its focus. In R. B. Stuart (Ed.), *Behavioral self-management* (pp. 1–48). New York: Brunner/Mazel.

Kanfer, F. H. (1980). Self-management methods. In F. H. Kanfer & A. P. Goldstein (Eds.), *Helping people change: A textbook of methods* (2nd ed.). New York: Pergamon Press.

Kanfer, R., & Zeiss, A. M. (1983). Depression, interpersonal standard-setting, and judgments of self-efficacy. *Journal of Abnormal Psychology, 92,* 319–329.

Kaplan, L. J. (1984). *Adolescence: The farewell to childhood.* New York: Simon & Schuster.

Karsten, A. (1928). Mental satiation. In J. de Vana (Ed.), *Field theory as human science.* New York: Gardner Press, 1976.

Kassin, S. M., & Lepper, M. R. (1984). Oversufficient and insufficient justification effects: Cognitive and behavioral development. In J. G. Nicholls (Ed.), *Advances in motivation and achievement: Vol. 3. The development of achievement motivation* (pp. 73–106). Greenwich, CT: JAI Press.

Katz, P., & Taylor, D. (Eds.). (1988). *Eliminating racism: Profiles in controversy.* New York: Plenum Press.

Kavanagh, D. J., & Bower, G. H. (1985). Mood and self-efficacy: Impact of joy and sadness on perceived capabilities. *Cognitive Therapy and Research, 9,* 507–525.

Kazdin, A. E. (1978). Covert modeling: Therapeutic application of imagined rehearsal. In J. L. Singer & K. S. Pope (Eds.), *The power of human imagination: New methods in psychotherapy. Emotions, personality, and psychotherapy* (pp. 255–278). New York: Plenum Press.

Kegan, R. (1982). *The evolving self.* Cambridge, MA: Harvard University Press.

Kegan, R. (1983). A neo-Piagetian approach to object relations. In B. Lee & G. G. Noam (Eds.), *Developmental approaches to the self.* New York: Plenum Press.

Kelley, K.; Byrne, D.; Przybyla, D. P. J.; Eberly, C.; Eberly, B.; Greendlinger, V.; Wan, C. K.; & Gorsky, J. (1985). Chronic self-destructiveness: Conceptualization, measurement, and initial validation of the construct. *Motivation and Emotion, 9,* 135–151.

Kent, G. (1987). Self-efficacious control over reported physiological, cognitive and behavioral symptoms of dental anxiety. *Behaviour Research and Therapy, 25,* 341–347.

Kent, G., & Gibbons, R. (1987). Self-efficacy and the control of anxious cognitions. *Journal of Behavior Therapy and Experimental Psychiatry, 18,* 33–40.

Khan, M. (1972). The finding and becoming of self. In *The privacy of self* (pp. 294–305). New York: International Universities Press.

Kihlstrom, J. F. (1987). The cognitive unconscious. *Science, 237,* 1445–1452.

Kihlstrom, J. F., & Cantor, N. (1984). Mental representations of the self. In

L. Berkowitz (Ed.), *Advances in experimental social psychology* (Vol. 17). New York: Academic Press.

Klein, M. (1932). *The psycho-analysis of children.* London: Hogarth Press.

Klein, M. (1934). A contribution to the psychogenesis of manic-depressive states. In M. Klein (Ed.), *Contributions to psychoanalysis, 1921–1945* (pp. 282–310). London: Hogarth Press, 1948.

Klinger, E. (1975). Consequences of commitment to and disengagement from incentives. *Psychological Review, 82,* 1–25.

Kobasa, S. C. (1979). Stressful life events, personality, and health: An inquiry into hardiness. *Journal of Personality and Social Psychology, 37,* 1–11.

Kohlberg, L. (1969). Stage and sequence: The cognitive developmental approach to socialization. In D. Goslin (Ed.), *Handbook of socialization: Theory and research.* New York: Rand McNally.

Kohlberg, L. (1971). From is to ought: How to commit the naturalistic fallacy and get away with it in the study of moral development. In T. Mischel (Ed.), *Cognitive development and epistemology.* New York: Academic Press.

Kohut, H. (1971). *The analysis of the self.* New York: International Universities Press.

Kohut, H. (1977). *The restoration of the self.* New York: International Universities Press.

Kohut, H. (1984). *How does analysis cure?* Chicago: University of Chicago Press.

Kohut, H., & Wolf, E. S. (1978). The disorders of the self and their treatment: An outline. *International Journal of Psychoanalysis, 59,* 413–425.

Kolligian, J., Jr., & Sternberg, R. J. (1989). *Perceived fraudulence in young adults: Is there an impostor syndrome?* Manuscript submitted for publication.

Kramer, Y. (1977). Work compulsion: A psychoanalytic study. *Psychoanalysis Quarterly, 46,* 361–385.

Krueger, D. W. (1984). *Success and the fear of success in women.* New York: Free Press.

Krueger, D. W. (1989). *Body self and psychological self: Developmental and clinical aspects of disorders of the self.* New York: Brunner/Mazel.

Kuhl, J. (1985). From cognition to behavior: Perspectives for future research on action control. In J. Kuhl & J. Beckmann (Eds.), *Action control from cognition to behavior.* New York: Springer-Verlag.

Kuhl, J., & Beckmann, J. (Eds.). (1985). *Action control from cognition to behavior.* New York: Springer-Verlag.

Kun, A. (1977). Development of the magnitude-covariation and compensation schemata in ability and effort attributions of performance. *Child Development, 48,* 862–873.

Kuypers, J. A., & Bengston, V. L. (1973). Social breakdown and competence. *Human Development, 16,* 181–201.

Ladd, G. W., & Price, J. M. (1986). Promoting children's cognitive and social competences: The relation between parents' perceptions of task difficulty and children's perceived and actual competence. *Child Development, 57,* 446–460.

Langer, E. J. (1975). The illusion of control. *Journal of Personality and Social Psychology, 32,* 311–328.

Langer, E. J. (1979). The illusion of incompetence. In L. C. Perlmutter & R. A. Monty (Eds.), *Choice and perceived control* (pp. 301–313). Hillsdale, NJ: Erlbaum.

Langer, E. J. (1982). Old age: An artifact? In S. Kiesler & J. McGaugh (Eds.), *Aging: Biology and behavior.* New York: Academic Press.

Langer, E. J. (1983). *The psychology of control.* Beverly Hills, CA: Sage.

Langer, E. J. (1989a). *Mindfulness.* Reading, MA: Addison-Wesley.

Langer, E. J. (1989b). Minding matters. In L. Berkowitz (Ed.), *Advances in experimental social psychology, 22,* 137–173. San Diego, CA: Academic Press.

Langer, E. J., & Avorn, J. (1981). The psychosocial environment of the elderly: Some behavioral and health implications. In J. Seagle & R. Chellis (Eds.), *Congregate housing for older people.* Lexington, MA: Lexington Books.

Langer, E. J., & Benevento, A. (1978). Self-induced dependence. *Journal of Personality and Social Psychology, 36,* 886–893.

Langer, E. J., & Chanowitz, B. (1987). A new perspective for the study of disability. In H. E. Yuker (Ed.), *Attitudes towards persons with disabilities.* New York: Springer Press.

Langer, E. J.; Chanowitz, B.; Palmerino, M.; Jacobs, S.; Rhodes, M.; & Thayer, P. (1989). Nonsequential development and aging. In C. Alexander & E. J. Langer (Eds.), *Higher stages of human development: Perspective on adult growth.* New York: Oxford University Press.

Langer, E. J.; Dillon, M.; Kurtz, R.; & Katz, M. (1987). Believing is seeing: Using mindlessness to improve vision. Prepublication manuscript, Harvard University.

Langer, E. J.; Hatem, M.; Joss, J.; & Howell, M. (1987). The mindful consequences of teaching uncertainty for elementary school and college students. Prepublication manuscript, Harvard University.

Langer, E. J., & Imber, L. (1979). When practice makes imperfect: The debilitating effects of overlearning. *Journal of Personality and Social Psychology, 39,* 360–367.

Langer, E. J., & Piper, A. (1987). The prevention of mindlessness. *Journal of Personality and Social Psychology, 53,* 280–287.

Langer, E. J.; Rodin, J.; Beck, P.; Spitzer, L.; & Weinman, C. (1979). Environmental determinants of memory improvement in late adulthood. *Journal of Personality and Social Psychology, 37,* 2014–2025.

Langer, E. J., & Thompson, L. (1987). Mindlessness and self-esteem: The observer's perspective. Prepublication manuscript, Harvard University.

Langer, E. J., & Weinman, C. (1981). When thinking disrupts intellectual performance: Mindlessness on an overlearned task. *Personality and Social Psychology Bulletin,* 7, 240–243.

Langlois, J. H. (1981). Beauty and the beast: The role of physical attractiveness in the development of peer relations and social behavior. In S. S. Brehm, S. M. Kassin, & F. X. Gibbons (Eds.), *Developmental social psychology: Theory and research.* New York: Oxford University Press.

Lapsley, D. (1985). Elkind on egocentrism. *Developmental Review, 5,* 218–227.

Lapsley, D., & Murphy, M. (1985). Another look at the theoretical assumptions of adolescent egocentrism. *Developmental Review, 5,* 201–217.

Lapsley, D., & Rice, K. (1988). The "new look" at the imaginary audience and personal fable: Toward a general model of adolescent ego development. In D. Lapsley & C. Power (Eds.), *Self, ego, and identity: Integrative approaches.* New York: Springer-Verlag.

Larsen, G. Y. (1977). Methodology in developmental psychology: An examination of research on Piagetian theory. *Child Development, 48,* 1160–1166.

Lasch, C. (1979). *The culture of narcissism.* New York: Norton.

Latham, G. P., & Lee, T. W. (1986). Goal setting. In E. A. Locke (Ed.), *Generalizing from laboratory to field settings* (pp. 101–117). Lexington, MA: Heath.

Lazarus, R. S. (1983). The costs and benefits of denial. In S. Greznity (Ed.), *Denial of stress.* New York: International Universities Press.

Lazarus, R. S.; DeLongis, A.; Folkman, S.; & Gruen, R. (1985). Stress and adaptational outcomes: The problem of confounded measures. *American Psychologist, 40,* 770–786.

Lazarus, R. S., & Folkman, S. (1984). *Stress, appraisal, and coping.* New York: Springer Press.

Leahy, R. L. (Ed.). (1985). *The development of the self.* New York: Academic Press.

Leahy, R. L., & Hunt, T. M. (1983). A cognitive-developmental approach to the development of conceptions of intelligence. In R. L. Leahy (Ed.), *The child's construction of social inequality* (pp. 135–160). New York: Academic Press.

Leggett, E. L. (1985). *Children's entity and incremental theories of intelligence: Relationships to achievement behavior.* Paper presented at the annual meeting of the Eastern Psychological Association, Boston.

Lenny, E. (1977). Women's self-confidence in achievement settings. *Psychological Bulletin, 84,* 1–13.

Lent, R. W., & Hackett, G. (1987). Career self-efficacy: Empirical status and future directions. *Journal of Vocational Behavior, 30,* 347–382.

Lepper, M. R., & Green, D. (1978). Turning play into work: Effects of adult surveillance and extrinsic reward on children's intrinsic motivation. In M. R. Lepper & D. Greene (Eds.), *The hidden costs of reward* (pp. 109–148). Hillsdale, NJ: Erlbaum.

Levine, J., & Redlich, F. C. (1960). Intellectual and emotional factors in the apprehension of humor. *Journal of General Psychology, 62,* 25–35.

Levy, D. M. (1943). *Maternal overprotection.* New York: Columbia University Press.

Lewin, K. (1935). *A dynamic theory of personality.* New York: McGraw-Hill.

Lewin, K. (Ed.). (1948). *Resolving social conflicts.* New York: Harper & Row.

Lewin, K.; Dembo, T.; Festinger, L.; & Sears, P. (1944). Level of aspiration. In J. Hunt (Ed.), *Personality and the behavior disorders.* New York: Ronald Press.

Lewin, K., Lippitt, R., & White, R. (1939). Patterns of aggressive behavior in experimentally created social disasters. *Journal of Social Psychology, 10,* 271–299.

Lewinsohn, P. M.; Mischel, W.; Chaplain, W.; & Barton, R. (1980). Social competence and depression: The role of illusory self-perceptions. *Journal of Abnormal Psychology, 89,* 203–212.

Lewis, C. N. (1971). Reminiscing and self-concept in old age. *Journal of Gerontology, 26,* 240–243.

Lewis, H. B. (1979). Shame in depression and hysteria. In C. E. Izard (Ed.), *Emotions in personality and psychopathology* (pp. 371–396). New York: Plenum Press.

Lewis, M., & Brooks-Gunn, J. (1979). *Social cognition and the acquisition of the self.* New York: Plenum Press.

Licht, B. G., & Dweck, C. S. (1984). Determinants of academic achievement: The interaction of children's achievement orientations with skill area. *Developmental Psychology, 20,* 628–636.

Lichtenberg, J. (1985). *Psychoanalysis and infant research.* Hillsdale, NJ: Analytic Press.

Liebert, R. M., & Sprafkin, J. (1988). *The early window: Effects of television on children and youth* (3rd ed.). Elmsford, NY: Pergamon Press.

Linville, P. W. (1982). Affective consequences of complexity regarding the self and others. In M. S. Clark & S. T. Fiske (Eds.), *Affect and cognition.* Hillsdale, NJ: Erlbaum.

Linville, P. W. (1985). Self-complexity and affective extremity: Don't put all of your eggs in one cognitive basket. *Social Cognition, 3,* 94–120.

Locke, E. A.; Frederick, E.; Lee, C.; & Bobko, P. (1984). Effect of self-efficacy, goals, and task strategies on task performance. *Journal of Applied Psychology, 69,* 241–251.

Locke, E. A.; Shaw, K. N.; Saari, L. M.; & Latham, G. P. (1981). Goal setting and task performance: 1969–1980. *Psychological Bulletin, 90,* 125–152.

Locke, H. J., & Wallace, K. M. (1959). Short marital adjustment and predictive tests: Their reliability and validity. *Marriage and Family Living, 21,* 251–255.

Loevinger, J. (1976). *Ego development.* San Francisco: Jossey-Bass.

Loevinger, J. (1978). *Scientific ways to the study of ego development.* Heinz Werner Lecture Series, XII. Worcester, MA: Clark University Press.

Loewald, H. W. (1960). On the therapeutic action of psychoanalysis. *International Journal of Psycho-Analysis, 41,* 16–33.

Loewald, H. W. (1970). Psychoanalytic theory and the psychoanalytic process. *Psychoanalytic Study of the Child, 25,* 45–68.

Lowenthal, M. F., Thurnher, M., & Chiroboga, D. (1975). *Four stages of life.* San Francisco: Jossey-Bass.

Luria, A. R. (1976). *Cognitive development: Its cultural and social foundations.* Cambridge, MA: Harvard University Press.

Lynch, J. J. (1977). *The broken heart: The medical consequences of loneliness.* New York: Basic Books.

Maccoby, E. E., & Martin, J. A. (1983). Socialization in the context of the family: Parent-child interaction. In P. H. Mussen (Series Ed.) & E. M. Hetherington (Vol. Ed.), *Handbook of child psychology* (Vol. 4, 4th ed., pp. 643–691). New York: Wiley.

MacCorquodale, K., & Meehl, P. E. (1953). Preliminary suggestions as to a formalization of expectancy theory. *Psychological Review, 60,* 55–63.

MacKay, D. G. (1981). The problem of rehearsal or mental practice. *Journal of Motor Behavior, 13,* 274–285.

Maehr, M. L., & Braskamp, L. A. (1986). *The motivation factor: A theory of personal investment.* Lexington, MA: Lexington Books.

Main, M., & Weston, D. R. (1981). The quality of the toddler's relationship to mother and to father: Related to conflict behavior and the readiness to establish new relationships. *Child Development, 52,* 932–940.

Markus, H. (1977). Self-schemata and processing information about the self. *Journal of Personality and Social Psychology, 35,* 63–78.

Markus, H. (1980). The self in thought and memory. In D. M. Wegner & R. R. Vallacher (Eds.), *The self in social psychology.* London and New York: Oxford University Press.

Markus, H. (1983). Self-knowledge: An expanded view. *Journal of Personality, 51,* 543–565.

Markus, H., & Kunda, Z. (1986). Stability and malleability of the self-concept. *Journal of Personality and Social Psychology, 52,* 858–866.

Markus, H., & Nurius, P. (1986). Possible selves. *American Psychologist, 41,* 954–969.

Markus, H., Porter, C., & Nurius, P. (1986). *Possible selves and coping with crisis.* Unpublished manuscript, University of Michigan.

Markus, H., & Sentis, K. (1982). The self in social information processing. In J. Suls (Ed.), *Social psychological perspectives on the self* (Vol. 1, pp. 41–70). Hillsdale, NJ: Erlbaum.

Markus, H., & Wurf, E. (1987). The dynamic self-concept: A social psychological perspective. *Annual Review of Psychology, 38,* 299–337.

Marmor, J. (1962). Psychoanalytic therapy as an educational process: Common denominators in the therapeutic approaches of different psychoanalytic schools. In J. H. Masseman (Ed.), *Science and psychoanalysis: Psychoanalytic education* (Vol. 5, pp. 286–299). New York: Grune & Stratton.

Marold, D. (1987). *Correlates of suicidal ideation among young adolescents.* Unpublished doctoral dissertation, University of Denver.

Marshall, V. W. (1980). *Last chapters: A sociology of aging and dying.* Monterey, CA: Brooks/Cole.

Marteau, T. M., & Johnston, M. (1986). Determinants of beliefs about illness: A study of parents of children with diabetes, asthma, epilepsy, and no chronic illness. *Journal of Psychosomatic Research, 30,* 673–683.

Matas, L., Arend, R. A., & Sroufe, L. A. (1978). Continuity of adaptation in the second year: The relationship between quality of attachment and later competence. *Child Development, 49,* 547–556.

McArthur, L. Z., & Baron, R. M. (1983). Toward an ecological theory of social perception. *Psychological Review, 90,* 215–238.

McClelland, D. (1961). *The achieving society.* Princeton, NJ: Van Nostrand.

McCranie, E. W., & Bass, J. D. (1984). Childhood family antecedents of dependency and self-criticism: Implications for depression. *Journal of Abnormal Psychology, 93,* 3–8.

McDermott, R. P. (1974). Achieving school failure: An anthropological approach to illiteracy and social stratification. In G. Spindler (Ed.), *Education and the cultural process.* New York: Holt, Rinehart, & Winston.

McGuigan, F. J. (1978). *Cognitive psychology: Principles of covert behavior.* Englewood Cliffs, NJ: Prentice-Hall.

McGuire, W. J. (1984). Search for the self: Going beyond self-esteem and the reactive self. In R. A. Zurcher, J. Arnoff, & A. I. Rabin (Eds.), *Personality and the prediction of behavior* (pp. 73–120). New York: Academic Press.

McGuire, W. J., & McGuire, C. V. (1981). The spontaneous self-concept as affected by personal distinctiveness. In M. D. Lynch, A. Norem-Hebeisen, & K. Gergen (Eds.), *The self-concept* (pp. 147–171). New York: Ballinger.

McGuire, W. J., & McGuire, C. V. (1982). Significant others in self space: Sex differences and developmental trends in social self. In J. Suls (Ed.), *Psychological perspectives of the self* (Vol. 1, pp. 71–96). Hillsdale, NJ: Erlbaum.

McGuire, W. J., & McGuire, C. V. (1987). Developmental trends and gender differences in the subjective experience of self. In T. Haness & K. Yardley (Eds.), *Self and identity across the lifespan* (pp. 134–146). New York: Routledge & Kegan Paul.

McKey, R. H., et al. (1985). *The impact of Head Start on families and communities.* Final Report of Head Start Evaluation, Synthesis and Utilization Project. Washington, DC: U.S. Government Printing Office.

Mead, G. H. (1934). *Mind, self, and society.* Chicago: University of Chicago Press.

Meichenbaum, D. H. (1977). *Cognitive-behavior modification: An integrative approach.* New York: Plenum Press.

Meissner, W. W. (1978). *The paranoid process.* New York: Jason Aronson.

Mento, A. J., Steel, R. P., & Karren, R. J. (1987). A meta-analytic study of the effects of goal setting on task performance: 1966–1984. *Organizational Behavior and Human Decision Processes, 39,* 52–83.

Messer, B., & Harter, S. (1985). *The self-perception scale for adults.* Unpublished manuscript, University of Denver.

Mettee, D. R., & Riskind, J. (1974). Size of defeat and liking for superior and similar ability competitors. *Journal of Experimental Social Psychology, 10,* 333–351.

Mettee, D. R., & Smith, G. (1977). Social comparison and interpersonal attraction: The case for dissimilarity. In J. Suls & R. Miller (Eds.), *Social comparison processes: Theoretical and empirical perspectives.* Washington, DC: Hemisphere.

Meyer, W-U.; Bachmann, M.; Biermann, U.; Hempelmann, M.; Ploger, F-O.; & Spiller, H. (1979). The informational value of evaluative behavior: Influences of praise and blame on perceptions of ability. *Journal of Educational Psychology, 71,* 259–268.

Midgley, C., Feldlaufer, H., & Eccles, J. S. (in press). Change in teacher efficacy and student self- and task-related beliefs in mathematics during the transition to junior high school. *Journal of Personality and Social Psychology.*

Mill, J. S. (1964). *Autobiography of John Stuart Mill.* New York: First Printing.

Miller, A. T. (1981). *The drama of the gifted child.* New York: Basic Books.

Miller, A. T. (1982). *Self-recognitory schemes and achievement behavior: A developmental study.* Unpublished doctoral dissertation, Purdue University.

Miller, A. T. (1985). A developmental study of the cognitive basis of performance impairment after failure. *Journal of Personality and Social Psychology, 49,* 529–538.

Miller, A. T. (in press). Changes in academic self-concept in early school years: The role of conceptions of ability. *Journal of Social Behavior and Personality.*

Miller, C. T. (1982). The role of performance-related similarity in social comparison of abilities: A test of the related attributes hypothesis. *Journal of Experimental Social Psychology, 18,* 513–523.

Miller, D. T., & Turnbull, W. (1986). Expectancies and interpersonal processes. *Annual Review of Psychology, 37,* 233–256.

Miller, D. T., Turnbull, W., & McFarland, C. (1987). *Particularistic and universalistic evaluation in the social comparison process.* Manuscript submitted for publication.

Miller, N. E. (1944). Experimental studies of conflict. In J. McV. Hunt (Ed.), *Personality and the behavior disorders* (Vol. 1). New York: Ronald Press.

Mills, M.; Puckering, C.; Pound, A.; & Cox, A. D. (1984). What is it about depressed mothers that influences their children's functioning? *Journal of Child Psychology and Psychiatry, Monograph Supplement, No. 4.* Oxford: Pergamon Press.

Minuchin, S., Rosman, B. L., & Baker, L. (1978). *Psychosomatic families: Anorexia nervosa in context.* Cambridge, MA: Harvard University Press.

Mischel, W. (1973). Toward a cognitive social learning reconceptualization of personality. *Psychological Review, 80,* 252–283.

Miura, I. T. (1987a). A multivariate study of school-aged children's computer interest and use. In M. E. Ford & D. H. Ford (Eds.), *Humans as self-constructing living systems: Putting the framework to work* (pp. 177–197). Hillsdale, NJ: Erlbaum.

Miura, I. T. (1987b). The relationship of computer self-efficacy expectations to computer interest and course enrollment in college. *Sex Roles, 16,* 303–311.

Montemayor, R., & Eisen, M. (1977). The development of self-conceptions from childhood to adolescence. *Developmental Psychology, 13,* 314–319.

Montour, K. M. (1977). William James Sidis, the broken twig. *American Psychologist, 32*(4), 265–279.

Moore-Ede, M. C., Sulzman, F. M., & Fuller, C. A. (1982). *The clocks that time us.* Cambridge, MA: Harvard University Press.

Moos, R. H. (1974). *Family environment scale* (Form R). Palo Alto, CA: Consulting Psychologists Press.

Moos, R. H., & Moos, B. (1981). *Revised family environment scale.* Palo Alto, CA: Consulting Psychologists Press.

Moretti, M., & Higgins, E. T. (1988). *Relating self-negativity to self-esteem: The contribution of "discrepancy" beyond global negativity.* Unpublished manuscript, University of Waterloo.

Morris, W. N., & Nemcek, D., Jr. (1982). The development of social comparison motivation among preschoolers: Evidence of a stepwise progression. *Merrill-Palmer Quarterly of Behavior and Development, 28,* 413–425.

Morrison, A. P. (Ed.). (1986). *Essential papers on narcissism.* New York: New York University Press.

Morrison, H., & Kuhn, D. (1983). Cognitive aspects of preschoolers' peer imitation in a play situation. *Child Development, 54,* 1041–1053.

Mullener, N., & Laird, J. D. (1971). Some developmental changes in the organization of self-evaluations. *Developmental Psychology, 5,* 233–236.

Muller, E. N. (1979). *Aggressive political participation.* Princeton, NJ: Princeton University Press.

Murphy, L. (1962). *The widening world of childhood.* New York: Basic Books.

Murray, D. M., & Bisanz, J. (1987). *Children's concepts of intelligence: Relations between prior knowledge and subsequent judgments.* Unpublished manuscript, University of Alberta.

Murray, E. J. (1956). A content-analysis method for studying psychotherapy. *Psychological Monographs, 70*(13, Whole No. 420).

Myers, I. B. (1986). *Introduction to type* (3rd ed.). Palo Alto, CA: Consulting Psychologists Press.

Nadelson, C., & Notman, M. (1981). Child psychiatry perspectives: Women, work, and children. *Journal of the American Academy of Child Psychiatry, 20,* 863–875.

Navon, D. (1984). Resources—a theoretical soup stone? *Psychological Review, 91,* 216–234.

Neemann, J., & Harter, S. (1986). *The self-perception profile for college students.* Manual. University of Denver.

Neisser, U. (1985). The role of invariant structures in the control of movement. In M. Frese & J. Sabini (Eds.), *Goal-directed behavior: The concept of action in psychology.* Hillsdale, NJ: Erlbaum.

Neugarten, B. L. (1964). *Personality in middle and late life.* New York: Atherton Press.

Neugarten, B. L. (1968). Adult personality: Toward a psychology of the life cycle. In B. L. Neugarten (Ed.), *Middle age and aging.* Chicago: University of Chicago Press.

Neugarten, B. L. (1970). Adaptation and the life cycle. *Journal of Geriatric Psychiatry, 4,* 1.

Nicholls, J. G. (1978). The development of the concepts of effort and ability, perception of own attainment, and the understanding that difficult tasks require more ability. *Child Development, 49,* 800–814.

Nicholls, J. G. (1979a). Development of perception of own attainment and causal attributions for success and failure in reading. *Journal of Educational Psychology, 71,* 94–99.

Nicholls, J. G. (1979b). Quality and equality in intellectual development: The role of motivation in education. *American Psychologist, 34,* 1071–1084.

Nicholls, J. G. (1980). The development of the concept of difficulty. *Merrill-Palmer Quarterly, 26,* 271–281.

Nicholls, J. G. (1984a). Achievement motivation: Conceptions of ability, subjective experience, task choice, and performance. *Psychological Review, 91,* 328–346.

Nicholls, J. G. (1984b). Conceptions of ability and achievement motivation. In R. Ames & C. Ames (Eds.), *Research on motivation in education* (Vol. 1, pp. 39–73). New York: Academic Press.

Nicholls, J. G. (1989). *Competence and accomplishment: A psychology of achievement motivation.* Cambridge, MA: Harvard University Press.

Nicholls, J. G.; Cobb, P.; Wood, T.; Yackel, E.; & Patashnick, M. (in press). Dimensions of success in mathematics: Individual and classroom differences. *Journal for Research in Mathematics Education.*

Nicholls, J. G., Licht, B. G., & Pearl, R. A. (1982). Some dangers of using personality questionnaires to study personality. *Psychological Bulletin, 92,* 572–580.

Nicholls, J. G., & Miller, A. T. (1983). The differentiation of the concepts of difficulty and ability. *Child Development, 54,* 951–959.

Nicholls, J. G., & Miller, A. T. (1984a). Development and its discontents: The differentiation of the concept of ability. In J. G. Nicholls (Ed.), *Advances in motivation and achievement: Vol. 3. The development of achievement motivation* (pp. 185–218). Greenwich, CT: JAI Press.

Nicholls, J. G., & Miller, A. T. (1984b). Reasoning about the ability of self and others: A developmental study. *Child Development, 55,* 1990–1999.

Nicholls, J. G., & Miller, A. T. (1985). Differentiation of the concepts of luck and skill. *Developmental Psychology, 21,* 76–82.

Nicholls, J. G.; Patashnick, M.; Cheung, P. C.; Thorkildsen, T. A.; & Lauer, J. M. (in press). Can theories of achievement motivation succeed with only one conception of success? In F. Halisch & J. van den Berken (Eds.), *International perspectives on achievement motivation.* Lisse, Holland: Swets & Zeitlinger.

Nicholls, J. G., Patashnick, M., & Mettetal, G. (1986). Conceptions of ability and intelligence. *Child Development, 57,* 636–645.

Nicholls, J. G., Patashnick, M., & Nolen, S. B. (1985). Adolescents' theories of education. *Journal of Educational Psychology, 77,* 683–692.

Nicholls, J. G., & Thorkildsen, T. A. (1987). *Individual and classroom differences in motivational orientations.* Paper presented at the meeting of the Society for the Experimental Study of Social Psychology, Charlottesville, VA.

Nigro, G. N. (1983). *Improvement of skill through observation and mental practice.* Unpublished doctoral dissertation, Cornell University.

Norem, J. K. (1987). *Strategic realities: Optimism and defensive pessimism.* Unpublished doctoral dissertation, University of Michigan, Ann Arbor.

Norem, J. K. (1989). Cognitive strategies as personality: Effectiveness, specificity, flexibility and change. In D. M. Buss & N. Cantor (Eds)., *Personality psychology in the 1990's: Recent trends and emerging issues.* New York: Springer-Verlag.

Norem, J. K., & Cantor, N. (1986a). Anticipatory and post-hoc cushioning strategies: Optimism and defensive pessimism in "risky" situations. *Cognitive Therapy and Research, 10*(3), 347–362.

Norem, J. K., & Cantor, N. (1986b). Defensive pessimism: Harnessing anxiety as motivation. *Journal of Personality and Social Psychology, 51*(6), 1208–1217.

Notz, W. W. (1975). Work motivation and the negative effects of extrinsic rewards: A review with implications for theory and practice. *American Psychologist, 30,* 884–891.

Ogilvie, D. M. (1987). The undesired self: A neglected variable in personality research. *Journal of Personality and Social Psychology, 52,* 379–385.

Orvaschel, H.; Walsh-Allis, G. A.; & Ye, W. (1988). Psychopathology in children of parents with recurrent depression. *Journal of Abnormal Child Psychology, 16,* 17–28.

Orvaschel, H., Weissman, M. M., Padian, N., & Lowe, T. L. (1981). Assessing psychopathology in children of psychiatrically disturbed parents. *Journal of the American Academy of Child Psychiatry, 20,* 112–122.

Ozer, E., & Bandura, A. (in press). Mechanisms governing empowerment effects: A self-efficacy analysis. *Journal of Personality and Social Psychology.*

Parker, G., Tupling, H., & Brown, L. B. (1979). A parental bonding instrument. *British Journal of Medical Psychology, 52,* 1–10.

Parsons, J. E., Adler, T. G., & Kaczala, C. (1982). Socialization of achievement attitudes and beliefs: Parental influences. *Child Development, 53,* 310–321.

Parsons, J. E., Frieze, I. H., & Ruble, D. N. (1976). Introduction. *Journal of Social Issues, 32,* 1–5.

Parsons, J. E., Kaczala, C., & Meece, J. (1982). Socialization of achievement attitudes and beliefs: Teacher influences. *Child Development, 53,* 322–339.

Parsons, J. E., & Ruble, D. N. (1977). The development of achievement-related expectancies. *Child Development, 48,* 1075–1079.

Parsons, J. E.; Ruble, D. N.; Hodges, K. L.; & Small, A. W. (1976). Cognitive-developmental factors in emerging sex differences in achievement-related expectancies. *Journal of Social Issues, 32,* 47–61.

Patterson, G. R. (1982). *Coercive family process.* Eugene, OR: Castalia Press.

Paulhus, D. L., & Martin, C. L. (1987). The structure of personality capabilities. *Journal of Personality and Social Psychology, 52*(2), 354–365.

Pcakc, P. K., & Ccrvonc, D. (1989). Sequence anchoring and self-efficacy: Primacy effects in the consideration of possibilities. *Social Cognition, 7,* 31–50.

Pedro, J. D.; Wolleat, P.; Fennema, E.; & Becker, A. D. (1981). Election of high school mathematics by females and males: Attributions and attitudes. *American Educational Research Journal, 18,* 207–218.

Perry, D. G., & Bussey, K. (1979). The social learning theory of sex differences: Imitation is alive and well. *Journal of Personality and Social Psychology, 39,* 1699–1712.

Perry, D. G., & Bussey, K. (1984). *Social development.* Englewood Cliffs, NJ: Prentice-Hall.

Pettigrew, T. F. (1979). The ultimate attribution error: Extending Allport's cognitive analysis of prejudice. *Personality and Social Psychology Bulletin, 5,* 461–476.

Phillips, D. A. (1981). *High-achieving students with low academic self-concepts: Achievement motives and orientations.* Unpublished doctoral dissertation, Yale University.

Phillips, D. A. (1984). The illusion of incompetence among academically competent children. *Child Development, 55,* 2000–2016.

Phillips, D. A. (1987). Socialization of perceived academic competence among highly competent children. *Child Development, 58,* 1308–1320.

Piaget, J. (1926). *The child's conception of physical causality.* New York: Littlefield, Adams, 1960.

Piaget, J. (1937). *The construction of reality in the child.* New York: Basic Books, 1954.

Piaget, J. (1951). *Play, dreams and imitation in childhood.* New York: Norton.

Piaget, J. (1965). *The moral judgment of the child.* New York: Free Press. (Original work published 1932)

Piaget, J. (1972). *The psychology of intelligence.* Totowa, NJ: Littlefield, Adams.

Pipp, S., & Harmon, R. J. (1987). Attachment as regulation: A commentary. *Child Development, 58*(3), 648–652.

Pittman, T. S., Ruble, D. N., & Boggiano, A. K. (1983). Intrinsic and extrinsic motivational orientation: Interactive effects of reward, competence feedback, and task complexity. In J. Levine & M. Wang (Eds.), *Teacher and student perceptions: Implications for learning* (pp. 319–340). Hillsdale, NJ: Erlbaum.

Pollins, L. (1983). The effects of acceleration on the social and emotional development of gifted students. In C. Benbow & J. Stanley (Eds.), *Academic precocity: Aspects of its development.* Baltimore, MD: Johns Hopkins University Press.

Post-Kammer, P., & Smith, P. (1985). Sex differences in career self-efficacy, consideration, and interests of eighth and ninth graders. *Journal of Counseling Psychology, 32,* 551–559.

Pressey, S. (1967). "Fordling" accelerates ten years after. *Journal of Counseling Psychology, 14*(1), 73–80.

Pringle, M. L. K. (1970). *Able misfits.* London: Longman.

Provence, S., & Lipton, R. C. (1962). *Infants in institutions.* New York: International Universities Press.

Raaheim, K. (1974). *Problem solving and intelligence.* Oslo, Norway: Universitetsforlaget.

Ramey, C. T., & Finkelstein, N. W. (1978). Contingent stimulation and infant competence. *Journal of Pediatric Psychology, 3,* 89–96.

Raps, C. S.; Peterson, C.; Jonas, M.; & Seligman, M. E. P. (1982). Patient behavior in hospitals: Helplessness, reactance, or both? *Journal of Personality and Social Psychology, 42,* 1036–1041.

Raymond, C. L., & Benbow, C. P. (1986). Gender differences in mathematics: A function of parental support and student sex typing? *Developmental Psychology, 22,* 808–819.

Raynor, J. (1982). A theory of personality functioning and change. In J. O. Raynor & E. E. Entin (Eds.), *Motivation, career striving, and aging* (pp. 249–302). Washington, DC: Hemisphere.

Rees, W. D. (1975). The bereaved and their hallucinations. In *Bereavement, its psychosocial aspects* (pp. 66–71). New York: Columbia University Press.

Rehm, L. P. (1977). A self-control model of depression. *Behavior Therapy, 8,* 787–804.

Rehm, L. P. (1982). Self-management in depression. In P. Karoly & F. H. Kanfer (Eds.), *Self-management and behavior change: From theory to practice* (pp. 522–567). New York: Pergamon Press.

Reiss, A. J., Jr. (1965). *Social organization and socialization: Variations on a theme about generations.* Working paper 1, Center for Research on Social Organization, University of Michigan.

Rholes, W. S.; Blackwell, J.; Jordan, C.; & Walters, C. (1980). A developmental study of learned helplessness. *Developmental Psychology, 16,* 616–624.

Rholes, W. S., Jones, M., & Wade, C. (in press). Children's understanding of personal dispositions and its relationship to behavior. *Journal of Experimental Child Psychology.*

Rholes, W. S., & Ruble, D. N. (1984). Children's understanding of dispositional characteristics of others. *Child Development, 55,* 550–560.

Rholes, W. S., & Ruble, D. N. (in press). Children's impressions of other persons: The effects of temporal separation of behavioral information. *Child Development.*

Richardson, A. (1967a). Mental practice: A review and discussion, Part I. *Research Quarterly, 38,* 95–107.

Richardson, A. (1967b). Mental practice: A review and discussion, Part II. *Research Quarterly, 38,* 263–273.

Roberts, G. C. (1984). Children's achievement motivation in sport. In J. G. Nicholls (Ed.), *Advances in motivation and achievement: Vol. 3. The development of achievement motivation* (pp. 251–281). Greenwich, CT: JAI Press.

Robinson, H. (1981). The uncommonly bright child. In M. Lewis (Ed.), *The uncommon child.* New York: Plenum Press.

Robinson, H. (1983). A case for radical acceleration. In C. Benbow & J. Stanley (Eds.), *Academic precocity: Aspects of its development.* Baltimore, MD: Johns Hopkins University Press.

Robinson, N., & Robinson, H. (1982). The optimal match: Devising the best compromises for the highly gifted student. In D. Feldman (Ed.), *New directions for child development: Developmental approaches to giftedness and creativity (no. 17).* San Francisco: Jossey-Bass.

Rodin, J. (1986). Health, control, and aging. In M. M. Baltes & P. B. Baltes (Eds.), *The psychology of control and aging* (pp. 139–165). Hillsdale, NJ: Erlbaum.

Rodin, J., & Langer, E. J. (1977). Long-term effects of a control-relevant intervention with the institutionalized aged. *Journal of Personality and Social Psychology, 35,* 897–902.

Rodin, J., & Langer, E. J. (1980). Aging labels: The decline of control and the fall of self-esteem. *Journal of Social Issues, 36,* 12–29.

Rogers, C. R. (1961). *On becoming a person.* Boston: Houghton Mifflin.

Rogoff, B., & Lave, J. (Eds.). (1984). *Everyday cognition: Its development in social context.* Cambridge, MA: Harvard University Press.

Rorer, L. G., & Widiger, T. A. (1983). Personality structure and assessment. *Annual Review of Psychology, 34,* 431–463.

Rorty, R. (1979). *Philosophy and the mirror of nature.* Princeton, NJ: Princeton University Press.

Rosenberg, M. (1965). *Society and the adolescent self-image.* Princeton, NJ: Princeton University Press.

Rosenberg, M. (1979). *Conceiving the self.* New York: Basic Books.

Rosenberg, M. (1985). Self-concept and psychological well-being in adolescence. In R. L. Leahy (Ed.), *The development of the self.* New York: Academic Press.

Rosenholtz, S. J., & Rosenholtz, S. H. (1981). Classroom organization and the perception of ability. *Sociology of Education, 54,* 132–140.

Rosow, I. (1973). The social context of the aging self. *Gerontologist, 13,* 82–87.

Ross, A., & Parker, M. (1980). Academic and social self-concepts of the academically gifted. *Exceptional Children, 47*(1), 6–10.

Ross, M., & Conway, M. (1986). Remembering one's own past: The construction of personal histories. In R. M. Sorrentino & E. T. Higgins (Eds.), *Handbook of motivation and cognition: Foundations of social behavior* (pp. 115–143). New York: Guilford Press.

Rubin, K. H., & Lollis, S. P. (in press). Origins and consequences of social withdrawal. In J. Belsky & T. Nezworski (Eds.), *Clinical implications of attachment.* Hillsdale, NJ: Erlbaum.

Ruble, D. N. (1983). The development of social comparison processes and their role in achievement related self-socialization. In E. T. Higgins, D. N. Ruble, & W. W. Hartup (Eds.), *Social cognition and social development: A sociocultural perspective* (pp. 134–157). Cambridge: Cambridge University Press.

Ruble, D. N., Feldman, N. S., & Higgins, E. T. (1986). *Developmental changes in ability evaluation for self and others.* Manuscript submitted for publication.

Ruble, D. N., & Flett, G. L. (1988). Conflicting goals in self-evaluative information seeking: Developmental and ability level analyses. *Child Development, 59*(1), 97–106.

Ruble, D. N., & Frey, K. S. (1987). Social comparison and self-evaluation in the classroom: Developmental changes in knowledge and function. In J. C. Masters & W. S. Smith (Eds.), *Social comparisons, social justice, and relative deprivation* (pp. 81–104). Hillsdale, NJ: Erlbaum.

Ruble, D. N., & Frey, K. S. (in press). Changing patterns of comparative behavior as skills are acquired: A functional model of self-evaluation. In J. Suls & T. A. Wills (Eds.), *Social comparison: Contemporary theory and research.*

Ruble, D. N.; Grosovsky, E.; Frey, K. S.; & Cohen, R. (in press). Developmental changes in competence assessment. In A. K. Boggiano & T. Pittman (Eds.), *Achievement and motivation: A social-developmental perspective.* New York: Cambridge University Press.

Ruble, D. N., & Rholes, W. S. (1981). The development of children's perceptions and attributions about their social world. In J. D. Harvey, W. Ickes, & R. F. Kidd (Eds.), *New directions in attribution research* (Vol. 3). Hillsdale, NJ: Erlbaum.

Ryan, R. M. (1982). Control and information in the intrapersonal sphere: An extension of cognitive evaluation theory. *Journal of Personality and Social Psychology, 43,* 450–461.

Ryff, C. D., & Dunn, D. D. (1983). *Life stresses and personality: A life span developmental inquiry.* Unpublished manuscript, Fordham University, New York.

Salili, F., Maehr, M. L., & Gillmore, G. (1976). Achievement and morality: A cross-cultural analysis of causal attribution and evaluation. *Journal of Personality and Social Psychology, 33,* 327–337.
Salk, L. (1973). The role of the heartbeat in the relations between mothers and infant. *Scientific American, 228,* 24–29.
Salkovskis, P. M., & Harrison, J. (1984). Abnormal and normal obsessions—a replication. *Behaviour Research and Therapy, 22,* 549–552.
Salomon, G. (1984). Television is "easy" and print is "tough": The differential investment of mental effort in learning as a function of perceptions and attributions. *Journal of Educational Psychology, 76,* 647–658.
Sameroff, A. J., Baracos, R., & Seifer, R. (1982). The early development of children born to mentally ill women. In N. F. Watt, E. J. Anthony, L. C. Wynne, & J. Rolf (Eds.), *Children at risk for schizophrenia.* New York: Cambridge University Press.
Sameroff, A. J., & Seifer, R. (1983). Familial risk and child competence. *Child Development, 54,* 1254–1268.
Sandler, J. (1960). The background of safety. *International Journal of Psycho-Analysis, 41,* 352–356.
Sandler, J., & Joffe, W. G. (1965). Notes on childhood depression. *International Journal of Psycho-Analysis, 46,* 88–96.
Sarason, I. G. (1975). Anxiety and self-preoccupation. In I. G. Sarason & D. C. Spielberger (Eds.), *Stress and anxiety* (Vol. 2, pp. 27–44). Washington, DC: Hemisphere.
Sarnoff, C. (1976). *Latency.* New York: Jason Aronson.
Schafer, R. (1968). *Aspects of internalization.* New York: International Universities Press.
Schaie, K. W. (1974). Translations in gerontology—from lab to life: Intellectual functioning. *American Psychologist, 29,* 802–807.
Scheier, M. F., Weintraub, J. K., & Carver, C. S. (1986). Coping with stress: Divergent strategies of optimists and pessimists. *Journal of Personality and Social Psychology, 51*(6), 1257–1264.
Schneider, K. (1984). Subjective uncertainty and achievement and exploratory behavior in preschool children. In J. G. Nicholls (Ed.), *Advances in motivation and achievement: Vol. 3. The development of achievement motivation* (pp. 57–72). Greenwich, CT: JAI Press.
Schofield, J. W. (1981). Complementary and conflicting identities: Images and interaction in an interracial school. In S. R. Asher & J. M. Gottman (Eds.), *The development of children's friendships* (pp. 297–321). New York: Cambridge University Press.
Schulz, R. (1980). Aging and control. In J. Garber & M. E. P. Seligman (Eds.), *Human helplessness: Theory and applications* (pp. 261–278). New York: Academic Press.
Schulz, R., & Hanusa, B. H. (1980). Experimental social gerontology: A social psychological perspective. *Journal of Social Issues, 36,* 30–46.
Schunk, D. H. (1984). Self-efficacy perspective on achievement behavior. *Educational Psychologist, 19,* 48–58.

Schwarzer, R. (Ed.). (1986). *Self-related cognitions in anxiety and motivation.* Hillsdale, NJ: Erlbaum.

Sears, R. R. (1981). The role of expectancy in adaptation to aging. In S. B. Leisler, J. N. Morgan, & V. K. Oppenheimer (Eds.), *Aging: Social change* (pp. 407–430). New York: Academic Press.

Sears, R. R., Maccoby, E. E., & Levin, H. (1957). *Patterns of child rearing.* Evanston, IL: Row, Peterson.

Selig, K. (1959). Personality structure as revealed by the Rorschach technique of a group of children who test at or above 170 IQ on the 1937 revision of the Stanford-Binet. *Dissertation Abstracts, 19,* 3373–3374.

Seligman, M. E. P. (1972). Learned helplessness. *Annual Review of Medicine, 23,* 407–412.

Seligman, M. E. P. (1975). *Helplessness: On depression, development, and death.* San Francisco: Freeman.

Seligman, M. E. P., Abramson, L. Y., Semmel, A., & von Baeyer, C. (1979). Depressive attributional style. *Journal of Abnormal Psychology, 88,* 242–247.

Seligman, M. E. P.; Peterson, C.; Kaslow, N. J.; Tanenbaum, R. L.; Alloy, L. B.; & Abramson, L. Y. (1984). Attribution style and depressive symptoms among children. *Journal of Abnormal Psychology, 93,* 235–238.

Sell, M. (1985, September). Stalking the "speedy turkey." *Oklahoma Runner,* p. 15.

Selman, R. L. (1980). *The growth of interpersonal understanding: Developmental and clinical analyses.* New York: Academic Press.

Serpell, R. (1977). Strategies for investigating intelligence in its cultural context. *Quarterly Newsletter of the Laboratory of Comparative Human Cognition, 1*(3), 11–15.

Shantz, C. U. (1983). Social cognition. In P. H. Mussen (Series Ed.) & J. H. Flavell & E. M. Markman (Vol. Eds.), *Handbook of child psychology* (Vol. 3, 4th ed., pp. 495–555). New York: Wiley.

Shatz, M., & Gelman, R. (1973). The development of communication skills: Modification in the speech of young children as a function of the listener. *Monographs of the Society for Research in Child Development, 38*(5, Serial no. 152).

Shavelson, R. J., Hubner, J. J., & Stanton, G. C. (1976). Self-concept: Validation of construct interpretations. *Review of Educational Research, 46,* 407–441.

Shaver, K. (1970). Defensive attributions: Effects of severity and relevance on the responsibility assigned for accidents. *Journal of Experimental and Social Psychology, 16,* 100–110.

Sherman, J. (1980). Mathematics, spatial visualization and related factors: Changes in girls and boys, grades 8–11. *Journal of Educational Psychology, 72,* 476–482.

Sherman, R. T., & Anderson, C. A. (in press). Decreasing premature termination from psychotherapy. *Journal of Social and Clinical Psychology.*

Showers, C. (1986). *Anticipatory cognitive strategies: The positive side of negative thinking.* Unpublished doctoral dissertation, University of Michigan.

Showers, C., & Cantor, N. (1985). Social cognition: A look at motivated strategies. *Annual Review of Psychology, 36,* 275–305.

Shrauger, J. S., & Schoeneman, T. J. (1979). Symbolic interactionist view of self-concept: Through the looking glass darkly. *Psychological Bulletin, 86,* 549–573.

Shrauger, S. (1975). Responses to evaluation as a function of initial self-perceptions. *Psychological Bulletin, 82,* 581–596.

Siegler, R. S., & Richards, D. D. (1982). The development of intelligence. In R. J. Sternberg (Ed.), *Handbook of human intelligence* (pp. 897–971). New York: Cambridge University Press.

Simon, K. M. (1979). *Effects of self-comparison, social comparison, and depression on goal setting and self-evaluative reactions.* Unpublished manuscript, Stanford University.

Singer, J. L., & Kolligian, J., Jr. (1987). Personality: Developments in the study of private experience. *Annual Review of Psychology, 38,* 533–574.

Singer, M. T. (1974). Engagement-involvement: A central phenomenon in psychophysiological research. *Psychosomatic Medicine, 36*(1), 1–17.

Skinner, B. F. (1987, September 13). B. F. Skinner insists it's just matter over mind. *New York Times,* p. E6.

Snyder, M. (1979). Self-monitoring processes. *Advanced Experimental Social Psychology, 12,* 85–128.

Snyder, M. (1987). *Public appearances, private realities: The psychology of self-monitoring.* New York: Freeman.

Spearman, C. (1927). *The abilities of man.* New York: Macmillan.

Spence, J. T., & Helmreich, R. L. (1983). Achievement-related motives and behaviors. In J. T. Spence (Ed.), *Achievement and achievement motives: Psychological and sociological perspectives* (pp. 7–74). San Francisco: Freeman.

Sperber, Z., & Weiland, I. H. (1973). Anxiety as a determinant of parent-infant contact patterns. *Psychosomatic Medicine, 35*(6), 472–483.

Spitz, R. A. (1946). Anaclitic depression. *Psychoanalytic Study of the Child, 26,* 316–352.

Spivack, G., Platt, J. J., & Schure, M. B. (1976). *The problem-solving approach to adjustment.* San Francisco: Jossey-Bass.

Sroufe, L. A. (1979). The coherence of individual development: Early care, attachment, and subsequent developmental issues. *American Psychologist, 34,* 834–841.

Sroufe, L. A. (1983). Infant-caregiver attachment and patterns of adaptation in preschool: The roots of maladaptation and competence. In M. Perlmutter (Ed.), *Minnesota symposium on child psychiatry* (Vol. 16). Minneapolis: University of Minnesota Press.

Sroufe, L. A. (1984). The organization of emotional development. In K. R. Scherer & P. Ekman (Eds.), *Approaches to emotion* (pp. 109–128). Hillsdale, NJ: Erlbaum.

Sroufe, L. A., & Waters, E. (1977). Attachment as an organizational construct. *Child Development, 48,* 1184–1199.

Stanley, J. (1976). The case for extreme educational acceleration of intellectually brilliant youths. *Gifted Child Quarterly, 20*(1), 66–76.

Stanley, J., & Benbow, C. (1983a). *Academic precocity: Aspects of its development.* Baltimore, MD: Johns Hopkins University Press.

Stanley, J., & Benbow, C. (1983b). Extremely young college graduates: Evidence of their success. *College and University, 58*(4), 361–371.

Steele, C. (1988). The psychology of self-affirmation: Sustaining the integrity of the self. In L. Berkowitz (Ed.), *Advances in experimental social psychology.*

Steele, C. M., & Liu, T. J. (1983). Dissonance processes as self-affirmation. *Journal of Personality and Social Psychology, 45,* 5–19.

Stein, A. H. (1971). The effects of sex-role standards for achievement and sex-role preference on three determinants of achievement motivation. *Developmental Psychology, 4,* 219–231.

Stern, D. N. (1985). *The interpersonal world of the infant.* New York: Basic Books.

Sternberg, R. J. (1984). Toward a triarchic theory of human intelligence. *Behavioral and Brain Sciences, 7,* 269–315.

Sternberg, R. J. (1985a). *Beyond IQ: A triarchic theory of human intelligence.* New York: Cambridge University Press.

Sternberg, R. J. (1985b). Implicit theories of intelligence, creativity, and wisdom. *Journal of Personality and Social Psychology, 49,* 607–627.

Sternberg, R. J. (1989). Mental self-government: A theory of intellectual styles and their development. *Human Development, 31,* 197–224.

Sternberg, R. J.; Conway, B. E.; Ketron, J. L.; & Bernstein, M. (1981). People's conceptions of intelligence. *Journal of Personality and Social Psychology, 41,* 37–55.

Sternberg, R. J., & Wagner, R. K. (Eds.). (1986). *Practical intelligence: Nature and origins of competence in the everyday world.* New York: Cambridge University Press.

Stevenson, H. W., & Newman, R. S. (1986). Long-term prediction of achievement attitudes in mathematics and reading. *Child Development, 57,* 646–659.

Stipek, D. J. (1981). Children's perceptions of their own and their classmates' ability. *Journal of Educational Psychology, 73,* 404–410.

Stipek, D. J. (1984). Young children's performance expectations: Logical analysis or wishful thinking? In J. G. Nicholls (Ed.), *Advances in motivation and achievement: Vol. 3. The development of achievement motivation* (pp. 33–56). Greenwich, CT: JAI Press.

Stipek, D. J., & Hoffman, J. M. (1980). Development of children's performance-related judgments. *Child Development, 51,* 912–914.

Strack, S.; Blaney, P. H.; Ganellen, R.; & Coyne, J. C. (1985). Pessimistic self-preoccupation, performance deficits, and depression. *Journal of Personality and Social Psychology, 49,* 1076–1085.

Strauman, T. J. (1987). *Self-discrepancies in clinical depression and social phobia: Cognitive structures that underlie affective disorders?* Unpublished manuscript, University of Wisconsin.

Strauman, T. J., & Higgins, E. T. (1987). Automatic activation of self-discrepancies and emotional syndromes: When cognitive structures influence affect. *Journal of Personality and Social Psychology, 53,* 1004–1014.

Strauman, T. J., & Higgins, E. T. (in press). Self-discrepancies as predictors of chronic vulnerability to different syndromes of emotional distress. *Journal of Personality.*

Strayer, F. F., & Strayer, J. (1976). An ethological analysis of social agonism and dominance relations among preschool children. *Child Development, 47,* 980–989.

Strube, M., Berry, J., & Moergen, S. (1985). Relinquishment of control and the type A behavior pattern: The role of performance evaluation. *Journal of Personality and Social Psychology, 49,* 831–842.

Suchmann, R. G., & Trabasso, T. (1966). Color and form preference in young children. *Journal of Experimental Child Psychology, 3,* 177–187.

Sullivan, H. S. (1953). *The interpersonal theory of psychiatry.* New York: Norton.

Suls, J. M. (1986). Comparison processes in relative deprivation: A life-span analysis. In J. M. Olson, C. P. Herman, & M. P. Zanna (Eds.), *Relative deprivation and social comparison: The Ontario Symposium* (Vol. 4, pp. 95–116). Hillsdale, NJ: Erlbaum.

Suls, J. M., Gaes, G., & Gastorf, J. (1979). Evaluating a sex-related ability: Comparison with same-, opposite-, and combined-sex norms. *Journal of Research in Personality, 13,* 294–304.

Suls, J. M., & Miller, R. L. (1977). *Social comparison processes: Theoretical and empirical perspectives.* Washington, DC: Hemisphere.

Suls, J. M., & Sanders, G. S. (1982). Self-evaluation through social comparison: A developmental analysis. In L. Wheeler (Ed.), *Review of personality and social psychology* (Vol. 3). Beverly Hills, CA: Sage.

Surber, C. F. (1980). The development of reversible operations in judgments of ability, effort, and performance. *Child Development, 51,* 1018–1029.

Surber, C. F. (1984). The development of achievement-related judgment processes. In J. G. Nicholls (Ed.), *Advances in motivation and achievement: Vol. 3. The development of achievement motivation* (pp. 137–184). Greenwich, CT: JAI Press.

Sutherland, J. D. (1980). The British object relations theories: Balint, Winnicott, Fairbairn, Guntrip. *Journal of the American Psychoanalytic Association, 28,* 829–860.

Tabachnik, N., Crocker, J., & Alloy, L. (1983). Depression, social comparison, and the false-consensus effect. *Journal of Personality and Social Psychology, 45,* 688–699.

Taylor, M. S.; Locke, E. A.; Lee, C.; & Gist, M. E. (1984). Type A behavior and faculty research productivity: What are the mechanisms? *Organizational Behavior and Human Performance, 34,* 402–418.

Taylor, S. E., & Brown, J. D. (1988). Illusion and well-being: A social psychological perspective on mental health. *Psychological Bulletin, 103*(2), 193–210.

Taylor, S. E., Wood, J. V., & Lichtman, R. R. (1983). It could be worse: Selective evaluation as a response to victimization. *Journal of Social Issues, 39,* 19–40.

Terman, L. M. (1925). *Genetic studies of genius: Vol. 1. Mental and physical traits of 1000 gifted children.* Stanford, CA: Stanford University Press.

Terman, L. M., & Oden, M. H. (1947). *Genetic studies of genius: Vol. 4. The gifted child grows up: 25 years' follow-up of a superior group.* Stanford, CA: Stanford University Press.

Tesser, A. (1980). Self-esteem maintenance in family dynamics. *Journal of Personality and Social Psychology, 39,* 77–91.

Tesser, A. (1986). Some effects of self-evaluation maintenance on cognition and action. In R. M. Sorrentino & E. T. Higgins, *The handbook of motivation and cognition: Foundations of social behavior* (pp. 435–464). New York: Guilford Press.

Thorkildsen, T. (1988). Theories of education among academically able adolescents. *Contemporary Educational Psychology, 13,* 323–330.

Thurnher, M. (1974). Goals, values, and life evaluations at the preretirement stage. *Journal of Gerontology, 29,* 85–96.

Thurstone, L. L. (1938). *Primary mental abilities.* Chicago: University of Chicago Press.

Tolman, E. C. (1955). Principles of performance. *Psychological Review, 62,* 315–326.

Tomkins, S. S. (1962). *Affect, imagery, consciousness* (Vol. 1). New York: Springer Press.

Topping, M. E. H. (1983). *The impostor phenomenon: A study of its construct and incidence in university faculty members.* Unpublished doctoral dissertation, University of South Florida.

Trevarthen, C. (1984). Emotions in infancy: Regulators of contact and relationships with persons. In K. R. Scherer & P. Ekman (Eds.), *Approaches to emotion* (pp. 129–157). Hillsdale, NJ: Erlbaum.

Trilling, L. (1971). *Sincerity and authenticity.* Cambridge, MA: Harvard University Press.

Tronick, E. Z., & Gianino, A. F. (1986). The transmission of maternal disturbance to the infant. In E. Z. Tronick & T. Field (Eds.), *Maternal depression and infant disturbance: New directions for child development* (No. 34, pp. 5–11). San Francisco: Jossey-Bass.

Trope, J. Y. (1986). Self-enhancement and self-assessment in achievement behavior. In R. M. Sorrentino & E. T. Higgins (Eds.), *The handbook of motivation and cognition: Foundations of social behavior* (pp. 350–378). New York: Guilford Press.

Truax, C. B. (1966). Reinforcement and nonreinforcement in Rogerian psychotherapy. *Journal of Abnormal Psychology, 71,* 1–9.

Turner, R. H., & Gordon, S. (1981). The boundaries of the self: The relationship of authenticity in the self-concept. In M. D. Lynch, A. A. Norem-Hebeisen, & K. J. Gergen (Eds.), *Self-concept: Advances in theory and research* (pp. 39–57). Cambridge, MA: Ballinger.

Turner, S. M., Beidel, D. C., & Costello, A. (1987). Psychopathology in the offspring of anxiety-disorders patients. *Journal of Consulting and Clinical Psychology, 55,* 229–235.

Ullman, C. (1987). From sincerity to authenticity: Adolescents' views of the "True Self." *Journal of Personality, 55,* 583–595.

Uphoff, J. K. (1985, September). Age at school entrance: How many are ready for success? *Educational Leadership,* pp. 86–90.

Vallacher, R. R., & Wegner, D. M. (1985). *A theory of action identification.* Hillsdale, NJ: Erlbaum.

Van Hook, E., & Higgins, E. T. (1988). Self-related problems beyond the self-concept: The motivational consequences of discrepant self-guides. *Journal of Personality and Social Psychology, 55,* 625–633.

Verbrugge, L. M. (1980). Health diaries. *Medical Care, 18,* 74–95.

Veroff, J. (1969). Social comparison and the development of achievement motivation. In C. P. Smith (Ed.), *Achievement-related motives in children* (pp. 46–101). New York: Russell Sage.

Vitaliano, P.; Russa, J.; Cart, J.; Maiuro, R.; & Becker, J. (1985). The ways of coping checklist: Revision and psychometric properties. *Multivariate Behavioral Research, 20,* 3–26.

Volpert, W. (1985). Epilogue. In M. Frese & J. Sabini (Eds.), *Goal-directed behavior: the concept of action in psychology.* Hillsdale, NJ: Erlbaum.

Wachtel, P. L (1973). Psychodynamics, behavior therapy, and the implacable experimenter: An inquiry into the consistency of personality. *Journal of Abnormal Psychology, 82,* 324–334.

Wallace, A. (1986). *The prodigy: A biography of William James Sidis, America's greatest child prodigy.* New York: Dutton.

Waters, E.; Noyes, D. M.; Vaughn, B. E.; & Ricks, M. (1985). Q-sort definitions of social competence and self-esteem: Discriminant validity of related constructs in theory and data. *Developmental Psychology, 21,* 508–522.

Watson, D., & Clark, L. A. (1984). Negative affectivity: The disposition to experience aversive emotional states. *Psychological Bulletin, 96,* 465–490.

Weary, G. (1979). Self-serving attributional biases: Perceptual or response distortions. *Journal of Personality and Social Psychology, 37,* 1418–1420.

Weinberg, R. S., Gould, D., & Jackson, A. (1979). Expectations and performance: An empirical test of Bandura's self-efficacy theory. *Journal of Sport Psychology, 1,* 320–331.

Weinberg, R. S., Yukelson, S., & Jackson, A. (1980). Effect of public and private efficacy expectations on competitive performance. *Journal of Sport Psychology, 2* 340–349.

Weinberg, W. A.; Rutman, J.; Sullivan, L.; Penick, E. C.; & Dietz, S. G. (1973). Depression in children referred to an educational diagnostic center: Diagnosis and treatment. *Journal of Pediatrics, 83,* 1065–1072.

Weiner, B. (1982). An attribution theory of motivation and emotion. In H. Krohne & L. Laux (Eds.), *Achievement, stress, and anxiety.* Washington, DC: Hemisphere.

Weiner, B.; Graham, S.; Stern, P.; & Lawson, M. E. (1982). Using affective cues to infer causal thoughts. *Developmental Psychology, 18,* 278–286.

Weiner, B., & Peter, N. (1973). A cognitive-developmental analysis of achievement and moral judgments. *Developmental Psychology, 9,* 290–309.

Weinstein, N. D. (1980). Unrealistic optimism about future life events. *Journal of Personality and Social Psychology, 39,* 806–820.

Weissman, M. M.; Gammon, G. D.; John, K.; Merikangas, K. R.; Warner, V.; Prusoff, B. A.; & Sholomskas, D. (1987). Children of depressed parents: Increased psychopathology and early onset of major depression. *Archives of General Psychiatry, 44,* 847–853.

Weissman, M. M., & Paykel, E. S. (1974). *The depressed woman: A study of social relationships.* Chicago: University of Chicago Press.

Weissman, M. M., Paykel, E. S., & Klerman, G. L. (1972). The depressed woman as a mother. *Social Psychiatry, 7,* 98–108.

Weisz, J. R. (1983). Can I control it? The pursuit of veridical answers across the life-span. In P. B. Baltes & O. G. Brim (Eds.), *Life-span development and behavior* (Vol. 5, pp. 233–300). New York: Academic Press.

Weisz, J. R. (1984). Contingency judgments and achievements behavior: Deciding what is controllable and when to try. In J. G. Nicholls (Ed.), *Advances in motivation and achievement: Vol. 3. The development of achievement motivation* (pp. 107–136). Greenwich, CT: JAI Press.

Weisz, J. R. (1986). Understanding the developing understanding of control. In M. Perlmutter (Ed.), *Social cognition: Minnesota symposia on child psychology* (Vol. 18). Hillsdale, NJ: Erlbaum.

Weisz, J. R.; Weiss, B.; Wasserman, A. A.; & Rintoul, B. (1987). Control-related beliefs and depression among clinic-referred children and adolescents. *Journal of Abnormal Psychology, 96,* 58–63.

Weisz, J. R.; Yeates, K. O.; Robertson, D.; & Beckman, J. C. (1982). Perceived contingency of skill and chance events: A developmental analysis. *Developmental Psychology, 18,* 898–905.

Werner, H. (1957). *Comparative psychology of mental development.* New York: International Universities Press.

Werner, H., & Kaplan, B. (1963). *Symbol formation.* New York: Wiley.

West, R. L., Berry, J. M., & Powlishta, K. K. (1988). *Self-efficacy and prediction of memory task performance.* Unpublished manuscript, University of Florida.

Wever, R. (1970). Zur Zeitgeber-Starke eines licht-dunkel Wechsels für die circadiane Periodik des Menschen. *Pfleugers Arch., 321,* 133–142.

Wever, R. (1979). Influence of light on human circadian rhythms. *Nord Counc Arct Med Res Rep, 10,* 33–47.

Whitbourne, S. K. (1985). The construction of the life span. In J. E. Birren & K. W. Schaie (Eds.), *Handbook of the psychology of aging.* New York: Van Nostrand Reinhold.

White, J. (1982). *Rejection.* Reading, MA: Addison-Wesley.

White, R. W. (1959). Motivation reconsidered: The concept of competence. *Psychological Review, 66,* 297–333.

White, R. W. (1963). *Psychological issues: Vol. 3, No. 3, Monograph II. Ego and reality in psychoanalytic theory.* New York: International Universities Press.

Wicklund, R. A. (1975). Objective self-awareness. In L. Berkowitz (Ed.), *Advances in experimental social psychology* (Vol. 8). New York: Academic Press.

Wicklund, R. S., & Gollwitzer, P. M. (1982). *Symbolic self-completion.* Hillsdale, NJ: Erlbaum.

Wiener, N. (1953). *Ex-prodigy: My childhood and youth.* New York: Simon & Schuster.

Williams, S. L. (1987). On anxiety and phobia. *Journal of Anxiety Disorders, 1,* 161–180.

Wine, J. D. (1971). Test anxiety and direction of attention. *Psychological Bulletin, 76,* 92–104.

Wine, J. D. (1980). Cognitive-attentional theory of test anxiety. In I. G. Sarason (Ed.), *Test anxiety: Theory, research, and applications* (pp. 349–385). Hillsdale, NJ: Erlbaum.

Winne, P., Woodlands, M., & Wong, B. (1982). Comparability of self-concept among learning disabled, normal, and gifted students. *Journal of Learning Disabilities, 15,* 470–475.

Winnicott, D. W. (1956). Primary maternal preoccupation. In *Through paediatrics to psychoanalysis* (pp. 300–305). New York: Basic Books, 1975.

Winnicott, D. W. (1958). The capacity to be alone. In *The maturational processes and the facilitating environment* (pp. 29–36). New York: International Universities Press, 1965.

Winnicott, D. W. (1960). Ego distortion in terms of the true and false self. In *Maturational processes and the facilitating environment* (pp. 140–152). New York: International Universities Press, 1965.

Winnicott, D. W. (1971). *Playing and reality.* New York: Basic Books.

Wolfe, T. (1982). The me decade and the third great awakening. In T. Wolfe, *The purple decades.* New York: Farrar, Straus, & Giroux.

Wolfe, V. V.; Finch, A. J.; Saylor, C. F.; Blount, R. L.; Pallmeyer, T. P.; & Carek, D. J. (1987). Negative affectivity in children: A multitrait-multimethod investigation. *Journal of Consulting and Clinical Psychology, 55,* 245–250.

Wood, J. V. (in press). Contemporary theory concerning social comparison of personal attributes. *Psychological Bulletin.*

Wood, J. V., Taylor, S. E., & Lichtman, R. R. (1985). Social comparison in adjustment to breast cancer. *Journal of Personality and Social Psychology, 49,* 1169–1183.

Wood, R. E., & Bandura, A. (1989). Impact of conceptions of ability on self-regulatory mechanisms and complex decision-making. *Journal of Personality and Social Psychology, 56,* 407–415.

Wortman, C. B. (1976). Some determinants of perceived control. In J. H. Harvey, W. J. Ickes, & R. F. Kidd (Eds.), *New directions in attribution research* (Vol. 1). Hillsdale, NJ: Erlbaum.

Wortman, C. B., & Brehm, J. (1975). Responses to uncontrollable outcomes. In L. Berkowitz (Ed.), *Advances in experimental social psychology.* New York: Academic Press.

Wortman, C. B.; Panciera, L.; Shusterman, L.; & Hibscher, J. (1976). Attributions of causality and reactions to uncontrollable outcomes. *Journal of Experimental Social Psychology, 12,* 301–316.

Wurf, E. (1987). *Structure and functioning of regularity in the self-concept.* Unpublished doctoral dissertation, University of Michigan.

Wurf, E., & Markus, H. (1983). *Cognitive consequences of the negative self.* Presented at the annual meeting of the American Psychological Association, Anaheim, CA.

Wurf, E., & Markus, H. (1987). *Self-schemas and self-definition: The importance of being different.* Unpublished manuscript, University of Michigan.

Wurf, E., & Markus, H. (in press). Possible selves and the psychology of personal growth. In D. Ozer, A. Stewart, & J. Healy (Eds.), *Perspectives on personality: Theory, research and interpersonal dynamics.* Greenwich, CT: JAI Press.

Wylie, R. C. (1961). *The self-concept.* Lincoln: University of Nebraska Press.

Wylie, R. C. (1974). *The self-concept: A review of methodological considerations and measuring instruments* (Revised ed., Vol. 1). Lincoln: University of Nebraska Press.

Wylie, R. C. (1979). *The self-concept: Theory and research on selected topics* (Vol. 2). Lincoln: University of Nebraska Press.

Yarrow, L. J., Rubenstein, J. L., & Pedersen, F. A. (1975). *Infant environment: Early cognitive and motivational development.* New York: Halsted.

Yussen, S. R., & Kane, P. T. (1983). Children's ideas about intellectual ability. In R. Leahy (Ed.), *The child's construction of social inequality* (pp. 109–133). New York: Academic Press.

Zigler, E. (1987). *Is paranoid schizophrenia really camouflaged depression?* Address given at the annual meeting of the American Psychological Association, New York City.

Zigler, E., & Glick, M. (1984). Paranoid schizophrenia: An unorthodox view. *American Journal of Orthopsychiatry, 54,* 43–70.

Zigler, E., & Glick, M. (1986). *A developmental approach to adult psychopathology.* New York: Wiley.

Zigler, E., & Glick, M. (1988). Is paranoid schizophrenia really camouflaged depression? *American Psychologist, 43,* 284–290.

Zigler, E., Levine, J., & Gould, L. (1967). Cognitive challenge as a factor in children's humor appreciation. *Journal of Personality and Social Psychology, 6,* 332–336.

Zorbaugh, H., Boardman, R., & Sheldon, P. (1951). Some observations on highly gifted children. In P. Witty (Ed.), *Gifted children.* Boston: Heath.

Zung, W. W. K. (1965). A self-rating depression scale. *Archives of General Psychiatry, 12,* 63–70.

Zuroff, D. C., & Mongrain, M. (1987). Dependency and self-criticism: Vulnerability factors for depressive affective states. *Journal of Abnormal Psychology, 96,* 14–22.

CONTRIBUTORS AND EDITORS

Albert Bandura is the David Starr Jordan professor of social science in psychology at Stanford University.

Sidney J. Blatt is a professor of psychology and psychiatry at Yale University.

Nancy Cantor is a professor of psychology at the University of Michigan.

Susan Cross is a doctoral student in social psychology at the University of Michigan.

David Elkind is a professor of child study and senior resident scholar at Tufts University.

Karin S. Frey is a research associate in psychology at the University of Washington.

Susan Harter is a professor of psychology at the University of Denver.

E. Tory Higgins is a professor of psychology at New York University.

Paul M. Janos is assistant director of the Early Entrance Program at the University of Washington.

John Kolligian, Jr., is a doctoral student in clinical/developmental psychology at Yale University.

David W. Krueger is a clinical professor of psychiatry at the Baylor College of Medicine.

Ellen J. Langer is a professor of psychology at Harvard University.

Hazel Markus is a professor of psychology at the University of Michigan.

Marlene M. Moretti is an assistant professor of psychology at Simon Frasier University.

John G. Nicholls is a professor of education at the University of Illinois.

Julie K. Norem is an assistant professor of psychology at Northeastern University.

Kwangyang Park is a doctoral student in social/organizational psychology at Harvard University.

Deborah A. Phillips is an assistant professor of psychology at the University of Virginia.

Diane N. Ruble is a professor of psychology at New York University.

Carrie E. Schaffer is a doctoral student in clinical psychology at Yale University.

Robert J. Sternberg is the I.B.M. professor of psychology and education at Yale University.

Elissa Wurf is an assistant professor of psychology at Lehigh University.

Marc Zimmerman is an assistant professor of public health at the University of Michigan.

NAME INDEX

SUBJECT INDEX